NEW HAVEN PUBLIC
NEW HAVEN FREE PUBLIC LIBRARY
3 5000 05307 6955

P9-CEB-272

MAY 1 8 2023

THE JOHN HARVARD LIBRARY

Howard Mumford Jones
Editor-in-Chief

THE AUTOBIOGRAPHY
OF
Lyman Beecher

Edited by Barbara M. Cross

IN TWO VOLUMES

Vol. II

THE BELKNAP PRESS OF
HARVARD UNIVERSITY PRESS
Cambridge, Massachusetts
1961

Distributed in Great Britain by Oxford University Press, London

Library of Congress Catalog Card Number 61-6348

Printed in the United States of America

CONTENTS

Volume II

ILLUSTRATIONS

VOLUME II

THE AUTOBIOGRAPHY OF LYMAN BEECHER

VOLUME II

I

INTRODUCTION

It has already been made apparent that the one idea of Dr. Beecher's life was the promotion of revivals of religion, not merely in his own congregation, but as a prominent instrumentality for the conversion of the world, and the speedy introduction of the millennial reign of our Lord Jesus Christ.

As we are moving on in the present volume toward more controversial eras, it is our desire still to keep this great idea uppermost, as the real ground of all his interest and concern in those discussions in which it was his destiny to bear a part. It is not strange that the attempt to carry forward revival work should lead to controversy, and even to divisions among good men. Our Savior distinctly declared that he had not come to send peace, but division.

The work of conviction and conversion of sinners, in a world like this — the work of building up a Church on principles entirely superior, and even opposed to those of selfish society, can not be carried on without resistance on the one side and mistake on the other. It was natural that the primitive churches should make mistakes, and incorporate errors into their teaching. It was natural that the adversary should take advantage of those mistakes as one important means of prolonging the conflict. So it was natural that the Reformation from popery should not be absolutely perfect, and that even in Puritan theology errors should lurk which the adversary should employ, together with other means, to cause that theology to be undermined, even in the strong-hold of its power, as the world has seen at Geneva, and in the city of pilgrims.

It was inevitable, then, that any one of Dr. Beecher's ardent and uncompromising character, who should attempt, under the circumstances in which nominal Christendom was placed, to carry on revivals, on a broad and comprehensive scale, would sooner or later be involved in controversy. With sinners, of course, he would be in controversy from the beginning, endeavoring to convince them that they are rebels against God, whose instant duty is submission, and that all their objections are unreasonable.

With all sects, of whatever name, who, as the necessary and

consistent result of their having discarded the theology of the Reformation, might avowedly condemn and oppose revivals, he would be at earnest war, that, if they could not be converted themselves, they might be disabled from preventing the conversion of others. With churches organized on the Episcopal plan he would come in collision, because they assail the fundamental principle of Apostolic church organization as understood by the Puritan founders, viz., that only those giving evidence of saving faith should be admitted to the communion.

And, lastly, he might be involved in earnest controversy with brethren of his own denomination, who might, on some important points, differ as to the best method of awakening sinners, answering their objections to the doctrines of grace, and bringing them to Christ.

One thing, however, a calm and comprehensive estimate of all his sermons, letters, and actions must convince a candid mind is true, namely, that if he went into controversy, he went into it because he felt that his business of saving souls was in some way obstructed, and he must remove the obstruction. If he attacked either systems, or institutions, or men with severity, it was because he felt that the eternal interests of immortal souls were at stake.

In the colloquial language of familiar conversation he was sometimes truculent in his modes of expression to a degree. Hundreds of times have we heard him "hew down" antagonists, "wring their necks off," "hang them on their own gallows," and do other sanguinary things too dreadful to mention. But there was always something in his eye and manner which told that he was speaking in a highly figurative sense of the logical demolition of error. His familiar correspondence, not designed for immediate publication, may be found to contain some such expressions, which have not been expunged, because it was hoped the reader would prefer to see the man as he was in unrestricted intercourse with trusted friends, and would be able to make all needful allowance.

In preparing this second volume for the press, under all the difficulties — truly appalling — that must attend the undertaking, we have endeavored to work by a very simple plan. We have endeavored to be in that frame of mind, and see all things from that point of view which to Dr. Beecher himself were most habitual. Without proposing to paint an elaborate portrait, without aspiring to be the historian of his life and times, restricted by the plan of our work mainly to his autobiography and correspondence, we have humbly tried, with earnest prayers for divine aid, to permit a faithful soldier of the Cross, toil-worn and scarred in a life of service, to tell, as far as possible in his own words, the story of his campaigns, and live his life over again before the reader.

A life based on an idea such as we have indicated is not easily comprehended, as it is not easily lived. How many, even in this land of revivals, have never breathed, or have breathed but for a moment, the inspiring atmosphere of a genuine work of grace, and, therefore, realize faintly, if at all, what it is! Something the dwellers in the arctic zone may know of summer, but they can form no adequate conception of the incense-laden breath of tropical climes. As little can a denizen of the world's bleak arctic — the ice-bound zone of unbelief — imagine the fresh, sweet, vital, tender, loving, joyous feeling diffused through a whole community bathed and baptized by the special influences of the heavenly Comforter. In that atmosphere of heaven, redolent of a Savior's genial presence, Dr. Beecher habitually lived; out of it, he languished and pined like the exile in Siberian deserts. Against whatever threatened the continuance and spread of this — to become the spring, the summer of the world — he fought with all the energy of his being.

May the sovereign Spirit on whom alone he relied for success in his warfare deign to accept this imperfect memorial, and seal it with a blessing, so that thereby it may be said in Zion, "He being dead, yet speaketh."

II

THE *CONNECTICUT OBSERVER*

THE state of the Congregational churches in Connecticut in the opening of the year 1824 was, on the whole, prosperous. The storm which overthrew the standing order had cleared away. The churches had easily adapted themselves to circumstances, and were thriving on the voluntary plan. Considerable alarm, however, was excited by the movements of other denominations, whose rising influence might prove injurious to the interests of Puritan institutions unless some organ could be provided for their defense. This led to the establishment of the Connecticut Observer, as follows.

AUTOBIOGRAPHY.

The Episcopalians were driving ahead with a popular rush. They had got such control of the Hartford paper that the editor would not admit our articles. I wrote to Hawes that they must be headed. Went to Hartford, and had a meeting at Hawes's of about a dozen ministers. What was to be done? We talked the matter over, and resolved to have a paper of our own. We subscribed forty dollars each on the spot. Then I went to Middletown, and talked with ministers there; spent the Sabbath; got a caucus Sabbath eve, and kindled fire in their bosoms.

Then I went to New Haven, to the editor of our paper, and talked to him. "Oh," said he, "they have got ahead of us. It is of no use to do anything." "Well," said I, "you may do what you please, but I tell you before God and high heaven we will have a paper in which the children of the Pilgrims can speak." At that he began to yield. "Oh, well, I'll publish any thing you please!" I went to Goodrich, and told him to send a piece. He did, and that paper was saved.

The General Association was to meet in about a week or ten days at Goshen, I believe. It was a large meeting, and I rose and expounded the whole business, and what we were doing, and the effect on our churches, and all their interests, to have our hands tied and our mouths stopped.

I let off as I never did before, for I felt indignant. They appointed me and one other on committee. Committee met, and what should —— do but talk just as that editor had. I turned in and gave him such a thrashing as I never did any body, up hand and down, hip and thigh, till at last he knocked under and said, "You go back and talk to them just as you have to me, and I'll agree." "Well," said I, "you go in and talk so like a fool as you did to me, for nothing else would make me say what I have been saying to you."

We reported what had been done at Hartford, Middletown, and New Haven, and what Litchfield county ought to do. Some flinched; but I told them, "If you don't take hold now, you'll find emissaries before long in your own congregations. You've got to fight, and to fight you must have money." So they subscribed on the spot enough to begin with and carry on. We sent out agents to get subscriptions in every county in the state, and it was carried.

Then I went down to Watertown, where a friend, Mr. Hooker,[1] had been settled not long after I came to Litchfield. I loved him very much, and he me. He was of first-rate abilities, and had been tutor in college. I talked with him about the paper, and asked him to be editor; he fell in and took it. Our paper then began to travel and thunder.

In Litchfield I spent two days and more, and got sixty subscribers. I went clear out to Mount Tom. Many of them never took a paper before or after. That, for that time o' day, was about equal to things going on now in our nation.

CATHARINE TO EDWARD.

"July 18, 1824.

"I have not enjoyed coming home as much in many years as now, for we are all in health, cheerful, and happy. I hope this summer we shall be able to fix up the old house, and make it look rather more neat and comfortable. It needs paper within and paint outside very much.

"Yesterday I heard two of father's very best sermons. The afternoon sermon perfectly electrified me. I wish it could be heard by all young men in the country. Among other things, he exhibited the ways in which they might do good, and the blessedness of it.

[1] Horace Hooker (1793–1862), student of Fitch, secretary of the Home Missionary Society, pastor at Watertown, Conn. (1822–1824), editor of the *Connecticut Observer* (1825–1841).

We saw a small specimen of its effect this afternoon, when, in playful obedience to some exhortations to a laudable public spirit, a party of our young townsmen turned out to transplant forest trees wherever they are needed through our streets. Father hopes a young men's library will also grow out of it.

"The fact is, I never hear any body preach that makes me feel as father does; perhaps it may be because he is father. But I can not hear him without its making my face burn and my heart beat."

DR. BEECHER TO EDWARD.

"August 10, 1824.

"I am glad you go to Boston. William is engaged in Boston in a good place. Harriet will come to Hartford next quarter. George goes to New Haven. I expect to get him through college, though not without difficulty.

"I have labored hard and preached well this summer, I believe. My Bible-class numbers two hundred and upward, and prospers. The week after Commencement I am to be in Hartford, and make a speech before the Foreign Mission Society."

THE SAME TO WILLIAM.

"1824.

"I am gratified to perceive by your letter to Mary that you are pleased with your place, and have a prospect of employment. So God takes care of the children of his ministers who serve and trust in him. Silver and gold have they for their children none, but, if they are faithful, their children are beloved for the father's sake. God raises up friends who answer instead of capital. I hope you will always eye the hand of God both in affliction and in prosperity.

"I have just returned from Guilford. Left all well. Could not find any trout where we caught so many.

"I preached yesterday my sermons on Depravity, written last winter. They are point-blank shot. I work and study hard, but carefully. My reply to the review of my sermon will be done soon. I think I shall like it, which is commonly a good recommendation, and that Unitarians will not be over-much pleased, which is another recommendation."

III

CORRESPONDENCE, 1824–1825

DR. BEECHER TO DR. CORNELIUS.

"August 31, 1824.

"YOUR letter was received, and, amid the pressure of very urgent and incessant application of mind, was laid down and forgotten, until I concluded that my silence would be as a negative answer to your request. I long to come — feel the importance of the moment, and am inclined to believe that as much good might be done to souls by my labor at such a time with you, as in a year or more in Litchfield. But if it is the will of God that I should be a stated pastor, I can not be an evangelist, though I sometimes think I would, if a regular and permanent support could be secured. And if it is the will of God that I should be an author, I must stay at home and write. Besides, we have enough to do, just now, to defend ourselves, and can not well go abroad to fight. I am committed for this and the next week in urgent public business, and, when that is ended, must hasten home to prepare sermons for the press.

"So the case stands. You have all my heart and soul, but you can not have my hand and tongue."

CATHARINE TO EDWARD.

"January 8, 1825.

"The paper goes on finely. Father has prepared some rare pieces for it. He is much animated with the success of the paper. There is nothing makes me feel so happy as to be with him, and nothing so stimulates my intellect as his conversation."

DR. BEECHER TO EDWARD AT ANDOVER.

"Middletown, January, 1825.

"DEAR SON, — I have been so pressed by public concerns at Danbury, at home, at Hartford, and here, that I have been literally unable to write to you. * * * The *Observer* begins with about 1400 subscribers. The first number strikes well, and the second, third, and fourth will be still better. It is, in my judgment, one of the grandest strokes of holy policy we have ever attempted for the Church of God. It will compel other papers to rise to our standard if they can, and thus control extensively that irresponsible organ of good and evil, the press. I wonder holiness has not been stamped on it before. It belongs to God, and must be consecrated. Our example will, I have no doubt, as in the Domestic Missionary Society, be followed, and our best and ablest men be placed at the head of the press in different districts of our land. There is so much of your father in the paper after the first No., and will be for some time, that I have directed the paper to be sent on. * * * Tell me all about your health and your studies, and whether they are making such strides to German infidelity as some good women in the world do tremble about. Say to me confidentially whether you observe in Brother Stuart, or any of the students, a leaning to rash criticism, calculated in its tendencies to make coxcombs in divinity, and break up foundations. Be honest and faithful in your reply. * * *

" * * * I am, for the first time for six or seven years, at ease in respect to the general course of events which concern the Church in Connecticut. The tide of toleration is ebbing, and Congregationalism is emerging from the floods of ungodliness which have rolled over it with waves and foam. They have broken themselves and recoil, but the rock remains, not a fragment broken off nor its base shaken. 'Why do the heathen rage, and the people imagine a vain thing?' "

DR. BEECHER TO DR. WISNER.

"1825.

"It is so long a time since I have spoken to you or been spoken to by you, either orally or by pen, that I feel somewhat impatient to intrude a claim upon your time.

"The first number of my reply to the review of my sermon has gone to press, and will be out in the *Christian Spectator* of next month, as I suppose. The second will follow in due order. I could not send them to Boston first, but they have been read by Stuart and Taylor, and will again be revised by the brethren at New Haven, if need be.

"I want you to ascertain whether Rev. Mr. Walker,[1] of Charles-

[1] James Walker (1794–1874), Unitarian minister and editor of the *Christian Examiner* (1831–1839), disparaged reforms and controversies. Professor at Harvard after 1839, he became its president in 1853.

town, is, or is reported to be, the author of pieces entitled "Notes upon the Bible," in the first three numbers of the *Examiner* for 1824, especially the third, as, if he is, I shall be able to slay him with his own sword on the subject of obvious meaning. I have read the controversy about Cambridge College, and think that the abominations of her secret history are coming to light, and that she who sat a queen, and felt that she should see no sorrow, is destined to feel the calamities of a long-delayed retribution.

"I rejoice to perceive unequivocal evidence that orthodoxy in Massachusetts is becoming a phalanx terrible as an army with banners, and that our adversaries shall no more be able to frame iniquity by law, and draw sin as with a cart-rope."

DR. BEECHER TO REV. E. CORNELIUS.

"February 16, 1825.

"I never subscribe for books, nor recommend them, unless I really like them, as among the very best, and I go by the same rule in giving commendation to writers, and even to my best friends. I give no commendations on the score of courtesy, none on the score of private friendship, none only because I like what I commend. And I am somewhat difficult to please. It never satisfies me that a writer has written tolerably well, or pretty well. The world is full of such writing, and would experience no great loss if it were emptied of it all. There are a few minds that see clearly, and speak directly and energetically to the point. These are the writers I love to read, and whom I can never too much admire or commend. They create no envy, and afford me unmingled pleasure. But I must acknowledge that my pleasure in reading such a work has been greatly heightened lately by the consideration that it came from your hand. Possibly you may have felt as if I did not pay to what you have published before the tribute of parental regard which you might justly have expected. I have now explained the reason. They were good, but not good enough for one of your capacity to write, or, rather, not good enough to acquiesce in as having attained.

"You have now given a specimen of vigorous writing, which, in the pending polemics, enrolls your name among the threes, and leaves the way open to find a place among the first three.

"I have read the sermon, which is the prating of a young religious coxcomb, knowing not what he says nor whereof he affirms, and you have done him ample justice. * * *

"Allow me to inquire about myself, and the first part of my reply to Walker.

"Am I a Calvinist, do you think, and will my claim be admitted as proved, and will Walker and his friends feel as if my gun was loaded deep enough for the first shot, and will the orthodox think I have done so far sufficient execution? I ask not this as food to my vanity, for I should abide by my own judgment, let the world think what they will. Still, as the game is out of sight, I must depend on those who are near to tell me what are the effects of the first fire. I hope the man is not dead, for I have some terrible things in reserve that I should not like to hurl at a dead man. I can not but think myself that, since the controversy opened between us, it has moved on with singular power and success on our part, and that, though Unitarianism, intrenched in Cambridge, and Boston, and Salem, with little redoubts all around, has had a better chance, on the score of talents, learning, wealth, and popular favor, than ever in the world before, these all will be of no avail in this enlightened community, but that gradually and at no distant day the victory will be achieved, and Unitarianism cease to darken and pollute the land."

IV

CORRESPONDENCE, 1825

On the following letter was endorsed by Dr. Beecher, under date September, 1856, the following explanatory statement: "This letter was written to arrest, and get time to quench, the first spark which was struck in the controversy between Goodrich and Taylor, of New Haven, and Nettleton, Tyler, and Dr. Woods; but, before I had time to write and send the letter, the fire was in the leaves, and outran all efforts to quench it. The parties on both sides were my special friends, and my labors were unceasing to explain and mitigate, and prevent explosions in the churches of Connecticut and Massachusetts."

DR. BEECHER TO REV. A. HOOKER.

"Litchfield, March 13, 1825.

"Dear Brother, — I have understood in several ways that some of the brethren were alarmed and dissatisfied in some points in the examination of Leavet[1]; that the delegates, also, were alarmed; and that fears have been expressed that Brother Taylor is Leavetical.

"Will you have the goodness to state to me what were the points in the examination of the candidate which create uneasiness, and will you allow me to express my earnest hope that nothing will be said or done which shall have a tendency to exasperate brethren, or to alarm the community, or to commit us, at this time, with the insupportable calamity of a theological controversy among ourselves? The reasons for avoiding a public controversial schism in Connecticut are obvious and powerful. We are watched by enemies within and without, and our condition is critical. Sectarians without and heretics within would gladly see us fall out by the way, and avail themselves of our confusion to put down our Theological Seminary, our College, and our churches; and I really fear that

[1] Probably Joshua Leavitt (1794–1873), who was in Taylor's first graduating class and became editor of the N.Y. *Evangelist* and home editor of the *Independent*. Active in the temperance and anti-slavery movements, he supported Finney.

our triangular brethren at the South would not put on sackcloth should we come into troubled water. The strength and glory of our Church has been and now is the cordial and efficient co-operation of the clergy, and our plans for self-defense and the augmentation of strength which are in operation and in a course of preparation are noble, powerful, and certain, if we fall not out by the way. The *Spectator*, the *Observer*, the Domestic Missionary Society, with a system for evangelists, for tracts, and for the improvement of our common schools, can not, with our revivals, fail of glorious results. But a controversial spirit, corroding the hearts and diverting the minds of ministers and churches, would, I have no doubt, put an end to our revivals, and leave us without strength in the presence of an insolent enemy. They have tried in vain to bind us with cords and withes; but still we have waxed valiant in fight, putting to flight the armies of the aliens. Evangelical doctrine, and peace, and love are the secrets of our Nazariteship, and it is only a controversial spirit, with its alienating and diverting influence, which can cause our glory to depart, and make us weak as other men. The reformation was stopped by the sacramental controversy; and the orthodox in the eastern parts of Massachusetts begin to have revivals only as they begin to dismount their hobby-horses, and to love one another and act in concert.

"I have said our churches are in a critical situation. We have just passed, or are, rather, now passing through a revolution, the object of which was, by withdrawing the support of law, and creating facilities and temptations to withdraw from our societies, to scatter and destroy us. And a great effort has been made to shake the confidence of the community in the clergy, and, if this could be done, I know not what would save us. But a controversy which would produce so much feeling, and such action and reaction as must attend the attack and the defense of such a man in such a station as Brother Taylor, could not be carried on without impairing the confidence of the public in the ministry. Inevitably we should first or last walk naked, and they would see our shame.

"If there are exceptionable points in Brother Taylor's system which need to be modified and guarded, that at present is, I have no doubt, entirely practicable. But we know what human nature is, even when partly sanctified, and how easy it is to confirm a man in his opinion by a course of treatment which to him shall appear precipitate or unkind.

"If I had the confidence of my good brethren sufficiently to render the pledge of any avail, I should not hesitate to pledge myself to produce statements and explanations from Brother Taylor on every point entirely satisfactory. I do not mean statements in which every brother would concur, for perhaps no two of us would explain ourselves entirely alike; but I mean statements which would release the mind of every brother from the apprehension of any dangerous error.

"I have heard that a brother has said that Brother Taylor 'is a Socinian,[2] and would avow himself to be so in a year,' and that the charge of heresy had been either made or insinuated by others. I presume such things, if they have been said, have been said inconsiderately, and perhaps under the influence of momentary excitement, as it would be an obvious violation of Gospel rule to make or to insinuate such charges before any steps had been taken to convince and reclaim, and as such liberties taken by ministers who differ with each other's character would tear us all to pieces.

"I have understood, also, that it is supposed by some that I am opposed earnestly to Brother Taylor on the subject of original sin. I have known his opinions perhaps for ten years, and have agreed in part, and in part differed with him, without supposing for a moment that his views or mine set aside the doctrine of original sin. The point on which I have differed with the most earnestness has respected two or three terms, with the view of preventing just such misapprehensions and alarms as have now probably happened. If any one supposes that I have regarded Brother Taylor as fundamentally erroneous on the subject of original sin, their impression is without foundation. *I have regarded him as adopting one of the half a dozen ways in which orthodox men explain and defend that difficult doctrine*, and I have censured him only as changing phraseology needlessly in a few particulars.

"But, in respect to the entire doctrine of original sin, though I believe it *ex animo*, I have long been of opinion that the policy is unwise of making that doctrine the hinge of controversy between the orthodox and Arminians, because, as it respects the character and destiny of infants, it gives to the enemy the advantage of the popular side; because the discussion carries us unavoidably into darkness and depths where the enemy have as good a chance as ourselves, and where both must return to *terra firma* or be swamped.

"Original sin, in respect to infants, is to be held so far as respects the existence in them of a nature which makes it certain that whenever they act accountably they sin. But the doctrine of man's

[2] Socinianism denied the divinity and atonement of Christ and interpreted the crucifixion as God's method of drawing men to Himself.

entire depravity from the commencement of his accountable agency, leaving it for God to decide when, that is the battle-ground. On this foundation the superstructure of Calvinism stands unshaken by any diversity of speculations. That nature in infants which is the ground of the certainty that they will be totally, actually depraved as soon as they are capable of accountable action — which renders actual sin certain, I call a depraved nature; and yet I do not mean by 'depraved nature' the same exactly which I mean by the term as applied to the accountable sinful exercises of the hearts of adult men. Nor does Edwards or Bellamy. Edwards calls it 'a prevailing effectual tendency in their nature' to that sin which brings wrath and eternal undoing; but he does not consider it as being sin in itself considered, in such a sense as to deserve punishment, for he says, 'Infants would be sinners in no other way than in virtue of Adam's transgression.'"

DR. BEECHER TO EDWARD.

"March 16, 1825.

"I am gratified that my review is satisfactory. There will be two numbers more, and, if I do not misunderstand their effect, they will make for Unitarians work for repentance, and, I hope, for reformation.

"I was much comforted by William while at home. He affords, as I conceive, great evidence of a change of heart, and yet something is not right with him. He does not see his evidence, nor rely on what he does see — is forever hunting after feeling, feeling, feeling, when he has had so much of it already as to shatter his nerves. I did something to correct his views on that subject, but he is not wholly recovered from worrying himself about want of feeling produced by feeling."

CATHARINE TO EDWARD.

"April 20, 1825.

"You can not imagine how much I enjoy this visit at home. You know how happy it makes us to be with father. His society seems always to give a new impulse to the affection of the heart, and to every intellectual power. He is now very much engaged in finishing off his answer to the review, and I think his last will make all smoke again."

MRS. BEECHER TO EDWARD.

"July 19, 1825.

"I thought last evening our street presented the most solemn scene I had ever witnessed. I left the house of the dying saint (Mrs. S——) about nine o'clock. Many persons were hanging about the doors and yard in perfect stillness. I crossed the street, and stepped softly into the anxious meeting, where a hundred poor sinners were all on their knees before God, and your father was in the midst, pleading with strong cries and tears for the mercy of God upon them. Around the doors were a number of people, solemn as death. I could not but say, 'How awful is this place! This is none other than the house of God and gate of heaven!'

"We thought the revival assumed a deeper appearance than at any former period."

—— TO EDWARD.

"August 28, 1825.

"How different will Litchfield be! We hope ——, and ——, and —— are born again. 'It is the Lord's doing, and is marvelous in our eyes.' The attention is spreading to Bradleyville and Goshen. Father's health is tolerably good. Few ministers exert themselves so much for the salvation of their people as he does. I fear after the call for effort is over he will sink."

WILLIAM TO EDWARD.

"August 31, 1825.

"The revival goes on steadily. Father works as hard and harder than ever. His health is just so that he can keep about. He is going to Danbury for the Church."

DR. BEECHER TO WILLIAM.

"October 26, 1825.

"The pressure of business has rendered it extremely difficult for me to write.

"Catharine recovered so as to be in her school examination, which surpassed in the number, respectability, and interest of those present any preceding one. The prospects of a winter school are good.

"Edward has been a great help to me and a great comfort. His piety and talents demand our united thanksgivings to God. His labors have been well received by our people, as also were yours.

"But for his and your aid much must have been omitted which I have been able to accomplish.

"George returns this week on Monday. He is impressed considerably, but has no hope. The revival continues, and is becoming now for six weeks more and more prosperous. The subject is pressing hard upon a number of young men, of whose ultimate conversion we entertain some hope. The Church is more extensively acquainted with the revival by inspection, and feeling, and prayer. Six were admitted to the Church last sacrament; twenty-four now stand propounded, among whom are Mary and Harriet. * * * May Jesus watch over you, and all of us, and give us favor and usefulness before man and God."

THE SAME.

"November 1, 1825.

"This has been a good day; twenty-five have been added to the Church, and the work of awakening and conversion moves on and increases, on the whole, both here and in Milton. We have been this three weeks in a state of deep sympathy for George, whose distress precluded sleep, almost, for many nights, and his voice of supplication could be heard night and day. But to-day, and especially this evening, he seems to be very happy, and, so far as I can judge by conversation, on good grounds. He is now with the girls, singing louder than he prayed. What shall we render to the Lord! Mary and Harriet communed to-day for the first time, and it has been a powerful and delightful day."

THE SAME.

"November 6, 1825.

" * * * George seems to be one of the happiest creatures ever I saw. All his quickness and characteristic ardor seems now to be heightened by the contrast of joy with recent distress. He talks rapidly, and with much and unaffected simplicity, and is exceedingly interested now in the meetings, and begs he may stay a little longer to enjoy them. * * * God has done for me exceeding abundantly in giving me such children as he has, and in giving me their hearts, as well as taking them himself."

THE SAME.

"November 9, 1825.

"Our family concert of prayer was held in the study, on Thanksgiving day — your mother, Aunt Esther, Henry, and Charles. It was a most deeply solemn, tender, and interesting time. The prayer which your mother made exceeded almost anything which I hear of supplication from the lips of any one. She is a holy woman, and eminently gifted in prayer. I trust the results of the concert will not be transient, but will be seen in time and in eternity.

"Henry and Charles have both been awakened, and are easily affected and seriously disposed now. But as yet it is like the wind upon the willow, which rises as soon as it is passed over. It does not grapple, but the effect is good in giving power to conscience and moral principle, producing amendment in conduct."

DR. BEECHER TO DR. TAYLOR (*after the Danbury Council*).

"Litchfield, December, 1825.

"DEAR BROTHER, — I have been at home only just long enough for my brain to get still after the whirl it was in while we were together, and for my intellectual eye to see clearly after the smoke passed away which filled the atmosphere.

"As it seems not improbable that we both may be called again to act as counsel in this wicked world — though I hope not on opposite sides — I have concluded to volunteer for your consideration several of the maxims which have regulated, and I believe, in time to come, will continue to regulate my conduct.

"I will never undertake the defense of a cause which I do not believe to be founded in truth and equity.

"As a general rule, I will confine my advocacy to the defense of ministerial innocence, and the assistance of the churches in the administration of discipline.

"As a general rule, I will not undertake for individuals against the pastor and the Church. The presumption is that the pastor and the Church are right, and, if not, the injured may obtain lay counsels; and it is better for the unity of the cause that ministerial counsel be for the Church, and not against her.

"I have never felt myself at liberty to go into another man's parish, and interfere directly or indirectly with a case of unfinished discipline, or to break up a settlement already made. This would lead to much evil, and call forth a general disapprobation justly unfavorable to my influence in the churches. Though we got along marvelously well in our treatment of each other, and in our temper as advocates, it is my firm resolution to get along still better, if ever called to manage a cause again.

"I am resolved to avoid all indication of impatience, and all tokens of my light estimation of an argument, and to use always only the language of candor and dispassionate courtesy, and to maintain and express only kind and Christian feeling. Doubtless I shall come short, but certainly less than if I had not a high rule, and strong resolution to conform to it."

A very pretty anecdote has been sent to the editor concerning the mutual relations of Dr. Beecher and Dr. Taylor when engaged on opposite sides in a certain famous ecclesiastical council. The feeling waxed so high in the place that the opposing parties would not speak to each other, and it was supposed their respective advocates would share the same feeling. They were lodged each respectively with the leading family of the party they represented. When dinner-time came the first day neither of the doctors were to be found, and search was made far and near, till a little girl found them quietly sitting in an orchard, with their arms thrown over each other's necks, concocting their plan of operations together. Such a beginning ended in peace in the parish. Our informant is the little girl who found them.

DR. BEECHER TO EDWARD.

"December 30, 1825.

"Henry and Charles have both had slight awakenings, which have increased the power of conscience, but promise no immediate saving results. Mr. L—— has been faithful with Henry, and, I trust, successful. He says in a letter, 'His observance of my regulations relating to study has become exact and punctual. His diligence has all along gradually increased, and I think he has arrived at that full purpose which will insure his making a scholar. My method of instruction for beginners is a system of extended, minute, and reiterated drilling, and the make of his mind is such as fits him to receive benefits from the operation.'

"I have given all my time to the *Connecticut Observer*, and, including my pastoral labors, have never labored more entirely up to the line of possibility in my life, minding always not to step over. Do you read the *Observer?* It would take away part of my pleasure in writing if you do not.

"The revival — I have never said it, or allowed myself to think it or feel it — is probably, for the time, nearly concluded. There are one or two districts where I shall make an effort, and then the whole ground will have been gone over, and will probably yield no more fruit at present; so I shall soon organize the Bible-class, and endeavor to make the most of what we have gained, and to prepare the way for another onset as soon as new materials shall rise up, which will not be long. It is never worth while to chase a revival after it is gone by. The laws of mind and of divine sovereignty are in unison, and after the greater stimulus has been applied and failed, it will do no good to apply the less. After one battle and victory, it remains to clear the decks and prepare for another. This I shall attempt to do. As to my prospects here I shall say but little. If the society here would not hinder, but would co-operate with me, I should desire no better situation; but, for a year past, they have occasioned me much trial and discouragement, and raised in my mind doubts about my duty which I never expected to feel. At such a crisis in my own mind, rumors are floating here from Boston of the purpose of the Hanover Society to give me a call; and it has been said they would do it if they knew I would accept. On that point I can not speak to any one, can not even decide for myself; and yet, if I am to see it my duty to go hence, that, perhaps, is the place to which, above all others, I should prefer to go. But I dare not stir; so I have made up my mind to do my duty here, and leave the event to God, believing that, if he has any thing for me to do here, he will make my way prosperous, or, if elsewhere, he will open the door himself, and not leave me to push it open. My people, with the exception of two or three, are, I doubt not, cordial, and whether they would unship me if they could, I can not tell; some things lately have looked that way."

V

SIX SERMONS ON INTEMPERANCE

THE occasion which called for these sermons is thus described by Dr. Beecher:

"There was a neighborhood about four miles out, called Bradleysville, where I used to preach on Sabbath afternoon, and have a lecture in the week. The first time I went it was connected with a revival of religion, and —— —— and his wife became pious. He was nearly the first male convert I had after I went to Litchfield, and was always most affectionate and kind. 'Twas my home there when I went out to preach and spend the night. He gave me more presents than any two or three, and was one of my most useful and excellent young men. The meetings, about this time, had been discontinued for some cause for a time. On setting them up again, I preached at his house as usual, but it did not go as it used to, and the second time the same. After lecture I went out doors a few moments, and when I came in, found he was abed, and his wife was weeping. I felt a shock of presentiment. I drew up my chair by her side and said, 'What is the matter?' 'Oh, matter enough,' said she. 'Who is it? Is it your father?' I knew he had some liabilities that way. She told me it was her husband too. 'Is it possible? is it possible?' 'Yes, it is possible!'

"I thought to myself as I rode home, 'It is now or never. I must go about it immediately, or there is no chance of their salvation.' These sermons I had projected early. I rather think it was at East Hampton that I struck out a considerable skeleton. They were laid by to be finished when I could get time. I knew where they were; I had laid them up; so I began the next Sabbath, and continued as fast as I could write them — one every Sabbath, I think. I wrote under such a power of feeling as never before or since. Never could have written it under other circumstances. They took hold of the whole congregation. Sabbath after Sabbath the interest grew, and became the most absorbing thing ever heard of before. A wonder — of weekly conversation and interest, and, when I got through, of eulogy. All the old farmers that brought in wood to sell, and used to set up their cart-whips at the groggery, talked

about it, and said, many of them, they would never drink again.

"The father was rescued, but the son was carried away. But when he died he was in possession of his mind, and seemed to have Christian feeling. And there is this hope about it: his mother was an habitual drinker, and he was nursed on milk punch, and the thirst was in his constitution. He was a retailer, and so became bound hand and foot. He reformed for a season, but went back. I indulge the hope that God saw it was a constitutional infirmity, like any other disease."

EXTRACTS FROM SERMONS.

"What, then, is this universal, natural, and national remedy for intemperance?

"IT IS THE BANISHMENT OF ARDENT SPIRITS FROM THE LIST OF LAWFUL ARTICLES OF COMMERCE BY A CORRECT AND EFFICIENT PUBLIC SENTIMENT, SUCH AS HAS TURNED SLAVERY OUT OF HALF OF OUR LAND, AND WILL YET EXPEL IT FROM THE WORLD.

1825–1860.

"Nothing should now be said by way of crimination for the past; for verily we have all been guilty in this thing, so that there are few in the land whose brother's blood may not cry out against them from the ground on account of the bad influence which has been lent in some way to the work of destruction.

"We are not, therefore, to come down in wrath upon the distillers, and importers, and vendors of ardent spirits. None of us are enough without sin to cast the first stone; for who would have imported, or distilled, or vended, if all the nominally temperate in the land had refused to drink? It is the buyers who have created the demand for ardent spirits, and made distillation and importation a gainful traffic; and it is the custom of the temperate, too, which inundates the land with the occasion of so much and such unmanageable temptation. Let the temperate cease to buy, and the demand for ardent spirits will fall in the market three fourths, and ultimately will fail wholly, as the generation of drunkards shall hasten out of time.

"To insist that men whose capital is embarked in the production or vending of ardent spirits shall manifest the entire magnanimity and self-denial which is needful to save the land, though the example would be glorious to them, is more than we have a right to expect or demand. Let the consumer do his duty, and the capitalist, finding his employment unproductive, will quickly dis-

cover other channels of useful enterprise. All language of impatient censure against those who embarked in the traffic of ardent spirits while it was deemed a lawful calling should therefore be forborne. It would only serve to irritate, and arouse prejudice, and prevent investigation, and concentrate a deaf and deadly opposition against the work of reformation. No *ex post facto* laws. Let us all rather confess the sins which are past, and leave the things which are behind, and press forward in one harmonious attempt to reform the land, and perpetuate our invaluable blessings.

"This, however, can not be done effectually so long as the traffic in ardent spirits is regarded as lawful, and is patronized by men of reputation and moral worth in every part of the land. Like slavery, it must be regarded as sinful, impolitic, and dishonorable. That no measures will avail short of rending ardent spirits a contraband of trade is nearly self-evident. * * *

"Could all the forms of evil produced in the land by intemperance come upon us in one horrid array, it would appal the nation, and put an end to the traffic in ardent spirit. If, in every dwelling built by blood, the stone from the wall should utter all the cries which the bloody traffic extorts, and the beam out of the timber should echo them back, who would build such a house, and who would dwell in it? What if in every part of the dwelling, from the cellar upward, through all the halls and chambers, babblings, and contentions, and voices, and groans, and shrieks, and wailings, were heard day and night! What if the cold blood oozed out, and stood in drops upon the walls, and, by preternatural art, all the ghastly skulls and bones of the victims destroyed by intemperance should stand upon the walls, in horrid sculpture, within and without the building! Who would rear such a building? What if at eventide and at midnight the airy forms of men destroyed by intemperance were dimly seen haunting the distilleries and stores where they received their bane, or following the track of the ship engaged in the commerce — walking upon the waves, flitting athwart the deck, sitting upon the rigging, and sending up, from the hold within and from the waves without, groans, and loud laments, and wailings? Who would attend such stores? Who would labor in such distilleries? Who would navigate such ships?

"Oh! were the sky over our heads one great whispering-gallery, bringing down about us all the lamentation and woe which intemperance creates, and the firm earth one sonorous medium of sound, bringing up around us from beneath the wailings of the damned, whom the commerce in ardent spirit had sent thither —

these tremendous realities, assailing our senses, would invigorate our conscience, and give decision to the purpose of reformation. But these evils are as real as if the stone did cry out of the wall, and the beam answered it; as real as if, day and night, wailings were heard in every part of the dwelling, and blood and skeletons were seen upon every wall; as real as if the ghostly forms of departed victims flitted about the ship as she passed over the billows, and showed themselves nightly about stores and distilleries, and with unearthly voices screamed in our ears their loud lament. They are as real as if the sky over our heads collected and brought down about us all the notes of sorrow in the land, and the firm earth should open a passage for the wailings of despair to come up from beneath."

VI

REQUEST FOR DISMISSION, READ BEFORE THE CONGREGATION

When I gave myself to God in the Gospel of his Son, it was done with the following views:

That all expectation of accumulating property for myself and family be relinquished, leaving it to God in his own way to take care of me when sickness or age should supersede active labor. That it would be my duty to live in family state, and to obey the injunction of providing for my own household, and of training my children in the nature and admonition of the Lord with reference to their piety and usefulness. I never expected or desired to give them any thing but their own minds and faculties, properly cultivated and prepared for active usefulness.

That for my support I must rely wholly upon the cultivation of my own intellectual and moral powers, and my fidelity in the pastoral office and in the Church of God, and on his promised blessing to render these means effectual, leaving it entirely to his providence to indicate where I should serve him, and in what manner I should be supported.

With these views I gave myself to the ministry, first at East Hampton, on Long Island, with a salary of $300 and my fire-wood, which, after five years, was raised to $400; and then, as my family increased, proving incompetent, at the end of another five years I obtained a dismission, and settled in this place May 29, 1810, upon a salary of $800, with an understanding that I might calculate upon a voluntary supply of wood. Early after my settlement my wife (of beloved memory) informed me, from year to year, that my income did not meet the unavoidable expenses of the family, and advised me to communicate the fact to the society. I replied that I had come hither with the determination of removing no more, and that, in my judgment, the condition of the society forbade a request for the increase of my salary. She suggested the expedient of my keeping school, to which I replied that my views of pastoral duty did not allow me. Her reply was, "Something must be done, and, with your permission, I will appropriate my own income to enlarge our dwelling, and rent the rooms, and keep boarders." To this, with some reluctance, I consented. At this time our arrears amounted to about $600. She made the attempt, lost her property, and by undue exertion, as I suppose, her life, and brought me into a condition of inextricable embarrassment, from which, ten years since, you relieved me with a generosity unparalleled.

From this time until the public education of my sons commenced, my income just yielded me a support. The extra expense of educating my sons I expected to meet by keeping boarders, and the disposal of a little property left me at Guilford, which, as yet, is not at my control. In the past instance I succeeded without any alarming accumulation of debt, on receiving from my son Edward $225, and from another child, Catharine, $160. About this time my health failed, which made a difference of at least $200 in my expenses in the course of two years. The state of my health demanding diversion of mind and manual labor, I made a purchase of land, by which my health has been regained, and which now may be disposed of, I trust, without loss. In my attempt to educate a second son I am brought to a stand. For three years I have perceived, each year, an arrearage, which it was my hope, by special exertions, to retrieve the next year. That expectation exists no more. My late investigation of my concerns has convinced me that there is an annual deficiency in my salary of $200, wholly irremediable by any possible efforts of my own, or by any authorized reliance upon Providence in my present condition; that I can not possibly, with my present income, cancel the past arrears of deficient support, nor continue the education of my children, nor maintain my credit for punctuality, nor my ministerial influence, nor my health nor spirits to prosecute the duties of my ministry; and, on looking at the condition of the society, it was my deliberate opinion that it could not be expected that they would meet these exigencies of my condition with any such degree of unanimity and cordiality as would not render the attempt useless to me and injurious to the society. The abandonment of the public education of my sons, painful in itself, seemed to furnish no prospect of relief; the expense of their support still resting upon me for no inconsiderable period, and being as *really*, if not as much beyond my ability, in my present circumstances as their public education. For several days and nights, while agitated by this subject, I endured what I shall not attempt to describe only by saying that a few days more of such suspense and mental agitation must for the time have prostrated me entirely.

I came, however, at length to the conclusion that I must ask for a dismission, sell my property, pay my debts, and cast myself upon the protection and guidance of heaven. Twelve hours after this determination was made, and without any agency, directly or indirectly, of mine, I received a communication, of which the following is an extract:

"Boston, January 2, 1826.

"Rev. and dear Sir, — The Committee appointed to recommend to the Hanover Church a suitable person to take the pastoral charge of them, have determined to report your name, provided there is a reasonable prospect that a call from the Church will be successful, and they have no doubt but that such a report would meet the cordial approbation of their constituents. But we have not the means, dear sir, of knowing the prospect of your accepting our invitation without writing you confidentially on the subject, which I now do by the order of the Church committee, of which I am a member. You will not think the question we put to be indelicate or disrespectful, since in our circumstances it seems expedient and necessary. A call, properly speaking, can not be given confidentially. It will, as a thing of course, be soon known abroad. In the present case it would excite much notice, and be the topic of much remark, and, if not successful, would greatly injure us; hence our cautionary measures.

"Permit me, then, respectfully to ask you, dear sir, whether, should our Church invite you to become their pastor, you would be able and willing to express an opinion before your Consociation that the Head of Zion called you to this city? I only remark that we have come to our present decision after looking a long time and very attentively, with many prayers, at the indications of Providence, and we cry to you with the utmost earnestness to come over and help us. We shall wait with some anxiety for your answer, which we hope you will send as soon as your convenience will permit it."

On the subject of this communication I would not consult my friends, nor ascertain the feelings of my people. It became indispensable to return an answer *yea* or *nay* upon my own responsibility. Therefore, making it a subject of prayer, and bringing to the consideration of it all the means of forming a correct decision in my power, I returned the following answer:

"DEAR SIR, — In reply to yours, I have to say that, when I came to Litchfield, it was both for the purpose of spending my days with the people, should it please God in his providence to enable me to provide for my household, and serve him without distraction in the Gospel of his Son. Experience has proved, however, that I accepted of a salary, as I did in my first settlement, which can not by me be made to cover the unavoidable expense of rearing up my family for usefulness. I do not regret either settlement, believing that I have had the approbation of my God, as I have had of my conscience and heart, and that, if I am saved, I shall meet many from both my pastoral charges whom I may present to Jesus Christ as the children he has given me.

"It is, however, more than a year since I have become alarmed at the disproportion between my expenses and my income, and have regarded my continuance here as doubtful. It was not, however, more than twelve hours before your communication arrived that I had come to the *full conclusion* that it would be my duty to remove, should God in his providence open my way to some place where I might be useful and unembarrassed with secular perplexities. I regard your letter, therefore, as a providential indication of the divine will concerning my duty."

I have not come to this conclusion from motives of ambition, or a desire or expectation of secular gain, nor hastily, under the influence of dissatisfaction with my people. You have done for me what you promised, and more. Nor with the expectation of escaping from trials here to live without them elsewhere. Nor with the expectation of stronger attachments than bind me to you. Nor have I looked only at my own interest, regardless of yours, but have weighed with as much solicitude the effect of my removal on you as on myself. Nor is it the plea of greater usefulness alone which has brought me to this conclusion; for, though it may be a sufficient reason in some cases, still the difference in this case might not have been sufficient, by apparent and certain things, to have satisfied my mind, and therefore I have not heretofore encouraged overtures for a removal which I might have encouraged, and have sometimes prevented their being made, and always chose to have it understood that my removal was not to be expected. Whatever suspicions any of you may have had on this subject, they have been without foundation. I have always dealt fairly and truly with you in this respect, and I can say with the utmost sincerity that, had my support here been such as that I could have been exempt from solicitude which I could not endure, and have fulfilled, as I understand it, my duty to my family, I would not have consented to receive a call fom any Church or people on earth. I am aware of the unfavorable impression which my repeated embarrassments are likely to have on myself in respect to prudence and economy, and it is probable that some men might have lived and perhaps even thriven upon my income; though I can not perceive how any man, with the family I have had, could give himself as exclusively to study, to pastoral labor, and to the public concerns of the Church as I have done, and rendered his income more available than mine has been. I have known a few ministers who have been wealthy farmers and money-lenders, but their people in spiritual things were as poor as their pastors were rich in the things of this life; and I am sure I would not exchange the souls which God has given me, and the blessedness of bringing them to Christ, and the hope of meeting them in heaven, for all the farms and money in creation.

In respect to the education of my sons, I have no aversion to their being farmers or mechanics, if this was the way in which Providence seemed to indicate that they should serve their generation; nor do I feel as if I had any claim on you to furnish for me the means of giving a public education to them all. But the fact is, I have not the means of making them agriculturalists, and their turn of mind does not seem to lead them to be artisans. It has pleased God to bless them with intellect, and most of them, I hope, with piety, and all of them with the love of study. They have been dedicated to God with many prayers that they might become ministers of Christ, and I do feel as if in these circumstances it is my duty to make every effort in my power to give them an education, and to give them to Jesus as ministers in the Church which he has purchased with his blood. For this end I have practiced as rigid an economy as I was able to do; have denied myself in equipage and dress more than otherwise I should have deemed it my duty to do; and, besides the accumulating arrears of debt, have permitted my buildings and fences to fall into decay for want of repairs. All this, however, will now no longer avail; and, as it has appeared to me, I must abandon their education and run the risk of their ruin, or remove, to continue the effort to educate them under more favorable auspices.

Placed, then, in a situation in which I could no longer move onward with my family establishment, and subjected, as I believed, to the necessity of a removal, I received the inquiry whether I would accept a call, and in the fear of God, and, as I suppose, in accordance with all just rules of interpreting the indications of his providence, I answered in the affirmative. I hope you will do me the justice to believe that I have endeavored to conduct uprightly and in the fear of God, and that the friendship between us, which has been confirmed by the joys and the sorrows of fifteen years, may not all in a moment be sacrificed, but that you will extend to me, in this heart-breaking moment, the consolation of believing that I have not forfeited your confidence, your affection, and an interest in your prayers. And it is my earnest prayer to God that we may, in the season of peculiar temptation and trial, escape those exhibitions of human frailty, folly, and wickedness which sometimes attend the separation of a pastor from his people, and afford to the world one cheering illustration of the fact that a minister and his people can be separated without exasperation and evil speaking, and under the influence of meekness, and resignation, and Christian love. For you, my dear people, if I should be dismissed, I shall cherish an unwavering affection to my dying day; shall always speak of you with affection and commendation, and always rejoice in your prosperity, and rejoice to contribute to it in any way which shall be in my power.

DR. BEECHER TO EDWARD.

"January 8, 1826.

"It is probable I shall myself and family be in Boston in two months or less. In looking into my concerns a short time since, I found it impossible to support my family and educate my children on $800, and that I must remove, or take George out of college immediately.

"I determined on the former with my heart, and conscience, and judgment, and without a moment's wavering, taking in, at the same time, the state of things here.

"In twenty-four hours after I had come to the determination, letters arrived from the committee of the Hanover Church, Boston, asking if I would accept a call.

"Mr. Evarts also wrote, as did the committee, with great urgency. My letters have reached Boston to-day, saying I will accept a call.

"Aunt E—— will go with us, and is, after the first shock, I believe, not displeased. When I went to Sag Harbor to send a letter to Dr. Dwight that I must leave East Hampton, I found a letter in the office inquiring if I would receive a call from Litchfield. And while your mother was writing to Boston that I should now move somewhere, I found in the post-office the above letters — a remarkable coincidence. God has been exceedingly gracious in saving me from a call before I could have decided, and in sending me one twenty-four hours after I had decided."

—— TO EDWARD.

"Hartford, February, 1826.

"It is pretty much decided that father will go the second week in March. The prospect of usefulness is very flattering, but still the idea of leaving Litchfield makes me sad. * * * Litchfield walks, and hills, and woods, the old house, and orchard, and mowing-lot, and many other things, will be painful to leave forever, and feel they are no more ours. The scenes where we have passed our earliest years are full of the feelings of youth. The beautiful lakes and woods, Bantam, Benvenue, the delightful walks and prospects, are all dear to me. I never knew before how strong was my love for inanimate nature, though to me it is not entirely inanimate, for I have conversed more with it in Litchfield than with living beings."

DR. BEECHER TO DR. TAYLOR.

"March 1, 1826.

"I wish to secure your presence and influence with my late charge Saturday after next, and as many Sabbaths as may be agreeable to you and to them. * * * It will comfort my people much, and bring them around you for advice, and give you a commanding power to aid them in the settlement of a minister. * * *

"Don't fail to go and do good a few times. I want to see you much. Want a man of your formation for Litchfield. Do you know of any one? I set out for Boston on Monday. * * * I should not have left Connecticut without consulting you but that Providence made the necessity of a removal too plain and indispensable to require consultation or leave any doubt.

"But in Massachusetts I shall not forget Connecticut, and may do something still to help. How comes on Brother H——'s cry of heresy? What was the result of your conference? Is he acting badly still? Is he gaining strength, or going down? Don't fail to write soon."

VII

BOSTON

In some respects the Boston of to-day is a different city from the Boston of 1826. At that time it was a much smaller city, with a more nearly homogeneous population, and, therefore, far more susceptible of being influenced perceptibly by a single mind.

Boys then skated in winter where now rise some of the finest public buildings and most sumptuous private residences in the country. It is estimated that the Back Bay lands alone will have added in 1870 two hundred acres to the city area.

East Boston, now a beautiful part of the city, was then a thinly settled pasture on what was called Noddle's Island. The Worcester Dépôt, that vomitory of the travel and the trade of the Great West and South, with its spacious freight and passenger accommodations, and numerous blocks of buildings adjoining, stand on ground obtained by filling up what was then known as South Cove.

While the area of the city has been greatly enlarged by these and other additions, the population has advanced from fifty to not far from two hundred thousand.

The character of the population has, at the same time, been materially affected by the introduction of the railroad system. Stages then were in their glory, and a visit to Andover or Groton, or some such suburban town, occupied a good half day or more. One can almost hear even yet the rattle of hoofs, crash of wheels, and impatient thundering at the front door at two o'clock in the morning, when such a journey was to be undertaken.

Now stages, with all their poetical associations, are gone, and seven principal lines of railway converge in Boston. Space is partially annihilated. Practically, the city suburbs are extended an hour's ride by rail in all directions.

The consequences are incalculable. The wealthier classes, once inhabiting the older-built portions of the city, where streets are narrow and crooked, and houses dingy, have moved to the newly-built portions of the city, or are distributed in the surrounding towns, leaving the ground to business and immigration. Thus the material on which the mind of Dr. Beecher energized is largely deposited as a fertilizing alluvium over all the surrounding district, while the scenes of his activity are silted up, as it were, with barren detritus of Old-World formations, giving to Boston in some quarters almost the air of a foreign city.

But Boston was already in 1826, in some respects, a changed city as compared with its former self. A single century had sufficed for a total revolution in religious belief.

"It is now," said Increase Mather[1] in 1722, "the dying wish of one that has been about threescore and six years * * * serving the best of masters in the blessed work of the Gospel, that the churches may stand fast in the faith and order of the Gospel, and hold fast what they have received, that no man take away their crown. * * * And, considering the relation which I have heretofore sustained as a president for twenty years, * * * it is my more particular desire that the tutors in our colleges, from whence the churches expect their supplies, would see to have the students well informed in the points which they must know and serve, that so the work of God among us may not be marred by falling into unskillful and unfaithful hands. * * *

"And, therefore, from the suburbs of that glorious world into which I am now entering, I earnestly testify unto the rising generation that if they sinfully forsake the God, and the hope, and the religious ways of their pious ancestors, the glorious Lord will severely punish their apostasy, and be terrible from his holy places upon them."

With what emotions would this dying saint have seen, at the distance of a single century, that university over which he had presided, to use the language of a recent writer, "from turret to foundation stone illuminated by the calm blaze of that rational religion in whose light all distinctions of Christian doctrine fade away like phosphorescent objects in the sunshine?" With what emotions would he have seen her sending forth the flower of her classes "to oppose in the pulpits of Massachusetts their philosophy of religion, their rhetorical grace, their soothing or animated elocution, and the flowers which they had culled from the field of nature or the Scriptures, to the honest interpretation, the downright argument, the urgent zeal, and the rigid sternness, now, indeed, learning to be less rigid and less stern, of ancient orthodoxy?" What if he had witnessed the "mightier aid given to the principle in which Unitarianism had its origin by the army of educated men who passed

[1] Increase Mather (1693–1723), influential Puritan minister, for a time president of Harvard.

from Cambridge to the highest seats of life, almost sure, whether they believed or not with their academic teachers, at least with them to disbelieve!" *

What if he could have foreseen the hour when "all the old churches in the metropolis of New England, with one exception, which might cease to be an exception, had passed through the old Arminianism of 1750 into Unitarianism, some of them to the extreme of that empty and Christless theory of which Belsham and Priestley were the apostles!" † [2]

The feelings with which Dr. Beecher entered upon the metropolitan arena, after having witnessed afar the successive steps of portentous change, were as though in him one of the old Puritans had risen from the dead. When he came sometimes into his Tuesday-evening lecture, after a visit to the burial-ground on Copp's Hill, there was that in the prayer and in the sermon that seemed like the rolling in of the Atlantic upon the beach.

Every step of the controversy — the election of Ware to the Hollis professorship in 1805; the establishment of the Panoplist; the founding of Amherst College and the Theological Seminary at Andover; the opening of Park Street; the thunder of Griffin's eloquence, startling the death-slumber of the children of the Pilgrims like an archangel's trump; the dark day of discouragement when he retired disheartened, and the whole enterprise seemed to have well-nigh failed; ‡ the ordination in his place of a son of the beloved instructor, Dr. Dwight; the mask torn off in 1815 from Unitarian concealment by the pamphlet entitled "American Unitarianism;" the letters of Channing and Worcester, Stuart, Woods, and Ware; the decision of Chief Justice Parker, annihilating at a blow the legal tenure of the Puritan churches; the letters of Miller, Sparks,[3] and Stuart — he had watched with intense and ever-increasing emotion. "It was as fire in my bones," he said; "my mind was all the time heating — heating — heating."

Thrice already, in 1817, 1819, and in 1823, had he been per-

* Pages from the Ecclesiastical History of New England. J. B. Dow, Boston, 1847.

† Dr. Bacon's Commemorative Discourse, Andover Memorial, p. 88.

‡ Andover Memorial, p. 216.

---

[2] Joseph Priestley (1733–1804) and Thomas Belsham (1750–1829), English Unitarians, taught that Christ was a man. Most American Unitarians then considered Christ as more than a man, though subordinate to God.

[3] Jared Sparks (1789–1866), Unitarian pastor in Baltimore (1819–1823), editor of the *North American Review* (1817–1818) and the *Unitarian Miscellany* (1821–1822). Professor of History at Harvard (1838–1849), president of Harvard (1849–1853), he wrote many volumes on American history.

mitted to lift his voice in Eastern Massachusetts. Now the sacred city of the Pilgrims became the appointed scene of his labors. The posture of affairs is thus sketched by a pen not over-partial to Puritan peculiarities, however loyal to the Trinitarian faith:

"The Christian Examiner became the chief and the able organ of those doctrines for whose promulgation it was destined and designed to labor with the spirit that beseemed its title. It leaned upon the Baltimore sermon of Channing, and reproached the orthodox for the separation which eight years had now decided. But its first volume contained a report of the 'Massachusetts Evangelical Society,' a Unitarian body — a report which was plainly intended to be a landmark which might either bound encroachment, or demonstrate the falsehood of the charge of encroachment. It thus protested against the progress of that mode of thinking which delights to represent 'a God all mercy.'

" 'The prevalence,' it said, 'of the modern sect of Universalists, who deny the doctrine of a future retribution, and who do not consider a pious and holy life essential to happiness hereafter, is particularly alarming, and calls for the special notice of all serious Christians. We think this system to be most injurious to the interests of good morals, and to the welfare of civil society, as well as fatally dangerous to the souls of men, and we believe it directly contrary to the plainest declarations of the holy Gospel.' The clerical trustees whose signatures were affixed to this document were Bancroft, Thayer, Foster, Lowell, Pierce, Kendall, Parkman, Ripley, and Ware. It had the fate of many other landmarks, and remains to denote the period and the men.

"In 1825 the American Unitarian Association was formed, for the concentration of Unitarian efforts and the propagation of Unitarian sentiments through books, and tracts, and missionaries. There were, indeed, grave questions which might have been expected to divide those efforts, as they certainly separated those sentiments. There was a higher and a lower class of Unitarians, and still beyond these a highest and a lowest. But it was calmly announced that, concerning these lowest doctrines, 'those who agreed in the great point of the simple unity of God differed, and should differ in peace.' Only the phrase 'the eternal Son of God' was unscriptural and absurd; every thing else might claim an undisturbed tolerance. In its first year the Christian Examiner announced to the world that he believed enough who believed no more than the humanity of Jesus Christ, who denied the existence of the devil, and who deemed the allusions of the New Testament to evil spirits to be a mere indulgence of the language of popular superstition.

"The Christian Examiner of 1827 was content to acknowledge that its editors 'thought they should prefer to the speculations of the infidel theologians of Germany even Calvinism itself, in a mitigated state, though they might hesitate about some of the more odious and mischievous forms in which it had lately appeared.' It acquiesced in the reasoning that 'to worship Christ as God was to deny him,' one of the shameless absurdities of Whitman of Waltham; [4] and in the statement which the life of Norton [5] was given to sustain, that the New Testament was not a revelation, but the history of a revelation. The most powerful and popular arguments, however, were still aimed at distorted pictures of Calvinism, for which the most grim of ancient Calvinists hardly furnished an outline. If the resemblance was denied, it was said that orthodoxy had changed its features, and was preparing to attach itself to the triumph of rational religion. But not the less was the picture assailed with triumphant indignation.

"Channing, in the noonday of his renown, Pierpont,[6] with his air of undaunted frankness, and Dewey,[7] with that eloquence which could invest with 'a glory and a glow' sentiments the most earthly and frivolous, all denounced the Calvinistic system as ascribing to the Maker of mankind acts which would dishonor the throne of a human tyrant. It was no preference for abstract Unitarianism that reconciled men to the surrender of all which it denied. But one writer thus clothed the opposite doctrine with the most revolting and terrific aspect. Another spread out a charming landscape in contrast, embracing all which is lovely and of good report, without one stern passage of the pilgrimage. Another hastened to allow the claims of all worldly business, and the innocence of all worldly pleasures within the limits imposed by a moderate temper and a wise regard to personal interest. Another had not a severe word for any opinion, and owned that he might himself be

[4] Bernard Whitman (1796–1834), advocate of temperance and slavery, became Unitarian pastor of Waltham, Mass., in 1826, after a division of the liberally inclined church over the issue of the dismission of the Calvinist minister.

[5] Andrews Norton (1786–1853), Professor of Sacred Literature at Harvard Divinity School, critic of Trinitarians and of Transcendentalists, wrote a history of the New Testament canon based on outside evidence.

[6] John Pierpont (1785–1866), poet and business man, studied at Litchfield Law School (1810–1812) before graduation from Harvard Divinity School. His Boston congregation disliked his reforming zeal, and he was dismissed in 1845.

[7] Orville Dewey (1794–1882), Andover graduate, became a prominent Unitarian minister in Boston and N.Y.

in error on any topic, however momentous might seem the necessity of truth. It would have been wonderful if the undecided, the indifferent, the inexperienced, the prosperous, the light-hearted, all who were as far as possible from being weary and heavy laden, had not been swayed like the trees in the wind. To such, and to those who honestly abhorred the Calvinistic creed and knew no other, were now added a company of speculative minds, that went forth, like the raven from the ark, over the ocean of free inquiry, and too often, like the raven, returned no more." *

It is scarcely necessary to add that the system of Unitarianism, in all its forms, Dr. Beecher regarded as the deadly foe of human happiness, whose direct tendency was to prevent true conviction and conversion, stop revivals of religion, and leave men bound hand and foot under the power of the adversary.

He could not be loyal to Christ, benevolent to man, or true to his own convictions without making war on such a system by every means consistent with the injunction, "Be wise as serpents, harmless as doves."

Subsequent developments, and the meteoric descent of star after star toward the vapors of Pantheism and infidelity, have more than justified the course he pursued and the sentiments he expressed.

* Pages from the Ecclesiastical History of New England, pp. 87–93.

VIII

CORRESPONDENCE, 1826

WILLIAM TO EDWARD.

"April 11, 1826.

"* * * I SPENT a week in Boston at the installation. Father was quite unwell with dyspepsia; he suffered much from fear, and does still. I never knew him more cast down. He felt as though his course was finished. He had serious thoughts of sending for you, and had even written the letter, but concluded to wait and see how he got over the Sabbath. This was Friday. He took a chair, and turned it down before the fire and laid down. 'Ah! William,' said he, 'I'm done over! I'm done over!' Mother told him he had often thought so before, and yet in two days had been nearly well again. 'Yes; but I never was so low before. It's all over with me! I only want to get my mind composed in God — but it is hard to see such a door of usefulness set open and not be able to enter.' You may be sure I felt this deeply. He seemed so sure that I almost feared it was so. I never saw him so low before.

"But we at length succeeded in cheering him some, and on Saturday I rode with him to Marblehead, and he was very much better, and preached on the Sabbath quite well, without much fatigue; on Monday I left, and he has continued, with much fear and trembling, to preach since. * * * The house where he preaches is crowded, and the vestry meetings also. He has twenty or twenty-five inquirers; and there seems to be a revival spirit in the churches. They board at Deacon Lambert's, in Pitt Street."

DR. BEECHER TO WILLIAM.

"Boston, March 31, 1826.

" * * * The pews sold, it is said, well — eighty-five, I believe, which covered about two thirds the expense of the house. The premium given on choice of pews was $1200 to $1300. All seem gratified and encouraged. * * *

"I hope that by still closer attention to regimen I shall relieve the acid which eating generates, and which so annoys me with restlessness and pain, all of which I could endure and submit to but for the dispossessing, agitating nature of the disease. I make no disclosure of my situation as yet, and wish you not to, hoping to grapple through once more, as I have often done. Should necessity, however, require, I shall hire a horse and chaise and depart for Connecticut, hoping to stave off the present turn, and take care and not get another; for the door here is wide, and I need only health to enter into an abundant harvest. There were twenty in the inquiry meeting this evening after you left. This eve the vestry was as full and solemn as on Sabbath. But how I shall stand it I know not, being held from day to day in suspense and fear.

"*Saturday morning*. We had a good Church meeting last evening. There is, I trust, a revival spirit rising among them. Pilsbury,[1] one of my old acquaintances and friends, and a Nettletonian, was with me, and is stationed within my diocese as a missionary, and hereafter we shall plan and act in concert."

THE SAME.

"Boston, April 10, 1826.

"It is with a deep sense of the divine goodness that I am able to say that my most distressing malady is yielding to prayer and regimen, and, I hope, passing away. Through the last week my convalescence was so slow that I could scarcely perceive it, only in its results of labor which I was able to perform. But I preached on fast-day two long sermons on Intemperance, attended several other meetings in the week, and at the close found myself evidently gaining strength.

"The sermons on Intemperance struck well, and it is the wish of many that I should preach them all, which I have concluded to do.

"Yesterday was a good day, though full of care and labor. Three baptisms in the morning, and the admission to the Church of five members from the world. In the afternoon the ordination of deacons before the congregation, and subsequently the administration of the sacrament. There were, besides our own, nearly a hundred communicants upon invitation, and not many of them from the

[1] Ithamar Pillsbury (1794–1859), evangelist among the poor of N.Y. and Boston (1825–1830), in 1835 founded a colony in Ill. that he hoped would bring piety and learning to the West. President of a new, impoverished Western college (1850–1855), he finally took charge of an Old School church.

three orthodox churches; persons probably who, since they came to the city, have formed as yet no connection with any church, though some of them were known to belong to Unitarian churches. But if they will commune with us, under such instruction as I gave in the sermon, it will be an omen for good.

"I was weary, but became refreshed after tea, and attended vestry meeting, and exhorted with more strength and pleasure than at any time before. The meeting crowded and solemn, though Dr. M'Auley [2] preached in Park Street. Most who attend are strangers to all our people, which shows that the light is beginning to shine into darkness, and creates the hope that the darkness will comprehend it.

"To-day I feel as well as on any Monday since I came to the city, and better. The pain and tenderness of my bowels have not ceased, but I am able to take more food, and digest and sleep better, and exercise more. My face is recovering its color, and my eye its firmness, and my heart courage, hope, and purpose of action.

"*You,* who alone, except your mother, know through what extreme debility, and distress, and depression, and fear I have passed, will know how, with me, to render praise to God for his goodness in turning my fears into hope, my debility into strength, and the region of the shadow of death into the light of life.

"If I ever felt my own emptiness, and unworthiness, and insufficiency, or any earnestness of desire to consecrate all my powers to the service of God, it seems to me that I feel all these things eminently now. The field here is truly ample and white to the harvest, and my past preparations and experience seem to render it hopeful that I may yet be permitted to reap an abundant harvest.

"But, though my ministry call out Unitarians of distinction, it is not on this kind of celebrity that I chiefly rely. It is, indeed, desirable to be able to create a curiosity among intelligent men to come and hear the truth, because it enables us to become the expounders of our own doctrines, and to wipe away aspersion and prejudice, and some arrows may hit and stick, even in high places. But, after all, the kingdom of God cometh not with observation; and I rely more on my vestry meetings on Sabbath and Tuesday eve, and on my chapel meetings on Friday eve at the North, and on my visits and labors among the middle class and the poor, than upon all the éclat of reputed talents and eloquence, and all the

[2] Thomas M'Auley (1780–1842), then pastor in Philadelphia, later took charge of the Murray St. Church in N.Y.C. and served as president of Union Seminary (1836–1840).

running to hear, and all the movements and talk from that source among the mighty and the noble. My plan is to retire and go to work silently, until the results shall tell in 'souls renewed and sins forgiven.' You will not fail to pray for me, that my health and faith fail not, as I shall not cease to give thanks that I have so many and so dear children to care for and co-operate with me in promoting the religion of Jesus Christ."

DR. BEECHER TO WILLIAM.

"Boston, April 13, 1826.

"Catharine arrived Friday, and left all well at Hartford. She has been and is a comfort to me. Her examination was royal, and all her prospects of a school and of great usefulness are exceeding good. * * * For all these mercies let the Lord be praised.

"We shall set out for Litchfield on Monday of next week. I can not pay your stage fare, but, if you are willing to walk, which I think will be much for your health, I will pay your traveling expenses. I hope you will accept this offer, as I shall go first to Guilford and New Haven, and shall need your assistance with your mother at Litchfield both before and after my arrival. * * * We have taken the house at North End — new, airy, and delightful within (No. 18 Sheafe Street), though surrounded by dreary roads to get to it. Can not have every thing in one place."

DR. BEECHER TO EDWARD.

"Boston, April 19, 1826.

"There is, I find, an earnest desire at Park Street to have you supply them. As things now stand there is no impediment, but a manifest providential indication that you should come. And my advice and my request now is that you will do it without fail; first, because your presence will be a great consolation to me just at this time, and, secondly, as to ulterior consequences, it is only following the leadings of Providence. And as we are not to push open doors before Providence opens them, so neither are we to refuse to enter when they are opened, but simply take ground as fast as Providence indicates, as the means by which the further purposes of Heaven concerning us may be disclosed.

"Another reason is that there are the little clouds of a revival in every orthodox Church, which four weeks of exertion such as you, with myself and others, may make, might produce an overpowering shower. And the public feeling here now is such that another revival would tell wonderfully."

DR. BEECHER TO EDWARD.

"June 11, 1826.

"The work here progresses, I believe, though the last inquiry meeting it rained hard, and yet there were twenty-five. The two last Tuesday evenings have been most deeply solemn, as was the last Sabbath, though the election week preceded. Brother Wisner has got home, and I hope, in concert with him and Brother Green,[3] soon to get under way in some general movement.

"Miss V—— and E—— called yesterday. I talked and prayed with E—— alone. She wept, but I fear the work does not grapple. Sometimes it seems as if persons had too much, and sometimes too little intellect to be converted easily. But all things are possible with God."

MRS. BEECHER TO ——.

"June 25, 1826.

" * * * I am happy to say we are beginning to be really comfortable. * * * I know not how a minister can desire any thing better than to preach the Gospel in Boston. * * * The four youngest children are with us. The girls are at Hartford, established as a family, with Aunt Esther at their head. Edward and George are at New Haven, William at Andover. My husband's health is pretty good. He has some dyspepsia at times, but it always leaves him on the Sabbath. He preaches a good deal, and with much encouragement.

"There is a secret history of Boston which is very interesting — the history of minds and moral influence. Of this we have learned some already, and shall, probably, much more. We are at the North End, to which at first I felt reluctant. Mr. Beecher is enthusiastic in regard to this situation. This soil was pressed by the feet of the Pilgrims, and watered by their tears, and consecrated by their prayers. Here are their tombs, and here are their children who are to be brought back to the fold of Christ. Their wanderings and dispersions are lamentable, their captivity long and dark, but God will turn it, we hope, and reclaim these churches; this dust and ruin shall live again."

[3] Samuel Green (1792–1834), pastor in Reading, Mass. (1820–1823), and in the Union St. Church, Boston (1823–1834).

DR. BEECHER TO CATHARINE.

"June 30, 1826.

"Your last letters, giving an account of the state of things in your school, have been read with deep interest and much thanksgiving, though not without some solicitude.

"The very high state of excited feeling, though extremely natural among young Christians, and powerful in its effects while it lasts, is too hazardous to health to be indulged, and necessarily too short-lived to answer in the best manner the purpose of advancing a revival. In my early efforts I gave myself up to strong feeling, which I have since learned to economize, or I should long since have been in my grave or been useless.

"You must, therefore, all of you, instantly put yourselves upon a different system, which I will describe and hasten to send you, or you will all be prostrate, I have no doubt.

"The state of feeling to be cultivated in those who superintend a revival is a mild, but constant and intense desire of heart for the awakening and conversion of sinners.

"When I say intense, I do not mean agitating, but strong and steady. A fullness and strength of desire, which does not ruffle the passions, and is compatible with the most cool and collected state of mind, both for planning and for action, and, at the same time, predisposes for earnest prayer, and for speaking to stupid and awakened sinners a word in season.

"It is a genial warmth of heart, of steady benevolent temperature, compared with the more intense heat and flashings of holy and animal affections and passions, all boiling at once in the heart.

"It is calm and tranquillizing, for it is full of hope and confidence, and deliberate, unagitating, and unexhausting action. It is more like the cool, determined, comprehensive zeal, and courage, and determination of a general in the day of battle. It is a state of feeling in which the mind and body can both endure for any length of time, for it is benevolence in such quantity as does not demand effort to get it up to the point of intense desire. It is there when at rest on its own level, and does not require all the rivulets of feeling in the soul to pour their contributions in to create power enough to move the wheels of the soul. Animal affection may be comparatively quiet, and yet a mighty, steady energy will keep the wheels of the soul in motion without effort, and without nervous friction.

REV. LYMAN BEECHER D. D.

"This is the state of heart which has carried me through all the revivals I have been in but the first, and that broke me down, and induced nervous habits which I shall never wholly retrieve. It is this self-possession of benevolence, burning mildly and constantly, but with undeclining heat, in the middle of the heart, which has enabled me to go through labors in revivals before which a man of my ardent temperament must otherwise have been prostrated; and it is the letting in to mingle with this the excitement and agitation of too much emotion which has rendered revivals so often fatal to the health of ministers and others.

"Another thing, also, is to be carefully shut out of your souls — I mean an overpowering weight of responsibility and care. We can neither carry the world on our shoulders nor govern it, nor even govern the wants of a very small part of it, which are most immediately under our own eye. Settle it in your heart, therefore, that you are to exercise your best judgment, and perform in the best manner you can your duty, and leave the whole in the hands of God. You can not be accountable for consequences.

"Again, beware that you do not borrow trouble, and create solicitude, and wear and tear, by events in anticipation, one in ten of which may never happen. Sufficient to the day is the evil thereof, as well as the good, pre-eminently in the period of a revival, and especially to those who superintend it. Be therefore quiet. Let not your heart be troubled. Give thanks greatly for the good; and, at whatsoever time you are afraid, trust in the Lord.

" * * * We are all getting better health. Our prospects, I think, are daily more hopeful. The door of usefulness is wide, and, if I may have health to enter in, I have no more for this world to ask. There are glorious things ahead, and, as it seems to me, within reaching distance if I live and have health. But this will be as God sees best, in whom it is ever good to trust."

DR. BEECHER TO EDWARD.

"July, 1826.

"I have kept up the same strain of revival preaching, with the same results, as when you were here. Fifty and sixty attend the inquiry meeting, and from two to five new cases and new hopes each week. There are probably between thirty and forty who have hope. The congregation is full and solemn, and seems to be amalgamated into a homogeneous mass of belief and solemnity by the power of truth.

"As I become more acquainted with the state of Unitarian congregations, I find that there is in them a precious remnant who have not bowed the knee to Baal, and who long to hear the voice of the prophet of God. Events are ripening fast for some result. The light can not be excluded; the stream can not be stopped, and moves as fast, perhaps, as is safe and desirable. The more I become acquainted with my work and opportunity, the more I am satisfied that my opportunity to do good is increased tenfold. For example: at these united prayer meetings I can instruct and influence all the orthodox churches in Boston on the subject of revivals with more ease and as much effect as my own single church in Litchfield. I am now occupied in preparing a result of council for advice at Groton, which leads me to review all the perverse Unitarian judgments against orthodox churches, and to set forth the nature and rights of the churches of Massachusetts, one of the most interesting and important labors I have ever been engaged in, and I expect from it great and good results.

"To conclude, every circumstance in my present condition is agreeable, prosperous, and cheering, and, I have no doubt, operating favorably on my health. Let us be grateful, and do what we can."

DR. BEECHER TO EDWARD.

"August 3, 1826.

"I have again just read your letter at the Missionary Rooms,* and, as it laid me under the necessity of giving definite advice, and on short notice, I considered it proper to consult confidentially Mr. Evarts and Brother Anderson, who is my Judge Reeve, both as counselor and as an affectionate friend.

"They together counsel as I could find if I might have my choice on earth. I read your letter, and the following is their opinion: By no means accept or consent to be invited to the professorship at Dartmouth. * * *

"Last evening a young man of intelligence from a Unitarian society called on me confidentially. He is anxious: has been vehemently prejudiced against orthodoxy: sees that he is coming to it, and revolts; yet feels his depravity, and the need of a change of heart. He calls again on Saturday evening. I think the Lord intends to call him, and make him the harbinger of many more."

* Basement of Hanover Church.

WILLIAM TO EDWARD.

"August 27, 1826.

"I hope to begin to preach in about five years, and so our dear mother's prayers will be answered. I found a paper the other day written by her, in which I find she used to rise before day to pray, and that she used to dedicate her sons to God, to be his servants in his cause.

"Father works hard, and is quite popular, and is doing great good; his meetings are crowded to overflowing."

DR. BEECHER TO EDWARD.

"September 4, 1826.

"The work in Hanover Society is becoming of a more decided cast. The number of inquirers last evening doubled, and things look more like the letting out of waters. About sixty have hope, and appear well — such as we have examined for admission, better than I expected. My heart melted to hear their discreet and satisfying answers before the committee. I have had one young converts' meeting, much to the joy of my heart, and of all present. The shaking among Unitarian societies has, as I judge, but just begun. But it is going on. Two accomplished young ladies called on me to-day for advice. They belong to Unitarian societies, and can not live under the preaching, and wish to join our Church. One is a late convert. I know of five others who are about to leave, persons of high standing, to unite with Hanover Church, and of some others who are coming to consult me on the subject.

"An intelligent young man of Mr. Ware's society has called on me privately three times, and last evening attended the meeting of inquiry, almost, if not quite, in a state of submission.

"This is only a sketch. A wide and effectual door is open, and Unitarians are evidently alarmed, and know not what to do. It would be easy to kindle a fire in all their congregations around Boston and through the state like that which Whitfield [4] kindled in old Arminian congregations."

[4] George Whitefield (1714–1770), English evangelical preacher, leader of the Calvinist Methodists, conducted large, emotional revivals in America during the Great Awakening.

THE SAME.

"September 5, 1826.

"Just as I was about to send a letter last evening, Mr. Evarts called on me to say that the deacons of Park Street, by agreement of the committee, have written to request you to supply four Sabbaths, with a prospect, as he thinks, of their being united to give you a call.

"As to the importance of the stand in Boston, as the centre of extended and powerful action, I have never stood in such a place before, and do not believe that there is, all things considered, such another, perhaps, on earth. It is here that New England is to be regenerated, the enemy driven out of the temple they have usurped and polluted, the college to be rescued, the public sentiment to be revolutionized and restored to evangelical tone. And all this with reference to the resurrection of New England to an undivided and renovated effort for the extension of religious and moral influence throughout the land and through the world.

"All this, under God, is to be accomplished here by intellectual power upon an intellectual people, who are captivated with vigorous intellect and powerful argument, and will come to hear it, and will be influenced by it.

"And when I consider the similarity of our minds, and views, and systems of action, I can not but feel as if the concentration of our resources in a system of preaching and action would give additional momentum to our individual power. * * * You were pleased to say once that nothing brought out your mental vigor and energized your soul like my society. The effect of your society, for obvious reasons, is the same on my mind; and if it please God to place us where the action and reaction of intellectual power may be habitually experienced by us both, the public results may be great and good.

"I write as disinterestedly on this subject as if the social enjoyment of your society would be no greater than that of another. I have not, and shall not allow that to come in as a motive at all; it shall be a consequence, if God please, of my having sought first and only the kingdom of God and his righteousness.

"But, with all these considerations in view, if God moves in a manner which indicates it may be his will to call and fix you here, I should not dare to resist. * * *

"But it is my hope that you will not fail to take hold of the end of the rope that is put into your hand, and pull it, till we see what is on the other end."

DR. BEECHER TO CATHARINE.

"September 8, 1826.

"Yours of the 6th came duly, and awakened many recollections. I was not, however, sick when you was laid in my arms, but young, and fresh, and well. It was a year from that time that I was invaded by sickness. Since then, with a constitution part of iron and part of miry clay, I have been permitted, for the most part, to preach and labor in my vocation, and to see a family of beloved and affectionate children rise up around me, some of whom, with my most beloved Roxana, are not, while most of them remain to be my crown and my comfort to this day. I am a man of many obligations daily multiplying.

"I can neither speak of them nor feel them to their extent. In your life and prosperity I rejoice, being, after Aunt Esther, my nearest contemporary among the ancients of the early days. William, Edward, Mary, George, and Harriet, all in their time and place, have come to be my most affectionate companions and fellow-helpers.

"If earthly good could fill the soul, mine might be running over; and as it is, my consolations are neither few nor small.

"Your request some time ago that I would come on to Hartford I could not find time to answer, and nothing but the urgency and goodness of your motive saved you from the reaction of vexation and rebuke that you should think of such a thing.

"Events have proved it to be needless, as here they have proved it would have been a wanton dereliction of a most interesting and pre-eminently important post of duty. Every Sabbath many persons come on purpose to hear me, brought by curiosity or the invitation or influence of friends, who, so far as I have experience, for the most part feel an abatement of prejudice, and not unfrequently surprise, approbation, solicitude, and ultimately conversion.

"The course I have taken of declining exchanges, and being always at home, favors this method of disseminating truth and removing false impressions, and is producing, if I may judge from all I hear incidentally one way and another, 'no small stir' among

Unitarians, with some doubts whereunto the thing may grow; which doubts the Lord will solve, I fully believe, before many years, if I am permitted to live and enjoy health, together with my fellow-workers here and around. The revival has added about sixty to the number for whom we hope, and is now putting on a more interesting appearance than ever. Our last inquiry meeting was nearly double in numbers to any preceding one."

IX

THE REVIVAL

AUTOBIOGRAPHY.

When I commenced in Hanover Street, the first three Sabbaths the seats were free to all, and thronged above and below. Then they sold the pews, and the fourth Sabbath I preached to the Church and congregation specifically. The house was not thinned. There was a flood of young people of the middle classes that kept the congregation overflowing.

The Church numbered only thirty-seven; but there were many excellent young men in it, such as Lambert, Noyes, Palmer, Stone, Anderson, and others. Lambert was quick to take care of any thing in the house — quick as a cat to see. Noyes was a deliberate, deep, correct thinker. Then there was a fine set of women. There came in speedily a steady stream by letter, so that the house kept full.

The Church had had charge of their own affairs, property, etc., a year before I came, so that they were used to business; and, for fear it might fall into the hands of Unitarians, as other Church property had done, they had a trust deed, giving it entirely and forever to the Church. It was as finely organized a Church as ever trod shoe-leather. Extremely wise they were; I never knew them make a mistake.

When I began among them they were pleased, and more than pleased. I remember, one Sabbath, Anderson came smiling after sermon, and said with emotion, "You will overset us if you are going to preach at this rate!" I never shall forget that. I knew nobody then. I took those subjects that were unquestionable, but solemn, to make them tell on the conscience. I began with prudence, because a minister, however well known at home, and however wise and successful he *has* been, has to make himself a character anew, and find out what material is around him.

They had a Church prayer meeting, which they conducted themselves. I told them they had been able to go alone, and take care of Church business, and I had tried every where to make the Church do something in the prayer meeting, and it was the hardest thing I ever tried; if I went others would go, and if not, not; never could make the weekly prayer meeting succeed. Hence I told them they must take it and sustain it. That went through. Oh, how well it went! 'Twas the best Church I ever saw.

From the beginning my preaching was attended with interest. I could take hold. There was very earnest hearing in the congregation. I saw it was taking hold. Deep solemnity, not mere novelty. I felt in my own soul that the word went forth with power. It was a happy season, hopeful and auspicious. Not long after Dr. Chaplin [1] began to attend. He had been in the habit of listening to a dead, feeble fellow on the wrong side, but who didn't do much on any side. Shall never forget how Chaplin heard. He was of quick, strong feeling, and was wide awake to hearken. He made me think of a partridge on a dead limb, watching me when I was trying to get a shot at him. He began to bring over his family and his patients from Cambridgeport; and, as the seriousness increased, he came in with three or four carriages — some thirty persons — every Sabbath.

I kept watch from the first among my hearers. They told me of a young lady who had been awakened. I found her out, conversed with her, and she was converted. The next was Dea. P——'s daughter, and they kept dropping in. I tell this that you may know how to *begin* a revival. I always took it by word of mouth first, talking with single cases, and praying with them. Went on so till I found twelve, by watching and picking them out. I visited them, and explained what an inquiry meeting was, and engaged them, if one was appointed, to agree to come. I never would risk a blank attempt.

I began, early in this course, to intimate to the Church the probability of more interest. I grew in importunity, and roused the Church to take hold. At that time many ministers did not understand about this. I began to say to the Church, "I think there is a work begun. Fire in the leaves — not only among us, but in the community." I made no attack on Unitarians. I carried the state of warm revival feeling I had had in Litchfield for years. I carried it in my heart still with great success. They came to hear; there was a great deal of talk about me — great curiosity. They would hear, and then run me down — they would never go again. But they did

[1] James Chaplin (1780–1826), M.D., member of the American Temperance Society.

come again, till they were snared and taken. Many that came to scoff remained to pray.

Finally, my soul rose to it, and I preached to the Church one afternoon, explained to them the state of interest and opposition, and what an inquiry meeting was, and that they must be ready, and gave out an invitation to a long list of persons, whom I described. There were fifteen the first week, twenty the second, thirty-five the third, and the fourth time three hundred. The vestry was filled. Lambert met me at the door, when I came to meeting, with his eyes staring:

"It's a mistake; they've misunderstood, and think it's a lecture. You must explain."

"No," said I, "it's not a mistake; it's the finger of God!"

But I made an explanation, and only one person left.

I parceled out the room to ten individuals, to see every person, and make inquiries of their state, and bring back to me the report. (Oh, that was glorious! It lasted all that winter.) They brought back reports of awakenings and conversions. I talked with forty or fifty myself; and if there were special cases, I went and visited. I said just a word, or a few — not many. I *struck* just according to character and state.

It was really almost amusing to see the rapid changes in language and manner I underwent as I passed from one class to another. A large portion, on being questioned, would reveal their state of mind easily, and, being plain cases, would need only plain instruction. They believed the Bible, and they believed what I told them as if it was the Bible — as it was; and therefore the truth was made effectual by the Holy Spirit as well as if more conversation was had.

Another class would have difficulties. Could not see, realize, feel any thing. Did not know how to begin. To such a course of careful instruction was given.

Another class would plead inability — can not do any thing. Many of these told me their ministers told them so. Now I rose into the field of metaphysics, and, instead of being simple, I became the philosopher, and began to form my language for purposes of discrimination and power.

Next came the infidel and skeptical class, whom I received with courtesy and kindness; but, after a few suggestions calculated to conciliate, I told them the subject was one that could not be discussed among so many, but that I should be happy to see them at my house, and succeeded in that way many times. They had the idea that ministers scorned them, and that ministers were this, that, and the other. But it was necessary to go over with them, and trip up their arguments; for, until they were tripped up and crippled, logic was of little avail. So I put myself on the highest key with them, used the highest language and strongest arguments, and made them feel that somebody else knew something besides themselves; and then they came, meek as lambs, and were easily gained. Sometimes I had all these in a string. There were some pretty hard cases occasionally. There was ——, a vile fellow, who came. They used to have balls, and swap wives, and that sort of thing. I treated them politely, and they me, but I never made out any thing with them.

While I was in the inquiry meeting the Church held prayer meeting in a room near by, and, as conversions happened every night — ten, twenty, thirty — I went in and reported to them. That was blessed. They were waiting in hope and prayer, and I went in to carry glad tidings.

The Baptists came in to see what was going on, and pretty soon they began to revive. When I first set up evening meetings not a bell tingled; but, after a few weeks, not a bell that didn't tingle. The Unitarians at first scouted evening meetings; but Ware found his people going, and set up a meeting. I used to laugh to hear the bells going all round.

In this thing of revivals, you would find all these things came by *showers*. Each shower would increase, increase, increase; and when I saw it was about used up by conversion, I would preach so as to make a new attack on mind and conscience, varying with circumstances, and calculated to strike home with reference to other classes, and bring a new shower. The work never stopped for five years.

I was once with Dr. Jackson at the Hospital, and went the rounds with him. His secretary read from a book in which he kept short notes about the patient. After we got through he said, "Well, Dr. Beecher, how do you like it?" "Why," said I, "it's almost an exact image of my inquiry meeting. I have my book, where I note down my cases and their symptoms, just as you do."

"Well," said he, "you have more fanaticism there."

"No, sir, not an atom; but we have God, and the influence of his Spirit. But there is no more fanaticism there than you have here."

You see, in the revival, the numbers increased so fast it was overwhelming, so I kept a record.

When the time came for admission of converts to the communion, some seventy at once, it produced no small excitement. Till then all had been the butt of ridicule. The enemy had kept whist, except a few outlaws, at first, although the higher classes — the Cambridge College folks — had their spies abroad to see what was going on.

But, as the work deepened, I told my Church one of two things would come: either the revival would burst out through all these churches, or else there would be an outbreak of assault upon us such as could not be conceived. It was the latter. In one day after the seventy joined, the press belched and bellowed, and all the mud in the streets was flying at us. The upper class put mouth to ear, and hand to pocket, and said *St-boy!* There was an intense, malignant enragement for a time. Showers of lies were rained about us every day. The Unitarians, with all their principles of toleration, were as really a persecuting power while they had the ascendency as ever existed. Wives and daughters were forbidden to attend our meetings; and the whole weight of political, literary, and social influence was turned against us, and the lash of ridicule laid on without stint.

"Well," said I to the Church, "I have only one thing to say — Don't you let your fears be excited about *me*. God helping, I shall take care of myself. But watch your own hearts and pray; watch for the serious, and keep up a system of fervent, effectual prayer." And they did.

As for me, I cared for it all no more than for the wind. I knew where I was, and what I was doing, and knew that I was right. I used to think as I walked the street, "If you could know any thing that was vile about me you would scream for joy; but you don't." All sorts of vile letters were written to me by abandoned people. But all this malignity did us no harm. They only rung the bell for me. It was two years before the leaders of the Unitarians began to change their tactics and treat me gentlemanly.

My first series of sermons in my own vestry was doctrinal and explanatory. The effect was that many minds were satisfied. They cut their way. They were sermons made for the purpose, new every one of them, as if I had been running bullets in a mould.

When I revised and preached my six sermons on Intemperance, they took strong hold, and made my audience even fuller. My young men were for having them printed. Marvin did it well, and a number of editions were sold. Then the Tract Society bought the copyright. They offered fifty dollars; but I said they ought to give a hundred, and they did. These sermons made a racket all around, more than I had any idea they would. They stirred up the drinkers and venders all over the city. There was a great ebullition of rage among a certain class. And from that commenced a series of efforts among my people and others in Boston to promote this reform.

X

THE GROTON CASE

AMONG the first acquaintances I made in Boston was old Dr. Chaplin,[1] of Groton, father of Dr. Chaplin, of Cambridgeport. He happened to be in at Deacon Proctor's soon after I came, consulting on the state of matters in his parish. He had asked a colleague, and the Church had voted to call John Todd; [2] but the society refused, and employed Unitarian ministers from Boston. In fact, the society, with a minority of the Church, turned the Church out of doors, and took the property. They were backed up by recent legal decisions, which declared that the parish was the Church.*

By means of those decisions the Unitarians had been playing the mischief with our churches, and I was as eager to get at them as a hound on a fox's track. I advised a council. When the council was called a committee was appointed, of which I was chairman, to draw up a report. This gave me a chance to overhaul the courts.

REV. JOHN TODD TO DR. BEECHER.

"Groton, September 22, 1826.

"We are dying with impatience to see your report. We are sitting on the banks of the rivers of Babylon, harps still on the willows, our enemies requiring of us a song, and yet we are too heavy to sing. I want to have your report out, and that prodigiously, for you must know that all the orthodoxy in this town has been raked out of the ashes; no breath of heaven has yet breathed on them.

"My congregation increases — it is now a great congregation; some few are anxious, one or two rejoicing in hope. Meeting-house goes forward well. The Unitarians are going to have a splendid

* Mass. Reports, vol. ix., p. 299, and vol. xvi., pp. 479, 500.

---

[1] Daniel Chaplin (1743–1831) was orthodox pastor at Groton until a new church was formed as the result of this dissension.

[2] John Todd (1800–1873) was ordained pastor of the church formed by the Groton dissidents in 1827. Active in the temperance and missionary movements, a successful revivalist, he later had churches in western Mass. and Philadelphia.

installation; a ball in the evening, and probably R—— one of its gayest. They have not a single individual who prays in his family, and probably not one who prays in his closet. A few of them used to pray in the family once a week, but since they have become more enlightened they have left that off. We have excommunicated *nine*, all the Unitarian members. They howl about persecution, and cry John Calvin and Servetus,[3] popery, and what not. You would have been amused to see our Church meeting on the door-steps by the meeting-house.* It was a bright day, and a glorious sight for the sun to look upon. Once more, in behalf of this people, and, as I believe, in behalf of the churches of this state, *do*, Dr. Beecher, *do* let us have the report immediately."

EXTRACT FROM RESULT — THE RIGHTS OF CONGREGATIONAL CHURCHES.

"Much has been said about the rights of towns and parishes, and the effect of 'restoring to the churches the power they once enjoyed of electing the minister without the concurrence of the people or congregation, or by the aid of a council which they might select to sanction their choice; and it is said the people never would consent to be taxed for the support of men in whose election they had no voice;' as if the churches now claimed the sole power of electing the minister, and there were no alternative but to take it from the churches, and give it to towns and parishes. But the fact is that the law of 1692, giving equal powers to churches, and towns, and parishes in the settlement of a minister, had been for eighty-five years the practical rule. And the law of 1695, enabling churches to settle a minister, in opposition to a vote of the town, had, during all this entire period, remained a dead letter, and might have been unanimously repealed at the time the Constitution was formed, instead of making it the occasion of taking away wholly the rights of the churches, and giving them to towns and parishes.

"We shall never understand the merits of this question, or do justice to the memory of our fathers, without going back to the age in which they lived, and considering the circumstances in which they were placed. Then doctrinal controversies had no being, and the papal Church was the mighty power which shook

* The doors being locked against them.

---

[3] Michael Servetus (1511–1553) was condemned by Calvin for his views on the Trinity and after a long trial was burned in Geneva.

the earth. And this tremendous usurpation of the rights of God and man had come upon the world, as all history testified, by means of a corrupt priesthood, introduced into the churches by secular and ecclesiastical despotisms, established by the usurpation of the rights of the churches in the election of their pastors. Beholding then, as they did, the anti-Christian apostasy, deriving the nucleus of its terrific power from the usurpation of the rights of the churches in the election of their pastors; and smarting, as they did, in their recent escape from Episcopal despotism; and coming hither, as they did, to restore the Church of God to her primitive purity and liberty; and threatened, as the Reformation still was, by the gigantic power of Popery, and as even New England itself was, bounded by French colonies on the north, and south, and west — is it wonderful that our fathers should guard the door of the Church, and the spiritual rights of the Church, from secular intrusion, with great decision? They regarded the independence and purity of the Church of God, and justly, as the only means of restoring civil and religious liberty to the world. The question of Church organization, rights, and duties was therefore the great question between Protestants and Papists, and one of greater moment never agitated the world.

"When, therefore, an event, as unexpected as it was alarming, came on our fathers toward the close of the first and the beginning of the second generation, viz., a suspension of renewing grace, and the multiplication of men who, though respectable for character, could not join the Church, and were impatient of taxation without a voice in the election of their minister, they knew not what to do. To admit unrenewed men to the Church they could not; and at that day they would not come in if they might; and to give to secular communities the power of electing church officers, especially the pastors of the churches, by a joint vote with the Church, would soon subject the Church to the will of a secular community, and throw her back into the same state from which she had just been delivered by her exile. It was the apparent inconsistency and impossibility of permitting a civil body to vote in the election of a church officer which made the resistance of the churches for a long time so determined, and held back the churches in Boston long after those of the country had compromised in 1692. This difficulty was created by insisting upon universal taxation for the support of ministers, which they did not dare to give up, and their refusal of a voice in their election, which they did not dare to grant. But as soon as the compromise of 1692 had time to disclose its results, the fears of the churches, and the discontents of towns and parishes subsided, and a happier state of society never existed until the late exposition of the Constitution swept away the conditions of concord, and let out again upon churches and societies the occasions of strife and alienation. But even now there is no need that churches, and towns, and parishes should fall out by the way. There is, in fact, no contrariety of rights or interests between them, and no occasion for jealousy or strife. The churches have no desire to possess the sole power of electing a pastor, nor do they desire the right given by the law of 1695 of overruling the voice of the congregation by the advice of a council. They are content with what the law of 1692 gave them — the right of a concurrent vote in the election of their pastors; a right which the law of 1754 confirmed to them, when it made them, by express enactment, what they had been from the beginning in fact, corporations known in law, with rights of property and of pastoral election. So much power in the churches is indispensable to their existence as religious associations; and towns and societies are as really interested in the preservation of the churches as purely religious communities, as the churches themselves are. All the great interests of society are best promoted by falling into hands which are most deeply interested in them, and best acquainted with them. Physicians should doubtless superintend the interests of the medical profession, while agriculture, commerce, and manufactures may be expected to thrive best under the auspices of farmers, and merchants, and artisans. And can any reason be assigned why the dictates of common sense should not prevail in assigning to men professedly pious a precedence, at least, in the concerns of religion?

"No calamity is greater to a town than the existence of a Church in a low state of religious feeling, lax in discipline, lax in morals, few in numbers, and inefficient in religious enterprise. In such a state, every thing that is good runs down, and every thing that is wicked rises. The light in such a Church is darkness, and it is great darkness. And yet the tendency of giving to secular communities the sole power of electing the minister is to multiply such churches, as the tendency of the concurrent vote of the churches is to maintain their purity and moral vigor for the benefit of themselves and of society around them.

"It has been objected that the town is bound by law, under a penalty, to settle a minister, which the Church, if allowed a concurrent vote, may prevent. But who does not know that in eighty-five years' experience such an event never happened; that the law now is nearly, if not quite, obsolete; and, if it were not, that it would only assimilate our religious to our civil polity, which is by design not a democracy, but a system of checks and balances. The President of the United States may arrest the passage of a law; so may the Senate or the House of Representatives; and when it is passed the Supreme Court may declare it unconstitutional. Why, then, should the pure and holy interests of religion be thrown into the hands of the unmingled democracy of town and parish meetings, without a single check or balance to stay the fury of passion or defeat the purposes of intrigue, by giving time for piety, and deliberative wisdom, and cool reflection to operate? Towns are as really benefited by the senatorial influence of the churches in the election of pastors, as the churches are by civil aid in the support of the Gospel; and in all cases of collision which have come to pass between the towns and the churches, a way out has been indicated by the resolution of moral forces. Necessity has dictated a compromise which has ended in peace."

XI

CORRESPONDENCE, 1826–1827

DR. BEECHER TO EDWARD.

"November 21, 1826.

In reference to the main question of your accepting the call to Park Street, my mind has come to the same conclusion with yours. We have waited for Providence to speak, and it has spoken. * * * In respect to the other subject, of an authorized ministry, baptism, etc., what you do know from the Bible on those subjects is enough, without ecclesiastical history and combats with windmills in the fog of distant ages.

"No doctrine, and no institution which can not be found in the Bible without the aid of ecclesiastical history, can be recognized as of divine appointment. And in the Bible no diocesan bishop crosses your track, and no instance in which it is certain that baptism was performed by immersion, and no evidence, if it was, that immersion was the exclusive mode. And as to infants, it may suffice that once, by divine appointment, the seal of His covenant was to be applied to them, and that, though the seal has been changed under the new dispensation, the application of it to infants has not been revoked.

"I say this, not to confirm your opinion, which does not waver, but to express the ground of my own. * * * The revival progresses in my congregation, and in all the churches. The Church in Park Street is in a fine state; I believe the field before you is white to the harvest. God send you soon to reap."

EDWARD TO DR. BEECHER.

"December 4, 1826.

"I hope that you will be able to preach my ordination sermon. As there is no one whom I love better, so there is no one I should more desire to have preach for me on so interesting an occasion. * * * The committee speak of the third Wednesday of December. Were it not for one reason I should willingly accord. My mind has been troubled as to the mode of baptism. * * * I can not administer this ordinance until I am satisfied that I can conscientiously adhere to the present mode. * * *

"I have read or heard all the arguments which can satisfy Dr. Dwight and such men, and I know the common arguments of our denomination; but my mind refuses to act, and my conscience is unsatisfied until I can survey the field so as to satisfy myself."

DR. BEECHER TO EDWARD.

"December 7, 1826.

"I will take care of the business of the delay of time, if need be. I shall not mention to any one the occasion of delay — it is unnecessary; and, as publicity could do no good and might do harm, I should advise you not to communicate unless quite confidentially.

"There is no cause for alarm or solicitude. Your present state of mind is occasioned not by any perceived cause for change of views, but from a tender conscience, and the necessity imposed upon you of grasping, condensing, and weighing circumstantial evidence, scattered over a vast field, in so short a time and under such serious responsibilities. If you were leisurely pursuing the subject it would open upon you, and progress to its conclusion without solicitude. There is only one thing which you will have occasion to watch and pray against, and that is the morbid sensibility of what may be termed *nervous conscience*, by which I mean a conscience made preternaturally sensitive and fearful. This I have reason to believe has worried many a man till he became a Baptist through excess of conscience.

"I have no doubt of what is true on the subject, and do not expect that you will have any when you shall have had time calmly to examine it. But to me it seems as if you had better come home and be with me, and supply by exchanges, and attend the inquiry meeting, and a few such things, and be ordained when you are ready, especially if your mind should be veering to the Baptist side of the question. I should be sorry to have it acquire any considerable momentum that way till I see you. * * *

"I think you had better meet me at Providence on Tuesday of next week, where I shall be on an ordaining council, to preach next day the sermon for Waterman [1] — your classmate, I believe. I shall return on Thursday."

[1] Thomas T. Waterman (1801–1873), pastor of several Eastern churches, served churches in Ill. and Minn. from 1852 to 1857.

DR. BEECHER TO CATHARINE.

"February 3, 1827.

" * * * I preach every Thursday evening at Cambridgeport, a mile only this side of the college, in the Baptist meeting-house. The house is full, and exceedingly silent and solemn, and there is a revival begun — about a dozen inquirers, and five cases of recent and joyful hope. * * * Many come down from Cambridge, and some from Brighton, Newtown, and Roxbury.

"In Newtown is a revival begun, and in the region round there is a shaking among the dry bones. My eye and heart are on Cambridge, where the Congregational Church is low, and the college is as you know. But the revival of evangelical sentiments in the community around the college can not be without effect, and possibly yet the fire may break out in the institution itself; for this we wait and pray, and, as far as we may, use the means.

"Channing's sermon *[2] is doing good among the more sober part of Unitarians. It is quite too much for them. They are alarmed; and when they see what sort of folks it is who chuckle and swallow it, it scares them still more, 'for these fellows,' they say, 'we know have no religion.' It will be reviewed in due time, and in a manner, I trust, which will make him wish he had spoken more truth concerning the sentiments of others and less concerning his own."

MRS. BEECHER TO ——.

"February 26, '27.

"The religious interest has been gaining and unwavering. Every week brings evidence of the presence of God's Spirit, giving efficacy to truth. I say every day to myself, 'Oh, the glorious Gospel of the ever-blessed God! What results are these, and all by means of this simple, blessed truth.'

"It has been a season of many tears, and we have wept with those that weep, and rejoiced with those that do rejoice. It has been a season of wonderful *talking*. We have been obliged to stop our ears and go straight forward, lest our minds should be drawn away. And it has been a remarkable season for fabricating and

* At the dedication of the Second Unitarian Church, New York. — *Works*, vol. iii., p. 163.

[2] The sermon described God as "infinite and universal Mind" and accused Trinitarians of worshipping a corporeal God subject to human passions.

vending lies. The revival went on perfectly still till we received seventy-five into our Church, and the lecture at Cambridgeport began to tell; since that the commotion has been very great. Almost every minister of every denomination has set up evening meetings, and preach against us without mercy. The enemy is helping us wonderfully, particularly Dr. Channing's late sermon."

XII

NEW MEASURES

THE year of Dr. Beecher's removal to Boston (1826) was signalized by powerful revivals in different parts of the land. Among these, none were more remarkable than those in central New York, particularly within the bounds of the Presbytery of Oneida. From week to week the columns of the Boston Recorder and other religious journals contained glowing accounts of the wonderful outpourings of the Holy Spirit.

Whole towns, in some instances, were said to be converted. In other cases, all the professional and leading men were gathered in. The mightiest opposers and unbelievers were in some places changed to friends, or stirred up to wrath. "It does seem," says one (Feb. 21), "that there never was a time like the present since Pentecost — such wonderful displays of divine grace, such multitudes flocking to Christ."

The Presbytery of Oneida speak of it as "a work of divine power, of which we have witnessed no parallel in this country, and such as we have seldom discovered in the history of the Church."

"In these revivals," they say, "we have discovered no instance of the use of artifice to excite mere human feeling or to influence the passions. In most cases convictions were very pungent and deep. These were the effects of the simple word of God, the sword of the Spirit piercing the conscience and the heart. The Word has generally been presented in plain and pointed language. Boisterous speaking and loud declamation have been studiously avoided. Private visiting, faithful discipline, and setting apart days of fasting and prayer, have been eminently blessed. The effectual, fervent, agonizing prayer of faith has been found the immediate forerunner of the operation of divine power."

The Synod of Albany say that, "in consequence of this display of divine power, the theatre has been deserted, the tavern sanctified; blasphemy has been silenced, and infidelity confounded." Twenty-five congregations had shared in the work. Not a town in Oneida county had been passed by. Not less than twenty-five hundred were subjects of hopeful conversion.

A correspondent from Rome, New York, remarks, "The revival commenced here in such a powerful manner that our good pastor almost sunk under the labors it called for. But God sent us a Mr. Finney [1] to help gather in this precious harvest of souls."

This, perhaps, was the first introduction of a name, since so distinguished, to the Eastern public. Rev. C. G. Finney, then at the outset of his career, was the most prominent instrument in promoting these revivals. "After he came here," says the writer last quoted, "the Spirit of God was shed down with a power that nothing seemed able to resist."

Soon after (Sept. 22), the Recorder states that "the Christian Register has employed such strong assertions respecting *Mr. Phinney*," that the following statement is quoted from "a highly respectable paper of Utica:" "The gentleman in question has been in this part of the country ever since the days of his childhood; his character has been intimately known among us; and the Oneida Presbytery received him a few days since by a unanimous vote."

Rarely, it is believed, has the Holy Spirit raised up an instrument more formidable than Mr. Finney to the repose of the careless in Zion. But no human instrument is without defect. His boldness and severity appeared to some to verge upon rashness and denunciation; pungency assumed at times the guise of personality; agonizing earnestness in prayer was scarcely distinguishable in some instances from irreverent familiarity.

"When I first became acquainted with him," writes Rev. S. C. Aikin [2] to Dr. Beecher, April 20, 1827, "I think he used too frequently the word 'devil,' and harsh expressions; but he is greatly reformed, and I apprehend that reading those very quotations which you make from Edwards on Revivals was the means of his reformation. Until he came to my house (at Utica) he had never read the book, and here it was frequently in his hands during the revival; also other volumes of that great writer; and he often spoke of them with rapture. Indeed, next to the Bible, no book was read

[1] Charles Grandison Finney (1792–1852) gained fame by his spectacular revivals in western New York. He believed in "scaring" sinners, and his controversial "New Measures" included calling on specific sinners to repent, the public prayers of women, the denunciation of unregenerate ministers, and protracted meetings. Conservatives identified his doctrines that men could instantly submit to God and could "make themselves a new heart" with Taylor's New Divinity. In 1834 the Broadway Tabernacle Church was organized for him. A reformer opposed to slavery, he headed the Theological Department at Oberlin after the Lane crisis, and was Oberlin's president from 1851 to 1865.

[2] Silas Aiken (1799–1869), minister at Boston's Park St. Church (1837–1848), was not a popular preacher but was a devoted pastor.

so much in my family as Edwards on Revivals and on the Affections."

It was said, also, that certain measures were introduced not hitherto of good repute among Presbyterians and Congregationalists, such as women praying in public, the intrusion of evangelists upon the parishes of settled ministers, and other fanatical practices.

How much truth there may have been at the bottom of these charges we shall not undertake to determine. That there was some foundation for them seems probable. That they were greatly exaggerated seems no less probable.

As the revival spread, and many laborers entered into the field, it is natural to suppose that Mr. Finney would have imitators, who, as usual in such cases, would find it easier to exaggerate his defects than equal his excellencies. And as no one mind could know all that was transpiring in different places, so many exceptionable things may have occurred of which the principal leaders could have no knowledge, and which, when reported in an exaggerated form, they might with perfect sincerity deny to have happened.

Perhaps the waters of the river of life, discolored at first and made turbid, might, had circumstances been auspicious, presently have worked themselves free from sediment without being checked in their exuberant flow. But no such movement is allowed to take its natural course in a world like this. A sleepless adversary not only stirs up the enemies, but divides the friends of truth, as he can easily do, since some are naturally more struck by the faults and others by the excellencies of any measures whatever.

Few men have been more blessed in revivals than Mr. Nettleton. Yet he it was who stood foremost in opposition to the movements of Mr. Finney and his colaborers. Mr. Nettleton was at that time laboring at Jamaica, L. I. In his early ministry he had been called to move in the track of Davenport's wild-fire a century previous, and had conceived an almost morbid horror of any thing approaching to fanaticism. Yet now he heard that his own name was used at the West as sanctioning irregularities he had always disapproved.

At an earlier period he might have been able to bear the inexpressible pain this gave him with comparative equanimity; but his illness in 1822, as his biographer informs us, "gave a shock to his constitution from which it never recovered. For a considerable part of the time during the remainder of his life he was exceedingly feeble, and at no time was he able to engage in arduous labor." *

* Memoir of Dr. Nettleton, p. 302.

He had himself labored with happy results in the vicinity of Saratoga and Albany a few years before, and felt, of course, a livelier interest in what was now transpiring.

At length, being fully convinced "that irregularities were prevalent to such an alarming extent that the character of revivals had gone back half a century," * and, as it would seem, unconsciously impelled to a method kindred to that employed on the prairies to arrest conflagrations by setting a back fire, he accepted an invitation to visit Albany, where, in the opening of 1827, he writes to Dr. Beecher, "from two to three thousand souls assemble every Sabbath evening to hear a feeble, dying man preach."

When Mr. Finney heard of his presence at Albany, we are told, he "set out immediately to go and sit at his feet and receive instruction. On arriving there he was disappointed and grieved to find Mr. Nettleton very reserved and distant, so much so that he was unable to approach him, or to enter much into conversation." †

The disappointment appears to have been mutual. Mr. Nettleton's biographer states, "He had two interviews with Mr. Finney, hoping that by a free consultation their views might be brought to harmonize so far, at least, that they might co-operate in promoting the interests of Christ's kingdom. But in this he was painfully disappointed. He found that Mr. Finney was unwilling to abandon certain measures which he had ever regarded as exceedingly calamitous to the cause of revivals." ‡

Mr. Nettleton thus refers to this interview in a letter to Dr. Beecher of May 10, 1827: "You may think it strange that I did not receive him and run the risk of moulding him. But I could not do it without sanctioning all that he had done, and joining with disorganizers all over the world; for my name was already in their service at the West; and besides, if I should not succeed, it would ruin us both, and if I should have succeeded, the disorganizers would say I had spoiled him."

The truth seems to be that Mr. Nettleton's mind was made up before he visited Albany. Nor, considering the dissimilarity of the two individuals, is it likely he would have succeeded, or strange he did not feel inclined to try.

He himself was old and broken, Mr. Finney young and robust. The one was reverential, timid, secretive; the other bold, striking, demonstrative. The style of the one was subdued, that of the other

* Memoir, p. 269.
† Rev. S. C. Aikin to Dr. Beecher, April 20, 1827.
‡ Memoir, p. 238.

full of eclat. The atmosphere most congenial to Mr. Nettleton was one of hushed, mysterious stillness. "I love to talk to you," he would say, "you are *so still.*" Often, in dismissing an assembly, he would say, "Go away *as still* as possible." Mr. Finney is described by an admirer as "frank, open, giving his opinion without solicitation in a strong style, somewhat dictatorial. He keeps nothing to himself. In this respect he is perfectly at antipodes with Mr. Nettleton." *

Mr. Nettleton himself thus forcibly contrasts the two styles of operation: "Seven years ago about two thousand souls were hopefully born into the kingdom, in this vicinity, with comparative stillness. But the times have altered. The kingdom of God now cometh with great observation."

It is not probable that any course of measures Mr. Finney could have adopted would have failed to jar more or less painfully on Mr. Nettleton's susceptibilities. Both were originals, both had their eccentricities, but their eccentricities were of opposite kinds.

Mr. Nettleton's secrecy and love of stillness, with other peculiarities, in his palmier days, were doubtless an excellence. He resembled, in the conduct of a revival, a skillful performer playing with exquisite touch upon some delicate instrument. After his health was broken, however, there was a heightening of these tendencies to a species of fastidiousness peculiarly quaint and remarkable.

If we might presume to illustrate the difference of the two men in their styles of labor by a comparison, we should say that the latter set snares for sinners, the former rode them down in a cavalry charge. The one, being crafty, took them with guile; the other, being violent, took them by force.

Yielding to this powerful antagonism, and flying apart from his younger brother evangelist like an electric pith ball, forming his judgment mostly on the testimony of others, and usually those unfavorable to the movement, it is not strange Mr. Nettleton should come to regard him as sustaining to himself the relation of a Davenport to a Whitefield, and exclaim, "Whoever has made himself acquainted with the state of things in New England near the close of the revival in the days of Whitefield can not but weep over its likeness to the present."

It was in this state of mind that, January 2, 1827, he composed a long and elaborate letter to Dr. Beecher, afterward revised and enlarged, and addressed to Rev. Mr. Aikin. In this very able

* Letter of Rev. S. C. Aikin to Dr. Beecher, April 20, 1827.

composition, which our limits forbid us to publish,* he weaves together with surprising skill the mass of rumors and reports he had accumulated from various sources, in a texture so fine that omniscience only could draw the line between exactness and exaggeration, and winds up with the irresistible appeal, "Dr. Beecher must write to these men. Somebody must speak, and *who,* WHO, I ask, shall do it, if not some one from New England?"

Now it is by no means strange that the effect of such an appeal upon Dr. Beecher's mind should be deep. It was just the view of the subject calculated to strike his mind as both probable and alarming. As the adversary had done such things in other days, so he might be expected to attempt them now. With Mr. Finney he was personally unacquainted; with Mr. Nettleton he had been intimate for years, and cherished an exalted opinion of his wisdom. If but a moiety of that resumé of reports was true, too well he could anticipate the comments of the Unitarian press,† and the bearing of the whole on that revival in which all his energies were absorbed.

So averse, however, was he to any thing that threatened controversy among the friends of revivals, that it was not till after careful inquiry and consultation with Dr. Porter, Dr. Woods, Professor Stuart, and others, that at last he composed his well-known letter to Messrs. Beman [3] and Finney.‡

"My object in that letter," he writes soon after to Rev. J. Frost,[4] "was to justify them against the opposition of formalists and the haters of revivals of religion, and to suggest emendations where to me it seemed they might be needed, and yet without checking the ardor, and boldness, and moral momentum with which I did not doubt Brother Finney was moving on."

* The reader will find the chief portions in the Memoir of Mr. Nettleton, pp. 238–249.

† The Examiner for May and June, 1827, considers it profane to call the New York revival a work of God; describes Mr. Finney as "the principal instigator of these disturbances," "distinguished for an inflammatory or rather ferocious style of preaching;" speaks of "Beman, another of these incendiaries," and represents them as shaking their fists in people's faces, and saying, "You lie! You are going to hell!" etc., etc.

‡ See Appendix A.

---

[3] Nathan Beman (1785–1871) was called to the First Presbyterian Church, Troy, N. Y., in 1823. "The warhorse of the New School," he invited Finney to Troy, and vociferously shared Finney's criticisms of the dry or unregenerate Eastern ministry. He was moderator of the General Assembly in 1831 and president of R.P.I. from 1845 to 1865.

[4] John Frost (1783–1842), pastor in N. Y., also acted as agent for the American Board of Missions and the Oneida Institute.

A single sentence at the close of the same letter shows his conviction of what was indispensable to a mutual understanding: "*This, however, makes it necessary that Brother Finney should come upon ground on which we can sustain him, for we can not justify his faults for the sake of his excellencies.*"

A copy of the letter to Messrs. Beman and Finney was sent to Mr. Nettleton, accompanied by a short letter, in which, says Dr. Beecher, "I poured out my feelings, and thoughts, and fears in respect to principles and prospective evils in such language as the occasion inspired and my habits of confidential intercourse with Brother Nettleton justified."

It seems that Mr. Nettleton furnished an extract of this latter epistle to the moderator of the Presbytery of Troy, who loaned it to a gentleman to read and show to others, and in this manner it soon found its way to the press in the form of a hand-bill.

It is remarkable that so shrewd a judge of human nature as Mr. Nettleton should not have foreseen the probability of some such result. We will not assert that, with Dr. Beecher's elaborate effort at conciliation before him, he deliberately planned to defeat it; but, if such had been his design, he could scarce have accomplished it more effectually. "I regret," he writes, "the surreptitious publication of that letter of yours to me. * * * Yet I am not sure but we should all have kept silence unless you had been made to speak, contrary to your own and the wishes of your friends."

The effect of the letter, observes Dr. Beecher shortly after, "is as if a man should throw a firebrand on a train of powder which another was attempting to guard against ignition." The letter to Messrs. Beman and Finney remained unanswered, but from the published extract he heard in every direction. In vain he protested against its publication as "an outrageous violation of authorized confidence for which neither Brother Nettleton nor myself are accountable." The "fire was in the leaves," and a public controversy seemed inevitable.

"Had it come," wrote Mr. Gillet, of Rome, "from an obscure minister, I should have set him down as an enemy of revivals. * * * What I lament is that it strengthens the hands of opposers; — published in the first number of a Universalist paper at Utica!"

"There is one admonition contained in his letter," said the Christian Examiner, "which we can adopt, though it is expressed too strongly, and betrays something too much like a panic, viz., 'We are on the confines of universal misrule and moral desolation, and no time is to be lost in forestalling and holding public sentiment correctly, before the mass shall be put in motion by fierce winds before which nothing can stand, and behind which, when they have swept over the land, nothing will remain.' "

In his reply to Mr. Gillet, Dr. Beecher says, "I am not surprised that the letter should have pained you or given the enemy a momentary exultation; for though it contains nothing to which I do not believe the earnest attention of ministers should be called, it by no means contains *all* that ought to have been said on that subject by a friend of revivals, who first spoke out and called the attention of the public to the subject; nor is the language such as I should have selected in any other than an unrestrained confidential communication with one with whom, on such subjects, I have been long in habits of the most unreserved intimacy.

"These circumstances ought to be known, though it is nearly impossible they should be, to all who have read my letter; for, though it contains the truth in reference to my apprehensions concerning certain revivals, it by no means contains the whole truth, and may, therefore, make an erroneous impression. But the thing I most deprecate is its tendency to get up a controversy on the subject, and produce a needless collision, which I believe may be superseded by correspondence and Christian conference."

But these hopes of conciliation gradually faded. The Western brethren, Dr. Beecher felt, had not met his overtures in the spirit in which he had offered them. Particularly the absence of any reply from Messrs. Beman and Finney operated unfavorably upon his feelings in regard to them. "I did expect," he wrote at the time, "that Brother Beman or Brother Finney would have written to me, and that the correspondence would have softened down into mutual explanation," etc.

In another letter, a little later, he says, "I am certain, for I have tried it for more than one whole year thoroughly, as my correspondence will show, if called for, that no kindness and magnanimity on our part will be appreciated."

How this silence was probably occasioned we have seen. Natural enough, and excusable under the circumstances, it was unfortunate, since it left Mr. Nettleton to be the channel through which impressions respecting them and their measures should mainly be communicated to Dr. Beecher's mind, tinged in their passage by the powerful idiosyncrasy of the medium.

And when, in addition to this, they seemed to attack Mr. Nettleton, and were understood to be combining "to destroy or neutralize his influence," nothing farther was necessary to commit Dr. Beecher unreservedly in his defense, and in the support of his views.

In short, Mr. Nettleton was clearly master of the position, and, for the space of a year, all that mortal man could do to create and intensify a panic, his letters show was done by one so weak and faint as to be continually on the point of retiring from the field.

"Take all possible care of your health," writes Dr. Beecher (March 14, 1827), "and also of your own spirit, that no provocation shall produce in word or look an asperity which we so much deplore in some. You will need to watch and pray. Especially be careful about letting the war get up as between young men and old ministers; for, brother, it will sound invidiously to young ears, and the young have the advantage of the old in respect to action and long life. We must save young men and not smite them. I mean, we must take care not to throw young men into the opposite scale."

"Every word of your excellent letter," replies Mr. Nettleton, "met my views and feelings. It certainly requires great patience to manage a denouncing spirit. But, if you will pardon the expression, I have found that the devil's backbone is prodigiously stiff ever since I have been in the ministry, so far as the introduction of similar measures is concerned, and I never have felt so strong a desire to write a history of my own experience on the subject as of late. But there is no one subject on which mankind have so little wit, and which it would be so difficult to make them understand, most ministers themselves not excepted."

Thus matters went on until, at length, said Dr. Beecher, in conversation on the subject, "the tide of public sentiment we raised against their measures began to make them feel. Beman came on to Boston to propose a convention for purposes of explanation. I fell in with it; sat down and wrote to ten or a dozen others to go by all means. We met at New Lebanon,* and discussed nine days. It

* The following members composed the Convention, which convened July 18, 1827: A. S. Norton, D.D., Clinton, N. Y.; Rev. Moses Gillet, Rome, N. Y.; Rev. N. S. S. Beman, Troy, N. Y.; D. C. Lansing, D.D., Auburn, N. Y.; Rev. J. Frost, Whitesboro', N. Y.; Rev. W. R. Weeks, Paris, N. Y.; Rev. H. Smith, Camden, N. Y.; Rev. C. G. Finney, Oneida Co., N. Y.; L. Beecher, D.D., Boston, Mass.; H. Humphrey, D.D., Amherst College, Mass.; Rev. A. Nettleton, Connecticut; Rev. J. Edwards, Andover, Mass.; Rev. J. Hawes, Hartford, Conn.; Rev. C. Tenney, Wethersfield, Conn.; Rev. G. W. Gale, Oneida, N. Y.; Rev. S. Churchill, Oneida, N. Y.

A careful perusal of the minutes of this Convention has satisfied us that there was no radical difference of views between the Western brethren and those from New England; and that, but for the influence of one individual, the same settlement might have been made then and there which was afterward effected at Philadelphia.

was a battle royal, though there was no venom, no breaking friendship. It was not a question of orthodoxy, nor of the reality of the revivals, but of wrong measures. They sought to explain, or deny what we had heard on credible testimony. We were not convinced. We stood out against them as having been disturbers of the churches.

I recollect that Hawes at one time was quite carried away with some of their statements. "Well," said he, "I profess I am satisfied." "Stop," said I, "Brother Hawes, don't be in a hurry and decide too quickly. Gentlemen," said I, "you need not think to catch old birds with chaff; it may be true that you don't go personally into ministers' parishes; but, in the noise and excitement, one and another of the people in the towns want you to come and preach, and you are mighty reserved, and say, 'Ah no, we can not come unless ministers invite us,' and so you send them back like hounds to compel them to call you."

Said I, "Finney, I know your plan, and you know I do; you mean to come into Connecticut and carry a streak of fire to Boston. But if you attempt it, as the Lord liveth, I'll meet you at the State line, and call out all the artillerymen, and fight every inch of the way to Boston, and then I'll fight you there."

So far as the prevention of controversy was concerned, this Convention was a failure. The Western brethren were indignant at the course pursued by Mr. Nettleton. Their statements on the subject were construed by him into a personal attack. He became increasingly urgent with Dr. Beecher to come out openly in his support. "We think," he writes, October 29, 1827, "to forestall public opinion by silent measures, but this is giving them all the advantage they want. We can correspond with our friends who are already firm and need no correction, but this does not touch the evil. It is the irregulars themselves, and the *ignobile vulgus*, and the whole host of insurgents, that need to know our opinion and our determination to make a firm and decided stand against these measures. A few letters like that of Dr. Porter would soon turn to flight the armies of the aliens. It is not mere argument, but names, that will turn the current against the ragamuffins." * * *

"I do think that you and Brother Edwards [5] ought to publish something in the papers — your views of Mr. Finney's sermon and of my 'Remarks' thereon, and of my efforts. To prevent the effect

[5] Justin Edwards (1787–1853), Boston minister (1828–1829), secretary of the American Temperance Society (1829–1836), president of Andover (1836–1842), secretary of the Sabbath Union (1842–1849). From 1849–1853, he worked for the American Tract Society.

of my 'Remarks,' and to hold public sentiment, and to turn it back, the old story is stirring harder than ever at the West, that 'Mr. Nettleton has recanted;' that he 'has made a humble and Christian confession.' I have received a number of letters from clergymen on the subject. * * * But I intend to remain silent until somebody speaks to divert public attention from me to the subject itself." * * *

"Letters have been circulated in Philadelphia and at the South saying that all the ministers of this region agree with Mr. Finney, and that Mr. Nettleton's Remarks have done himself more harm than they have Mr. Finney. Unless something is published, thousands will believe it."

Under date of December 29th he writes: "I never was attacked on so many *awkward* points. Silence is construed into sullenness, unwillingness to be corrected, envy, etc.; and so many good people are made to believe." * * *

"Your letters are a great comfort to me, but I do not deserve a hundredth part of what you say. I understand it as a defense of the cause of *revivals,* and I wish nothing more."

By these and similar appeals Dr. Beecher was prevailed on to publish his letter, composed a year before, to Messrs. Beman and Finney.* Events took place, however, soon after this, which led to an auspicious settlement.

"In the spring of 1828," said Dr. Beecher, in conversation on the subject, "I found out that Mr. Finney's friends were laying their plans to make an impression on the General Assembly, that held its session in Philadelphia, and to get one of their men in Mr. Skinner's [6] place. Skinner's Church had just asked me to preach for them, and I wrote back that I would supply, if they wished, while the Assembly was in session. That blocked somebody's wheels; it blocked a good many wheels. I staid till the close, when Beman preached half a day. That defeated their plans. They failed.

"But, while I was there, I prepared the way for a settlement. I consulted leading men on all hands whether the controversy might not be suspended where it was. I saw that if the war could only

* By a singular coincidence, it happened that a private letter of the same date, to the editor of the Christian Spectator, was subsequently, in a surreptitious manner, given to the world, in the form of an "Address to the Ministers and Churches of Connecticut."

---

[6] Thomas H. Skinner (1791–1871), professor at Andover (1832–1835), N. Y. C. minister (1835–1848). He sided with the New School in the 1837 schism, and in 1848 became professor at Union Seminary, which he helped establish.

stop they would grow cool. I proposed it to Beman and others, and they approved, and so it was settled.

"We drew up and published the following statement:

"The subscribers, having had opportunity for free conversation on certain subjects pertaining to revivals of religion, concerning which we have differed, are of opinion that the general interests of religion would not be promoted by any farther publications on those subjects, or personal discussions, and we do hereby engage to cease from all publications, correspondences, conversations, and conduct designed or calculated to keep those subjects before the public mind, and that, so far as our influence may avail, we will exert it to induce our friends on either side to do the same."

"The effect of this," continued Dr. Beecher, "was good. The excesses we had complained of, though real, were effervescent and evanescent. The men were beginning to be ashamed of them themselves. They soon sobered down. I wrote the same day to Nettleton, and explained the whole matter to him."

DR. BEECHER TO MR. NETTLETON.

"Philadelphia, May 28, 1828.

"I could not answer your expectations in replying to the late publications, for want both of time and of documents, such as your letter just received contains. Besides, I could not feel so certain that it was best, as I wish always to do in any measure which is to affect deeply the Church of God. I concluded, at length, to come on to New York and to this place, and to confer with our friends, and with brethren on the other side, to see if we could find a stopping-place, and if not, to make all due preparation for publication.

"I have conferred with Dr. Porter, of Andover, our brethren Wisner, Greene, Skinner, and my son, with Brother Hawes, Mr. Holmes, of New Bedford, Dr. Richards, Mr. Eddy, of Canandaigua, with Mr. Peters, Dr. Rice, and many others, and the opinion of every one is to forbear farther publication, if possible.

"1. Because, in respect to yourself, there is no need of it, no impression injurious to you having been made in New England, or to the west of Oneida county, and none in the Middle and Southern or Western States — none but among partisans on the other side.

"2. An attempt to rectify all their mistakes in your defense would injure you by keeping you before the public eye in a personal collision with Mr. Finney. We thought that your character and high standing in the Church is too important to be brought down into a protracted controversy of this kind.

"3. That controversy so much personal, and hinging so much on an individual, would help the wrong by giving notoriety, and enlisting public curiosity, and, if we press the subject beyond a certain time and point, public sympathy.

"4. It would tend to keep up a party in the Church, who, identified with their leader, might in self-defense be embodied to defend him, and might introduce a controversy into the Presbyterian Church, and by dividing ecclesiastical judicatures, involve and keep the whole Church in a blaze. We thought the best way to disarm our brethren of a dangerous power in the Church is to let them alone, and that every tub should be left to stand on its own bottom.

"5. We did deprecate the publication to the world of so many and such extravagant things as must come out should we enter on the work of proof; and there is no medium between immediate and entire silence and a thorough development, which, though it would justify us in our opposition, would, as much as it injured them, subtract from the cause, provided they will now stop. We wished to save them their character for the Church as well as ours.

"6. We could not but feel, from all that is past, that there can be no telling what sort of contrary testimony might on the other side be adduced to blast our own or their own character, to distract public sentiment, and to enable enemies to say that we are *all* liars. We thought that the general cause could not but be injured by such a contest. I do not say we anticipated willful falsehood, but we could not fail to apprehend that which would in reality be falsehood.

"7. We were inclined to believe that those brethren are tired of the controversy, and are now willing to get out of it if they can have a fair opportunity, and that not a few neutrals are urging them.

"8. We know that the public are becoming tired of the controversy, and that public sentiment is against publication.

"9. We considered it utterly impossible ever to come to a settlement by public discussion or private explanation, and that our own views on both sides being before the public, it was best to stop, and let the truth have its weight.

"10. They have denied so much in theory, and denied so many facts as being wrong and slanderous, that they stand bound before the public to good behavior in time to come, which must operate so far to restrain as to prevent the repetition, we hope, of any such excesses as will be as alarming as the past.

"11. There is such an amount of truth and power in the preaching of Mr. Finney, and so great an amount of good hopefully done, that if he can be so far restrained as that he shall do more good than evil, then it would be dangerous to oppose him, lest at length we might be found to fight against God; for, though some revivals may be so badly managed as to be worse than none, there may, to a certaint extent, be great imperfections in them, and yet they be, on the whole, blessings to the Church.

"12. We thought that the publication of Dr. Richards and others, though it does not include your name, is, on the whole, about a fair offset to their late publications, and that this is the best time we can ever expect to have in which to stop. We therefore, who were present in the city, have, in accordance with the general opinion of our friends above named that farther publication should cease, signed with the brethren on the other side the document which you will see in the Philadelphian.

"You probably will feel as if they will take advantage of it; but I am fearless on that point, believing that the course is right in the sight of God, best for your own peace and health, and altogether better than to have you and Finney coupled together, as you would be by a public discussion.

"Rest assured that your reputation does not and will not suffer. I wish to suggest to you the propriety, since your health seems to deny much revival enterprise, that you should move round among the theological seminaries, spending time enough near one and another in succession to imbue the young men with correct views. Such a course would be invaluable in its influence, and enable you yet to do more good by imparting the result of your observations and experience, than you did in the revivals where you obtained them.

"I commend this thought earnestly to your attention; it will do more than ten years of controversy, without the possibility of an answer. Dear brother, be of good cheer; take care of your precious life, and live as long as you can, to bless, as you have done eminently, the Church and the world."

"This letter, however," continued Dr. Beecher, "did not satisfy Nettleton. He wanted the battle to go on. He was one of those that never can give up their own will. He got the notion that the New Haven brethren were currying favor with Finney and Beman, and their followers, to secure patronage for the Christian Spectator. He felt as though he had fought a battle, and we had not duly appreciated it. That was the real origin of all his bitterness against Taylor.

"But the settlement worked well on the whole. The fact that after so much feeling and such deep excitement so happy an arrangement was made, shows real Christian principle in all concerned. It might, in former times, have led to martyrdom. There was real evil — there was real good on both sides. Nobody was finally injured. The evil was corrected; the good was saved.

"In about two years after that we had Mr. Finney in Boston. Some of our deacons wanted him to come, and Wisner had heard him preach somewhere. He did his best, and Wisner was much pleased. Somebody had written to him on the subject, and about the same time Catharine saw him, and he said to her, 'Your father vowed solemnly at the New London Convention he would fight me if I came to Boston, and I shall never go there till he asks me.' So we wrote and invited him, and he came (August, 1831) and did very well."

XIII

REMINISCENCES

FROM MRS. H. B. STOWE.

"MY DEAR BROTHER, — The looking over of father's letters in the period of his Boston life brings forcibly to my mind many recollections. At this time I was more with him, and associated in companionship of thought and feeling for a longer period, than any other of my experience, and it was the most active, glowing, and successful period of his life. It was the high noon of his manhood, the flood-tide of his powers; and a combination of circumstances in the history of Massachusetts brought him in to labor there just as a whole generation were on the return-wave of a great moral reaction. The strict theocracy founded by the Puritans in the State of Massachusetts had striven by all the ingenuity of legislation and institution to impress the Calvinistic seal indelibly on all the future generations of Massachusetts, so that no man of other opinions should minister in the Church or bear office in the state. As in Connecticut, so in Massachusetts, a reaction had come in and forced open the doors of the state, and rent the sole power from the clergy; but the revolution had gone deeper and farther, and extended to ideas and theologies.

"A system of protest and denial arose, which owed its vitality less to the assertion of new propositions than to the denial of old ones. Its life consisted more in demolition than in construction, and its followers were more certain as to what they did not than what they did believe.

"This party, called for convenience Unitarian, was, in fact, a whole generation in the process of reaction, and consisted of persons of the most diverse and opposite shades of opinion, united only in the profession of not believing Calvinism as taught by the original founders of Massachusetts.

"When Dr. Beecher came to Boston, Calvinism or orthodoxy was the despised and persecuted form of faith. It was the dethroned royal family wandering like a permitted mendicant in the city where once it had held court, and Unitarianism reigned in its stead.

"All the literary men of Massachusetts were Unitarian. All the trustees and professors of Havard College were Unitarians. All the élite of wealth and fashion crowded Unitarian churches. The judges on the bench were Unitarian, giving decisions by which the peculiar features of church organization, so carefully ordained by the Pilgrim fathers, had been nullified. The Church, as consisting, according to their belief, in regenerate people, had been ignored, and all the power had passed into the hands of the congregation. This power had been used by the majorities to settle ministers of the fashionable and reigning type in many of the towns of Eastern Massachusetts. The dominant majority entered at once into possession of churches and church property, leaving the orthodox minority to go out into school-houses or town halls, and build their churches as best they could. Old foundations, established by the Pilgrim fathers for the perpetuation and teaching of their own views in theology, were seized upon and appropriated to the support of opposing views. A fund given for preaching an annual lecture on the Trinity was employed for preaching an annual attack upon it, and the Hollis professorship of divinity at Cambridge was employed for the furnishing of a class of ministers whose sole distinctive idea was declared warfare with the ideas and intentions of the donor.

"So bitter and so strong had been the reaction of a whole generation against the bands too stringent of their fathers — such the impulse with which they broke from the cords with which their ancestors sought to bind them forever. But in every such surge of society, however confident and overbearing, there lies the element of a counter reaction, and when Dr. Beecher came to Boston this element had already begun to assert itself.

"The human mind can not long subsist merely on protest and denial. Enthusiasm can not long be kept up simply by not believing. By a power as inevitable as gravitation, the human soul is always tending, after every such era of revolutionary free inquiry, to fall back exhausted into the kindly arms of a positive belief. He who teaches a positive and definite faith, which he believes with undoubting certainty in every part, has therefore an infinite advantage in any such crisis of opinions as that which Dr. Beecher found in Boston.

"He had not been there many weeks before every leisure hour was beset by people who came with earnest intention to express to him those various phases of weary, restless, wandering desire and aspiration proper to an earnest people whose traditional faith has been broken up, but who have not outlived the necessity of definite and settled belief. From minds of every class, in every circle of society, the most fashionable and the most obscure, these inquirers were constantly coming with every imaginable theological problem, from the inspiration of the Bible out through all the minutest ramifications of doctrinal opinion or personal religious experience. There seemed to be an incessant ringing of the door-bell from morning till night. Inquirers and deputations came from many of the neighboring towns, spreading before him the cares and wants of feeble churches, exiled from their places of worship and deprived of their church property by the triumphant majority, who despised the faith of their fathers.

"The effect of all this on my father's mind was to keep him at a white heat of enthusiasm. Within a stone's throw of our door was the old Copp's Hill burying-ground, where rested the bones of the Puritan founders; and, though not a man ordinarily given to sentiment or to visiting of graves, we were never left to forget in any prayer of his that the bones of our fathers were before our door.

"His family prayers at this period, departing from the customary forms of unexcited hours, became often upheavings of passionate emotion such as I shall never forget. 'Come, Lord Jesus,' he would say, 'here where the bones of the fathers rest, here where the crown has been torn from thy brow, come and recall thy wandering children. Behold thy flock scattered on the mountain — "these sheep, what have they done?" Gather them, gather them, O good Shepherd, for their feet stumble upon the dark mountains.'

"My father's prayers in ordinary moods and those under excitement were as different as can be conceived, and there was a power sometimes in these daily supplications which seemed to shake our very souls. What was to be remarked of them was those direct and earnest addresses to the Savior and to the Holy Spirit, which, notwithstanding the orthodox belief of Congregationalists, are seldom heard except in the worship of the old liturgic churches. In hours of earnest excitement his petitions to the different persons of the Trinity would remind one of those antique, fervid invocations of the earlier Church. It must not be inferred from this that his air and manner was continually solemn. On the contrary, that hilarious cheerfulness which was characteristic of him was never more manifest; and it seemed perfectly wonderful, with his public labors, with what unfailing spring and vivacity, and with what a flow of ready sympathy he would converse with every one who came near him at any hour of day or night.

"He kept a load of sand in his cellar, to which he would run at odd intervals and shovel vigorously, throwing it from one side the cellar to the other, on his favorite theory of working off nervous excitement through the muscles, and his wood-pile and wood-saw were inestimable means to the same end. He had also, in the back yard, parallel bars, a single bar, ladder, and other simple gymnastic apparatus, where he would sometimes astonish his ministerial visitors by climbing ropes hand over hand, whirling over on the single bar, lifting weights, and performing other athletic feats, in which he took for the time as much apparent delight and pride as in any of his intellectual exertions.

"His care of what he called regimen, diet, sleep, exercise, etc., went on with all his other cares without seeming to interrupt them. He seemed to navigate his body, as an acute mariner would work his ship through a difficult channel, with his eye intent on every spar and rope, each sail kept trimmed with the nicest adjustment. The harsh climate of Boston, with its east winds, had long been famous for making all its literary workers dyspeptics; yet it was in this climate that his work lay; here he must conquer, notwithstanding he brought with him his life's disease. So careful was he of atmospheric influences upon the sensitive surface of the body, that he would often undress and dress again completely three or four times a day, to meet various changes of the mutable Boston weather.

"He had a different relay of garments for every turn of the weather-cock, till it stood at that harsh, dire east, which necessitated both flannels and a leathern jacket to keep out the chill and keep in the vital warmth.

"His theological and pastoral discussions with ministers and inquirers who thronged upon him were always mingled with abundant cautions and prescriptions in regard to the care of health, with minute directions drawn from his own personal experience.

"The time that he spent in actual preparation for a public effort was generally not long. If he was to preach in the evening he was to be seen all day talking with whoever would talk, accessible to all, full of every body's affairs, business, and burdens, till an hour or two before the time, when he would rush up into his study (which he always preferred should be the topmost room of the house), and, throwing off his coat, after a swing or two with the dumbbells to settle the balance of his muscles, he would sit down and dash ahead, making quantities of hieroglyphic notes on small, stubbed bits of paper, about as big as the palm of his hand. The bells would begin to ring, and still he would write. They would toll loud and long, and his wife would say 'he will certainly be late,' and then would be running up and down stairs of messengers to see that he was finished, till, just as the last stroke of the bell was dying away, he would emerge from the study with his coat very much awry, come down the stairs like a hurricane, stand impatiently protesting while female hands that ever lay in wait adjusted his cravat and settled his coat collar, calling loudly the while for a pin to fasten together the stubbed little bits of paper aforesaid, which being duly dropped into the crown of his hat, and hooking wife or daughter like a satchel on his arm, away he would start on such a race through the streets as left neither brain nor breath till the church was gained. Then came the process of getting in through crowded aisles, wedged up with heads, the bustle, and stir, and hush to look at him, as, with a matter-of-fact, businesslike push, he elbowed his way through them and up the pulpit stairs.

"As to his preaching, it consisted invariably of two parts: first, careful statement and argument addressed purely to the understanding, and, second, a passionate and direct appeal, designed to urge his audience to some immediate practical result. The first part was often as dry, condensed, and clear as a series of mathematical axioms. If preaching upon a doctrine, he commenced by the most clear and carefully-worded statement of what it was not and what it was, before attempting to prove or disprove. It very often happened that these simple statements disarmed prejudice and removed antipathy, and, to a people somewhat predisposed to return to the faith of their fathers if they could see their way, rendered the succeeding argument almost needless. I remember the introductory statement of a sermon on the doctrine of total depravity, in which, after telling much that it did *not* include, he reduced it simply to this proposition: *That men by nature do not love God supremely, and their neighbor as themselves.*

" 'All that is cultivated in intellect and refined in taste, much that is honorable in feeling and amiable in social relations,' he said, 'we concede. The temple is beautiful, but it is a temple in ruins; the divinity has departed, and the fire on the altar is extinct.'

"After this followed the scriptural argument, on which he always and unhesitatingly relied, without the shadow of a doubt that we do have, in our English translation, the authoritative, inspired declarations of God. Then came the answering of objections. Here he was conversational, sprightly, acute, and often drew the laugh by the involuntary suddenness and aptness of his replies and illustrations. Easy and colloquial in his dialect, he carried his audience with him through this part. They were stirred up and enlivened, and, as a plain countryman once said, 'he says it so that you feel you could have said it all yourself.' Last of all came what he considered the heart of his discourse — *the application.* A sermon that did not induce any body to *do any thing* he considered a sermon thrown away. The object of preaching, in his view, was not merely to enlighten the understanding, or even to induce pleasing and devout contemplation, but to make people set about a thorough change of heart and life. These closing portions of his sermons were the peculiarity of his preaching. He warned, he entreated, he pleaded, urging now this motive and now that, talking as if his audience were one individual, whom he *must*, before he left the pulpit, persuade to take a certain step. 'If these things are so,' he would say, 'you, my friend, have neglected this matter too long. Are you not convinced that you ought to do something now, to-night, this moment? Do you say, "What shall I do?" One thing I will tell you, that if you do not do something more than you have, you will be lost. *That* you acknowledge, do you not?' Then, changing the tone of his voice to the lowest key of personal conversation, he would say, 'Now there is one thing you can do: you can resolve before God, from this moment, that the salvation of your soul shall be your first object, and that, whatever it may mean to be a Christian, you will not rest till you are one. You can do *that.* Are you not conscious that you can? I put it to you — will you do it? You can not refuse without periling your salvation. When you leave this place to-night you can avoid distracting conversation. You can preserve this resolve as carefully as you would shade a lamp which the winds of heaven are seeking to extinguish. *Will you do it?* Will you go to some solitary place to-night, and there kneel down and pray? You are conscious you can do it. Will you do it? Will you open your Bible and read a chapter? and, lest you should not know where to look, I will tell you. Read the first chapter of Proverbs, and then kneel, confess your sins, and try to give yourself up to God for the rest of your life. Then seek the instruction of your minister or Christian friends; break off all outward and known sins; put yourself in the way of all religious influences, and I will venture to say you can not pursue this course a fortnight, a week, without finding a new and blessed life dawning within you.'

"I recollect one sermon that he preached in Boston addressed to business men — those who were so engrossed and hardened with cares that they were tempted to feel that they could not give the time necessary to become Christians. The practical point for which he pleaded was, that they would come to a resolution to give half an hour a day to religious reading and prayer. He pled with all his eloquence for this one thing. 'You can not give half an hour this week without giving an hour the next; your eternal life or death may turn on your granting or refusing this one thing.' The many business men who became members of his Church attest the practical value of this style of appeal.

"As he preached he watched the faces of his hearers, and when he saw that one was moved he followed him. 'A—— B—— has seemed to feel a good deal,' he would say, 'these several Sundays. I must go after him. Something seems to block his wheels.' Often he used to say to me, speaking of one and another with whom he had been talking, 'I've been feeling round to find *where the block is*. I put my finger on this and that, and it don't move; but sometimes the Lord helps me, and I touch the right thing, and all goes right.'

"After his evening services it was his custom to come directly home and spend an hour or two with his children, as he phrased it, letting himself 'run down.' This was our best season for being with him. He was lively, sparkling, jocose, full of anecdote and incident, and loved to have us all about him, and to indulge in a good laugh.

"Often his old faithful friend the violin was called in requisition, and he would play a few antiquated contra dances and Scotch airs out of a venerable yellow music-book which had come down the vale of years with him from East Hampton. Auld Lang Syne, Bonnie Doon, and Mary's Dream were among the inevitables; and a contra dance which bore the unclerical title of 'Go to the devil and shake yourself' was a great favorite with the youngsters. He aspired with ardent longings to Money Musk, College Hornpipe, and sundry other tunes arranged in unfavorable keys, although he invariably broke down, and ended the performance with a pshaw! In after years, after his mind began to fail, nothing would so thoroughly electrify him as to hear one of his sons, who was a proficient on the violin, performing those old tunes he had tried so many times to conquer.

"These musical performances sometimes inspirited him and his young audience to the verge of indiscretion. When mother was gone to bed before him, he could be wrought upon by the petitions of the children to exhibit for their astonishment and delight the wonders of the double shuffle, which he said he used to dance on the barn floor at corn huskings when he was a young man. But the ravages of these saltatory exercises on the feet of his stockings caused them to be frowned upon by the female authorities to such a degree that the exhibition was a very rare treat. These innocent evening gala hours, like every thing else, were a part of his system of regimen. 'If I were to go to bed,' he would say, 'at the key at which I leave off preaching, I should toss and tumble all night. I must let off steam gradually, and then I can sleep like a child.'

"In fact, he was an excellent sleeper, and usually knew of but one nap, which lasted from the time his head touched the pillow till the youngest child was sent to wake him up in the morning. This was invariably the department of the reigning baby, who was solemnly instructed by him that it was necessary to take him by the nose, and kiss him many times before the heaviness in his head would go off so that he could lift it. Oftentimes he would lie in bed after his little monitor had called him, professing fears that there was a lion under the bed who would catch his foot if he put it out, and requiring repeated and earnest assurances from the curly head that he should be defended from being eaten up if he rose; and often and earnestly the breakfast-bell would ring before he could be induced to launch forth. Great would be the pride of the little monitor, who led him at last gravely into the breakfast-room, and related in baby phrase the labors of getting him up.

"Of the ardent love and admiration which my father felt for the ministerial brethren with whom he was associated in this period of his labors I have a pleasant memory. His heart seemed able to take them all in with the fresh vivacity of early days, and he gave to the good parts of each the tribute of most sincere and enthusiastic admiration. He was constantly acting in counsel and concert; he relied on them for advice; he listened to their opinions, and never imposed his own upon them; and the great influence he exerted among them was always that of a brother and companion, and never that of a master.

"The weekly reunion of the Boston ministers was always full of social life, and often presented amusing scenes. The stranger who should have been called on to point out the great orthodox leader would hardly have picked out the short, square man in negligent undress, who sat among them apparently the favorite and boon companion of all, but the mark for all sorts of jokes and sly witticisms, which his little personal peculiarities would call forth, and which he always sent back with interest in sallies which carried the laugh through the circle. Occasionally, while sermons, or letters, or other communications were being read, he would be seized with sudden whiffs of inspiration, and after fumbling in his pocket for the pencil which was never there, would borrow his next neighbor's, dash off hasty notes, and pocket it. This process would sometimes occur till half the pencils of the company were lodged in one or other of his pockets, when one of the party would remark dryly, 'Well, doctor, how many pencils have you got in your pocket by this time?' When, suddenly recollecting himself, he would bring them out and begin a humorous distribution of them to their owners.

"The doctor's watch was a standard joke. He always wore one which never was going, and he, for his own part, had no more sense of time than the angel in the Revelations who declared that it should be no longer. Wherever it was good to be, there he staid till some one else woke him and reminded him that his hour was come. His watch was only wound up at such intervals when it would suddenly occur to him to inquire what time it was. Then he would pull out his old friend, hold it up, shake it, inquire the time of his next neighbor, wind it up and set it with an air of grave attention, and go on his way rejoicing.

"He was accustomed to carry about him two or three pairs of spectacles, to guard against the accidents to which his absent habits exposed him. At one time, in ministers' meeting, he was reading with great energy and commenting on a certain document, and, as his wont, was throwing his spectacles up on his head at intervals when making his own comments on what he read. Inflamed with zeal, he performed this customary motion with such ardor that the spectacles slipped over on to the back of his head, and when he would return to his manuscript, feeling for them in vain, he mechanically took another pair from his pocket, which he put on in front. 'Now, brethren,' said Dr. Wisner, 'we must look about us. The doctor has got on his spectacles behind and before; he means to look into the matter all round.'

"These pleasant days of ministerial fellowship in Boston were never forgotten by him. These friendships seemed to have all the ardor of those of his early days. In speaking of his friends, he would often break into expressions of enthusiasm — 'So and so is a wonderful creature!' And indorsed on their letters are often found little records, such as 'the man I loved best of all,' 'the best man God ever made,' and the like. His friendships were constant and imperishable, passing the love of woman."

XIV

THE SPIRIT OF THE PILGRIMS

TOWARD the close of the year 1827, arrangements were made for the establishment of the monthly periodical named at the head of the chapter. "You are aware," writes Dr. Beecher to the editor of the Christian Spectator (Dec. 18), "that this thing has been agitated before, and since my coming I have probably had some influence to keep it back. But we have advanced now to a point in which I am well convinced that we must have the aid of a local magazine. The mass of mind which is now awake to investigate and feel, and to receive impressions such as those will make who most frequently approach it, renders the pulpit unequal, and a new means of enlightening and forming public sentiment indispensable. Indeed, considering the growing reaction of virulence which our success creates, we can not, with only past means, maintain our own ground.

"These considerations produced a meeting for consultation last evening of ministers and laymen, to whom seem in providence to be committed the responsibility of deliberation and efficient action in the emergency here, in which the opinion was unanimous that the existing and prospective state of things demand a periodical magazine *sui generis* in the city; and a vote was passed that the thing be done as soon as may be, and the whole subject committed to a committee of nine to take all the requisite measures.

"It is in behalf of this committee that I write to give you and the associated minds of the Christian Spectator this information, and the assurance of our cordial estimation of that work, and of our purpose still, as far as it can be done, to secure the continuance of its subscribers. You will be assured that no alienation of feeling and no sinister motive operate with us in this thing, and that whatever can be done will be to give free course with us to your work."

The following are some of the reasons assigned, and the principles advanced by the new periodical in unfurling its banner to the breeze and clearing the decks for action. We give them as a fair exhibition of the then prevailing type of orthodoxy, in which such men as Porter, Woods, Stuart, Beecher, Taylor, Tyler, Fitch,

Nettleton, Hewitt, Harvey, and the New England ministry generally, sympathized fully with Dr. Beecher.

"There has been for several years past, and especially of late, a great increase of attention to religion in this city and the vicinity. * * * A spirit of investigation has gone forth — a spirit of free inquiry — a spirit that determines to examine for itself, to hear for itself, to think for itself, and not implicitly to confide in the representations of partisans; and this spirit is all the while adding to the number of those who hear orthodox preaching, who converse with orthodox ministers, who associate with the members of orthodox churches, who read the Bible with seriousness and with an anxious desire to ascertain its real meaning, and who admit the reasonableness of making religion the first, the constant, and the greatest object of attention. This spirit of investigation is a noble spirit, and it should be cherished, and cultivated, and satisfied. * * *

"It is undeniable that a large portion of the community has been totally deceived in regard to the doctrines and preaching of the orthodox. * * * The cause of truth has already suffered greatly in this way. Misrepresentations the most palpable and injurious, of the doctrines, preaching, and motives of the orthodox, have been common for many years, and the continual repetition of them has by no means ceased. The apparent object has been to keep the members of Unitarian congregations from entering the doors of an orthodox church, and this, to a very unhappy extent, has been the effect hitherto. There are not a few proofs, however, that these misrepresentations are soon to recoil upon their authors with unexpected violence. When those who have been misled determine to hear and examine for themselves, they find every thing different from what they had been taught to anticipate. They exclaim at once, 'This can not be orthodoxy. For aught that we can see, this is reasonable, scriptural, and in agreement with all that we observe within our breasts, or in the world around us. *There is nothing here that violates common sense or the experience of mankind.* Either this is not orthodoxy, or we have been grossly imposed upon respecting it.' * * *

"The Unitarian controversy, as it is now conducted in Great Britain, Germany, and the United States, embraces nearly all the great points of fundamental error. It is, as we firmly believe, *one of the last great controversies which is to afflict the Church;* and although we would by no means advise to have it introduced where it is unknown, still there is little doubt that it must, for a time, attract the attention of many individuals, in almost every part of our country. The history of this controversy, so far as it has already proceeded, does not furnish any ground of alarm for the future; but, in order to make a proper use of advantages, as well as to corect misrepresentations, it is necessary that the orthodox should have some regular channel of communicating with the public. * * *

"If it be asked, What do the orthodox believe, and how is the term now to be understood? we answer, that from the Reformation (and there is no need that we should go back farther) a certain system of doctrines has been called orthodox. These doctrines contain, as we believe, the great principles of revealed truth. Among them are the following, viz.:

"That, since the fall of Adam, men are, in their natural state, altogether destitute of true holiness, and entirely depraved;

"That men, though thus depraved, are justly required to love God with all the heart, and justly punishable for disobedience; or, in other words, they are complete moral agents, proper subjects of moral government, and truly accountable to God for their actions;

"That in the unspeakable wisdom and love of God was disclosed a plan of redemption for sinful men;

"That in the development of this plan God saw fit to reveal so much concerning the nature and the mode of the divine existence as that he is manifested to his creatures as the Father, the Son, and the Holy Ghost; and that these Three, each partaking of all the attributes of the Deity, and being entitled to receive divine worship and adoration, are the one living and true God;

"That the Son of God, laying aside the glory which he had with the Father from everlasting, came down from heaven, took upon himself man's nature, and by his humiliation, sufferings, and death, made an atonement for the sins of the world;

"That, in consequence of this atonement, the offer of pardon and eternal life was freely made to all, so that those who truly repent of sin and believe in the Lord Jesus Christ will be saved;

"That men are naturally so averse to God and holiness that, if left to themselves, they reject the offers of salvation, and neither repent of sin nor truly believe in a Savior;

"That God, being moved with infinite love and compassion, sends forth the Holy Spirit according to his sovereign pleasure, by whose beneficent energy an innumerable multitude of the human family are renewed, sanctified, and prepared for heaven; while others are suffered to pursue the course which they have freely chosen, and in which they obstinately persevere till the day of salvation is past;

"That God, in his providential dispensations, in the bestowment of his saving mercy, and in his universal government, exhibits his adorable perfections in such a manner as will call forth the admiration and love of all holy beings forever;

"That believers are justified by faith, through the efficacy of the atonement, so that all claims of human merit, and all grounds of boasting, are forever excluded;

"That the law of God is perpetually binding upon all moral beings, and upon believers not less than other men, as a rule of life; and that no repentance is genuine unless it bring forth fruits meet for repentance, and no faith is saving unless it produce good works;

"That those who have been renewed by the Spirit will be preserved by the power of God, and advanced in holiness unto final salvation; and

"That Christ, as the Great King of the Universe, the Lord and Proprietor of created beings, will judge the world at the last day, when the righteous will be received to life eternal, and the wicked will be consigned to endless punishment.

"The foregoing propositions have been drawn up in haste, neither in the words of Scripture nor of any human creed, nor with any design of exhibiting exact theological precision. We much prefer, on ordinary occasions, to express our views of religious truth in an unrestrained, popular manner. In this way the Scriptures announce religious doctrines, and in this way the same great truths may be communicated by different writers and speakers, who will naturally fall into an almost infinite variety of expression. We do not insist that others should adopt our form of words, but we have no doubt that the obvious meaning of these words is in accordance with the Bible, and can be sustained by an appeal to that infallible test. It is unnecessary to add that we have not attempted to present the reader with a summary which should comprise *all* the important truths of revealed religion.

"These doctrines, and all others necessarily connected with them and forming a part of the same system, have been received in all churches and by all individuals who have been understandingly called orthodox. These doctrines we believe, and in them we rejoice. We believe them because we think them to be clearly revealed in the Word of God, and not because they have been held and defended by such men as Luther and Calvin, Hooker and Owen, Baxter and Edwards, however pious and eminent these individuals may have been. We call no man master. We submit to no man's authority. We hold ourselves bound by the law and the testimony; and if any man's arguments or theories will not abide this ordeal, they are to be rejected. Our motto is, *Let God be true, but every man a liar*."

It is apparent, from these extracts, that the men engaged in this enterprise really believed the religion of the Redeemer to be a reasonable religion, whose fundamental doctrines would stand the test of the most free and thorough investigation.

As against the Unitarians, probably not an orthodox minister could be found but would have agreed with Dr. Dana "that the doctrines of the Gospel, while they are incontestably true, are likewise in perfect accordance with the dictates of *sober reason;* though by some reason and revelation are artfully set at variance, and unwearied efforts employed to persuade us that doctrines undeniably found in the Scriptures are at war with common sense." *

But while the New England divines at that day were unanimously convinced that no doctrine found in the Scriptures could be at variance with common sense, it is manifest, from the extracts above given, that they did not hold themselves responsible to the letter for those doctrines as stated in the creeds of the Reformation, but only for the substance of them, as surviving the discussion of two hundred years.

When the "Unitarians understood and avowed," as they claim to have done, "that they were assailing, not the undefined and modified substance now called orthodoxy, but *Calvinism,* which had expressed itself in positive formulas, and to which the orthodox party professed an unqualified and unequivocal allegiance," † the defenders of orthodoxy very properly pronounced it a "misrepresentation most palpable and injurious."

Never did the free churches and pastors of New England "profess an *unqualified* and unequivocal allegiance" to those "positive formulas." From the beginning they protested against such "unqualified" use of creeds as unlawful. From the beginning they avowed the expectation of "farther light" as the glorious privilege of the New England churches.

Whether or not they had really given up any part of the substance of doctrine in giving up imputation, inability, etc., as Dr.

* Sermon entitled "Evangelical Preaching is Rational Preaching," delivered at the ordination of Rev. W. K. Talbot as pastor of the Presbyterian Church and Society in Nottingham West, N. H., by Rev. Daniel Dana, D.D.

† Half Century of Unitarian Controversy, p. 55.

Hodge[1] and Dr. Ellis[2] so cordially unite in asserting, one thing is certain, they strenuously maintained that they had not, and that, so long as they held that man from the very womb was lost except through the blood of Christ, they held all that was essential. In so doing they acted in strict accordance with the doctrine of "farther light," and treated the creeds of the Reformation in the only legitimate manner known to pure Protestantism; and for the Unitarians, or any others, to attempt to rein them up sharply, and hold them accountable to the very letter of Calvin and of the Assembly, was not only an infringement of their ancient liberties, but a palpable misrepresentation, justly resented and protested against by the Spirit of the Pilgrims. As Dr. Nettleton well remarks,* "Why not take this ground with Unitarians? We feel no concern for old Calvinism. Let them dispute it as much as they please; we feel bound to make no defense. Come home to the evangelical system now taught in New England. Meet us, if at all, on our own avowed principles, or we shall have nothing to say to you."

The feelings and aspirations with which Dr. Beecher co-operated in the establishment of the new magazine are vividly expressed in the following lines extracted from a letter dated March 1, 1828, addressed to Dr. Griffin:

"The time has come when the Lord Jesus Christ 'expects every man to do his duty,' and when nothing is required to give to error a final discomfiture, and to truth a permanent victory, but a united and simultaneous effort to rescue from perversion the doctrines and institutions of our fathers, the fairest inheritance ever bestowed by Heaven upon men, and holding out to this nation and this world more prospective good than was ever committed to a merely human instrumentality.

"For a century or more there has been, as you know, a decline in evangelical doctrine and vital piety in this region; and so low did the pulse of life sink in this once holy city, that the enemy thought verily that the witnesses were slain, and began to exult over their dead bodies and fearlessly to divide the spoil. The college was given to Socinus, that he, by its perverted funds and

* See vol. i., p. 491, Letter to Dr. Beecher.

[1] Charles Hodge (1797–1878), professor in Princeton Theological Seminary after 1822, in 1825 started the *Princeton Review,* in which he attacked New School and other heresies.

[2] George Ellis (1814–1894), Unitarian pastor, editor of the *Christian Examiner* (1849–1855), overseer at Harvard (1850–1879), professor in Harvard Divinity School after 1857. In 1857 he published *A Half Century of the Unitarian Controversy.*

powerful influence, might corrupt the literature of the commonwealth and disciple all the cultivated intellect of the state, especially that which should be concerned in the formation and administration of law.

"Care also was taken that the initiated should be well provided with the loaves and fishes by governmental favor and a perverted political confidence, and that our aspiring youth whom the college had not perverted should be bribed to drink of the cup of sorcery as the only probable condition of political elevation. And while the servants slept the enemy sowed tares, till a large portion of the Eastern churches, with their funds, were subverted; and when the servants awoke, it was only to discover that what perverted majorities could not do fast enough in plundering and blotting out the churches of the Pilgrims, the law, by its kind accommodations, was enabling minorities of the churches, by the aid of secular societies of Unitarian fraternity, to accomplish.

"A single hand might unbar the gates of Zion, and let in her foes and give up her funds and records, and the law called it just and honest. Thus for a time 'judgment was turned away backward, and justice stood afar off, and truth was fallen in the streets, and equity could not enter.' And all the while at the corners of the streets they were sounding the praise of our fathers and their institutions, to keep off the public eye from the degenerations which were going on in secret, while the finger of scorn was every where pointed at their dejected children, and notes of exultation and contumely ascended on every side. 'And the Lord saw it, and it displeased him that there was no judgment, and he saw that there was no man, and wondered that there was no intercessor, therefore his arm brought salvation; when the enemy came in like a flood, the Spirit of the Lord lifted a standard against him.'

"Under the influence of truth and of the Holy Ghost a great attention is awakened to the subject of religion, and a public sentiment is formed and forming eminently favorable to free and fair discussion. We can now explain and assert our rights before a public that will hear and do us justice. We can uncover the deeds of darkness of past years to the wondering eye and the indignant heart of an honest community, whose confidence has been abused, and who can feel for our wrongs and indignities, and will not be partakers in other men's sins. The day of retribution now for a long time slumbereth not.

"All which is now needed is that the friends of the religion and institutions of our fathers read, and understand, and feel, and act in unison for the defense of those liberties, civil and religious, which had well-nigh been taken away forever. All the great designs which God has to answer by planting our fathers here in this nation and world depend, as I believe, on the efforts of this generation to rescue their institutions from perversion, and restore them to their native purity and glory. We have no sectarian views. We love all who love our Lord Jesus Christ in sincerity and truth.

"Consultation has been had as extensively as time and circumstances would allow, and but one sentiment and feeling prevails. We all seem to hear the voice from heaven saying, 'Arise, shine, for thy light is come, and the glory of the Lord is risen upon thee.' We dare not be disobedient. We only wish our brethren, and the churches, and friends of the institutions which are threatened by Unitarians, to respond to the call which we make upon them for their counsels, and prayers, and co-operation. The great point is to obtain readers, and for this we are determined to send out approved agents who can well explain our views and aid our union of efforts.

"Such a one is the bearer of this letter. We wish to obtain in every town in this commonwealth the reading of the Spirit of the Pilgrims by a considerable number, so that its light may shine and its influence be felt. More I need not say, nor even this, for your information, whom God employed to open this conflict which is now moving on to certain victory with such glorious rapidity and power."

XV

CALL TO PHILADELPHIA

About this time Dr. Beecher received a call from the Fifth Presbyterian Church [1] in Philadelphia, recently left vacant by Dr. Skinner's removal. "I got Skinner a call to Boston," observed Dr. Beecher, "and he came. His congregation, to be up with me, gave me a call to his place, and got several persons to write urgently. Among others, Dr. Miller, of Princeton, wrote an argument, very strong; and when it was read in my trial at Cincinnati it made a sensation."

"Before this letter reaches your hands you will have been apprised that the church of which our friend Dr. Skinner was lately the pastor has given you a unanimous call to become their minister.

"Some are disposed to smile at this measure as a sort of desperate effort at retaliation for robbing Philadelphia of Dr. Skinner. Others view it as a plan by no means hopeless. But ALL, so far as I know, in this region, would *most cordially rejoice* in the success of the application, and hail your arrival in Philadelphia as an event most devoutly to be wished by all the friends of Zion within the bounds of the Presbyterian Church.

"My dear brother, I beg, with all the earnestness which I am capable of feeling or uttering, that you will not either lightly consider or hastily reject this call. I do seriously believe that, however painful the step of removal to Philadelphia might be, both to the friends of religion in Massachusetts and to yourself, the residue of your days could not possibly be disposed of (so far as human views can go) in a manner so much calculated to unite the friends of Christ in the South and West with those in the East, and to introduce a new era of harmony, love, and co-operation in the American churches.

"It is not only a matter of immense importance that the individual church in Philadelphia which gives you this call should

[1] Skinner returned to the Fifth Church in 1828 after six months in Boston. When he left for Andover in 1832, a large majority seceded in protest against the calling of a New School pastor, George Duffield.

be supplied with a pastor wise, pious, peaceful, prudent, and acceptable, as far as possible, to all parties; but, if *you* will come to that place, I am most deeply persuaded that you will have an opportunity of diffusing a most happy and reviving influence all around you to a degree which very few men in our country have ever had; that you will be likely, humanly speaking, to bring together feelings and efforts which are now widely separated, and, in fact, to give a new impulse to all those great plans which I know to be near your heart.

"By removing to Philadelphia, unless I utterly miscalculate, you would not be likely to subtract very essentially from your usefulness in Massachusetts. You might still, by means of writing and occasional visits, continue to do there a large portion of what you now do, while your usefulness and influence in the Presbyterian Church, from New England to New Orleans, might, and probably would, be increased tenfold. I have no doubt that, by the acceptance of the station to which you are called, your opportunity for doing good in the American churches would be doubled, if not quadrupled at a stroke.

"Say not that these things are mere matter of human calculation. They are so; and yet, I think, the book of God and human experience furnish an abundant foundation for them to rest upon. The truth is, we want nothing for the benefit of our eighteen hundred churches, next to the sanctifying Spirit of God, so much as an individual in Philadelphia (our ecclesiastical metropolis) who should be active, energetic, untiring, comprehensive in his plans, and firm and unmoved in his purposes and efforts.

"Will you not cast yourself on the Lord's strength and faithfulness, and come and help us to unite all our forces in one mighty effort, in the name of our heavenly King, to promote his cause at home and abroad?

"With the cordiality of a brother, and the freedom of an old friend, I conjure you, when such an open door is set before you, not to refuse to enter it. As to your reception among us, I hope I need not say that it would be *universally*, with *glad hearts* and *open arms*. May the Lord direct and bless you."

The Church also sent on a committee to urge upon Dr. Beecher the acceptance of their invitation. Speaking of their visit, Dr. Beecher remarked:

"When the two gentlemen came on to see me about the call, I took them into my inquiry meeting. There was great variety of cases. Language of simplicity came along, and they'd see me talking 'way down in language fit for children, and then, the next moment, rise up into clear, strong, philosophical language. And then the language of free agency and ability came along, and then, they told me afterward, they thought I was going to be a — what d'ye call it? — Arminian, and they'd stick up their ears. I *made something* of free agency — more than a Calvinist would do usually — and brought folks up to *do* what they were able to. But next minute came along the plea of morality and self-dependence, and I took them by the nape of the neck and twisted their neck off. So they saw that I had my replies according to the subject, and in the course of the evening heard me touch on seven or eight or more different states of mind."

This invitation led to that visit to Philadelphia during the session of the General Assembly already referred to. During that visit he writes to Dr. Wisner:

"The mandamus by Brother Fay [2] arrived, but I can not obey it. I left home with the determination to be gone four weeks, and gave up the expectation of being in Boston at the anniversaries, and have made and can make no preparation. Besides, if there was reason for my coming here, which I can not doubt, there is more reason for staying as long as the Assembly stays than there was for coming; for the whole troop of New-Measure men are here, and are kept at bay, as yet, by a watchful Providence, but would doubtless clap hands and go pell-mell to work if the means were removed which Providence employs. * * * * Another reason for staying here is that the Sabbath cause needs touching in the General Assembly, and will, as I expect, be moved in a general meeting in the city, to be gotten up next week, at which I wish to be present. I learn from Lewis Tappan [3] that they have sent to you in Boston to move on the same subject, which I hope you will do, for much depends on the promptitude with which the annunciation of the general union and address is followed up in different parts, and especially in the cities of our land."

It is hardly necessary to inform the reader that the call to Philadelphia was declined, for reasons which need not be stated. As he afterward remarked when called to the West, "Aside from the seminary, there was not a place besides Boston I would have looked at for a moment."

[2] Warren Fay (1784–1864), minister in Conn. and Mass., was active in the temperance and missionary movements.

[3] Lewis Tappan (1788–1873), a convert from Unitarianism and a successful N. Y. businessman, generously supported abolition, missions, education, and revivals. He retired in 1849 to give all his time to charities.

XVI

INFANT SALVATION

It is already sufficiently apparent that Dr. Beecher's one idea was to do good by leading men to repentance. The statement of the apostle, "After that in the wisdom of God the world by wisdom knew not God, it pleased God by the foolishness of preaching to save them that believe," he accepted as a bona fide disclosure of the best method of saving and blessing mankind. It was his business, by preaching, to awaken men, answer all their objections, convince them that the doctrines of the Gospel were not at variance with common sense, and lead them to intelligent and honorable repentance.

His hostility to Unitarianism arose wholly from the obstacles cast by that icy system in his path. It took away the key of knowledge. It would not enter in itself, and those who were entering in it hindered. Among the means employed to check the progress of religious awakening to which Unitarians resorted were repulsive and distorted exhibitions of Calvinism, which, if even true to the letter, were certainly false to the spirit of the system by being taken out of their proper connection, and without due regard to the law of progress both at the time of the Reformation and since. Compared with Romanism, the doctrines of the Reformation were a wonderful step of progress. Compared with New England divinity as embodied, *e. g.*, in the lectures of Dr. Dwight, those same formulas, if rigidly imposed to the letter, would be a yoke of bondage and a turning back the wheels of lawful and necessary progress. We have already justified the Spirit of the Pilgrims in pronouncing such representations of orthodoxy to be misrepresentations. Among these, none, perhaps, was more common or more mischievous than the charge of believing in the damnation of infants.

The origin of the controversy on this point is thus stated by Dr. Beecher himself: "As evangelical religion increased in this city and the country around, I became satisfied that the people who were under Unitarian influence, and had not the means of knowing otherwise, were led to believe that the orthodox around them did hold to the doctrine that infants are lost, as a part of their system; and that, instead of relying on truth and argument, attempts were made to prejudice an honest and well-meaning community against their brethren, the children of the Pilgrims, by the circulation of such unfounded reports.

"In these circumstances, being requested to republish a sermon which had some reference to the number of the saved, I supposed it a duty indicated by the prevailing misapprehensions around me to disclaim, in behalf of myself and of the orthodox generally in this city and vicinity, and in New England, and in behalf of the great body of the Congregational and Presbyterian ministers in the United States, the believing or teaching any such doctrine.

"In the execution of this purpose I wrote and published the following note:

"I am aware that Calvinists are represented as believing and teaching the monstrous doctrine that infants are damned, and that hell is doubtless paved with their bones. But, having passed the age of fifty, and been conversant for thirty years with the most approved Calvinistic writers, and personally acquainted with many of the most distinguished Calvinistic divines in New England, and in the Middle, and Southern, and Western States, I must say that I have never seen or heard of any book which contained such a sentiment, nor a man, minister or layman, who believed or taught it. And I feel authorized to say that Calvinists, as a body, are as far from teaching the doctrine of infant damnation as any of those who falsely accuse them. And I would earnestly and affectionately recommend to all persons who have been accustomed to propagate this slander, that they commit to memory, without delay, the ninth commandment, which is, 'Thou shalt not bear false witness against thy neighbor.'"

In the controversy which ensued it has been recently claimed "that Dr. Beecher was utterly and most ingloriously vanquished, and that his opponent gained a complete and unquestionable victory." *

We submit, however, that the utmost the reviewer could claim to have proved was, that Dr. Beecher had rashly asserted more in respect to Calvinistic writers than he could maintain. How far even here such claim is valid we prefer to leave every one acquainted with the case to judge for himself. At best it was but a side issue, not the main point in controversy. In respect to the question which was of instant practical concern, and which caused the challenge to be thrown out in the original note, we are far from

* Ellis's Half Century, pp. 83, 84.

thinking the reviewer and his allies had any cause for self-felicitation.

"The reviewer," observes Dr. Beecher, "understood my denial to respect the whole Calvinistic party of present times, and my charge of bearing false witness to respect all who accused them of holding to infant damnation; admits that he is implicated in the charge of falsehood and slander, and bound to defend himself, and comes out for that purpose. By quoting the charge from the Christian Disciple * he repeats it, and there leaves it as he found it; says not a word to prove it true; comes and looks upon it, like Levite upon Jew, and passes by on the other side. But, in the mean time, he gathers up all his resources and puts forth all his energies to repel the charge of slandering his neighbor, 'the Calvinistic system,' whom no one ever suspected of being his neighbor, or had charged him with slandering; and feels indignant at being charged with bearing false witness against his neighbors, the Calvinistic writers, and compasses sea and land for evidence to clear himself.

"But, under the charge of bearing false witness against 'living Calvinistic men,' the whole Calvinistic party of modern times, in the sight of the nation, he meekly lies down — lies down deliberately under the acknowledged charge of falsehood and slander — lays his hand on his mouth, and his mouth in the dust, and pleads guilty — says he knew from the beginning that the charge against the living Calvinistic party could not be proved." †

Was it indeed a "complete and unequivocal victory," while convicting an antagonist of a mistake in a matter of book-learning, to be thus publicly impaled as a willful slanderer?

The reviewer failed utterly to show that the perdition of infants was either a doctrine of the creeds of the Reformation, or a necessary logical inference from them, even in their original strictness, much less from the system as modified by centuries of investigation and "farther light."

On the other hand, Dr. Beecher showed that, his enemies themselves being judges, the doctrine was of Unitarian origin, and received its death-blow at the hands of Calvin and the New England divines.

"The early Calvinists, as a body, did not, in any form, receive

* * * * "A doctrine, moreover, which follows necessarily from the Calvinistic system, and which would now be insisted on by all real and consistent Calvinists if they thought their people would bear it." — *Chris. Discip., May and June*, 1823, p. 220.

† Spirit of the Pilgrims, vol. iii., p. 23.

the doctrine of infant damnation. The reviewer himself has furnished conclusive evidence of this fact. The Lutherans, 'not content with condemning the Anabaptists, set down the position that *salvation does not depend on baptism* among the false and erroneous doctrines of the Calvinists.' That baptism is essential to salvation had, it appears, by a misinterpretation of John, iii., 5, come down from the early fathers (those undoubted Unitarians, as the Examiner would have them), and was the principal argument which went to compel the belief of infant damnation; and Calvin, it seems, was the first to explode the false Unitarian interpretation, which shut the kingdom of heaven against infants, and to give the interpretation adopted by his followers, which opens to them wide the kingdom of glory. I do not believe that the Christian fathers were Unitarians; but if they were, as the Examiner contends, why then the Unitarians introduced the doctrine into the Church, and Calvinists were the pioneers raised up by Providence to expel it." *

The work begun by Calvin, Dr. Beecher showed, was completed by the Edwardean divines in the rejection of the doctrine of imputation.

"Our Puritan fathers held to the doctrine of original sin as consisting in the imputation of Adam's sin and in a hereditary depravity, and this continued to be the doctrine of the churches of New England until after the time of Edwards. He adopted the views of the Reformers on the subject of original sin as consisting in the imputation of Adam's sin and a depraved nature transmitted by descent. But, after him, this mode of stating the subject was gradually changed, until, long since, the prevailing doctrine has been that men are not guilty of Adam's sin, and that depravity is not of the substance of the soul, nor an inherent physical quality, but is wholly voluntary, and consists in the transgression of law in such circumstances as constitutes accountability and desert of punishment. This change was not accomplished without discussion. It was resisted by those who chose to be denominated Old Calvinists, and advocated by those who were called Hopkinsians and New Divinity men, until for years these views of original sin have been the predominant doctrine of the ministers and churches now denominated evangelical."

This he then shows to have been well known to the Unitarians, and adds: "And yet, with all this knowledge that the phraseology and faith of New England Calvinists is changed on the article of

* Spirit of the Pilgrims, vol. iii., p. 187.

original sin, all those expressions which the Reformers adopted on that subject are quoted in evidence that the Calvinists of New England hold to the damnation of infants!" *

This discussion marks an era in theological advancement. Never before had the doctrine of infant damnation been so publicly and earnestly denied, and the salvation of infants, by implication, so distinctly maintained as the faith and hope of the churches. The charge so indignantly repelled as odious and slanderous fell into desuetude; or if occasionally renewed by some tyro in theology, in these numbers was laid a basis for its final and most inglorious discomfiture.

An illustration of these remarks will be found in an article in a religious journal, in which the following propositions are ably sustained:

"1. The dogma of the perdition of infants first arose from the reception, by a corrupt (patristic) Church, of the doctrine of baptismal regeneration.

"2. John Calvin was the first man who dealt a death-blow to the power of this dogma by refuting and repudiating the doctrine of baptismal regeneration.

"3. Ever after Calvin's time, and in consequence of his influence, this dogma retained but partial and feeble hold of the Reformed churches.

"4. The New England divines destroyed the last remnant of life lingering in this ancient dogma [by repudiating the doctrine of imputation], and now, for many years, the current orthodox faith has utterly and indignantly repudiated it." †

* Spirit of the Pilgrims, vol. i., pp. 158–161.

† Congregationalist, February 19, 1858.

XVII

YOUNG MEN — MUSIC

Dr. Beecher was remarkable through life for his youthfulness of feeling, and his consequent power to sympathize with the young, and stimulate them to active usefulness.

"When I came to Boston," he observed, "evangelical people had no political influence there, and in civil affairs those who joined them had but little chance. All offices were in the hands of Unitarians — perhaps a Baptist occasionally; hence, as young men came in from the town, there was a constant stream of proselytes to them. But, as the revival went on, I had a large number of young men that joined the Church — Anderson, Stone, George E. Head, Amasa Walker, Palmer,[1] and such — the finest set you ever laid eyes on.

"I invited Marvin to come to see me in Sheafe Street. Explained to him the operation of political patronage. The whole influence of Unitarianism a poisonous bribery. I said, 'What do you think of that?' 'I think it must be stopped, or we shall be stopped.' 'My opinion is, we can stop it. There are ten men in our Church — you one — that can assemble in a confidential meeting, and make such arrangements as will do it.' I named twelve to bring to me. He did. I explained to them, and said, 'You may exert a power that shall be felt through the United States. There is a set of smoking loafers who have been in the habit of attending primary meetings, and having it all their own way. Our people don't go. The cause of God is abandoned just here — the cause of souls. They come streaming in to this city from all directions to be perverted. Now organize a society. Go to the primary meetings; go to this and that man, and persuade them to go and do up the business.'

[1] I could find a record of only two of these young men. Amasa Walker (1799–1875) had been farm worker, clerk, and teacher in Woodstock, Conn., when he entered the shoe business in Boston. An abolitionist, he retired from business in 1840 and was Mass. secretary of state under the Free Soil Party (1852–1853). He lectured on political economy at Oberlin (1842–1848) and at Amherst (1859–1869). Julius Palmer (1803–1872), from rural R. I., was clerk and later partner in a hardware store. He was a deacon, superintendent of the Bowdoin St. Sunday School, and a founder of Mt. Vernon Church.

"They did so. First meeting they got an old Democrat as captain. On hand when the clock struck. Went to work. When the loafers came in, they stared: 'What — what — what's going on here?' and, seeing what was going on, moved to adjourn. Lost. Young men went on quietly and put on some of other denominations, and adjourned. The nominations were carried to the polls, and elected, and that was the last time they ever had to take care to put in orthodox men. From that time the orthodox have had an equal chance.

"These young men met monthly (the 'Hanover Association of Young Men' they called it), and had committees on various important matters relating to state of city and things needing to be done.

"One of their reports was on lotteries, and it was so well drawn that afterward, when it came into the Legislature, it was embodied in the law that was passed. Nobody ever knew where that movement came from. They never knew what hurt 'em.

"They got up a petition to sweep off the booths for ardent spirits on the Common on public days. They got Channing's name, and the deputy governor, and supreme judges, and lower judges, merchants, and carried into the city council the largest number of signatures ever known before that time to any such document. It failed the first year, but carried the year following. The next public day there was not one of the booths, and they have never been put back since. But they never knew where *that* came from either.

"They examined the number attending Unitarian congregations compared with ours, and found that we outnumbered them. They appointed committees to watch for young men who came to the city, and bring them under good influence. They wrote short paragraphs, and got them inserted in the papers, about any object they wanted to accomplish. The violation of the Sabbath by steam-boat excursions to Nahant was discussed and checked in this way. They had a committee on the colored population, and another on the Irish, and another on sailors.

"The Association was organized in January, 1827, and before the year was out there were four other Associations of the same kind formed in the city. One of the last things I did before going West was to address the young men of these Associations, some twelve hundred of them, in Tremont Theatre. The house was full, and a more interesting audience I never looked on."

We have been favored with a communication from a prominent member of the Association, Hon. Amasa Walker, of North Brookfield, Mass., of which the following is an extract:

"The first movement made in behalf of Lyceums in Massachusetts was by this Association.* The subject was introduced by the writer on the 3d of December, 1828. Prior to that time there had been no such thing as popular lectures or Lyceums. When courses of lectures were given, as they sometimes, but not very frequently were, they were attended only by the male sex. Ladies were not supposed to be interested in such things. The single or married man who attended went alone, and left his female friends at home.

"The idea of popular lectures for the mutual improvement of both sexes had just been started by Josiah Holbrook, of New Haven,[2] and he had come on to Boston to endeavor to bring his ideas before the public.

"The subject, as just stated, was presented before the Hanover Association, and a committee appointed, which reported strongly in favor of the measure, and within a short time the Boston Lyceum was formed, consisting at first of less than a hundred members, but which continued to increase, from time to time, for sixteen years, until the audience attending its meetings filled the largest hall in the city. This was the practical introduction of the important idea of combining popular improvement and amusement for both sexes — of furnishing some place of rational resort which the people might visit more beneficially than the theatre.

"The experiment was entirely successful; and, as your father witnessed its progress, he predicted 'that the time would come when he should preach in the Tremont Theatre;' a prediction which, as you know, was fully verified.

"It is quite difficult now to realize the great importance of this Lyceum effort in changing the public taste, and in giving a higher and better tone to the public mind. Individual voluntary associations pass away, but ideas become impressed upon society never to be obliterated. Lyceums, however transient as organizations, have produced a social revolution in a most essential particular, and the several lecturers who now traverse the broad territory of the United States, entertaining thousands with their eloquence, have

* It is stated, however, in the Appendix to Judge White's Ipswich Address, 1830, p. 50, that Lyceums were formed in the south part of Worcester county in the autumn of 1826.

[2] Josiah Holbrook (1788–1854), editor and itinerant lecturer, fostered the Lyceum movement.

been created by the new tastes generated by the Lyceum movement.

"I shall not attempt to say any thing of the strictly religious movements of which your father was the soul and centre while in Boston — of his great controversy with the learned and talented Unitarians, carried on with so much ability and success. Of that you have better authority than my own. I wish to confine myself wholly to the particular topic to which I have referred, because I feel that the vast influence which Dr. Beecher exerted while in Boston, through the various agencies he set in motion, is but little appreciated by the present generation. A great part of those who, while in middle life, were associated with him in Boston, have passed away; and only those who were then the young men by whom he was surrounded, and who participated in his labors, can fully realize the immense services he rendered to society, not only in Boston, but through the commonwealth. I speak not now of his denominational services, but of that great moral and social influence which he exerted.

"I have already intimated that other young men's associations had been formed in the different religious societies. These had given such an impetus to the public mind that societies of young men were formed for a great variety of kindred objects. A grand display of these was made on the 4th of July, 1833, when they joined together in celebrating the national anniversary.

"A large procession was formed, and marched through various streets to Chauncey Place Church, where an oration was delivered by the president of the Boston Lyceum, who was a member of the Hanover Association. Never, perhaps, did any man look down upon a nobler and more inspiring audience. The floor of the house was entirely filled with young men, mostly between the ages of eighteen and twenty-five — the galleries with ladies. It was a union celebration, without any reference to denominational differences. Dr. Frothingham[3] implored the divine blessing. It seemed to the writer then, as it does now, a kind of culmination of your father's efforts in behalf of young men; for although there were societies present at that time in whose formation he had no direct agency, yet, knowing as I did the various influences he had put in motion in the city, I felt that the demonstration was to be credited to his efforts.

[3] Nathaniel Frothingham (1793–1870), student of Ware, Unitarian pastor in Boston, translator, hymn writer.

"The societies present on the occasion were:

"The Boston Lyceum.

"The Franklin Debating Society.

"The Boston Young Men's Society.

"The Boston Young Men's Marine Bible Society.

"Young Men's Society for the promotion of Literature and Science.

"Boston Laboring Young Men's Temperance Society.

"Lyceum Elocution and Debating Society.

"Mercantile Library Association.

"Mechanics' Apprentices Library Association.

"Young Men's Temperance Society.

"Mechanics' Lyceum.

"The results of all these great efforts to improve the moral and intellectual condition of the city, and furnish the people with rational and elevating entertainments, were, that in a few years the theatre was in a great degree superseded. So many courses of lectures, so many interesting discussions were furnished by these various associations, that there was neither time nor taste for the entertainment of the drama. It fell, therefore, into desuetude, so that for some few years it nearly ceased to exist.

In this connection we insert a few of Dr. Beecher's reminiscences of Dr. Lowell Mason,[4] the distinguished composer, who presided over the choir of the Hanover and Bowdoin Street churches, and whose musical career may be said in some measure to have commenced in connection with the former.

"Lowell Mason was not with me at first, but came early, and staid while I was in Boston. He came to us from Savannah. Deacon Noyes, a far-reaching man, knew about him, and corresponded with him, and got him to come and take choir and classes. He did good. He took young converts and trained them to sing. They drew in the unconverted, and were instrumental in their conversion. His influence was not secular, but as efficacious as preaching. Almost all who went to his classes, instead of being decoyed by it and made frivolous, were converted."

Dr. Beecher's mention of Lowell Mason suggests a remark or two on some of the indirect results of the founding of Hanover Street Church on psalmody and sacred music in America. It was

[4] Lowell Mason (1792–1842) added music to the Boston public school curriculum, organized the Boston Academy of Music, composed and made collections of hymns.

here that Mr. Mason introduced that method of teaching classes upon the Pestalozzian[5] system which has revolutionized the profession and created a new era in public worship.

Here, or in Bowdoin Street it was, that the Church Psalmody was first substituted for the cumbrous Worcester's Watts' and Select, which still weighs down the psalmody of some antediluvian districts like a nightmare. Here, too, the Handel and Haydn Collection was introduced, in some respects unsurpassed by any of the numerous subsequent collections by the same author. In Hanover and Bowdoin Churches also, it is believed, were first heard many of those melodies and harmonies which have since acquired a world-wide renown, and are familiar, wherever Christianity is known, as household words.

An ardent lover of music himself, Dr. Beecher infused into that department, as he did into every other with which he had any thing to do, a portion of his own singularly progressive and buoyant enthusiasm. His full belief that the millennium was coming, that it was at hand, that the Church was just about to march with waving banners to final and universal dominion, imparted to music, as it had to theology, an entirely new spirit.

The music of New England had originally been plaintive and mournful to a remarkable degree. It was the natural tendency of persecution and exile to tune the harp of the daughter of Zion in the minor key; but, under the exhilaration of anticipated conquest, minor airs became distasteful and went out of date, and music assumed a bolder, livelier, more triumphant character.

It is believed that no single mind, not professionally connected with musical education, exerted so distinct and widespread an influence in this direction as that of the pastor of Hanover Church.

We insert here a few reminiscences kindly furnished us by Dr. Lowell Mason:

"Rev. C. Beecher: Dear Sir,

"I am ashamed to send you these blotted papers. When I wrote to you the other day I had already made the first drafts, but I thought I could, before this, find time to re-write.

"I thank you for causing me to think, and thus to bring up these things, and others more personal, relating to your beloved and honored parent, to my remembrance. I remember with much

[5] Johann H. Pestalozzi (1746–1827), Swiss educational reformer, urged that education should correspond with the child's development and experience.

satisfaction his visit to me a year or so before he died. Mrs. M—— and myself happened to be all alone. We had nothing to do but to devote ourselves to him, and all talked over old times in high glee."

"I was accustomed to go to Dr. Beecher before the time for the commencement of the public worship on Sunday morning. Such calls are often annoying to the minister, engaged, perhaps, in preparation for the services of the day. I often found him thus engaged. He would be always short and to the point with me, but I do not remember that he ever met me in an impatient or discourteous manner. One day I went as usual; it was very near the time for the commencement of the service, and just as I entered the room the bell began its call. He looked up, and, with a smile, said, 'I can't give you the hymns now; I don't know what I shall preach about yet, so I wish you to select any you think proper.' I left him to choose his subject and prepare his sermon while I went to select the hymns; probably in ten minutes afterward he came into the church. The hymns being of a general character, and adapted to direct worship, answered the purpose well, as such hymns always will. After this he requested me always to make the selection, and to send the numbers to him. This course was afterward followed; and, after much experience, the following seemed to be the result: It is better that the first and second hymns be those of direct worship, and that the subject of the sermon be not distinctly alluded to in either of them; but that the last hymn sung after the sermon shall always be closely connected with the sermon, following exactly in its wake — following out and deepening, if possible, the state of mind or emotions awakened by the preacher.

"Very often, for years afterward, did Dr. Beecher allude to the admirable effect produced in the carrying out of this principle. 'You seemed to take up,' he would say, 'the subject where I left it, and to carry it on beyond where I had the power to do.' Yes, blessed old man; but this can not be done unless the preacher has done his work somewhat as you used to do it. Unless the preacher awakens emotion, it can not be intensified by any hymn power. I used to tell the doctor, in reply to such remarks as the above, 'Sir, you laid the train, and there was nothing left for me to do but to apply the fuse.'

"He was one day preaching a most deeply interesting sermon to a house full of people, and while all were listening with the closest attention he suddenly paused. Lifting his spectacles, he looked forward to the organ gallery, and said, in a loud voice,

'Mr. Mason, sing Old Hundred.' The contrast was striking. The mandate was quickly obeyed, and the choir, rising, sang to the tune the doctor had named that stanza, than which there is not a better or more comprehensive in the language:

" 'Be thou, O God, exalted high,
And as thy glory fills the sky,
So let it be on earth displayed,
Till thou art here, as there, obeyed.'

"As soon as this was over the sermon was resumed. He had felt that he needed a moment's rest and cheer, and therefore called for the song.

"One Sabbath evening, when there was a meeting of such persons as desired personal conversation on the subject of religion, many persons being present, and while quite a number of those who used to come to his aid on such occasions were engaged in conversation with such persons as had come up for religious instruction and guidance, he came to me and said, 'I want you to sing now. We'll sing "The voice of free grace." ' He then called for the attention of all to the hymn, which was sung by all who were disposed to take a part. At its close he made a few remarks, and the conversations were resumed.

"The next day, or soon after, I met him, when he said to me, 'Well, one person gave up his heart during the singing of the hymn, as he told me afterward, and probably there were others of whom I have not heard.' He was fond of the song when judiciously introduced under such circumstances.

"Dr. Beecher, like Dr. Watts, desired a quicker movement in singing than was customary. He liked the tune of Old Hundred, even the slow movement then prevalent; but he would say sometimes to me, 'I wish you would sing faster.' He would have rejoiced to have heard the old tunes moving in equal tones, as The Old Hundredth, Dundee, etc., restored to their original time as now extensively sung.

"When a large organ was needed in the Bowdoin Street Church, it contained what no other organ before in the city had contained — a double diapason, a thirty-two feet stop, running down as low as the twice-marked capital G. When the doctor first heard its deep and majestic tone, as he afterward told me, not only was a new form of emotional expression opened to him, but his whole being seemed to be enlarged; a power of feeling was awakened within which before had always slumbered. His was a truly poetical and musical soul, and now, when the new organ poured forth its lofty tones,

> " 'Some chord in unison with what he heard
> Was touched within him, and the heart replied.'

"Dr. Beecher was in an uncommon degree free from such chains as early habits, custom, or prejudice often bind the spirit, and check investigation and progress. He could even tolerate alterations in hymns, if in them he could see improvement, and was ever ready to sacrifice early and long-cherished associations to truth and beauty. The following incident illustrates this fact. The 102d Psalm, by Watts, 5th stanza, reads thus:

> " 'He frees the souls condemned to death;
> And, when his saints complain,
> It sha'n't be said that praying breath
> Was ever spent in vain.'

To this Dr. Beecher had been accustomed from his youth, and it was a favorite hymn and stanza; but in the 'Church Psalmody,' the book used in the Bowdoin Street Church, this stanza is thus altered, by which it is relieved of the too colloquial and unpleasant elision in the third line:

> " 'He frees the souls condemned to death;
> Nor, when his saints complain,
> Shall it be said that praying breath
> Was ever spent in vain.'

The hymn in the original was very familiar to Dr. Beecher. One Sabbath it was given out, and was read by him. When he came to this stanza he read somewhat as follows:

> " 'He frees the souls condemned to death;
> And, when his saints complain,
> It sha'n't (looking at his book more carefully) — shall it —
> It sha'n't — shall it —'

I believe he tried the third time without success, when, turning to the light and looking closely at the stanza, he braced himself up, and, elevating his voice, made a final attack and won the victory, as he was wont to do in other things. After the service I walked up Bowdoin Street with him. I said, 'Doctor, the hymn seemed to give you some trouble in the reading.' 'Yes, it did, indeed; I began to fear I should not make out to read it.' 'And pray, sir, which do you think the better of the two, the original or the altered copy?' 'Oh, the altered copy is the best, but it bothered me much to read it.' How many are there with whom, putting intrinsic merit out of view, this inconvenience of reading would have been a sufficient reason for rejecting the hymn altogether. Not so the doctor, who was always on the look-out for the better — always ready to look at intrinsic worth, and to sacrifice his previous preferences when they came into competition with the right. Dr. Beecher was one of the few who, leaving the things which are behind, press forward toward the mark of perfection in the smaller as well as in the greater things."

XVIII

CORRESPONDENCE, 1829

WHILE the campaign against Unitarianism was being prosecuted with full vigor and promising auguries, suddenly there were symptoms of discord among the champions of orthodoxy, unaccountable and perplexing to themselves, and matter of rejoicing and ridicule to their enemies. To use their opponents' own language, "The Spirit of the Pilgrims was established to do battle with Unitarians; but just midway in its series of volumes it allowed us a breathing-spell, while it occupied its pages with the doctrinal contentions in its own household." *

This controversy was the more remarkable because so many of those prominently concerned in it had formerly been grouped together as intimate friends in Connecticut, of one heart and one mind in the development of the theology of revivals. Time was when Taylor, and Stuart, and Beecher, and Nettleton, and Tyler, and Porter, and Hewitt, and Harvey were all together, not only in local proximity, but in the warmest unity of belief and feeling. Let the reader turn to the letters of Dr. Hewitt † or Dr. Nettleton,‡ already given, as an illustration of the perfect accord then reigning.

The causes of their subsequent controversy are partly speculative and partly personal; for, good as they were, they were but men, and not wholly exempt from the bias of earthly motives.

"Our doctrine was," said Dr. Beecher, when questioned on this point, "that GOD GOVERNS MIND BY MOTIVE AND NOT BY FORCE.

"Edwards did not come up to that fair and square, Bellamy did not, and, in fact, nobody did until Taylor and I did, and the fact was, Taylor did it indiscreetly. We had got through with the slang of Old Side and New Side. The opposition to Hopkinsianism was all still, asleep, gone by. That was closed up until this thing about Taylor. Goodrich, in one of his lectures to the students, came out in a form that seemed to imply the denial of original sin — nothing sinful in infants. The minute I heard of that I saw the end. I never felt so bad. I wrote a long letter to him and Taylor, telling them they must take that back, or they would have the old fight over under new names.

* Ellis's Half Century, p. 64. † Vol. i., ch. I. ‡ Vol. i., ch. lxxi.

"Harvey attacked them, but they knocked him over easily.* He afterward assailed me in a book, and finally turned against Tyler. He was a shark in the net. They had to throw him off.

"Then there was Hewitt. He was at first friendly to Taylor, and intimate with him. For some reasons of a private nature, however, he was alienated, and predisposed to come into antagonism with Taylor's opinions. What Goodrich said about original sin gave him a handle, and he began to canvass against New Haven.

"I remember one day in Litchfield he called on me and told me where he had been, calling on this man and on that — some thirty or forty. I got up and looked him right in the face —

" 'Hewitt,' said I, 'do you know what you are about? Have you said any thing to Taylor about what you are doing?'

" 'No,' he said, 'I have not.'

" 'And why do you not? How dare you attempt to divide the churches in this peaceful state without an effort to obtain satisfaction?'

" 'Oh, it would be of no use. Dr. Taylor would not condescend to take notice of me. I am not big enough. But we will let him know that what we may lack in talents we will make up in numbers.'

"I had no sympathy with such feelings, and rebuked him severely, though without forfeiting his friendship. I never could approve of this mode of assailing character, and undermining confidence, and spreading alarms, and organizing honest men into a party, but always reproved it earnestly.

"But Hewitt went on, and was the chief agent in inflaming the opposition. Then, when Nettleton wanted us to break fellowship with the New-Measure men, and we would not, he became dissatisfied, and availed himself of what Hewitt had begun, and they began to work on Porter of Andover, and Tyler of Portland, and others. Nettleton never did much good after he got crazy on that subject.

"As for me, Old and New School folks had never quarreled with me. All had gone smooth. The revivals in which I was engaged were so powerful that nobody dared, nobody wanted to oppose. I struck hard against Emmons † on one hand, and Dr.

* "Mr. Harvey at first maintained," says Crocker, "that there is a sin which does not consist in the transgression of known law, but in the *nature* which the race derives from Adam." After being reviewed by the Christian Spectator, he "virtually yielded the point, and entered upon the new inquiry whether men are sinners from their birth."

† The Exercise Scheme.

Burton *[1] on the other. I stood between. But when my church blazed out so, they all praised God and cooperated. The fact is, when I preached free agency, and the Holy Spirit set it home and produced conviction, every body rejoiced, and there was no trouble until I would not denounce Taylor.

"There was some little jealousy just then between Andover and New Haven because Taylor was drawing away students, and this made Porter, without his being aware of it, more susceptible to their influence. After a while he sent me a letter † expressing alarm at a change in my doctrinal views and preaching, for which there was no foundation."

DR. PORTER'S LETTER.

"You are already aware," he said, "that I have felt some serious apprehensions respecting certain changes in your theological opinions which you profess to have made of late years — that is, as some of your remarks imply, changes gradually made during many years; others, that they are chiefly quite recent.

"I can not and need not spend time in *professions*. You are *my old friend*, and know that I have as much confidence in your integrity as a man and a minister as you could demand. I need not stipulate that you shall not misconstrue my motives. I know you will not, and whatever is amiss in my manner you will excuse. I claim no right to dictate how you shall think or preach, but I claim the right to tell you all my heart on any subject, as a man talks to his friend. It is several years since occasional remarks from Connecticut ministers, and one transient conversation with you, gave me some apprehension as to your views; but nothing serious existed in my mind till I heard and read some speculations of your son, in which I understood you to coincide, and heard the echo of your own sermons in Boston, and had from you in conversation some disclosure of your views, and what I understood as an acknowledgment of general coincidence with the published views of Dr. Taylor.

"If you ask me here to specify what I think wrong in your or Dr. Taylor's views, one of the worst faults I find is the in-

* The Taste Scheme.

† May 22, 1829.

[1] Asa Burton (1752–1836), minister to a large church in Vt., trained divinity students in his development of Edwardean theology, which identified regeneration with a "taste" for divine things.

definite and obscure character of those views. In all the annals of theological discussion, I have seen no match for Dr. Taylor's obscurity. I mean, when a man has good sense as he has, and can preach with perspicuity. And as for you, who certainly can speak and write as clearly as any man on common subjects, I understand that you, as well as Dr. Taylor, are beginning to complain (as system makers have been wont to do) that you are misunderstood.

"So far as I have any distinct conceptions of the new views embraced by you or ascribed to you, the faults I find are chiefly these, viz., that these views are not built on the BIBLE, but on philosophical theories as to man's mind and powers of agency; that your preaching does not draw its proof from the Scriptures, and therefore does not lead men to '*search the Scriptures*,' as much as the plain, serious preaching common in New England pulpits; that you exalt one part of Calvinism, viz., *human agency*, so as virtually to lose sight of its correlate, *human dependence*, and thus make regeneration a result of *means* and instrumentality, so that the sinner is born rather 'of blood, or of the will of man, than of God;' and, finally, that your views would cherish presumptuous reliance on means in ministers and impenitent sinners, so as (in direct contravention of your own meaning) to frustrate revivals of religion.

"It is certainly more consistent with the Bible to represent a well instructed, anxious, inquiring sinner as more likely to be saved than one who is ignorant and careless, or else means would be useless. And though I presume your meaning goes no farther than this, I apprehend your system goes much farther in effect, as you are understood; for you are understood to propose that you will take a sinner, careless though he be, and in a certain process of means, attended on with an unholy heart, you will, in a moderate period, return him a converted man. In other words, you are supposed to be thus unwittingly reviving the Arminian notion of gradual regeneration by light, or what has been sometimes termed reliance on *unregenerate doings*.

"Much of this, you will say, is mistake; this presents another aspect of the case. Whether you suppose your new views to respect the *substance of Calvinism*, or the modes of exhibition, is, perhaps, not very important, while you do make the impression on Calvinists and anti-Calvinists that you are modifying the system in its essential parts, and that, unconsciously to yourself, with an improper confidence that the Gospel, as you preach it, will awaken no objections in ungodly men. Your remarks to me implied that, in the general current of Calvinistic preaching in New England, there is a great and radical fault in making the Gospel offensive by the manner of exhibition. Now there always will be some rash and unskillful preachers, and I have no doubt that our venerable fathers, Mills and Hallock, sometimes strained points; but, as a general thing, it never was so, and never will be in our pulpits, that an indiscreet fidelity is the leading defect of preachers. A thousand causes will prevent it.

"I lament that you are making the impression to which I have alluded for several reasons:

"1. The real Gospel, however skillfully preached, if preached clearly, will be opposed. Experience has decided this. If you say this has resulted from the wrong mode of preaching, I add, God has decided in his Word that 'the carnal mind is enmity against himself.' Christ preached wisely, no doubt, yet to his hearers he said (not, you would have loved me and my Father if you had seen our character truly, but) 'you have *seen* and *hated* both me and my Father.' You alarmed me, Brother Beecher, when you explained, as Unitarians do, the opposition of Christ's hearers into their national prejudices as Jews, implying that Christ's preaching would not be opposed now. If this is so, then Paul made a great mistake when he classed Jews and Gentiles together as enemies to God.

"2. I regret the impression you have been making, because the grand danger of the ministry always has been a tendency to modify the Gospel to appease opposition. There is a large number of orthodox ministers in New England, who, from family alliances, from constitutional delicacy of temper, etc., etc., as I hinted above, will temporize and make smooth work, from an honest conviction that a full disclosure of the truth would alienate their hearers. The bitter revilings of base men have been gradually and insensibly leading Calvinistic ministers to hide their colors and recede from their ground. Dr. Spring's Church at Newburyport, Park Street, especially in Dr. Griffin's day, and a few others, have stood like the Macedonian phalanx. But others have gone backward. *Caution*, CAUTION has been the watchword of ministers. When they do preach the old standard doctrines, it is in so guarded a phraseology that they are not understood to be the same.

"You know as well as I, but, if I am not mistaken, thirty years ago, ten sermons were preached in New England on *total depravity* and *election* to one that is preached on those subjects now. I know well that fear and interest are not your motives as a preacher; but

I suppose you have honestly adopted a philosophical theory, which will lead you (and that with a view to man's salvation) to lean toward a modification of the truth by undue efforts of policy— (I can not get a better word) — to render it palatable to men. But to bring men's hearts to the Gospel is quite another thing from bringing the Gospel to their hearts.

"3. I lament the impression above stated, because, if it is a fact that your mode of preaching has led anti-Calvinists, whether Arminian or Unitarian, to say that you are not a Calvinist, it becomes you as a man of sense and piety to explain the fact to yourself. And the case becomes still more imperative if your most substantial and intelligent brethren are apprehensive too. These brethren, if I understand the case, are among the most discriminating and excellent ministers in the land. When I told you how one of them felt on hearing you preach at Haverhill, you said that probably three fourths of your brethren would have the same feelings in the same circumstances. Really, brother, you surprised me by that declaration, accompanied by another, that these good brethren must be brought to light by gradual, not by violent transition.

"But why should these good brethren be alarmed, should they hear your system preached out? Because they would misunderstand it? Then take care that its basis is not darkness. If you can not make clear heads combined with honest hearts comprehend your meaning, what sort of system must this be to enlighten and save the world! Why, then, would these brethren be alarmed? Because they understand your system and solemnly dissent from it? Take care, then, that its basis is not error.

"Three fourths of your brethren may dissent from you, and yet they be wrong and you right. But that dissent imposes a solemn claim on you to lay your foundation with care. Who are these brethren? Men whom God has blessed above all others since the apostles' days as his own chosen ministers. Men of capacity, and some of them not inferior to yourself in theological knowledge and power of discrimination. In New England there are three hundred ministers, who are men of thought, and some of them of extensive reading. I should not dare to say or think of such men that they would, on any important points of difference between them and me, renounce their own opinions and embrace mine, when mine should be disclosed to them.

"Brace up now, Brother Beecher, and bear a while with my plainness like a man as you are. Once in a century or two the Church needs a GREAT REFORMER to arise. Some of your remarks have seemed to mean (what Brother Beecher ten or twenty years ago would not have dreamed of) that you were born for that end, and that the theology of New England is the theatre for operation. I do not tax you with ambition or vanity. I have thought you uncommonly free from both, considering the high estimation you have honorably attained. Of the powers of your tongue and pen for popular impression no one has a higher estimation than I, and you must long have been conscious of these powers yourself. I have gloried and do glory in your usefulness as a champion of the Sabbath and other great and good objects.

"But then I do not think you a metaphysician born to tear up the foundations laid by Edwards. You are a rhetorician and a popular reasoner. Your forte is impression by vivid argumentation, and appeal from common sense and boundless stores of illustration. I praise God that he has given these talents to a man whom I so much love and respect. But I would much sooner trust Dr. Hyde,[2] for example, to search out the flaws in a system of metaphysics than Brother Beecher.

"4. I lament the above impressions, because conflicting speculations among the orthodox are peculiarly unseasonable at the present time. Arminianism received from the hand of Edwards its mortal blow, of which it lingered more than half a century in New England and died. You and I can remember its last moments in Connecticut till the race of wig men for the corporation of Yale was run out. Hopkins, with some hyper notions, helped to settle the work begun by Edwards on a firm footing, so that, except Cambridge folks, not an Arminian candidate has been to be found, or has been wanted in New England for many a year. Our orthodoxy has settled into a solid, tranquil, scriptural state, and perhaps no body of ministers since the world began have been so united, and so manifestly blessed of God, as the ministers of New England for the last thirty-five years.

"Massachusetts, indeed, has been an exception for a part of that time. Twenty-four years ago Dr. Azel Backus and I visited Boston, and found Old Calvinists (Arminians), Calvinists, and Hopkinsians all pulling different ways, while Connecticut was quiet as a clock. This state (Massachusetts) was then the region of *original geniuses*, every man having his '*psalm*' and his '*doctrine*,' every man putting forth his '*Bible news*,' or his book in some form, to show that he was an independent thinker. As the battle

[2] Alvan Hyde (1768–1833), an Edwardean who criticized Hopkins, was pastor in Lee, Mass.

has waxed warm with the Unitarians, all these parties have ranged under two banners, and for several years I have rejoiced to see Trinitarians and Calvinists in Massachusetts merging their common differences, and uniting in one phalanx against a common enemy.

"Judge, then, what must be my anxiety, when, just at this conjuncture of solemn interest to the Church, a battery is opened in Connecticut, and a standard raised, and a campaign begun that threatens to divide our forces; and judge what must be my regret when my most intimate associate (but one) in the Connecticut fraternity, called to Boston as a captain of the Lord's host against the enemies of our faith, gives me to understand that he feels bound to preach such a modification of his former sentiments as will seriously alarm his best brethren.

"It were vain to hope that all this alarm will subside in a few months, and that Unitarians will never learn the secret that we are divided. It were vain to hope that any change touching the vital points of New England orthodoxy can be accomplished silently, or can be accomplished *at all*, without public discussion. The thing has gone thus to its '*ne plus*' from a dread of division; but push it farther, and a battle royal is inevitable. Our hills will ring with the noise of conflict, our brethren of the South and West will turn away with sighing from this land of the Pilgrims as the region of theological speculation. The Spirit of God will foresake our churches, and Unitarians — ay, UNITARIANS! — what will they say?

"Dear brother, if necessity is not upon you, if you are not impelled by a constraining, overwhelming sense of duty to open this campaign, I beg you to pause, and think, and pray, and search the Bible still a few months longer before this Rubicon is passed. To these crude and hasty thoughts (which I should not dare to hazard in this rough manner except to you) I have but one more to add. If necessity is upon you, and you must go on without regard to the opinions of your brethren, in good conscience you can not use the *plural pronoun* in debate with Unitarians. You should speak for yourself only.

"You must be aware that on the subject of infant damnation, for example, your Calvinistic brethren would not have chosen you as an organ to express their views in many respects as you have done. Now, my dear brother, I must stop, as I have not another moment to spare. If all my apprehensions are *needless*, I hope they are also *harmless*, except as they may give pain to your heart, which I would gladly avoid. Your age and standing render you inaccessible to such remarks as I have made from brethren younger than yourself. From me, your old friend, you will take nothing amiss, and whatever is wrong in this letter you will forgive."

DR. BEECHER'S REPLY.

"Boston, June, 1829.

"DEAR BROTHER, — Yours of the 22d was received with feelings such as you anticipated, and with no regret, only that, instead of holding in to the *ne plus*, you had not used the same plainness earlier. The state of apprehension to which your mind has come, and the just cause for it, provided your apprehensions are well founded, is to me the occasion of as much surprise as it is of regret; for had I gone to sleep in Boston and waked up in Calcutta, I should not have found myself surrounded by more strange and unexpected associations than I was in being called upon by you, in such a tone, for explanations on such topics, to remove from your mind such apprehensions as you express.

"It is, however, due to friendship and to the cause of Christ, which is to some extent associated with our well or ill doing, that I should attend to your suggestions with great seriousness and candor. Be assured, also, that I not only admit your right to interrogate and admonish me, but appreciate your motive in doing so, and regard what you have said and done as high evidence of the reality and magnanimity of your friendship, while it affords to me no unflattering evidence of your confidence in mine.

"Instead, also, of being vexed at the fears of my anonymous brethren, I regard them as is just, with satisfaction, as an evidence of that zeal for the truth, for the want of which, in past generations, it has been in this region so vilely betrayed and bartered away. You can not, however, be insensible that close upon the confines of honest zeal lie the territories of twilight, and suspicion, and fear, and imagination, and amplification, and whisperings, and rumors, where, through our own imperfections, the enemy employs the influential friends of Christ to wound one another, and to propagate distrust, and alienation, and acrimony, almost as injurious to the cause of Christ as heresy itself.

"The strength of the Church depends upon our concentrated action, and this (like credit in the mercantile world) depends on confidence; whatever, therefore, propagates suspicion and distrust among brethren who have long acted together, paralyzes their power, as the failure of great capitalists undermines public confidence and propagates alarm in cities. Of this the great enemy of the Church is perfectly aware, and has never failed, when the concentration of forces against him had become too formidable for direct resistance, to ease himself of his adversaries by dividing them.

"Thus the sacramental controversy alienated the Reformers. The divisions of Presbyterians and Independents lost the vantage ground, and brought back the Stuarts, and High-Churchmanship, and dissoluteness, and infidelity in England, and the divisions occasioned in New England by getting in and getting out of 'the half-way covenant' paralyzed for seventy years the power of the Church, and exiled almost the special influences of the Holy Spirit.

"It would seem at present as if the Church had acquired in this country a moral influence no longer to be resisted by the Prince of Darkness but by dividing the leaders in the sacramental host, and that the ministers in New England who have seen eye to eye in all the essentials, and have moved shoulder to shoulder in the battle, are now selected as the objects of his malicious experiment. But in vain, I trust, is the net spread; it is, however, well set, and has nearly inclosed us, and will not probably be escaped without a due sense of danger, self-possession, prayer, and the wisdom which is both pure and peaceable.

"The Reformed churches made vigorous efforts to heal their divisions, and, as they say, but for a few restless and rash spirits the work of peace would have been accomplished. A little rashness now, or petulance of pride, or obstinacy of self-will, may do us corresponding injury. God grant we may be kept, and not throw away the victories of the past and the prosperity of coming generations by any indiscreet precipitation. The chief occasion of needless divisions in the Church of God has been the undue stress which good men have laid upon the *circumstantials* of religion, who were agreed in the fundamentals. I mean by circumstantials either the discipline and ceremonies, or the philosophy of religion. The first divided the Church of England, the second threatens to divide us.

"By the philosophy of religion I mean the different theories by which men illustrate and defend those doctrines in which they are agreed. This, you know, always has been, and, till men have more grace and knowledge, probably always will be, the *debatable ground*, the religion of hobby-horses, no two of which can be hitched together. On this ground the only condition of peace would seem to be, to let every man ride his own hobby without molestation or alarm, leaving it to experience and public sentiment to adjust the relative merits of the favorite animals. Unless we renounce wholly the teachings of experience, and give ourselves up to absolute infatuation, we shall avoid the substitution of our different *explanatory theories* of the doctrines for the doctrines themselves, and shall not fear nor suspect heresy, nor propagate alarm concerning any speculations, the authors of which hold fully and correctly all the fundamental doctrines.

"It is the opinion of Wilson, the evangelical Episcopalian, who has recently written an invaluable essay, introductory to 'Baxter's Reformed Pastor,' that uniformity in opinion, even in a single nation, is hopeless, considering the infirmity of man; but unity of heart on all essential points, with liberality and charity as to non-essentials, produces all the good consequences of such uniformity, besides many others peculiar to itself.

"The *argumentum ad invidiam* and the *argumentum ad terrorem* will do no good, but evil only; and the attempts to repress free inquiry and original investigation within the limits and cordial belief of the fundamental doctrines by combinations and practical resistance would produce something more than a conflict, which would make the hills and valleys of New England ring; it would be a volcano to rend the very bowels of the Church; for there always have been in the Church, and always will be, and always ought to be, men who will not be deterred by such influence. Uniformity in our theoretical expositions of the fundamental doctrines can be attempted successfully only by conversation and discussion in its kindest and most conciliating forms; for the more entire our agreement in fundamentals, the greater will be the sense of injury in being treated as if we were heretics.

"All these remarks, however, are irrelevant, provided your apprehensions concerning my designs, views, and preaching are well founded. If it be true that I have become a 'system maker;' that my views 'are not built on the Bible, but on certain philosophical theories as to man's mind, and powers, and agency;' that my 'preaching does not draw its proofs from the Bible,' and 'does not lead men to search the Scriptures;' 'exalts human agency so much as virtually to lose sight of human dependence; makes regeneration the result of means, to the exclusion of the Spirit's special influence; cherishes presumptuous reliance in ministers and in sinners so as to frustrate revivals;' that I propose to 'take a sinner through a course of means, and return him a saint without the Holy Spirit;' that I am 'reviving the Arminian notion of gradual regeneration; modifying the Calvinistic system in its essential parts; hold that the Gospel can be so preached as to render it palatable to the carnal heart;' that I regard myself as a 'reformer, raised up to modify the New England theology on points which concern its vital interests;' and that in the propagation of these views I am about to 'open a campaign and pass the Rubicon,' draw the sword and throw away the scabbard — if I am doing all this, there is foundation for your fears.

"But never, as in reading your letter, have the emotions of surprise, mirthfulness, and grief held such strange conflict in my mind. To refrain from laughing was impossible, and to refrain from tears equally so; nor has it been without constant vigilance that I have kept those feelings from rising which a sense of unmerited loss of confidence and distrust is calculated to wake up in our sinful hearts, but which I never have indulged, and trust I never shall indulge toward you; for, as you wrote evidently in haste, and as evidently under excitement of solicitude, I can not suppose you saw all your implications at one view as I have placed them.

"If you had employed your importunity to dissuade me from going on a crusade to recover Jerusalem from the Turks, I should not have been more astounded by its irrelevancy to any thought of my mind or feeling of my heart. Assuredly I have no campaign to open nor Rubicon to pass; and unless my friends thrust me forward, and come after me in battle, there will be no battle; for with me it is a fundamental maxim not to expend my strength in contending with the friends of Christ, when so much effort is needed to turn back his enemies. Should I find myself in the Hellespont, vexed with storms, doubtless, as I am able and as I am aided, I shall breast the waves with heart of oak and arms of controversy; for if I was not born to be a reformer (of which I never dreamed), it has always been my opinion that I was not born to be a coward.

"Before I attempt a particular explanation of your specifications, you must allow me to say that your apparent confidence in their truth seems to me disproportioned to your evidence; for certainly your letter contains specifications which go to the shipwreck of orthodoxy, and it states, also, the evidence, and brings in the verdict, and applies the admonition, and threatens the execution, in no equivocal terms, if I persist in my present course.

"Now, that these specifications are unfounded, I know, and that there is no evidence to sustain them which can justify their credence to the extent implied in your letter is my full belief. I can not, therefore, resist the conclusion that you have done me great injustice, and that, if the confidence of conspicuous men in the Church in each other is so easily to be given up, the adversary will make an easy defense, and Zion will, for a long time to come, sit in sackcloth.

"It is this panic which I witness, this suspicion among former friends, that alarms me more than all besides; for to all purposes of cordial co-operation, the suspicion of heresy is as fatal as open denunciation. I have said there is no foundation for your apprehensions on any of the points named. The elementary principles of my theology on all the topics concerning which any difference can be supposed between me and yourself have for a long time been published in my sermons on the Government of God, The Bible a Code of Laws, and The Faith once delivered to the Saints, my two sermons on Depravity, in the National Preacher, and the Gospel according to Paul. They have not, to my knowledge, been misunderstood or created alarm, and in their amplification and application in the pulpit and in the vestry I utter no sentiments at variance with them.

"To me, therefore, it appears both unjust and of dangerous tendency that you should permit parole testimony, 'the echo' of my sermons, to set aside my deliberate, guarded, published statements. The conversation I held with you was desultory and short, because, from indisposition, I could not enter the field of explanation. I therefore made a few detached remarks, some of which you misunderstood, and others, designed to qualify them, have forgotten. I perceived that farther explanation would be necessary, but, not fully apprised of the strength of your feelings, resolved to defer it to another opportunity. Had I understood your state of apprehension to be as it since appears, I should have said nothing, or said more, for I know not but that this is the first time I have ever had occasion to complain of being misunderstood.

"The direct remarks I have to make on the several topics contained in your letter must be laconic, and, to save time, I shall simply give a word or two as the index to the subject.

" '*System Makers.*' It has always been a predominant object of my heart to escape the sin and folly of such a charge in its invidious sense, and to apply rather to practicable purposes the great truths of the Bible; to make the weapons of our warfare bright by use, instead of spending my time in pointing and polishing them to be hung up in the armory of God for admiration; and I do not believe that I have been, or am likely to be, a system maker in any dangerous or undesirable sense of that term.

"'*Views built not on the Bible, but on philosophical views of man's free agency, etc.*' On this subject there are extremes on both sides, and not a little loose and inconsiderate speech. It is easy, for example, to idolize philosophy and set it above the Bible, and it is as easy, and almost as common, to slam it down by wholesale, as if it were mere moonshine. But philosophy is the nature which God has given to things, to mind, and to matter, with the laws of their operation; and so far as the attributes of things lie within the cognizance of our faculties, they constitute the basis of all knowledge and of all experience. The Bible itself assumes this philosophy and our knowledge of it, and can not be explained without it, nor lawfully explained against it. 'Tis only when philosophical theories are formed independently of facts, or when they respect subjects which lie beyond the ken of our faculties, that philosophy becomes contemptible and dangerous.

"Do you say, Why not let philosophy alone, and preach the plain doctrines of the Bible? My answer is, it can not be let alone, nor can the plain doctrines be preached without it; they never have been, and never will be. Can we teach the nature of God as a Spirit without philosophy? or of man as a free agent without any conception of the nature of law, and free agency and accountability? And if there be many things on these subjects which are hid, are there none which lie open and naked within the sphere of our knowledge? It is because we can and do understand the nature of things that the Bible does not teach them directly, but assumes them as known.

"Do we not understand, both from philosophy and the Bible, the difference between natural and moral government — natural and moral inability — and what is requisite to constitute accountability, and what may excuse from obligation and blame? And shall our ignorance on subjects that we do not understand set aside our knowledge on subjects that are comprehensible? Or shall the folly of theorizing *in terra incognita* beget the affectation of humble ignorance concerning those things which we were made to understand, and are bound to, and able to, and do understand?

"It was by discussion, deeply imbued with intellectual philosophy, that Edwards, and Bellamy, and Hopkins, and others, brought many truths out of relative obscurity, and gave us the quiet in New England of which you speak; a peace, however, neither then nor since based on exactly coincident philosophical expositions, but upon the catholicism which, within the fundamentals, would agree to differ. What now has come to pass, that the advocates of the exercise and taste schemes, so long tranquil and brotherly, must buckle on the harness and lift the bristling spear? a war in which the vanquished and the victors must stop where they begun, and sit down and weep together over the needless desolation they have made. If I understand my own mode of philosophizing, it is the Baconian. Facts and the Bible are the extent of my philosophy.

" '*That my preaching does not draw its proofs from the Bible.*' I appeal to my Portland sermon, my two on Depravity, and to every one of my manuscript sermons on doctrinal subjects. No charge could be more unfounded. The uniform shape of all my sermons is to show what God says, and that it is true in fact; corresponds with the nature and character of men, with the principles of moral government and the moral condition of the world, and with the actual experience of saint and sinner; sometimes by showing the facts in the case first, and that the Bible confirms the statement, and sometimes what the Bible says, and that facts confirm it. This is the heart and back-bone of my preaching.

" '*Exalts human agency so as virtually to lose sight of human dependence.*' You can not exalt human agency higher than free agency, and ability commensurable with divine requirements, as stated by Edwards and the New England divines, nor can you introduce a dependence consistent with accountability more absolute than that which results from the certainty of voluntary unbelief, without the special influence of the Holy Ghost. Both these I inculcate intelligibly, and often, and if not equally, it is because the circumstances in which I have been placed did not demand it. The preaching of dependence by hyper-Calvinists had been so disproportioned as required the reiterated inculcation of free agency and ability to obviate prejudice, gain a hearing, and give the relative proportions of truth to minds accustomed to disproportionate and distorted views.

" '*Makes regeneration the result of means to the exclusion of the special influence of the Holy Spirit.*' As unfounded as possible. I never thought so, said so, nor has ever a paragraph or sentence come from me, from which, by any fair construction, such an inference could be drawn; nor could such an apprehension be entertained by any one who heard attentively, for any length of time, my prayers, exhortations, and sermons.

"All of these not only imply no such thing, but exclude the possibility of any such supposition. If there be one point which my own experience, observation, and study of the Bible have taught me, it is the absolute dependence of saint, sinner, and minister upon the special influence of the Holy Spirit. The sermon which contains an epitome of my views on this subject is written out, and, so far as I know, has been approved. Since the reception of your letter, it has been read to Brother Nettleton and received his approbation. It does not encourage in ministers a presumptuous reliance on means, nor has it been the effect of my preaching to create any such reliance on means in sinners who have come under my inspection and care.

" '*Does not lead men to search the Scriptures.*' How can this be, if my preaching occasions a presumptuous reliance on means? But with some, the very head and front of my offending is that I do inculcate reading the Bible too much. It is four years since I have, in dealing with awakened sinners, recommended scarce a single book except the Bible, and all the while my confidence in its sufficiency and efficacy has been steadily increasing, as has also the urgency with which I enforce the reading and study of it. My Church have gone over the Confession of Faith twice, reading and expounding a chapter in the Bible which contains the subject of consideration in the Confession; and I have also a Bible-class, taught by influential members of my Church, besides Bible-classes in the Sabbath-school. On the whole, I think it must be admitted that my Church and congregation make considerable use of the Bible.

" '*Propose to take a sinner through a course of means and return him a saint.*' If by this it is meant that I propose to make him a saint, I deny ever having made such a proposal; if it means that I undertook to guarantee the conversion of every one who will follow my directions, I say I have never offered any such guarantee; if it mean that many who have followed my directions have in a short time afforded credible evidence of piety, this is what is common in a successful ministry; if it mean that in some respects I succeed better with particular classes of persons, and that I am more encouraged to attempt the conversion of sinners from the success which it has pleased God should attend my instructions, this is true; and if it mean that the more seriously and implicitly persons follow my advice, the stronger is my expectation of a favorable result, this also is true.

" '*Receiving gradual regeneration.*' By moral suasion I suppose is intended. I am doing no such thing, and no one would say this who ever heard me preach with his ears instead of his elbows. All my discourses are marked and explicit on the subject of instantaneous regeneration; and I have never preached or stated the subject so carelessly as to justify mistake, having been aware of the liability of being misunderstood, and spoken always with caution.

"And as the prevalent errors around us on the subject of regeneration admit the necessity of a change, only insisting that it is gradual, the doctrine of instantaneous regeneration has been, ever since my residence here, the Thermopylæ of the battle, and I have dwelt more on this than on any other topic in theology. As to moral suasion, I hold to none, and never have held to any of which revealed truth is not the means, and the special influence of the Holy Spirit the efficient cause. On this subject, also, I have always spoken with guarded precision, knowing the liability to misconception amid sagacious opponents.

"'*Modify the Calvinistic system in its essential parts and in its vital interests.*' If I am possessed of the powers you ascribe to me, it must be admitted that I understand what are the essential parts and vital interests of Calvinism, and of course have a better opportunity to judge of my own opinions and preaching than those who hear me transiently; and I deny that I am modifying or changing the essential doctrines, or affecting the vital interest of Calvinism. In respect to 'new views,' they had reference to my mode of stating, proving, and answering objections to those very doctrines. I appreciate, however, my folly in using such a term without more definite explanation of what I meant by it. But I never thought or said I had discovered any new fundamental doctrines, or given up any old ones, or so modified the Calvinistic doctrines as to affect the system vitally.

"I had in my mind, at the time, those fathers in the Church to whose mode of preaching on decrees and election you alluded as in some respects exceptionable, and to the very things which you admit to be defects. But on this subject I can not now express my meaning better than in a note to my review of the Christian Examiner, in which I reply to a similar accusation brought against modern Calvinists.*

* "The reviewer had pronounced the statement of doctrines in my sermon entitled 'The Faith once delivered to the Saints' decidedly anti-Calvinistic. Dr. Channing had said, 'It is a plain matter of fact that the hard features of that religious system which has been "received by tradition from our fathers" are greatly softened, and that a necessity is felt by those who hold it of accommodating their representations of it more and more to the improved philosophy of the human mind, and to the undeniable principles of natural and revealed religion. Unconditional election is seldom heard of among us. The imputation of Adam's sin to his posterity is hastening to join the exploded doctrine of transubstantiation. The more revolting representations of man's state by nature are

"My remark that three fourths of my brethren might be alarmed, etc., was, in the first place, a conversational hyperbole; and, in the next place, I merely meant that many, on hearing my expositions, would feel that my strokes fell upon their philosophy, which, having identified with their doctrines, they would be alarmed. But I did not say or think that three fourths of my brethren, or any portion of them, on understanding my views, would be alarmed at them as affecting the vital interests of Calvinism.

"And as to '*bringing my brethren right by gradual and not by violent transition*,' really, my good brother, your 'imagination runs riot;' all I meant was, that the discrepancies of our philosophy were not of such consequence as to justify the agitation of our churches by a public and perhaps an alienating controversy, and still less were it worthy of good men, at such a day, to obtrude their own peculiarities, and run a race of hobby-horses; but that whatever changes were needed, or assimilation of views, should, without

---

judiciously kept out of sight, and, what is of still greater importance, preaching is incomparably more practical than formerly.'

"In reply to this statement of Dr. C—— I say: 'If the meaning of Mr. Channing be that the doctrines which, as mere abstract positions, wear a repelling aspect, as now explained seem to be the regular parts of a great system of moral government, in the administration of which justice and mercy are reconciled, and that mental philosophy has lent her aid in this exposition; that the doctrine of election is now so stated as admits of accountability and punishment, and stops the mouths of gainsayers; that the imputation of Adam's sin and Christ's righteousness are so stated as to appear both practicable and rational; and that the doctrine of total depravity is now explained in a manner which shows both the falsehood and absurdity of the statements and objections made concerning it by its opponents, or that, as the doctrines of the Bible are better understood, they produce an increase of practical preaching — it might all be admitted as a concise account of what we believe to be true.

"'But if Dr. C—— intends to insinuate or to say any one doctrine of the Reformation has been given up, or the principle abandoned on which it has always rested, we request him to review this position, and to fortify it by evidence, or abandon it. Not one of the first principles of the doctrinal reformers has been abandoned, while every one of them has been corroborated by a more accurate knowledge of mental philosophy and of scriptural interpretation. The entire system never stood so impregnable as now, and never appeared so intelligible, so reasonable, so amiable, and, at the same time, so terrible to guilty consciences as now.

"'And if Dr. C—— supposes that the doctrine of man's depravity, or the doctrine of election, is not preached as often as they were, and that Calvinists are holding their peace on these points, he follows his own imagination instead of historical verity. All the great doctrines of the Reformation are preached more frequently, and more plainly and powerfully, by the orthodox in New England, than they were fifty or even thirty years ago, and their faithful exhibition is attended by the power of God in those increasing revivals of religion which are carrying salvation through our land.'"

sounding a trumpet before us, be left to work their way gradually, as the result of time, experience, and free inquiry, and the calm interchange of opinions among ministerial brethren.

"But, after all, I can not admit the existence of '*new views*,' or even explain my meaning without implying more in impression than is true in fact. The physician may by experience improve in the application of the general principles of his art, without changing them, or affecting seriously their vital interests, and the observing husbandman may through life be acquiring valuable information, and making improvement in his application of the general laws of nature; but should they say to a friend they had made some improvement in medicine or husbandry, would they be denounced as innovators or ridiculed as reformers, even though they should think it best to make no noise about the matter, but let their works speak for themselves? On this subject, brother, allow me to say that your irony is as unmerited as it is severe; and I find no occasion to 'brace up,' inasmuch as it has no sort of application to me.

"'*Gospel can be so preached as to make it palatable to the carnal heart.*' An entire mistake. I said the doctrines of the Bible are reasonable in fact, and can be so explained and vindicated as to be made to commend themselves to every man's understanding and conscience, and stop every mouth; but I did not say, nor have I ever said or thought, that the doctrines can be made palatable to the carnal heart. To see intellectually, and approve the right way, and pursue the worse, is a common phenomenon of sinful mind. Still, though the heart is carnal, it is possible to exasperate it with irritating and unreasonable expositions of the doctrines. And it is possible, by correct and judicious exhibitions in subject and manner, to allay the irritation which arises from misapprehension, and to bring the heart under such restraint by the convictions of the understanding, that its more *sensible* and outrageous enmity will not be apt to rise, while yet it is not reconciled, nor is the truth palatable.

"You do not surely mean to deny the influence of temptation from circumstances to create prejudice, and obstinacy, and opposition to the truth. This was the extent of my remark concerning the Jews. If their ignorance, and prejudice, and worldly sacrifices in giving up the Mosaic economy had no special influence on the rulers of the nation, over and above the natural opposition of the heart to the truth, how came it to pass that priests and rulers should be so virulent and obstinate, while the common people, influenced by no such temptation, heard our Savior gladly? And why is it that the Gospel does not in fact meet with the same opposition in orthodox congregations now that it met with from the Jews? The absence of powerful temptation does not reconcile, but the presence of it greatly invigorates and inflames its enmity.

"'*Tends to frustrate revivals.*' I can not but think that these tendencies of my views to frustrate revivals are of the same kind with those tendencies of the Unitarian system to produce effects that it never does produce, while it is attended with other effects in direct opposition to these. On this subject you must forgive me this boasting, for I speak as a fool; but the fact is even so, that for four years it has pleased God I should be constantly employed in revivals of religion, in which I can not but hope that upward of four hundred souls have been inclined and enabled to embrace Jesus Christ as he is offered to them in the Gospel; a number more than double the results of my ministry, during the same time, in any other period of my life.

"I only inquire how it would seem to you had you for the last four years been blessed to turn out an uncommon number of good speakers, to receive from me a solemn warning concerning your principles of elocution as tending to make bad speakers!

"In saying that I agreed with Dr. Taylor, I had reference to his views of *actual sin* as in all cases voluntary, and not the result of a natural necessity. Is this a novelty? is it a heresy? or a doctrine which is to tear up old foundations? Until recently, in saying this, I supposed I agreed with you and Dr. Woods, and the great body of New England divines, who hold to the doctrine of natural ability and moral inability.

"Am I to understand from your alarm that you think there are two sorts of actual sin, one voluntary, the other involuntary? and two sorts of qualifications for personal accountability, one including knowledge of law and natural ability, and the other utterly excluding it, so that one class of subjects may be sent to hell justly, in circumstances which would exonerate another class entirely from all blame? I am not an alarmist, but is it true, brother, that in the most important theological seminary in our land, the philosophy of free agency and the nature of sin are so explained as by implication to deny the distinction between natural and moral inability, and render it naturally impossible for a sinner to make to himself a new heart? And are we, who hold to different views of the nature of sin and free agency, already called upon for explanation on peril of being suspected of heresy?

"In uniting my friends at Andover in an argument with myself in discussing the subject of infant character and condition, I have certainly sinned ignorantly and in unbelief; but, as at present advised, your request will be sacredly regarded, and in time to come I shall speak for myself only, and such as may agree with me.

"You perceive, then, that I do say, as you anticipated I might, not only that much of your apprehension is groundless, but that all of it is the result of misapprehension and mistake. I admit, however, that if my preaching produces misapprehension in the minds of others, without any thing to account for it on their part, I ought to regard it as the result of some defect in my mode of exhibition. I am surprised, however, that you should think that the charge of Arminianism by hyper-Calvinists, or anti-Calvinists, should need an explanation.

"The latter have for a long time charged me with Arminianism because I preached free agency, which they insisted Calvinism denied, and so explained the doctrine of free agency and dependence as stopped their mouths and superseded their power of misrepresentation and proselytism; and this has been my sin against some of this class in this city. Others have claimed me for the same reason that they have claimed Brother Stuart, because it is hard to kick against the pricks, and much easier to claim an opponent than to answer him. Others have claimed me, also, because they have so long caricatured Calvinism, that when they hear it truly stated they have no way to shield themselves against the reaction of an abused public confidence but to cry out, Oh, that is not Calvinism, it is good Arminianism! This is the game which has been playing in this city, and I know of nothing but the interposition of such fears as you express that can avert the day of retribution, followed by a glorious reaction of public sentiment in favor of unperverted evangelical doctrine.

"But you will say, Why should Calvinists be alarmed? Hyper-Calvinists are alarmed for the same reason that some of them were alarmed in the beginning at Andover divinity as not up to the mark — as mere milk and water — as running down orthodoxy, and verging to Arminianism; and for the same reason that some of them are alarmed now at the alleged apostasy of Dr. Woods on certain points from New Divinity to Old Calvinism.

"Others, some ministers and more church members, who had been sitting for years in the quietude of Arminian inaction, waiting 'God's time' to come and move them, and liking God's time best of all, because it came so slowly and ended so soon, and gave such long and glorious intervals for covetousness and sloth, have been alarmed lest I should put men up to action before God's time, and have been pained at my reproof of their sloth and perversion of the doctrine of divine sovereignty and dependence, as well as by the earnest importunity with which I inculcated the duty and the motives to immediate action.

"They called it Arminianism, and went to sleep in their doctrinal sloth and profound self-complacency. It may be that it is the 'echo' of some such sermons which has reached your ears as being of Arminian tendency; for with some men all is Arminian which is not Antinomian. But my brethren who are not hyper-Calvinists, and who are my friends, why should any of them be alarmed? That is the question I wish them to answer, and I am all meekness to receive reproof or admonition, and all alacrity to reform, when my brethren, by whose confidence in me I have, under God, been sustained and carried through certainly the most arduous and difficult, and I hope it may yet prove to be the most useful part of my life, shall point out the well-founded, well-authenticated cause of their solicitude.

"I may here say that those of my brethren who have heard me most, and best understood my mode of expounding and vindicating the doctrines of the Bible, are not alarmed; and until the single exception of Dr. C—— was stated to me, I had no apprehension that any one in whose confidence I had a right to rely had any such fears as your letter indicates, or even any serious apprehensions at all; for the alarm of some of my brethren, those with whom for so long a time I had buckled on the harness, and with whom I took it for granted that my orthodoxy stood justly above suspicion, I can not account, except by the unusual concurrence of circumstances, and the facility with which fear and suspicion, once awakened, are propagated even among good men.

"It is true that in assailing error I have not, in animated argument, measured out my language with the accuracy of metaphysical definition, and it is very probable that metaphysical ears have been startled, and heard heresy in my hyperboles and metaphors; still, the common people have heard me gladly, and have smelt no heresy in my doctrine that I can learn, and my Rev. friend and brother, the Bartlett Professor of Sacred Rhetoric at Andover, will not, I am sure, hang or burn me for any sins of that sort.

"There may be another cause or occasion of misapprehension in those who hear me transiently, in the fact that my preaching, until recently, has been wholly adapted to the exigencies of a revival; consequently, knowing the state of the congregation, I have gone to the Bible for remedies, as the physician would go to the store of the apothecary, to be applied, not in contempt of system, but in the accommodation of elementary scriptural truth to personal exigencies, under the guidance of experience and common sense, rightly dividing the word of truth, and giving to every one his portion in due season.

"But, incidental to such preaching, and heard every Sabbath by from fifty to one hundred strangers, from all parts of New England, of all sorts of philosophy, orthodoxy, belief and unbelief, and unacquainted with my particular object and entire system of doctrine, and unacquainted with what I had preached and explained to prepare the way for what they then heard, or with what I might next preach to guard and balance it, it would hardly fail that some should misunderstand. From this cause, I can not doubt that rumors have gone abroad, occasioned, not by the faults of my preaching, but by its correct adaptation to the condition of my stated hearers.

"The state of the community in which my labors commenced and have been continued affords another occasion of misapprehension and alarm to some. I found it to be the fact that, between hyper-Calvinistic and philosophical necessitarian tendencies, the doctrine of dependence had been reiterated and overstated, till it had produced extensively in the community the results of fatalism with multitudes. If free agency was admitted at all, it was so out of sight or so dimly seen in the background that a large portion of the community had ceased to feel the practical influence of the doctrine of accountability, while many were in theory, and more in feeling, fatalists.

"In this condition the people did not need high-toned Calvinism on the point of dependence; they had been crammed with it, and were dying with excessive aliment, and needed a long and vigorous prescription of free agency to produce an alterative, and render the truth salutary by administering the proper portions in due season. Nor was there for a long time any danger of overaction on the subject of free agency and natural ability. The Antinomianism of perverted Calvinism, and the fatality of philosophical necessity, made it an obvious policy and an imperious duty to indoctrinate the community thoroughly in the true principles of God's moral government, and in the nature, reality, and responsibilities of free agency; it had been any thing rather than wisdom, it had been infatuation, to have swung out with such preaching as you commend. If it would have done good to some, of which I have no doubt it would, I am confident it would have done great evil to very many more. Anti-Calvinists would have been needlessly but certainly confirmed in their prejudices, and would have girded more closely their cloak of error, which now the balanced exhibitions of truth are inclining many to hold loosely, and not a few to cast away.

"I did not doubt, when my labors commenced here, that the time would come when the whole system in its just proportions might be exhibited without repellancy and with increased effect; and before I received your letter, I had felt the propriety of beginning to balance the overactings of free agency by giving more prominence, and frequency, and power to the doctrine of absolute dependence on the Holy Ghost.

"That I have made no mistake in judgment I will not say, but of this I am confident, that no man can be qualified to fill the station to which God has called me, and to meet the responsibilities that have rested on me, without acting for himself upon some general plan which he alone can fully comprehend, and can not stop at every step to vindicate and explain; and if I possess the capacity which you ascribe to me, I think my expectations were not unreasonable that my brethren would repose in me the confidence which is indispensable to success on the part of every man whom God calls to a high station and high duties in this eventful day.

"The equity of this principle you will not deny. The violation of it in respect to some of the faculty of your seminary you, I know, felt keenly; whether I have any cause to complain in this respect, I may be too much interested to decide. But I have too long delayed to mention what I regard as the '*sine qua non.*' All your fears concerning all the preceding were only concurring and amplificatory causes, which had never waked up and run together but for the attraction of this one. I allude to that 'battery,' as you call it, which 'just in this solemn conjunction is opened at New Haven,' and one of the great guns of which you seem to think I have engaged to man at Boston.

"Now against this assumed coalition between me and Brother Taylor I protest; for no man's opinions will I consent to be made answerable, by common fame or suspicion, and only as I specifically adopt and profess them. I love Brother Taylor and New Haven, and I love Brother Woods and Andover; with both I agree, as I suppose, in all the fundamental doctrines, and with both on some points of speculation I differ, as they do from one another.

"You conjure me, unless constrained by an overwhelming sense of duty, to pause, re-examine, read, and pray, before I pass the Rubicon. I have already told you I have no Rubicon to pass; and as to reading, and re-examination, and prayer, it is what I have been about, especially the three past years: it has been my chief employment to revise my sermons, and collect the cream of the last thirty years' labor; and if I have ever preached with truth and discretion, it is since I have been in Boston.

"On reviewing the whole of my course under the urgency of your expostulation, which avails with my heart and head more than that of almost any other man, I perceive but two things which demand my attention; the first is, to go on, as the state of this community admits, in adjusting the symmetrical proportions of the systems of free agency and dependence; the other is, since I am apprised of the need of it, to be as careful to explain and guard against misconception on the subject of dependence on the Holy Spirit as I have been in establishing the doctrine of free agency in opposition to fatalism; but as to my hyperboles and metaphors, alas! I shall despair of ever reducing them to logical precision, but shall probably go on sinning as I have done.

"It is my hope and expectation that the preceding explanations will be satisfactory; a work which for few men in this world, worn down and exhausted as I have been by other cares and labors, would I have attempted, almost, my good brother, for no one but yourself, whom certainly above most this side heaven I love and confide in.

"Should any point remain unexplained about which your fears still cluster, you will have the goodness to tell me in short metre, definitely, wherein you think me in error, and what you take to be the truth in the case. But should the account which I have given of myself and my stewardship be satisfactory, I need not ask you to take the responsibility of extending the satisfaction to all who have seen your letter to me, or whose fears your own fear and conversation may have excited."

Of this correspondence Dr. Beecher, in later years, wrote as follows:

"Dr. Porter's letter, falling in with other concurring circumstances, made it necessary for me to undertake a serious exposition of my views and vindication of my mode of preaching, and has served to call forth and embody in a permanent form thoughts, plans, views of doctrine, and a policy of ministerial action and of ministerial wisdom which otherwise must, by the stream of care, have been soon obliterated from my own recollection, and have remained distinctly only in the book of God.

"It was one of the greatest trials of my life to find the confidence of a tried friend failing me at a time when the clouds were dark, the waves of an angry controversy rolling on, the enemy exulting, and my own health failing under public and domestic troubles. But these and the death of Dr. Chaplin brought me low in health, and occasioned a year of darkness, bodily debility, and mental distress such as I shall not soon forget. The Lord delivered me, but the wormwood and the gall I have still in remembrance.

"This letter was carried by myself to Andover and read to Dr. Porter, in the presence of Dr. Woods, Prof. Stuart, Dr. Justin Edwards, Mr. Cornelius, and several others. Dr. Porter professed himself relieved and satisfied. He said there was one point, though not material, on which his mind was in suspense, and which he should like to look at again. A large portion of the next day was devoted to familiar, friendly conversation on the subject of the letter, in which he expressed the most cordial and entire satisfaction in respect to my soundness.

"I left the letter in his hands for perusal, with the understanding that it would be returned, as soon after it was, with a written note, reiterating, and in stronger terms than in conversation, his satisfaction with the sentiments I had expressed, and the explanations I had given in the letter.

"It was perhaps a year after that he signified his desire to read the letter again; and after a short time he returned it, with another note, increasing in the intensity and cordiality of the terms in which he expressed his unqualified approbation of my views and expositions contained in the letter, and his pleasure and gratitude at what he was pleased to call the very Christian manner in which I had borne and replied to the trying implications of his letter.

"I have only to add that these reiterated declarations of satisfaction and confidence of my brother, Dr. Porter, were never to me reversed, but were, on my consultation with him concerning my duty in accepting the call to Lane Seminary, renewed. I stated expressly that I would not go to the West without the confidence and support of those friends on whom I had been accustomed to rely, and he not only repeated his assurances of confidence as aforetime, but, on the conditions I had stated, advised me to accept the call."

The reader will bear in mind that this correspondence was unknown to the public at the time, a few individuals only being made acquainted with the facts, and that it was not until eight or nine years after that the letters were published, in a manner hereafter to be considered.

XIX

THE GOSPEL ACCORDING TO PAUL

IN April, 1829, Dr. Tyler was installed in Portland, Maine, over the church left vacant by the death of the lamented Payson. Dr. Beecher was invited to preach on the occasion. Many circumstances combined to make the occasion one of unusual interest — his long and intimate friendship with the candidate; the associations connected with Dr. Payson, under whose ministry Mrs. Beecher had been converted; and the present posture of the Unitarian controversy. The subject chosen, as the title of the sermon indicates, was one well suited to develop the peculiar characteristics of the speaker, and meet the demands of the moment. It was an elaborate argument to show that the evangelical system, as rejected by Unitarians, is the very substance of the Gospel. A few extracts from the discourse are here presented:

"I am now to show that the Gospel which Paul preached is the true Gospel. It is a strong presumptive argument of its truth that it is eminently a rational system. In natural philosophy, that is rational which accords with the laws of the material world, and in the divine moral government that is rational which corresponds with the principles of mind and the nature of law; and such, eminently, is the Gospel which Paul preached. It recognizes every where God as a lawgiver, and man as a free agent, perverted and ruined by sin; the law as unable to sustain its own moral power, and forgive and reclaim, while a substitute for the execution of the penalty is announced, originating in the wisdom and emanating from the love of God; offered on terms, and attended by aid, and guarded from perversion by moral checks, which, taken together, bring upon our depraved nature powerful restraints from sin, and concentrate upon the mind an amount of motive in favor of a return to loyalty as great as can be conceived to be possible, and such as must have at least a powerful tendency to do what the apostle declares the law could not do.

"The more the elements of this Gospel according to Paul are scrutinized, the more undeniable will their rationality appear. Is it not rational that God should create intelligent, voluntary, accountable beings? Why should his benevolence be satisfied with multiplying worlds and brute animals? Why not surround himself with moral beings, who can behold his glory, feel his goodness, obey his will, and celebrate his praise? And if it be wise and good to give being to an intelligent universe, why should it be abandoned to anarchy and misrule? How could intelligent beings, free agents, be governed but by the moral influence of law? and who could legislate for the universe but God? and what better rule of obligation than the moral law, adapted to all minds, and all worlds, and all periods of duration — a law which discloses the relations and duties of all rational beings to the Creator and to one another, and binds them in sweet fellowship, and moves them to a delightful, benevolent activity?

"And if this law, as the apostle declares, is holy, just, and good, and the bond of perfectness, is it not rational that its influence over moral beings should be sustained by rewards and punishments according to deeds? In what other way can free agents be governed, and the rational and social enjoyment of the universe sustained? Is it not rational that moral, accountable beings should be able to sin? Is it possible by force to prevent transgression and not destroy accountability? Does not the ability to obey include, necessarily, the ability to transgress? Is it possible to form free agents, and set up a moral government, without bestowing on creatures the terrific capacity of transgression and desert of punishment? And have not facts evinced, though Paul had not taught it, that all men have sinned, and come under the high penalty of the violated law?

"But, in such a case, is not the doctrine of the apostle rational, that by the deeds of the law no flesh can be justified? Would not the abolition of the rewards of law destroy utterly their influence? and would not the remission of the penalty, upon conditions which every subject believes he certainly shall comply with and escape punishment, equally abolish the penalty and destroy its power? Could God annihilate the attraction of gravity, and still govern the natural world by its agency? Could he at all more annihilate rewards and punishments, and yet maintain the moral government of the universe by his law? * * *

"Our first conclusion, in view of the past discussion, is, that we know with moral certainty what is the true Gospel. By moral certainty I mean that certainty which is the result of evidence, and can not be fallacious without throwing discredit on all our powers of reasoning, and establishing the dominion of universal skepticism. The secular concerns of the world move on by the guidance of such knowledge, which, if it be not as certain as demonstration, does nevertheless create and justify, for all practical purposes, a confidence as safe and unwavering.

"I am aware that pretensions to knowledge on the subject of religion are treated with derision when they go to set aside favorite opinions, and to disturb the conscience by the implication of criminal and destructive error. That, in the track of 'gifted minds,' who have examined and reasoned only to discover their past mistakes and present ignorance, any one should pretend to knowledge, is deemed the height of arrogance.

"What, then, is the meaning of these high pretensions to ignorance and uncertainty? Is it meant that man, half divine, almost infinite, can not reason? That reason itself, godlike reason, is but a meteor of the night, that 'guides to bewilder, and dazzles to blind?' Or is it meant that her eye is keen and comprehensive, and her decisions the basis of knowledge on all subjects of temporal interest, while sad eclipse and disastrous twilight have dimmed her vision and mocked her efforts to obtain knowledge on all the more important interests of eternity? On which horn of the dilemma will the advocates of uncertainty choose to hang? Will it be pretended that man is not capable of knowledge, and that there is no difference between the confidence inspired by sophistry, and that which is the result of valid evidence and sound reasoning? Of what use, then, is reason? and of what avail is evidence, as the means of knowledge? and what advantage has the truth above error? and what, after all, is the boasted illumination of the nineteenth century but an accumulation of doubtful doubts?

"If the subject of religion is made an exception, and reason, keen-sighted every where beside, is blind here, then by what fallacy has it come to pass that her vision should fail just where it is most needed, and that darkness and doubt should settle down upon those subjects which respect our eternal well-being? nay, should gather about the Bible, sent from heaven to shine as a light in a dark place; not on the law, whose precept is as plain as the fact is of its transgression, but upon the Gospel, which alone can answer the question, 'How shall man be just with God?' — a question which Socrates could not answer, and to which the heavens, with all their hosts of suns and stars, have sent down no reply; which no breeze has wafted to the listening ear, no breath of morning whispered, no grateful incense of rose or violet indicated, no 'smile of beauty told?' Yes, why has this darkness fallen upon the Gospel, *without* which we could have known our guilt and wretchedness, but *with* which, it seems, no man can discover the certain means of escape?

"Why, again would we ask, can we not *know* what is the Gospel with moral certainty? Can there be a subject on which certainty is more urgently needed? Did God make the Gospel obscure on purpose, or was he unable to make it plain? Does he not speak of it as if it were plain, and treat his subjects as if it were so, commanding his ministers to preach it, and their hearers to receive it, as the condition of eternal life? And yet is the whole to which it is possible to attain some modest conjectures about what may be the Gospel, which shall subject to the laugh of scorn all pretensions to knowledge on the subject? * * *

"That all do in reality reject the Gospel atonement who, through inattention, or want of information, or manifold temptations, can not be said positively to believe it, we do not say. Theirs, possibly, may be the sin of ignorance, or of wavering and doubt. Much less do we say that all renounce Christianity who attend the ministrations of those who deny the atonement and justification by faith. For these doctrines have been eradicated from the churches of the Pilgrims, not at first by opposing them, but by omitting to preach them; and the New Gospel has been introduced, not by the pulpit first, but by the press and at the fireside. A cautious silence was maintained on the subject until the more aged and evangelical portion of the congregation were gathered to their fathers, while the rising generation, uninstructed in the truth, and, by misrepresentation, prejudiced against it, were gradually initiated into the new faith.

"And even now there is remaining too much recollection and belief of early Biblical instruction to render the unequivocal denial of the atonement safe. To this hour there are not a few who can not be persuaded that their ministers reject the atonement in the evangelical sense; for their ministers have learned to use terms which the initiated understand in the anti-evangelical sense, and which persons evangelically inclined misunderstand in the evangelical sense — terms which by one class of the audience are understood to deny the atonement, and by another to teach it. If, at times, from the pulpit or the press, the atonement is denied and ridiculed with an explicitness which creates alarm, and these people apply to their ministers for explanation what was said and meant, and is still believed, is taken back, and modified, and explained away as no honest man — no Christian would dare to do. Our meaning is, that those who possess the means of knowledge, and who do, understandingly, reject the atonement, do reject the Gospel and renounce Christianity; and when we consider that some in this country have been understood to avow their unqualified disbelief in the inspiration of the Bible, and that, in the community which receives the instruction and illustrates the tendency of the New Gospel, much of the ancient implicit confidence in the Bible as the rule of faith is gone, and supplanted by irreverence and doubt, and to a fearful extent by absolute infidelity — when we consider these things, we are prepared to meet the reaction of invidious feelings which may be provoked by the avowal that the renunciation of the atonement is the renunciation of Christianity. We are not of the number who will stand idle and mute, while, in the name of Christ and by his nominal ministers, the fabric of Christianity is taken down piecemeal from the topstone to the foundation, and removed from the community, leaving behind a cheerless infidelity.

"It ought to be understood by the people — it will be understood, that the controversy which agitates New England respects not merely the doctrines of the Bible, but the Bible itself. To this length the same controversy has gone in Germany with a tremendous reaction; and to the same result it is fast hastening in this country, with a reaction still more glorious to the cause of truth and the Church of God; for, though some indications of alarm, and the return of a more cautious policy appear, it is too late to stop the causes which have been put in operation. The dark waters of infidelity will scorn and defy restraint, and will roll on, sweeping away, one after another, all forms of Christianity which are not built on the rock, and leaving only two parties, those who believe in the atonement and in the Bible, and open infidels."

While thus carrying on war in earnest against a real enemy, Dr. Beecher was extremely reluctant to be called off to engage in conflict with brethren who held the fundamentals of religion as firmly as himself. Yet it was in this same year (1829) that Dr. Tyler published his "strictures" on the views of Dr. Taylor, of New Haven. Already, in 1828, the latter had been openly charged by Messrs. Hewitt, and Harvey, and others with Arminian and Pelagian heresy,[1] and in the celebrated Concio ad Clerum had fairly thrown down the gauntlet to his assailants. Already the war of pamphlets and periodicals had passed through its earlier stages, when the Portland divine entered the lists, and smote with lance's point the shield of the New Haven professor, declaring, "He has adopted principles in his explanations and statements which will

[1] Pelagian heresy: fifth century doctrine that taught that men were born innocent, could win salvation by virtue, and could achieve perfection.

lead, by inevitable consequence, to the denial of important doctrines; and that his speculations will pave the way for the gradual influx of error upon the American churches."

At the same time he wrote to Dr. Beecher, saying that he hoped that what he had done would not exclude him from the pale of friendship. To this Dr. Beecher replied as follows:

"Boston, March, 1830.

"Nothing is farther from the reality than the forfeiture of my friendship by the course you have taken. You have only exercised the right of conscience and free inquiry, which we all must do unless we would sink down into nerveless, indiscriminating theology, or come under the power of a theological despotism as arbitrary as the power of caste or of popery. I know, too, you have acted conscientiously and with deliberation, and not without pain; and though on both sides, and from the beginning, I have exerted every atom of my influence to avert a rupture and a public controversy, yet, when I became convinced that it must come, there is no one on your side to whom I should have committed the responsibility of writing with as much cheerfulness as to yourself.

"My reason for not replying to your letter sooner was the utter impossibility of doing it. The solicitude I had felt, and the efforts I had made with Nettleton and at Andover, had brought me to the *ne plus*, and left me only to choose between letting the subject alone or absolute prostration. I did think that you misunderstood Dr. Taylor, and that it was a pity for two such men to come before the public to settle points some of which could not fail to be adjusted by correspondence or conversation. I think so still; for if a man is obscure, or may be understood differently from what he means, that does not authorize the charge or the suspicion of heresy until it be well ascertained that he does adopt the construction which is given to his words; and in this respect, however severely he may deserve to be censured as a philologist, as a theologian he has been not only misapprehended, but misrepresented in circumstances in which the means existed and the obligation of ascertaining his meaning correctly, and of preventing logomachy and vain jangling; and if I could have written to you, I should have urged you not to publish till you had submitted your remarks to Taylor and received his reply, and I believe that such was the verbal advice which I sent by Brother Pond.[2]

[2] Enoch Pond (1791–1882), student of Emmons, pastor in Mass., became editor of the *Spirit of the Pilgrims* in 1828. After 1832 he taught in Bangor Theological Seminary, where he advocated temperance, missions, revivals, and the New England Divinity, and opposed the "fogs" of German metaphysics.

"I disapproved and regretted that you began with notes of alarm, which in a controversy is begging the question in the outset, and, by exciting on the one part fear and feeling, and on the other a sense of unmerited distrust and injury, tends only to disqualify writers and readers on both sides for a fair and calm logical discussion. I therefore should have been better pleased with the *tocsin* at the close of this discussion, when you should have shown that you correctly understood Taylor, and that what he holds is wrong, and as wrong and dangerous as you supposed.

"I could have appreciated the extract from Connecticut better if you had given me the name of the Litchfield brother; but I have received representations even from Brother Nettleton which demanded afterward, as facts disclosed in his presence evinced, so much abatement and modification as convinced me that more has been and is still to be feared from excess of feeling, and prejudice, and precipitancy, than from all other causes. There has from the beginning been in the community a feverish state of feeling which has greatly pained and alarmed me, and which made me the more deprecate the introductory alarms of your letter. We may in this way make a fire which we can not put out, but, in my belief, shall never in this way make peace.

"I do not anticipate that the Christian Spectator is on its 'last legs,' or will be while efforts are made to arrest discussion and free inquiry by putting it down. And while I have never made myself responsible for all the opinions of Brother Taylor, or regarded his expositions as the most felicitous, and have regretted that the subject should have been brought up in the form of controversy, and have felt as if all which is material in his opinions might have been taught without alarm, I can not sympathize with you in the fears that his talents are employed in 'giving currency to dangerous errors.'

"The account of the conduct of his students in Litchfield county betrays, I should think, some excitement of feeling, and does not correspond with any thing which I have seen in any of them with whom I have been conversant, and is a loose, and, I should think, unfair way of testing the merits of doctrinal opinions in theology. If they are impertinent, and do declaim against old members, and boast of new light, etc., they have their reward for their folly in just public disapprobation, which probably will not fail to teach them better manners.

"But, brother, there are those whose conduct and conversation becometh the Gospel — very precious young men, whom God delights to honor, and who meekly delight to honor God; and my full belief is that no seminary has sent out more young men of piety and promise, according to numbers, than the seminary at New Haven; and, according to the best information I can obtain, they have been distinguished as revival men rather than otherwise; and if they have a few *isms,* they soon rub off in action, and they become most excellent ministers; and it grieves me to see you feel and hear you speak of such blessings to the Church, and so much needed, in such terms of alarm and depreciation. Your correspondent thinks the New Haven system radically Arminian. He is doubtless honest, and just as certainly mistaken, if I am competent to understand principles and language.

"I have examined the passages commented on by Brother Nettleton, and am grieved, and amazed, and alarmed that so good a man should be able to put upon them the construction which he does, and that in the teeth of the passages which he quotes, and, as it seems to me, in disregard of all the equitable rules of exposition — for a writer is not to be compelled to mean what, through inadvertence or obscurity, his language may be made to mean, but what, upon a fair comparison with his object and argument, and of his expressions one with another, he actually does mean; and I have never met with an instance, as it appears to me, of more flagrant injustice than the sentiment ascribed to Taylor by Brother Nettleton. Whether his sentiments are true or not, as I understand him they are precisely those which Nettleton himself has so triumphantly urged in favor of immediate submission against those who plead for waiting God's time.

"It is his object to reconcile exhortations to immediate duty with dependence, and the order of his thoughts, as I understand them, is as follows: 1. The sinner is authorized to regard actual obedience to divine requirement as an event which may attend an immediate attempt to do the duty. Not as a result, however, of unaided free agency and ability, and not as the result of common grace yielded to or used by the sinner without God's doing more at one time than another, but as the result of special grace, rendering present endeavor effectual; that no sinner has any evidence that this concurrence of special grace will not attend his immediate effort to obey, and that no minister has a right to assure him, or can prove that God may not attend an immediate effort with special grace; and that to tell the sinner that he will not submit of himself, and that God at any definite moment will not concur to make him willing, will unavoidably, for the time, preclude all effort to submit; for if it be certain that the sinner will not and that God will not subdue his will, what possible motive can there be to effort, and what possible alternative but waiting God's time?

"Brother Taylor says, then, that the possibility of divine special concurrence must be admitted as a rational ground of present effort; that the call, and special grace, and the sinner's own effort may be coincident; and Brother Nettleton represents him as saying that the sinner is authorized to believe that he SHALL repent, etc., without special grace. Not only that he is able, as a free agent, to make himself a new heart, but that he will do it without any thing special on the part of God. Now there is certainly a broad chasm between a sinner's having no evidence that special grace will act without an immediate effort to repent, and he being authorized to believe that he certainly shall succeed, and that, too, without special grace.

"If any thing Taylor has said can be made to mean this, the express contradiction of it in immediate connection, and his known opinions to the contrary, should have deterred Brother Nettleton from giving to his words such a construction. If he has sinned as a philologist, let him be punished by the critics, but let him not be charged by his theological brethren with holding what we know he does not hold, and what *I* can not perceive him to teach while he seems also to teach directly the contrary.

"Brother Taylor no more places the Holy Spirit in the background than you, or I, or Brother Nettleton, and I am grieved and alarmed that he should be so misapprehended and misrepresented.

"That Stuart and Emerson[3] do not agree on all points with Taylor I should think to be true. It is true of myself. But that they regard his sentiments, in which he differs from them as you do, as fundamentally erroneous, and a ground of great and just alarm, though you have evidence of it which satisfies you, there has none of it ever come to my knowledge, and I do not believe it to be so.

"As to the difficulties at the South and West, and New England's coming out, and Taylor's inability to stand or going down stream — as all these are events in futurity, and I must say at one sitting all I have to say for the present, I can, of course, say but little. That he can be stopped by me or any one, as things now are, is beyond hope. If he is radically wrong, the course which has been taken toward him from the time that Hewitt began to make the outcry until now, has, in my judgment, been calculated to do

[3] Ralph Emerson (1787–1863), Conn. minister (1816–1839), professor at Andover Seminary (1829–1853).

any thing rather than to arrest him or to check the prevalence of his sentiments; and much as I shall deplore the event if your views of his sentiments and their tendency are correct, it is my most full and deliberate belief that they will prevail and predominate, both in New England and elsewhere, if he continue to be treated as he has been.

"That I am wholly without apprehension when so many are alarmed, it would be the affectation of confidence to say. That the fears of evil are, however, greatly exaggerated, I have no doubt; and that Brother Taylor and his school will be eminently and permanently useful, is my hope and expectation. I wish I could say that I had, or could see that I had, no reason to fear that the theology of New England is running down again to natural inability, and old Calvinism, and waiting God's time, and formality, and triangularism.*

"But I do not permit myself to be agitated in this respect. I believe that God has seen reasons for having the system of Calvinism re-examined and discussed by a new and original investigation of all the points, and that the result will be the purging out of all the false philosophy which may have been mixed in with it, and leaving the mass like gold seven times purified. Who of us are to suffer the loss of the most wood and hay by the process I can not tell; but all mine is at the Lord's service at any time; and if all which is in New England should be brought out and laid in one pile, I think it would make a great bonfire."

* As some readers may not be familiar with this term, we insert a brief extract from Whelpley's Triangle, written in 1816:

"There are a few points which go perpetually into the strain of preaching of certain gentlemen, and their scheme may be compared to a triangle, from which they never depart, and in which, if they step out of one angle, their next step is into another, the succeeding one into the one from which they started."

Having enumerated the three points, viz., Imputation, Inability, and Limited Atonement, he observes:

"The whole of their doctrine, then, amounts to this, that a man is, in the first place, condemned, incapacitated, and eternally reprobated for the sin of Adam; in the next place, that he is condemned over again for not doing what he is totally, in all respects, unable to do; and, in the third place, that he is condemned, and doubly and trebly condemned, for not believing in a Savior who never died for him, and with whom he has no more to do than a fallen angel."

XX

CORRESPONDENCE, 1828–1829

EDWARD TO DR. BEECHER.

"October 15, 1828.

"*** My mind is and has been uncommonly tranquil. God has been and is very gracious to me, though I do not deserve the smallest favor, and is conducting me to a result which I have long expected from his mercy, while I have been daily becoming more conscious that from his justice I deserve nothing but disappointment, and mourning, and lamentation, and woe. I think I see the hand of God in all the events which have befallen me, and I find daily reason to believe that at no time has he left me or forsaken me. The promises of his covenant of love are sure, and stand fast forever and ever. ***

"I trust that you will pray for me, and have faith in God that he will remember and answer all your prayers, and make me even more useful than you had ever hoped; and that I may live and die humble and holy, depending alone on Christ, and doing all his will, and giving him all the glory."

CATHARINE TO EDWARD.

"March 12, 1829.

"What you suggested on the character of God has been of essential service to us, and we have read the Bible with more pleasure and comfort since. And now, in reference to another subject on your theory of a former state, what do you say of Adam? What is the reason that half the human race die in infancy, without any chance of being affected by a system of means, and what becomes of infants? Just answer these questions simply, and let us think it out; you do not know how much we speculate on these points.

"One more question: What do you do with that famous fifth chapter of Romans? How I wish you could help us in some of our speculations! For instance, how strange it would seem to us to be told in any other case, Here is a being you must love this very moment. If we found we did not love a person that we ought to love, we should consider it rational to take some time for it; but here is an invisible being whom we are persuading minds to love on the instant. We have some speculations about this strange inability.

"Oh how I wish you could sit by our fire, evenings, and help us out of our conjectures. One of our scholars, when pressed to love God immediately, said to Harriet, 'I don't see how people *can love right off* so as they do.' "

DR. BEECHER TO CATHARINE.

"March, 1829.

"A sinner never extinguishes obligation to love God, but he may so disqualify himself by ignorance or stupidity as that instruction and time shall be the only means by which, according to the laws of depraved mind, he can be brought back. And though it is proper to set up immediately the demand of the law to convince of sin, yet I do not suppose that we are bound, or that it is best to rely chiefly on peremptory demands of immediate submission, for it is by truth seen and felt that the event is to be secured as really as if God did nothing. And God acts also by your means in proportion as they are wisely adapted; and you will bring the sinner to submit by pressing him with the reasons, and shedding light, *light*, LIGHT, sooner than if you merely reiterate submit, *submit*, SUBMIT."

DR. BEECHER TO DR. WISNER.

"Boston, July 3, 1829.

"Not a word was said by any one at Andover, except Mrs. C—— inquired, in a manner which I understood, but should not if I had not known something, whether Dr. Wisner would accept.*

"In respect to your people, so far as I have heard, I should think there was a kind of taking for granted they have got to lose their minister.

"As to the reasons *for*, those which have occurred to me are,

"1. The great importance of such a department as pastoral theology, and your qualifications, in many respects, beyond any other man whom I know.

"2. The necessity of placing there immediately a man of weight, of character, discretion, and a business man.

"3. It is important that Andover and Boston should draw well

* An effort was made to obtain Dr. Wisner as professor of Pastoral Theology.

together in time to come as in times past, and no one could exert a happier influence in that respect than yourself.

"4. You have gone through with what may be called the first course of sermons on nearly all the subjects that occur in preaching to a congregation, and must preach old sermons, which will unharness your mind, or you must go over them by original study a second time, which, as the pleasure and excitement of discovery is superseded, will render the work, on some accounts, more irksome and difficult. The same discourse could much better be revised for another charge than be re-preached to the same people, who have gotten about all your ideas on particular subjects. I could preach very little which would be new to my people at Litchfield on any subject; they had got used to my thoughts.

"5. The admonitions in respect to your health. * *

"6. If, on account of health, or a call to some institution, it should be probable that you would remove soon, if not now, there would be strong reasons in favor of a present removal.

"7. So far as the interests of Old South are concerned, I believe they are, in the first place, safe, and, secondly, may be so well provided for as that, on the whole, your usefulness at Andover would be much greater than in your own congregation.

"8. I do not know who can go any better, if you do not, who is as well qualified, and I have some fears as to the next choice, if you do not accept. A bird in hand is worth two in the bush. You know I have great confidence in *you.*

"By this time you will begin to think I am for getting you off; but there is the other side to come.

"Brother Edwards is to be dismissed in a few weeks. We were constrained to give this advice in a confidential consultation last evening. Brother Green is laid by for the present by an affection of the throat or lungs — not sick, but hoarse, and is in a state of suspense, though we hope much, and yet not without fear. Edward will, I trust, get along, but his health is not perfect; his nervous system falters considerably. Dr. Jenks [1] I need not describe. Dr. Brown [2] is judicious and good, but, I fear, not so efficient and

[1] William Jenks (1778–1866), professor at Bowdoin College, became pastor of the Green St. Church, Boston, in 1826. He defended the New England theology, wrote a six volume *Commentary* on the Bible, and was active on behalf of the Indian, the Negro, and educational improvement.

[2] John Brown (1786–1839), a successful revivalist in Cazenovia, N. Y., proved too unbending in manners and doctrine for Boston tastes. After two years' service, he was dismissed from the Pine St. Church, and found a more appreciative audience in Hadley, Mass.

popular as to make Pine Street go up fast in these hard times. Dr. Fay has a call to New Connecticut.

"Dr. Beecher, you know, loves you as a son, and has leaned on you more than on any one else beside, and he can not but feel that, while new weights and responsibilities are coming on him, a main prop will be taken away; and if he consulted his heart only, or the peculiar condition of our churches just now, he would say you can not be spared, and you must not go. But, between this and the time of your final decision, Providence may throw farther light on the subject, and we may have more time and better means of forming a correct decision. It is immaterial where we live if it be where duty calls, and I doubt not that God will direct you to a correct decision, and continue, I trust, your life and usefulness many years."

DR. BEECHER TO CATHARINE.

"Boston, December 1, 1829.

"I have been up and down about Edward since you left, but more down than up, though now I think I am more up than down. * * * That Edward is not to have the support of his principal men I am confident. That he will have their real and secret, but most efficient opposition, is my full belief. I am not prepared to doubt the intentional rectitude of one of them; but I can not resist the evidence that defective preaching, etc., is only the ostensible, while personal dislike, and a fixed, determined purpose to get him dismissed, is the real cause. They are not willing he should succeed. They have no pleasure in his manifest improvement. They are afraid he will succeed, and, but for my letter, matters would have been brought to a crisis, in my judgment, in a few weeks.

"It is important, however, to his reputation, and to his usefulness to the Church, and to his safety and health, and to Park Street, and the general cause here, that, if possible, he stand it through; and, unless something new occurs, I think he has got by the pinch and will rise; and if he may have health, and write as I can advise and he execute, they may do what they please then."

XXI

LECTURES ON POLITICAL ATHEISM

THE commencement of these lectures is thus mentioned in a letter to Catharine:

"*November* 27, 1829. Yesterday, Thanksgiving, I preached upon Atheism — the causes, the kinds, the doctrines, the absurdities, the evil tendencies. The whole was, if I may say so, as good as I ever do such things. On the absurdities, for once, I opened the ground tier, and let out, without let or hinderance, all the caustics in the locker. In the evening preached in Park Street on the dangers which threaten the Church, and am to finish on the sources of safety next week."

The discourses referred to in the above letter were repeated in Cincinnati, and subsequently published, with the title, Lectures on Political Atheism, dedicated to the working men of America.

A single extract will be given from Lecture II., on the Causes of Skepticism. After considering some of the more prominent causes, he continues:

"With these remarks in view, I proceed to observe that the creeds of the Reformation are often made the occasion of perplexity and doubt to inexperienced minds.

"They contain, unquestionably, the system of doctrine taught in the Holy Scriptures; and they have stood through ages, against the encroachments of error, as the iron-bound shores to the ocean. But they were constructed amid the most arduous controversy that ever taxed the energies of man, and with the eye fixed upon the errors of the day, and on the points around which the battle chiefly raged. On some topics they are more full than the proportion of the faith now demands; some of their phraseology also, once familiar, would now, without explanation, inculcate sentiments which are not scriptural, which the framers did not believe, and the creeds were never intended to teach. They present, also, the results of investigations, without giving to the reader the intervening steps, without which minds not favored with leisure and undisciplined by study could not easily arrive at the conclusions.

"Of course they appear rather as insulated, independent abstract propositions than as the symmetrical parts and proportions of a beautiful and glorious system of divine legislation for maintaining the laws and protecting the rights of the universe, while the alienated are reconciled and the guilty are pardoned; and though, as abstract truths correctly expounded according to the intention of the framers, they unquestionably inculcate the system of doctrines contained in the Holy Scriptures; and though, as landmarks and boundaries between truth and error, they are truly important, yet, as the means for the popular exposition and the saving application of truth, they are far short of the exigencies of the day in which we live — mere skeletons of truth compared with the system clothed, and beautified, and inspired with life, as it exists and operates in the Word of God.

"Unhappily, also, some of the most important truths they inculcate are in their exposition so twisted in with the reigning philosophy of the day as to be, in the popular apprehension, identified with it, and are made odious and repellant by its errors, as if these philosophical theories were the fundamental doctrines of the Bible. There is no end to the mischief which false philosophy, employed in the exposition and defense of the doctrines of the Reformation, has in this manner accomplished. Good men have contended for theories as if they were vital to the system, and regarded as heretical those who received the doctrine of the Bible, and only rejected their philosophy. They have cried out against and renounced philosophizing, when it was their own philosophizing which divided and agitated the Church.

"In this manner the Church has been filled with controversies, and feuds, and jealousies; and intelligent men, offended alike by absurd philosophy and unchristian controversies about it, have, in the conflict of opinion, become discouraged and disgusted, and have either adopted heretical opinions or become skeptical. It is my deliberate opinion that the false philosophy which has been employed for the exposition of the Calvinistic system has done more to obstruct the march of Christianity, and to paralyze the saving power of the Gospel, and to raise up and organize around the Church the unnumbered multitude to behold, and wonder, and despise, and perish, than all other causes beside. There is no subject which so moves my compassion or fills my soul with regret, or my heart with the feeling, 'Oh that my head were waters, and mine eyes a fountain of tears, that I might weep day and night for the slain of the daughter of my people!'

"Nor is it to be expected that the Gospel will ever be attended with its primitive power in sudden and numberless conversions till it is again, as it was then, preached in demonstration of the spirit and with power, unobstructed by the clouds and darkness of a false philosophy. The points especially affected by this philosophy are vital to the principles of moral government, and involve the constitutional perceptions of truth, the universal dictates of common sense, and the unequivocal elements of accountability, as recognized in human government, as sanctioned in the Bible, and as employed by the Holy Spirit in convincing men of sin, and of God's justice in their condemnation. If the theories of this philosophy are not absurd, nothing is absurd; and if they are not false, nothing is false; and if, according to them, the conduct of God is not indefensible and unjust, it is only because what God does is right, simply and only because he does it, and therefore nothing which he does can be unjust.

"The points to which I allude as violated by a false philosophy are the principles of personal identity, by which the posterity of Adam are distinct from, and not to be confounded with their ancestor; the principles of personal accountability and desert of punishment; that men are not made accountable and punishable for the conduct of Adam, though liable to sin and misery as its universal consequence; the nature of sin and of holiness, considered not as material qualities, or the substance of the soul, or as instincts, but as the spontaneous action of mind under moral government, in the full possession of all the elements of accountability; and, above all, the doctrine of the decrees of God, and the universal certainty of all events to his foreknowledge; to which may be added, the nature of the atonement and its extent, and the doctrines of election and reprobation as they shine in the Bible, and not through the medium of a perverting philosophy.

"Whatever of these philosophical theories appertained to the system during the arduous conflict for civil and religious liberty against the papal despotism of modern Europe, men endured — even swallowed them unhesitatingly, almost unthinkingly, in the presence of a greater evil; but, since the conflict has passed away, and the nature of mind and moral government is better understood, and the numbers who think and will think for themselves multiply, the repugnance to this false philosophy has steadily increased, and will increase, till that which is adventitious and false is relinquished, and the truth is preached in its purity and unbroken power."

"These evils of philosophy have, however, been greatly aggravated by the caricatures of Calvinism which on all sides have been multiplied. I have never seen or heard a correct statement of the Calvinistic system from an opponent. Consult almost any oracle of opposition as to what is Calvinism, and the response will be, Calvinism is that horrible system which teaches that God has foreordained and fixed by physical omnipotence whatsoever comes to pass; that he has made a very small number of mankind on purpose to be saved, and all the rest on purpose to damn them; that an atonement by weight and measure has been made for the elect only, but which is offered to the non-elect on conditions impossible to be complied with, and they are damned for not accepting what did not belong to them, and could not have saved them if they had received it; and that infants as well as adults are included in the decree of reprobation, and that hell, no doubt, is paved with their bones. It is needless to say that falsehoods more absolute and entire were never stereotyped in the foundery of the Father of Lies, or with greater industry worked off for gratuitous distribution from age to age."

XXII

CORRESPONDENCE, 1830

DR. BEECHER TO WILLIAM.

"Boston, February 10, 1830.

"* * * The burning of our church will be confirmed to you long before this arrives; set on fire, probably, by the burning of the chimney that day, through some flaw or crack produced by the intense heat and the contact of some wood somewhere; but it is all conjecture. The feeling of the church and congregation is good — very good. They feel it, but are not cast down, and will soon rebuild. The insurance — $14,000 — will probably nearly cover the expense.

"We worship, in the mean time, at the Salem Church. They hire me for a stated supply, till our church is rebuilt, at fifteen dollars per Sabbath, and our Church make up the rest. They provide free 115 pews beside. Last Sabbath we met there for the first time. I preached from 'Our holy and our beautiful house is burned with fire, and all our pleasant things are laid waste.'

"It was a solemn and good day. There were over sixty inquirers in the evening, and four cases of hope the preceding week, and every indication of a real revival begun. My prospect of usefulness is, in my apprehension, greatly increased by this event."

It may be stated here that Salem Church at the North End, and Pine Street Church at the South End (subsequently removed to Berkeley Street), were formed as colonies from the Hanover Church in August, 1827. Seventy-nine members were dismissed to the former, five to the latter, making, together with twenty-five set off to form a church in Cambridgeport, a hundred and nine members colonized within the period of eighteen months.

DR. SKINNER TO DR. BEECHER.

"March 16, 1830.

"I am looking with greater concern than I can express at the present unprecedented state of things in the Presbyterian Church. The strange divisions and combinations which are now taking place among us are not unknown to you, and have probably a more definite meaning and issue in your apprehension than in mine.

"One thing, however, is becoming daily more evident, that the grand influence by which the Church has been advancing with matchless success and triumph the last forty years, namely, that of voluntary associations of Christians, is the secret of the marvelous doings of certain men, who have discovered the destructive bearing of that influence on all the interests of party zeal and private ambition. You will find the next Assembly, which I have heard with great joy you are to attend, such a one as no year has witnessed since that body was first formed.

"Brother Peters,[1] lately returned from a long journey in the West, can tell you some things which would fill you with concern for the cause of Christ in that region; and, if I had time, I would surprise you with a recital of movements now in progress in the two great cities and elsewhere.

"But something else must engage the few moments I have left. Many of us have been longing for your presence among us, believing that God has given you the qualifications for the peculiar task that some one must perform, of directing men's minds aright at this interesting crisis, when something of most disastrous or happy influence must speedily take place. You are wanted in Boston, I know, and where are you not wanted? But it is our full belief that you can do incomparably more for the general cause in New York at the present time than in any other spot in this world. And Providence will soon, it is probable, open a door for your entrance in among us. The Bleecker Street Church [2] will send you a call next week.

" * * * I want to be near you, to tell you some things which I am afraid to write. If I had your ear for half an hour, I should pour arguments into it which would command no common degree of conviction and interest. The Bible Society, the Tract Society, the Education Society, and, above all, the Home Missionary Society, all want you. You may do great good in Boston, but could you do as much good the next four years of your life any where on earth as in New York? You ought to remove at least once more, and when or where if not now?" * * *

[1] Absalom Peters (1789–1869) led in the formation of the American Home Missionary Society, defended Barnes, and was founder, director, and professor of Union Seminary. He was editor of the *American Biblical Repository* (1838–1841).

[2] Bleecker St. Church, founded in 1825, had forty-six members in 1828. Erskine Mason, a learned and argumentative preacher, became pastor (1830–1850).

DR. BEECHER TO WILLIAM.

"Within Point Judith, June 5, 1830.

"As I shall not be able to stop, and may not see you at the wharf, and could say but little if I did, I will just give you a little sketch of matters and things which you may wish to know. Generally the session of this Assembly has been auspicious, although more apprehension was entertained concerning it than any perhaps which was ever convened. But the very strength of apprehension created safety, all praying and striving for peace for fear of controversy, until it became one of the most devout and peaceable, good-tempered sessions I have ever known, a few instances excepted.

"The two points of chief interest were to adjust matters between the American Education and Assembly's Education Societies, and between the Home Missionary Society and the Assembly's board. The Triangulars wished to carry, in each case, a general recommendation for all their churches to patronize the exclusive Presbyterian boards. They were, however, defeated in both attempts, and a recommendation given for the churches to choose for themselves which should be the channel of their charities.

"They pretend that voluntary associations have no guarantee of orthodoxy, and that all charitable institutions ought to be accountable to the Church. But the real difficulty is the fear of the prevalence of our doctrines.

"Another measure, more exciting than any other, was a proposition for appointing an agency for the West, through which both Home Mission and Assembly's Mission should pass, to prevent collisions of the two boards in the West. This the Triangulars opposed bitterly, and finally threw it out of the house without discussion, to the great offense of many, and some of their own people at the West. A protest was signed by Dr. Rice[3] and many others, which scared them, and may have produced a compromise since I left, as they were in a great stew.

"My health has been and is good, and I have been constantly, and, I trust, not unprofitably occupied in preaching four sermons on the Dangers of the Church, and the Remedy.

"I preached for the Methodist Society of colored people last

[3] John Rice (1777–1831), editor of the *Virginia Evangelical and Literary Magazine* (1818–1828), advocate of Protestant cooperation, aided in the establishment of the American Bible Society. In 1824 he became Professor of Theology at Hampden Sidney College, Va.

Sabbath afternoon, at the invitation of their bishop. They had a Conference, with fifty preachers present from different parts of the Union, and four from Hayti. Two thousand blacks present. All a surface of black heads, wedged in — a solid mass almost. I came down to them and upon them in a way which made them cry 'Amen! amen!' 'True! true!' 'That's good! that's good!' 'That's preaching!' and clap hands, and jump up, etc.

"Two hundred came forward and subscribed a pledge of entire abstinence which I wrote for them — the largest Temperance Society, I believe, ever organized at once, and promising to carry it through all the colored families of the land. About as much good, *I guess,* as ever I did in so short a time.

"The sight of a black audience brought up afresh East Hampton and Freetown, where I used to preach to just such folks from 1800 to 1810.

"I gave an address for Sabbath Union in support of the motion to supply the Valley with Sabbath-schools in two years. Arthur Tappan [4] had promised $4000 in two years, and two individuals have guaranteed $5000 apiece. Nearly twenty thousand have been raised already in money, and agencies, and the right spirit is wide awake, and strong to preoccupy the Valley before his Holiness. So much good is to come out of popery, though it meant not so.

"I spoke also on the subject of Temperance, and the thing goes finely. Philadelphia henceforth, in doctrine and charity, will be predominantly with us. It is man's wickedness and the Lord's goodness which has hastened it. But the time has come when opposition seems to be as useful, if not more useful than direct patronage. The wrath of man praises him.

"We have had consultations about the Sabbath, and it is the prevailing opinion that we petition again, though not till fall, and with less noise, in the mean time pushing the thing in the papers by able writing. The Indian Bill [5] is gone wrong, yet there is much hope we can delay its execution till another Congress, and then block it. It passed against a real majority on account of peculiar

[4] Arthur Tappan (1786–1865), N. Y. businessman, supported the Sabbath School Union, the Bible and Home Missionary Societies, temperance, and Sabbatarianism. He contributed generously to the building of the Broadway Tabernacle for Finney, and to the establishment of Kenyon, Oberlin, Auburn, and Lane. At first an advocate of colonization of freed Negroes, he later became an active abolitionist and a founder of the American Anti-Slavery Society.

[5] A Georgia law (1830) ordered white residents among the Cherokees to secure a license from the government. Two New England missionaries refused to obey and were sustained by the Supreme Court.

circumstances, and the next day only after, when Jackson returned the Navy Bill and Road Bill, it would have been rejected by a large majority. But God will bring good out of evil.

"I shall be glad to hear from you next week, and know how you get along — whether you have got settled, and begin to get under way about study. I think you had better pursue my plan rigidly — *i. e.*, to confine your study to the forenoon; afternoon relax, attend to business and pastoral visits; evening, preach lectures, and *read*. In another thing you had also better follow my example for the first ten years of my life, in which I never planned and wrote a sermon scarcely which I did not read to your mother, and talk over with her. It was a great help to me, as often, in talking, my own mind was invigorated, and my heart warmed, and my thoughts made clear.

"You will not forget every week to make your sermons as good as you can, not depending on extempore readiness without careful and discriminating thought. Have one sermon every week that will tax your intellect and the intellect of your hearers."

DR. BEECHER TO DR. TAYLOR.

"June 16, 1830.

"I was disappointed in not finding you here. You were doing great good, and were much needed and much approved, and your going let the whole run back, so that I found things in a bad state when I got back. Hardly recovered yet, though I think rising. Thank you, however, for what you did do. The effect in other respects will be good.

"We have had a discussion in our Association to-day on the the question proposed by myself, 'What is the difference between a free agent who, being assisted by God, is able to act in and of himself, and the self-determining power?' It occupied three hours, and rambled over all the metaphysics of theology; and on *all* the points that came up no two agreed, though the result with Dr. Pond and others was to allay fear and diminish distance between them and us, and prevent squabble, and jealousy, and alienation, and prepare them to allay suspicions and outcries around them.

"Brother Fay stated, in a manner which implied that he had information on the point, that Dr. Woods would not publish his Pastoral Association sermon (which was a warning against philosophizing, and a prophesying of evil coming on the churches until maybe the Hindoos will have to send the Gospel to New

England), and, which is more, that he has concluded not to publish his letter, or treatise, or what not (to prove that sin, wherever it is, is better than holiness would be in its stead).

"He said, also, that there was considerable dissatisfaction at Andover among the young men about Dr. Woods, and that ten were about to leave for New Haven. Whether all this will be so, I know not. But I write, my dear son and brother, to say, 'Fret not thyself, and be not cast down.' You are now, perhaps, in the most critical state which you are to pass through — the last runnings of odium and vexatious opposition, and the risings of a tide still more dangerous. * * *

"For my sake, and your own, and the Lord Jesus Christ's sake, take care of your health, and when the fiery trial is past, and the flood of success begins to come in, take care of your heart.

"You must remember that Dr. Woods, as well as myself, is approaching old age; and if the tide should turn against him, a little asperity on your part would create sympathy for him and reaction on you."

DR. BEECHER TO CATHARINE.

"Boston, July 8, 1830.

" * * * While at Philadelphia and since, my interest in the majestic West has been greatly excited and increased, and my efforts have not been without effect to create a love and a waking up both there and here. The moral destiny of our nation, and all our institutions and hopes, and the world's hopes, turns on the character of the West, and the competition now is for that of preoccupancy in the education of the rising generation, in which Catholics and infidels have got the start of us.

"I have thought seriously of going over to Cincinnati, the London of the West, to spend the remnant of my days in that great conflict, and in consecrating all my children to God in that region who are willing to go. If we gain the West, all is safe; if we lose it, all is lost.

" * * * Write your thoughts to me as soon as you have time, and I will find time to write back to you; for this is not with me a transient flash of feeling, but a feeling as if the great battle is to be fought in the Valley of the Mississippi, and as if it may be the will of God that I shall be employed to arouse and help to marshal the host for the conflict; and if duty can be made plain, I am ready. But if I go, it will be part of my plan that *you* go, and another that Edward, and probably all my sons and all my daughters who are willing to go. This you must not show to any one. They are only my thoughts; but they are deep, and yet, withal, my ways are committed to God.

"In respect to the Indians the prospect brightens. The tide of the West is turning, and running strong against the Jackson administration. A great meeting has been held in Cincinnati, and one in another place, disapproving the measures of the present administration, and among the rest the Indian Bill, as Mr. Evarts says, exactly right, and proposing that their members of the Senate be requested not to ratify any treaty made in pursuance of it, and that their members in the House be instructed to make no appropriations. It is in contemplation to get up similar meetings in Philadelphia and New York, and Hartford, Northampton, and Boston, and through New England and the land. We shall succeed; the Indians will be saved!

"In respect to your mother, I perceive that you do not know that the whole family — Aunt Esther, children, mother, and all, have migrated for the summer to Wiscasset, Maine, three weeks ago to-morrow; and that I, with four or five young men, candidates for the ministry, keep bachelor's hall, but for which I should have talked about loneliness as emphatically as you; and as it is, I don't like it very much, and have not known time roll so slow since the sad year of solitude which passed over me once in other days. But, as I have so much to think about and do, time gets along somehow, and is gone as usual.

"Edward is well, though rather worn down by his long effort to rise in the face of opposition, which, however, he has achieved, and now writes, and has long since, so that if any grumble, it is manifest that they are unreasonable, and unwilling to be pleased.

"George goes to New Haven this fall to study with Dr. Taylor. How do you think Andover will like that? But it can not be helped. It will be the fault of Andover if I like her any less than I have always done. I trust I shall not be compelled to. * * *

"I believe I have now touched on all your topics and some more. There is much more that I might say, but can not now. There is an ocean of things which it would kill me to write down, both of what I am called to think, and say, and do, it being as much as I can bear to think, and say, and do so many things once over, and that is one reason why I am become so taciturn. I have to keep all the feeling I have for use, and that is why I write so little to my children or any body else. However, I am resolved to get out of the vortex a little, and to become my own self again, and to wrap around me the warm garment of natural affection instead of the cold one of public cares, though I must wear the latter no small part of the time, probably as long as I live; for when I stop I expect to stop in heaven, and not to linger long on earth after my active usefulness is ended." * * *

DR. BEECHER TO WILLIAM.

"Boston, Sept. 3, 1830.

"My journey East was pleasant, and my health was restored a little, though for a few days I am down with a fall cold. Harriet is better; Edward has a call to the presidency of Illinois College, and goes to Commencement at New Haven to confer and see about it. What result he will come to I can not tell. But there are many and great things in favor of his going, and nothing very inviting in his remaining where he is. I send you a number of newspapers. I would not preach nor talk much openly about Masonry,[6] though I have no doubt it will and ought to come down. * * *

Some time in the course of this year (1830) an incident occurred which may well be inserted here. It is narrated by Mrs. Homes, or, as always known in the family, "Aunt Homes."

"While Henry and Charles were in college, your father and Harriet * felt very much straitened for money. One evening particularly they were talking about it, and did not know what they should do to keep the boys along. At last your father said, 'Well, the Lord always has taken care of me, and I am sure he always will,' and retired to rest and was soon fast asleep. Harriet laid awake, she told me afterward, and cried. She cried because she did not see how they should get along; but what most troubled her was that her husband had so much faith and she had not any.

"The next morning was Sabbath morning. Some one rung at the door, and a letter was handed in containing a $100 bill, and no name. They came up to tell me, as they always did, but they did not know, nor I then, who gave it. I found out afterward it was Mr. Homes, a thank-offering at the conversion of one of his children."

* Mrs. Beecher and Mrs. Homes were sisters.

[6] Blamed for the mysterious disappearance of William Morgan, who had published an exposé of Freemasonry, the Masons were suspect as a secret, politically powerful order. William Wirt ran as Anti-Mason party candidate for president against Jackson in 1832.

Mr. Homes was always doing kind deeds. When the aforesaid Henry and Charles came home to spend their vacations, they always received some token of regard in the shape of a knife, or some other article from the hardware store on Dock Square. The first salutation they always met was, "Well, well! and which is Amherst, and which is Bowdoin?"

The following incident is also credibly related as having occurred about this time:

A certain Josiah Bissell attempted to establish a line of Sabbath-keeping stages through Central New York to Albany. He called to see Dr. Beecher about it. He was then living in Greene Street. The ladies had raised seventy-five dollars to purchase a carpet for the parlor, which was unusually large. The money had just been presented to Mrs. Beecher. Dr. Beecher was so enthusiastic about the plan, he ran up stairs to look for some money. He opened the bureau drawer where Mrs. Beecher had put the money, took out the roll without counting, and gave it to Bissell. By-and-by the ladies called to go and buy the carpet, and lo! the money was gone! The consequence was, the floor of the great parlor went bare.

In the opening of the chapter, allusion is made to the burning of Hanover Church, an event closely bearing upon Dr. Beecher's subsequent history. The circumstances attending the conflagration, as reported by tradition, were somewhat striking, and illustrative of the state of popular feeling in those days. It was said that the firemen sat idly by, refusing to work the engines, and singing,

"While Beecher's church holds out to burn,
The vilest sinner may return."

It was also told how the organ was seen through the blaze, when the gallery gave way, to spring forward, as it were, bodily, and fall into the flames. One of the basement rooms had been hired by a merchant, who, it seems, had stored there a quantity of spirits, unknown to any body but himself. The sudden flaming up of this excited no small merriment among the firemen, who hurraed for Beecher's broken "oil jug," referring to a well-known story then current. In the rear of the basement were the "Missionary Rooms," where a quantity of tracts were deposited. Numbers of these tracts, it is said, were carried by the firemen and others all over the city, and scattered on door-steps and sidewalks in a most efficient style of "home evangelization."

XXIII

CORRESPONDENCE, 1830, *Continued*

In 1830 Dr. Woods addressed a series of letters to Dr. Taylor on the question of the origin of evil and kindred topics involved in the New Haven controversy. Dr. Taylor, in his "Concio ad Clerum," had characterized the notion that sin is the necessary means of the greatest good, and that God could have prevented it, as a groundless assumption. Dr. Woods interprets him as affirming that sin is not the necessary means of the greatest good, and that God could not have prevented it. In the closing letter it is intimated that in some respects Dr. Taylor agrees with Arminians and Pelagians, in others with Unitarians, and even with French infidels. At the same time, he is exhorted to be calm and not lose his temper, to avow his real sentiments with perspicuity and clearness.

On reading these letters, Dr. Beecher wrote to Dr. Taylor (September 6) as follows:

"For six weeks I have been obliged to forego study and care. Dr. Woods's letters came out when I could neither endure nor let them alone. I think of them as Skinner does, and also as you do as to their temporary *ad captandum* effect. I hope, however, that while you have been *suaviter* as the case admits, you have been *fortiter;* for, brother, we are not to be browbeaten and driven off the ground of New England divinity — Bible divinity — by a feeble and ignorant philosophy into the three corners of the triangle. In respect to myself, I need no urging to commit myself, and nothing but time and strength to do it in the best manner; which, after Blagden's [1] settlement, and till my house * is finished, a period of three or four months, I hope to have, and mean to consecrate in the best manner I am able, which, in my opinion, will be the revision and publication of my lectures on 'Elements of Theology.'

* The Bowdoin Street Church.

[1] George Blagden (1802–1886), Andover graduate, was pastor of the Salem St. Church (1827–1830) and the Old South Church (1836–1883), both in Boston. He advocated Sabbath observance and educational reform, and stressed the value of the Puritan heritage.

"To dash in on any one point would answer little purpose and forfeit much influence. The thing needed is an elementary exposition, such as shall show the nature, and relation, and dependences of the system, remove difficulties, and allay fears, by showing at every step not a dark hole full of mysteries, but *terra firma* covered with light; and not mere speculation and vain philosophy, but the mainspring, back-bone, sinews, and muscle of revival preaching.

"This done, then, my particular sermons making a direct onset on the conscience would be understood, and not create starting and alarm. If it will please God to permit me to illustrate in this way our common views of theology, theoretical, experimental, and practical, as it has been done in my ministry for twenty years, and especially for the last four years here, I shall be satisfied, and I do intend that nothing shall delay or come in competition with the commencement and continuance of this effort; but if, as the case may be, the waves should beat on me here, and suspicion and odium make it needful, why, then, it is my fixed purpose not to stand on the defensive merely, but to attack, to exhibit the fallacy, the tendency, and the actual past and present effects of Dr. Woods's system. I am glad you are prepared for so prompt reply in Hart's review and its codicil.*

"It is my opinion, also, that some one among you should attack Dr. Woods in the style in which Dr. Alexander [2] was put down, never to peep again or mutter. You, if you must reply, must in your own way; but it is my wish and advice that Fitch make the main attack, and in a style which might not be so well for you. I have not read his review on Sin lately, but perhaps his attack on Woods might be softened a little as to courtesy; but I would have him exposed and pushed with great directness and power, and unsparingly, leaving of his temple not one stone upon another."

"Boston, September 23, 1830.

"My dear Brother, — At my request, we have had a consultation to-day in Dr. Porter's study; and as the result, also, was in no small degree owing to my instrumentality, and is so different from the tenor of my last letter, it will be necessary, to enable you to appreciate my reasons, to put you in possession, historically, of

* Dr. Woods's Letters were reviewed by Dr. Taylor in the Christian Spectator for September, 1830, in an article appended to a review of Bellamy on the Divine Permission of Sin.

[2] Probably a reference to Archibald Alexander (1772–1851), Philadelphia pastor, president of Hampden Sydney College (1796–1806), and Professor of Theology at Princeton after 1812. He was an effective critic of the New Divinity.

the circumstances which led to a change of opinion, and of the reasons which sustain it, lest I should seem to have acted capriciously.

"The advice in my last resulted from the conviction that no alternative remained but controversy, and that, however great the evil, it was forced upon us as the least of two.

"With the same opinion I went to Andover on Tuesday. On Wednesday morning I was notified by Brother Porter that an effort would be made to open the Spirit of the Pilgrims to controversy. I said, 'Very well, if opened for both sides, but there ought to be first a consultation.' To this be acceded, and commissioned me to get it up. It was accordingly put in motion. Toward evening Dr. Woods had a long talk on the subject with Brother Pond, which resulted in offering to confide to him the entire direction of managing the controversy, i. e., deciding how much space to give to it, and regulating the whole as to Christian spirit. To this, having full confidence in Brother Pond, I conceded.

"When the conference opened at eight o'clock this morning, we had prepared a resolution recommending to the conductors of the Pilgrims to open their pages as above, which was put round to say yea or nay. It was going unanimously till it came to Brother Greene, of Boston, who said he couldn't vote to continue the controversy; that in his opinion it was needless. He had no such fears as some had, and wished the whole controversy might stop on both sides; that the mischiefs of going on had not yet begun, but would be great; that the churches, to his knowledge, in Boston were alarmed at the prospect, and were saying, 'What do our doctors mean?' He was followed by Mr. Walker, of Vermont, who said that he knew what Mr. Greene had said to be true of the ministry in Vermont, some of whom were on one side and some on the other; but that they made nothing of it, and it gave them no trouble; and if it were needful, he would go on his knees to New Haven to present our advice, if we would give it, to prevent controversy. Mr. Jackson, from Vermont, confirmed Mr. Walker's statement, and spoke with great decision against controversy as needless and injurious.

"These were the last who were called on, and the vote was carried; and we were on our feet to come away, when, seeing this favorable time, I said, 'I have acceded to a regulated controversy as the least of two evils. If we can get along without, so much the better; for the least of the evils will, in my opinion, be great. Let us look at the question, 'Can all farther discussion on both sides be stayed?' Brother Hitchcock, of Randolph, a fine man, said, 'We have Unitarians in all our societies; the moment we open on one another they will clap their hands for joy, and we shall be faint-hearted and sick.' He begged the controversy might go no farther. Mr. Mitchell, of Maine, said that the statements from Vermont represented the feelings of the ministers generally in Maine. They were generally on one side (Andover), but they to a man, he believed, were opposed to controversy on the subject. Mr. Beckwith said he had traveled seven thousand miles, and could testify that the general feeling of ministers was regret at the controversy, and a wish that it might stop. Brother Peters made a similar statement. Emerson and Stewart were both opposed to continuing the controversy. By this time an article was drawn recommending the discontinuance of the controversy from this time.

"Dr. Porter came in about this time, and was rather in favor of the motion, and quite satisfied after it was passed. Dr. Woods seemed in favor, but started difficulties, which being obviated, he said that, having called on you to write, it would be indecorous now for him to advise to drop the controversy. He therefore should retire and not vote, but would pledge himself to pay all proper deference to pacific counsel if given.

"Dr. Church thought discussion necessary; there had been too little. I accorded, but said, 'There is now a feeling up that had better subside before we begin,' to which he acceded; and a number of others spoke in favor of 'dropping the subject,' as friend Nettleton says to sinners.

"On the whole, the question was taken on a written motion, and each man's name written down, and passed unanimously in favor of ceasing from controversy. The temper which characterized the meeting was excellent. I have given you but an outline. * * *

"The reasons which swayed my mind were,

"1. It is perfectly manifest to my mind that the public sentiment does not demand the controversy, but is opposed to having it, including the great majority of ministers and churches. Now this is a public concession that the New Haven theology is not a heresy, nor tending to heresy, and ought not to be assailed or made a breaking point, but left alone, to stand or fall by its own merits. What do you need more? What better could be hoped at the end of a controversy?

"2. I think there is on both sides, among those of us most deeply interested, a state of feeling which is too strong to be managed safely in a controversy. I think this soberly of myself, and of you, and of numbers on the other side; and if we do push the controversy now, as we shall if we let all loose, it will work up into a practical schism, which will refuse to license each other's candidates, set the churches all on fire, break up our charitable co-operation, and pull down on our heads the ruins of a glorious edifice now going up. I think also that our heat, and sense of injury, and of the importance of the point in dispute, will so far surpass that of the mass of the community that they will not sympathize with us, and that on both sides we shall, in their eyes, walk naked and expose our shame.

"3. If the controversy goes on, nearly all the public sentiment which is opposed to it will be apt, without much discrimination, to vent itself upon New Haven theology as being at least the needless occasion of existing troubles.

"4. There is also so much ignorance, and alarm, and fever up now, and so much temptation to keep it up, that I do not think we should stand a fair chance; i. e., points would be started and resisted which in a calm state of things would pass unquestioned.

"5. It is my deliberate opinion that you may now go on and instruct your students in your own way, and let Dr. Woods do the same, and all the sentiments we hold in common and regard as important be extended much faster than they can be by a controversy attended by such party spirit as will attend a keen and thorough discussion; for we must not calculate that such men as have and will commit themselves, with such power as they possess of organizing a party, will be driven from the field, or fail to set up a powerful barrier to the progress of what we believe to be truth. You have not appreciated, probably, the power that can and will be organized against you.

"6. In addition to this, if I thought there were no danger that they could push us into error, I am seriously apprehensive that we should, if we have not, push them back into errors which it may take fifty years to eradicate. Unpushed, they will not deny ability, though taste and exercise both virtually do it; but, hard pressed, I believe they would do it before they would yield to our arguments. I have seen symptoms of it which alarm me. But if we let things move more slowly, they will not and can not do it.

"7. Another reason which weighs greatly with me is, that we can not prevent it from becoming a war of theological seminaries, and, if virulence arises, can not prevent it from affecting Yale.

"8. In addition to all these, there is another reason for discontinuing controversy, which, more than all, commends itself to my sympathies. It is the very great and trying, and, had I been in your case, I might say insupportable responsibilities which have rested on you since the noise began about New Haven, and especially since you began to write. My dear brother, you need and ought to have rest; and if, while all other pens stop, you will stop, we can take care of you, and of your school, and of this truth, better, in my opinion, than it can be done by any thing you can do.

"There is another reason. Brethren in this city do not participate in the alarm about New Haven. Brother Pond, and all, if they do not adopt, do not denounce. Such a mediation is not lightly to be forfeited. But if, in opposition to the feeling and wishes of your friends here, the controversy should be persisted in, and its evils pushed upon us, you know how it would affect their minds. Stuart is gone over; and, if much more is done, Emerson will go, who is still our sincere friend, and need not be alienated and lost.

"I have drawn out these reasons at large, as if they might be necessary to persuade you to do reluctantly what, however, I trust you are ready and willing to do, and will be even glad to do; for, in my opinion, it is not safe for your health, nor safe to the proportions of the system of sound words, that so long and such intense interest should be concentrated with so much care, and solicitude, and feeling on one set of subjects. There is no possible danger in ceasing now. Your reply is sufficient. Dr. Woods's letter will be better understood as men cool, and we shall do well enough."

DR. BEECHER TO WILLIAM.

"Boston, November 1, 1830.

"I can not now write a long letter. Edward was dismissed on Thursday — all things pleasant; many presents from individuals — five hundred dollars by the Church; and yesterday, under his farewell sermon, a great many tears were shed. He preached at Cambridgeport a farewell last week, and at Old Cambridge last night. He comes to our house to-night, and leaves for the West on Wednesday or Thursday.

"Public sentiment is doing justice to him and to his friends, and to others. But all things in Park Street are quiet, and they want me to supply them for three months to come, which probably I shall do.

"I am entirely quiet in respect to Edward's removal. I believe it, on the whole, an ample field for all his powers to operate in to the best advantage for his country, and the Church, and the world, and, instead of feeling depressed by his removal, I feel an indescribable relief, and an ardent gratitude at the present state of his health, and spirits, and prospects, compared with what they were a year ago.

"I rejoice in your success and estimation. It is a most blessed remuneration. May God still preserve, and give you wisdom, and holiness, and success."

DR. BEECHER TO GEORGE (AT YALE THEOLOGICAL SEMINARY).

"November 5, 1830.

"I was glad to receive your letter, and hear of your pleasant accommodations, both for exercise, for piety, and for study—especially that you are aware of the temptation of intellectual pursuits to leave the affections to languish without constant care. It is our shame, and a deep evidence of the depravity of our hearts, that, during mental occupancy about God and divine things, the affections should run down. It is not so in heaven. There, while angels look into the system of redemption which we study, they veil their faces, and adore, and burn with admiration and with love, while we, the interested party, the subjects of so much compassion, and mercy, and glory to be revealed, lose our emotions by the intellectual contemplation of its objects.

"It need not, however, be so on earth to the extent which it is, as appears in the life and writings of Edwards, whose vigor of intellect, compass of thought, patience of investigation, accuracy of discrimination, power of argument, knowledge of the Bible, and strength of holiness, stand unrivaled. But for his piety, he might have been a skeptic more dangerous than Hume or Voltaire; and but for the command of his religion over all his powers, he might have been one of the most dangerous, as he certainly was one of the most original and fearless of speculators. But the attractions of his heart to God kept him in his orbit, and enabled him to go forth, and survey, and adjust the relations of the moral universe without becoming a wandering star; whose original investigation and deep piety, my son, follow. Next after the Bible, read and study Edwards, whom to understand in theology, accommodated to use, will be as high praise in theological science as to understand Newton's works in accommodation to modern uses of natural philosophy.

"Edwards and Fuller are the two best theological writers for a young man to study. But while Fuller, availing himself of his own powerful mind acting on Edwards's materials, has written with more conciseness and perspicuity than Edwards, he falls far below him in the ardor of his piety, and in his power of applying truth to the conscience. In this respect Edwards stands unrivaled. There is in his revival sermons more discrimination, power of argument, and pungency of application than are contained in all the sermons beside which were ever written. Study as models Edwards's applications. They are original, multiform, and powerful beyond measure."

XXIV

LANE

It was in October, 1830, that the idea was first suggested to Dr. Beecher of removing to the West. The history of the institution at that time may be briefly told.

"The charter had been obtained in the winter of 1829. A donation of sixty acres of land, furnishing an admirable location, had been secured, one condition of the title being that a theological institution should be established and maintained upon it. Five or six thousand dollars had been received, including $4000 from the gentleman whose name it bears.

"Agents had been sent East and South to collect funds, and had returned discouraged. The first professor in the theological department had been appointed, and about a year before had entered upon his duties. Three or four students were on the ground, but there were no conveniences for their accommodation. In the spring of 1830 the professor was sent to the East to obtain funds. He labored several months without any success, and early in September resigned his office and abandoned the enterprise.

"On the receipt of this intelligence, a special meeting of the board was called to consider what must be done. That was a solemn and memorable meeting. The institution existed only in name — without professors, without students, without funds or buildings, and their efforts to obtain funds having proved a failure, the prospect was dark enough to stagger the strongest faith. The foundations of one building were laid, but the means of completing it were not at command, and it seemed very doubtful whether the donation of land must not be given up, and the whole enterprise be abandoned.

"The record of that meeting, held September 30th, 1830, is brief: 'Much doubt rested on the minds of some,' says the secretary; 'the meeting was solemn, and, after much deliberation and consultation, it was resolved that one more effort be made to raise funds at the East.'

"From a full report of the financial operations of the seminary made some six years after, we are permitted to obtain a fuller acquaintance with that interesting meeting.

"The president of the board (Dr. Wilson) [1] said: 'I never had great confidence in obtaining aid from Eastern men and Eastern funds. We have made the experiment, and we have seen the result. We must now look to the West for professors and funds; and if we can not make a great institution, as we hoped, we must make a small one.' As little confidence, however, was felt by the members generally in obtaining aid from the West as the chairman had expressed in relation to the East. A member of the board said, 'I am an Eastern man; I know the hearts of Eastern Christians; I know they will give us money if we make a special appeal to them. We must have Dr. Beecher or Dr. M'Auley, and the means for his support will not be wanting.' The committee said, 'If the brother who has so much confidence in the East will go, we will send him, and make one more effort.' Dr. Wilson said 'Amen.' " *

That brother, the Rev. F. Y. Vail,[2] having accepted the mission, hastened to the East, from whence he wrote back to the board, October 14, as follows:

" * * * In visiting Philadelphia, New York, and Boston, it has been my first object to present, as fully as possible, the claims of our institution before a number of their leading men, in order to ascertain what ought and could be *done now* for our object. As the American Board was in session in Boston, I had the happiness to meet with many distinguished clergymen and laymen, among whom were Dr. Proudfit,[3] of Salem, New York, Drs. Alexander and Miller, and Professor Hodge, of Princeton. I was happy to find that there was but one deep and all-absorbing feeling among them respecting our great undertaking, and that was in accordance with our own; that Cincinnati, now at the heart of four millions, and in twenty years to be at the heart of twelve millions, is the

* Commemorative Discourse, by Dr. Allen, pp. 4, 5.

[1] Joshua Wilson (1774–1846), pugnacious minister of the First Presbyterian Church, Cincinnati, Professor of Moral Philosophy at Cincinnati College, attacked New School doctrines and pastors, and advocated Presbyterian control of missions. As editor of the *Standard*, he criticized abolitionists and eventually defended slavery as a divine punishment of sin.

[2] Franklin Y. Vail, member of the Board of Trustees for Lane, agent for the American Education Society in the West, joined the New School Presbyterians after the 1837 schism.

[3] Alexander Proudfit (1770–1843), a founder of the American Tract Society, became head of the N. Y. Colonization Society in 1835.

most important point in our nation for a great central theological institution of the first character. * * *

"That one of the very first men in our nation ought to be called to the head of our seminary, and that he ought and must be willing to go, and his people to give him up. After much consultation, it appeared to be the common impression of those consulted that Dr. Beecher, of Boston, if he could be obtained, would be the best man. That, as he is the most prominent, popular, and powerful preacher in our nation, he would immediately give character, elevation, and success to our seminary, draw together young men from every part of our country, secure the confidence and co-operation of the ministers and churches both east and west of the Alleghany Mountains, and awaken a general interest in the old states in behalf of the West.

"Having previously consulted with those men who would be likely to be called in as advisers respecting his dismission if Dr. Beecher should be elected, we had a meeting at his house on Saturday last. I opened the subject for the first time to Dr. Beecher; each brother there expressed his opinion; all felt that it was one of the greatest subjects ever brought before them; that Boston and the East generally would sustain an irreparable loss in giving up Dr. Beecher, and yet that the good of the Church, the awakening of the East in behalf of the West, loudly demanded that one of their best generals should occupy the very seat of Western warfare while the enemy is coming in like a flood; and that, if his people would give him up, he ought to go where Providence so obviously leads. Dr. Beecher could not but accord with these views of his duty in the case, seeing, as he thought he did, the hand of God in the whole matter; and he expressed the confident conviction that his people — their strong feelings to the contrary notwithstanding — would cheerfully give him up for such an object.

"The result is, that scarcely any doubt remains that the Lord and the Church have given us and the West Dr. Beecher, if he is now called. To secure an object so desirable, our dear Brother Tappan, of New York, will give us $20,000, to be connected with Dr. Beecher's appointment, and on the farther condition that two other professorships be obtained at the East, and from $10,000 to $20,000 more at the West, for buildings. I have preferred these conditions, as well as himself, that the great work should be done speedily, and the institution be placed on a permanent basis for future ages. I have pledged myself to raise the two other professorships as soon as practicable, and will now pledge myself to raise the sum requisite at the West, with the divine blessing, if there be no other one to do it. I have a prospect of the second professorship in a few days, and trust that the third will be obtained without much delay. Brother Tappan's plan is to pay the interest of $20,-000, and give us his obligation for the principal. His documents I will either bring myself soon, or send them."

"On the receipt of this intelligence," remarks Dr. Allen,[4] "the board assembled October 22d, 1830, and unanimously elected Dr. Beecher President and Professor of Theology. The following extract from the letter of the corresponding secretary, Dr. James Warren, in which he communicated to the agent the action of the board, will show the state of feeling at that time: 'Your success was entirely unexpected, and it gave a thrill to the soul of every member of the board, and others whom I have seen are rejoicing with tears in their eyes. Is it possible, say they, that this Western world is to be blessed with the presence of Dr. Beecher? And we give thanks to the Lord that he has made you the honored instrument of conferring so great a blessing upon us. The resolution was passed with *reverential silence;* not a word was spoken but 'Ay.' " *

"Early in 1831," remarks Dr. Allen, "solicitude began to be felt lest Dr. Beecher might not obtain the consent of his people to his leaving them, and Dr. Wilson, Rev. Messrs. Vail and Gallaher,[5] were appointed a committee to correspond with them on the subject."

From this letter, addressed "To the Hanover Church and Congregation of Boston," we present the following extract:

" * * * Having presented this general view of the character, claims, and prospects of our seminary, permit us, dear brethren and friends, to specify a few of the particular reasons why we believe Dr. Beecher is called by divine Providence to this institution.

"The strong conviction of many of our wisest and best men east and west of the mountains is, that the great interests of the Church, and especially of the West, require Dr. Beecher's labors at the head of our seminary. A large number of our ministerial and lay brethren have expressed their deliberate conviction that the

* Commemorative Discourse, p. 8.

[4] Darcia H. Allen (1808–1870) attended Andover Seminary, and after teaching at Marietta College, Ohio (1835–1840), became professor at Lane (1840–1867).

[5] James Gallaher (1792–1853) held several churches in Tenn. before coming to the Third Presbyterian Church in Cincinnati in 1830. After 1835, he acted as itinerant evangelist among the poor in the Mississippi Valley. Though he had little skill or interest in theology, he joined the New School.

HANOVER CHURCH.

LANE SEMINARY.

enterprise of building up a great *central theological seminary* at Cincinnati, soon to become the great Andover or Princeton of the West, and to give character to hundreds and thousands of ministers which may issue from it, is one of the most important and responsible in which the Church is ever called to engage; and that no man in our country, in many important respects, is so well fitted to give character, energy, and success to such an institution as Dr. Beecher.

"Never has the presentation of a similar subject excited more deep and lively interest, and called forth a more general and cordial approbation among the friends of religion at the East and the West, than the announcement of Dr. Beecher's appointment as our President and Theological Professor, and the consequent prospect of our securing ample funds for the endowment of the institution. This voice of public opinion and of the ministers and Church of Christ, we think, is to be regarded as no unimportant indication of the will of Providence in this matter. * * *

"The last reason we shall mention for Dr. Beecher's connection with our institution is, that the securing of funds pledged on this condition, and the consequent existence and prosperity of the seminary, depend upon it. We need not inform you that the strong convictions of the importance of our institution among our brethren at the East have led them to undertake its endowment. Three professorships, amounting in all to $50,000, are nearly secured on condition that Dr. Beecher becomes our professor, and that we at the West raise from $10,000 to $20,000 more for buildings, etc. These funds, thus liberally offered to us, are to be given on account of the special confidence which the donors place in Dr. Beecher to preside over and give character and success to our seminary. Shall it be, then, the painful calamity of the West, and of the Church generally, that some $60,000 or $70,000, which would place our institution on a high and permanent basis for ages, and bless our increasing and perishing millions, must be lost, and our now brightening prospects be blasted for want of the man with whom the friends of Zion and the West have identified their benefactions? Should we fail of securing Dr. Beecher and the funds connected with him, we see not how our institution can be sustained, as extensive funds are indispensable, and can not possibly be obtained here among our infant churches. Dear brethren and friends, permit us to appeal to your piety and philanthropy in behalf of the perishing multitudes around us, and the future millions which are quickly to rise up here and decide the destiny of our nation. When you consider the deplorable evils of a failure of this institution, and contrast them with the infinite benefits to our country and to the world likely to result from its success, we will confidently hope that your convictions on this subject will agree with our own, and that Dr. Beecher will find his people ready to make the sacrifice required, if he shall regard it his duty to accept our call."

Dr. Beecher thus describes his first emotions on being made acquainted with the plan in view:

"One day, after the building of the Bowdoin Street Church was commenced, I saw Vail and Cornelius coming along in the street toward me, talking earnestly about something. I knew a theological seminary had been talked of, and that Vail was the agent, and the thought struck me, 'Now they are going to pitch upon me!'

"They let some things drop that showed me it was so. There was not on earth a place *but that* I would have opened my ears to for a moment. But I had felt, and thought, and labored a great deal about raising up ministers, and the idea that I might be called to teach the best mode of preaching to the young ministry of the broad West flashed through my mind like lightning. I went home and ran in, and found Esther alone in the sitting-room. I was in such a state of emotion and excitement I could not speak, and she was frightened. At last I told her. It was the greatest thought that ever entered my soul; it filled it, and displaced every thing else.

"One thing that indirectly occasioned my being thought of, I have no doubt, was a little circumstance that had happened not long before on one of the North River boats. I was coming down the river, when I saw a crowd where a pert fellow, a skeptic, was talking. I drew near the ring to hear and see what he was doing. I soon saw that his antagonist was not his match, and needed help. He was showing up the contradictions of the Bible; among others, that Judas hanged himself, and in another place fell headlong, etc.

" 'And how do you reconcile *that?*' said he.

" 'Why, sir,' said I, 'the rope broke, I suppose.'

" 'How d'ye know?' said he.

" 'How d'ye know it didn't?' said I, and that dashed him. People began to laugh. Then I stepped up close to his side and kindly said, 'I venture to say you are a child of pious parents, and are fighting against your conscience. That is a dangerous thing, and you had better give it up.' I told him if he ever came to Boston to call on me. 'Why,' said he, 'I don't know who you be,' and half a dozen voices cried 'Dr. Beecher — Dr. Beecher.'

"I told this to Taylor; Taylor told Arthur Tappan eulogistically; and so, when Vail came on to New York, he found Tappan so well affected to me that he offered to give $20,000 on condition I would go. That, with what he had known of me before, I always thought settled it. So great things often grow out of little. I had had my interest excited toward the West already, and had said, in a meeting of the General Association at Groton, 'We must not only send money, but go ourselves — fathers, mothers, sons. But perhaps you will say, 'Physician, heal thyself;' why do not you go? I answer, 'When the Lord calls I will go, and I will send my children.'

"Now, in less than a year, Edward was gone, and here came Vail and Cornelius quoting my own words to me. But the difficulty was that Hanover Church had been laid in ashes only a short time before, and my congregation, though united and harmonious, was much scattered; but, in concurrence with my advice, and relying on my promise to stand by them while rebuilding, they had paid out several thousand dollars already, and incurred a debt of between eighteen and twenty thousand more. Moreover, they had thrown up their trust deed by my advice, and organized by a simple act of incorporation, giving the Church and society a concurrent vote. My promise, therefore, was not to the Church alone, but to the society, who would not be likely to be convinced it was my duty to go.

"I called together a few of my best friends — Evarts, Wisner, Greene, and Cornelius — and they came to the conclusion that I was bound in honor to remain; and that, even if I were not, it would not be for the public good for me to remove at that time. So I was constrained to decline the invitation, and had all the care and anxiety of going forward with the church until the dedication. But the doubt and perplexity of my mind in deciding this question was such that, with all the other things pressing upon me, it affected my nerves and health, and was a very, very severe thing."

The following letter from Dr. Taylor will be read with interest in this connection:

"Yale College, November 8, 1830.

"Your secret at Sherburne caused me almost a sleepless night. I can not think that the cause of Christ calls you to Cincinnati; nor, if I may interpose in this case, on the ground conceded before you left Litchfield, can I give my consent. Suppose, now, that the man in New York could be induced to give his $20,000 to found a professorship for you at Yale, would it not be better? * * *

"The cause of truth and the interests of religion require that you come here. You have tried to qualify yourself to do what must be done in this part of the country. Your influence and power on the heresy, the atheism, and the infidelity of the land; on the cause of revivals, the charitable enterprises of the age, can not, I think, be withdrawn from this part of the country without great loss on the whole. * * *

"Now, if you say it would be better for you to come here, Goodrich and I will go and see Tappan, to persuade him if we can. It would be better still if you went with us. I know how the interests of the West fall on the heart of that good man; but *we three*, I think, could satisfy him that more would be done in this way than in that proposed. Now why will not you think so too, and come right on to New Haven, and we will go with you to New York? * * Besides all this, we feel as if we had a prior claim; and we have, in fact, a plan under way, which was to furnish a fund as soon as you would be ready to leave Boston. Now, brother, don't come to any final conclusion without farther conferring with us."

While deliberating on this great question Dr. Beecher was by no means idle. In January, 1831, he commenced a series of lectures on Catholicism, in which he sounded an alarm in respect to the designs of Rome upon our country. About that time Professor Stowe [6] succeeded Asa Rand [7] as associate editor of the Boston Recorder, in which capacity he made his mark upon the thinking of the day. In April Dr. Taylor visited Boston, to assist in a protracted meeting. In June the Bowdoin Street Church was dedicated; sermon by Dr. Beecher on the text 1 Kings, viii., 27: "But will God indeed dwell on the earth? Behold, the heaven of

[6] Calvin Stowe (1802–1886), editor of the *Boston Recorder* (1829–1831), professor of Greek at Dartmouth (1831–1833), went to Lane as Professor of Biblical Literature in 1833. His marriage to Harriet Beecher took place in 1836. He helped found the College of Teachers at Cincinnati, and in 1837 he published a report on European elementary schools for the state of Ohio. In 1850 he went to Bowdoin, and in 1852 to Andover as Professor of Sacred Literature. A student of Hebrew and German criticism, he published *Origin and History of the Books of the Bible* in 1867. A scholarly man who saw visionary people, he suffered from such ill health that he resigned from Andover in 1864, and he and his more famous wife thereafter spent their winters in Florida.

[7] Asa Rand (1785–1871), editor of the *Boston Recorder* (1826–1830), critic of Finney's New Divinity.

heavens can not contain thee, how much less this house that I have builded?"

In August Mr. Finney commenced preaching in Park Street and other churches in Boston with success. Throughout this whole interval the religious interest in Dr. Beecher's congregation never entirely ceased. It may be said that from the time of his settlement to the time of his removal to the West there was one continuous, unbroken revival — less powerful, indeed, at some times, but never wholly intermitted.

The following is an extract from a letter to a young minister discouraged in a hard field. It is a specimen of numbers of the same kind which he was continually called to write in various directions:

October 18, 1831. "You say, 'It is necessary a young man should succeed when he begins, and be where he can.' Answer: There is no place where, if faithful, he can not succeed, for there are two ways of succeeding; one is success in building up, the other is such mental discipline and pastoral fidelity as will raise *him*, though Israel be not gathered.

"But you say, 'The grand difficulty is, the churches do nothing — only willing to be boosted.'

"This may be, but it is a fault very common in most churches. What did I do at Litchfield but to 'boost?' They all lay on me, and moved very little except as myself and God moved them. I spent sixteen of the best years of my life at a dead lift in boosting. I could not get my salary paid quarterly or half yearly. I could not and did not get a vestry, but held conferences in that old West schoolhouse, dark and dirty, lighted with candles begged or contributed among the neighbors, and stuck up on the side walls with old forks; and at last we grew so liberal and extravagant as to buy half a dozen tin things to hang on the wall and put candles in. I can not revert to the scene without shuddering. My soul hath it in remembrance, and is humbled within me.

"On the whole, I remark, it is a *common thing*, *almost universal*, for a person newly settled to get discouraged and run low somewhere about the close of the second year. Some break down. Others work up all their ideas, and grow discouraged and lazy, preach hasty, extempore sermons, neglect study, and are either dismissed, or, living through and seeing the danger, begin to rise and grow. And this has been the turning-point with many a man."

XXV

CORRESPONDENCE, 1832

After a year's delay the call was renewed, and urged upon Dr. Beecher's acceptance. The following is an extract from the letter of the secretary of the board:

January 23, 1832. "A desperate effort is making to ruin the seminary and the board in the estimation of the public. Your own character, too, has been assailed in the public papers of this city. Your theological opinions have been pronounced contrary to our Confession of Faith, and dangerous to the purity and peace of the Presbyterian Church. The idea is now busily inculcated that you can not renew your connection with our Church without the basest hypocrisy. This is working like leaven on the minds of a part of Western Christians, and if you do not now come on to the ground, you will have, at a subsequent period, a host of prejudices to encounter of the most formidable kind.

"Besides, the cause of Christ is suffering by this delay. The minds of many Western Christians are becoming alienated from their brethren at the East by the fierce and bitter controversies which now agitate the public mind. Missionaries who come out from New England are held up as heretics, and every obstacle is thrown in the way of their efficiency and success. In the mean time the cause of Christ languishes, the Spirit's influences have been withdrawn, infidelity, popery, and every hurtful error are striking their roots deep in this fruitful soil, the wave of population rolls on, iniquity and vice are becoming loud and turbulent, and moral desolations are spreading out in wide and dreary prospect around us. A large portion of our ministers neglect their pastoral duties, and are busily engaged in hunting heresy, in defaming the character of their brethren, and in blowing the coals of strife and division. Will you not, under these circumstances, come over and help us? Will you not come immediately? The case is pressing and urgent. The armies of Israel need a leader. The land is before us in the length and the breadth of it, but the Amalekite and the Canaanite dwell there, together with the sons of Anak, and the people's heart is discouraged because we have no Joshua to say, 'Go up, for the Lord will deliver it into our hand.' "

Among the influences brought to bear upon Dr. Beecher's mind in the decision of this question was the following letter from Dr. Skinner:

"Philadelphia, February 16th, 1832.

"You doubtless know that your appointment to the Professorship of Theology in the Lane Seminary is regarded throughout our country with deep interest. Many fear you will accept it, more that you will not. For my own part, I can not *imagine* any reasons so powerful against, as those which are palpably obvious for your accepting it. We can not see with God's eye; peradventure it may not be best for you to leave Boston; but you will act against the conviction of all the friends of anti-sectarian theology and religion in this and (as far as I know) every other part of the land if you decline this call to the West.

"Our eyes are fixed upon you as God's chosen vessel, eminently fitted and furnished for the great work which is to be done by some one in the place to which you have been invited; and we are perfectly confident that you can not, in the remaining days of your life, do half the amount of good anywhere else. The efficient piety of the Church is Calvinistic; by Calvinistic Christians the world is to be converted; they know this, and they have undertaken the work; but *you, at least,* have eyes to see that the *philosophy* of Old Calvinism is a great mountain which impedes these Christians, and will impede them forever if it be not removed. All things in the universe beside do not hinder the progress of the Gospel so much as this one obstacle.

"Arm the spirit which now reigns in the evangelical churches with just views of moral government and agency, and you bring the Millennium to the very doors. Now where in all the world can you do half as much to impart and disseminate such views as in the great Western Valley — the Valley of Decision in respect to this, and probably all other nations?

"How wonderfully, too, do all things seem to be conspiring in favor of this movement! Hear the doleful complaints, the long-drawn sighs of fatalism. Behold what transformations in the very heart of the old system! How does public sentiment gain strength as revivals give their divine sanction to the simple and consistent preaching of our brethren! What dementations are taking place among prelatical and Diotrephesian [1] Presbyterians! Oh, for such a mind and heart as yours, to lay hold of the opportunity now afforded you for making an impression on the Church in this land! Do not, my most estimable friend, suffer this opportunity to pass away unimproved. No local Church ought to think of raising an objection. The people would deserve a distinguished curse who should refuse to give you up.

"I have never seen so much of your excellent son Edward as I have done during his late visit to this place. Providence sent him to us just at the time when we most needed him, and when he could do most for his object. He preached like an apostle, and we shall never forget him. If he could stay here we should instantly build a church for him; but we must let the West have him. Our revival is still advancing."

A very elaborate letter was also received from Messrs. Mahan,[2] Vail, and Blanchard,[3] urging, on behalf of the board, an immediate acceptance of the call. To this Dr. Beecher replied as follows:

"Boston, March 17, 1832.

"The scenes of a four days' meeting and a subsequent revival, and the conflict between two such great demands, rendered it impossible for me, until now, to bring my mind to any settled conclusion; but in what I now say I am fixed, and move on solid ground.

"My views and feelings concerning the importance of the Lane Seminary remain unchanged, and I am willing to relinquish any thing and to do any thing during the remainder of my days to raise up the institutions of the West which God shall indicate to be my duty.

"The question of *comparative* usefulness has, however, considerably changed since my former call. Then I thought my special work here nearly done; now it seems to be but beginning, as it respects a favorable access to the public mind. Then it was the condition of my own people which hindered; now it is the condi-

[1] Diotrephes: an ambitious Christian. John 3:19.

[2] Asa Mahan (1799–1899), revivalist, pastor in Cincinnati (1831–1835). A trustee of Lane, he opposed the seminary's action in the slavery crisis, and in 1835 became president of Oberlin, where eighty of Lane's anti-slavery students enrolled. In 1839 he published a book on the possibility of a perfect Christian life.

[3] Amos Blanchard (1800–1869), agent of the American Tract Society (1828–1829), editor of the Cincinnati *Christian Journal* (1830–1831), after 1832 held various New England pastorates.

tion of the city which remonstrates, almost emptied of ministers. These, however, as I hope, are only temporary exigencies, and probably not to be laid in the balance against those of the West. It will not, however, be prudent, as I think, to decide until I shall have surveyed the premises, and seen those with whom I am to act face to face, and by consultation have attained to a thorough and mutual understanding; for if I come, I can not come to change or to *conceal* my theological opinions, or to teach and preach them without a cordial co-operation.

"I have therefore concluded to come on and see you as soon as possible, setting out probably by the first of April. The removal of my family will not be prudent or practicable till fall; but, should I conclude to return to Cincinnati, I might prolong my stay, if needed to assist in consultations and preliminary arrangements, so as to answer nearly the same purpose as if I had made a permanent removal. In the mean time I have some thoughts, of which it may not be improper to put you in possession, whether myself or another shall be employed by heaven to rear up the institution.

"I should exceedingly deprecate the annual drilling of a class one year in Biblical literature, the next in theology, and lastly in composition and eloquence — one stratum of knowledge piled on another, without any cement between; about as wise as if a man should eat his meat one day, and his vegetables the next, and his pies and cake on the third. My desire would be to blend the united services of all the professors in raising up the student to a perfect man, that 'all the body fitly framed, having nourishment ministered and knit together, might increase with the increase of God.'

"I think it highly important that the theological instructor should, if possible, sustain the pastoral relation, and the students worship with him in a popular assembly — that while in the acquisition of doctrine they might witness its application, and feel its power, and observe its effect. How can the full and warm tide of piety be maintained in the hearts of students shut up to be preached to, and to preach to one another, without the variety of instruction and social influence which appertains to a popular assembly? The soul of eloquence is *feeling*, and in the ministry *holy* feeling; but feeling without social excitement is impossible, and all eloquence unprompted by it is but parrot eloquence, alike offensive to God and man. Of all the mistakes made by great and good men, that of shutting up theological students on the Sabbath in a chapel, to be edified by classical accuracy at the expense of feeling and untrammeled eloquence, is one of the greatest — a kind of preaching having no more relation to that for which they should be preparing, than a sham fight with friends bears to a real battle.

"It is no less important that he who preaches to theological students should himself feel the inspiration which the pastoral relation alone affords, and bring forth the treasures new and old which the ever-varying exigencies of a church and congregation can alone suggest. And how, without some such living stimulus, is his heart to be kept on fire and his lips made apt to teach? Of all the men of talents and piety who have ceased from the pastoral relation, I have never known one who made any advance, or held his own, or did not manifestly retrograde as a preacher — who, like Samson, was not, to some extent, shorn of his locks, or, like the channel of a summer brook, comparatively emptied.

"Nor is the reason obscure. By the pastoral relation a wakeful interest is created for which there is no substitute. Habits of mental discipline, also, are preserved by the demands of the Sabbath constantly occurring, and a variety of subjects, and freshness and vivacity of illustration, and argument, and application, in no other way to be obtained. No artificial stimulus can so speak in eye, and action, and intonation as benevolence travailing in birth for souls, and exulting in the midst of renovated, rejoicing minds. My estimation of the wisdom of God in the foolishness of preaching, as putting in requisition to the highest point both the energies of mind and heart, has been continually increasing with time and observation; and after what I have witnessed of retrograde movement, as preachers, in those who have relinquished the pastoral relation, it would not be without fear that I should place myself in such circumstances.

"Indeed, so long have I lived, and moved, and had my being as the soul of an affectionate people, that to be unclothed at my time of life would seem almost like attempting to act on men in a disembodied state. Whether the pastoral care and theological instruction can be united in the same person I can not tell; but if it can be, nothing, in my opinion, can be more desirable; for, as I judge, the bold character of the West, midway between the fiery ardor of the South and the more phlegmatic North, provides the noblest possible material for the formation of a class of preachers who shall combine a power of intellect, an ardor of piety, a power of eloquence, and energy of action such as the world has not seen, and which not only the West, but the world itself, can not fail to feel.

"In respect to the probability of my removal, I have only to say that the *chief* uncertainty, in my opinion, will have reference to the *state of my health*. For the present routine of duties I am competent, but how much the excitements and perplexities of a removal may occasion disease beyond the power of the will to avert, I can not tell. I can only say that if, after a full view of the subject, there shall appear to be a rational prospect of success in the establishment of such a seminary as we desire, it is my purpose, as at present advised, to accept the call and come on with my family in the fall, provided the condition of my health shall render it practicable and prudent. May the Lord preserve and guide us all to do his will and trust his promises!"

XXVI

CONCILIATION

In the early part of 1832 the pages of the Spirit of the Pilgrims were opened to a discussion between Dr. Tyler and Dr. Taylor, forming the fourth stage of the New Haven controversy. About the same time a correspondence commenced between Dr. Beecher and Dr. Woods in the same periodical, preceded and accompanied by an active interchange of letters in private, the object of which was, if possible, to allay excitement and dissuade from controversy. From the unpublished correspondence a few extracts are here given:

June 6, 1832, Dr. Woods writes: "Thanks for your letter, in which you utter your whole heart so frankly. What you write has touched my heart. I know well what it is to be full of anxiety, and distress, and fear, and I can sympathize with you most sincerely and tenderly as far as my heart goes. Your heart, I believe, is much more enlarged, and disinterested, and holy than mine; so I have thought and felt uniformly. I never converse with you or hear you without having my love toward you kindled. Though I have sometimes doubted the propriety of what you have said or done, I have always esteemed and loved you; and I trust I always shall, if I gain a place among the inhabitants of heaven; and it seems to me it will be what I shall be greatly pleased with, to sit down there and talk over with you the things which are now taking place, and particularly those things in which we are jointly concerned. Oh, how high will be our emotions of gratitude toward God for carrying us through these scenes of labor, and fear, and anxiety, and grief! * * *

August 8. "I have been reading your letter again to-day, and find my heart drawn out toward you in love and confidence. Your sincerity, and kindness, and generosity command my strongest affections. I am ready to weep when I think how much happiness we might have enjoyed, and how much good we might have done, had we been united in our efforts for these few years past. But I bless God the time for co-operation has come, and I hope we shall do much in a little time.

"On my part there are many and stubborn difficulties. I shall be obliged to go against the feelings of many of my dearest friends. I have already done this in engaging in a correspondence with you in this way. I have many cautions given me, hear of many fears, and expect to see signs of decided disapprobation, and of the withdrawment of confidence. These things make my heart ache; but they don't move me in the least. Firm as a rock I feel this heart of mine to be, being fully persuaded that we are doing what God approves. I have counted the cost. I suppose you have. I mean to be perfectly honest and fair; I know you do. I suspect myself more than I do you. But you will have some severe trials with your particular friends.

"I heard a man who loves and esteems you highly say lately, 'Depend on it, Dr. Beecher will neither say nor do any thing which will make against Dr. Taylor, or in any way displease him.' I told him you did not agree with Dr. Taylor in all his points, and never had. He replied, 'Well, you won't get him to say so.' I told him that he was mistaken; that I believed you would say out honestly and unreservedly just what you believed on any subject, whether you agreed with Dr. Taylor or not. He said you would not do it. I told him I could not believe you capable of any servility; that I believed you had true, manly independence.

"I have started with the determination not to cover over or spare what is wrong in myself or in my party. My dear brother, I have made up my mind to act for Christ, and for the judgment day. As for any respect of persons, love of man's favor, fear of his displeasure, or reluctance to deny myself and suffer, I tell these things, 'Stand by, and hinder me not in what I have undertaken, with my dear brother, for the cause of truth and love.' "

About this time Dr. Beecher published his sermon on Dependence and Free Agency, the proofs of which were sent to Dr. Woods for his suggestions, and subsequently forwarded to Dr. Beecher at New York by Dr. Wisner, who had kindly assumed the final revision, to whom Dr. Beecher writes as follows:

October, 1832. "Yours was received in New York, and read with an entire reciprocation of affection and interesting recollection, and had I not for some time sealed up the fountain of feeling and tears as things for the present too expensive to be indulged, I should have shaken with emotion and poured out a flood. As it is, I read it with great delight, and warmth of heart, and sweet comfort, and gratitude to God that we had been given to one another for so long a time in so many, and such difficult and grievous enterprises, whose results yet to come will be, I doubt not, as the bounteous harvest exceeds the penurious seed which is sown. And amid the temporary shipwrecks of many hopes by the frost of this untimely controversy, it is cheering to reflect that no shade has passed over our minds creating suspicion, and no wave dashed upon and sunken the immovable foundation of our friendship, which, I doubt not, will be perpetual. It would be easy to fill many pages with the overflowings of my heart in delightful yet painful reminiscences which must not be indulged on earth, but for which there will be time and strength in heaven. Till then we shall be constrained to think much of each other and the past, and say but little.

"I send back by Eastman [1] the proof-sheets of my sermon, with Dr. Woods's letter. There is some foundation for his remarks about the unfinished state of the manuscript, but not in sentiment, of which in no respect would I authorize any alteration, for it is mature, and for good cause that I have written, as I judge. A sentence obscure you may make plain, or too long break into two, and you may substitute any word more acceptable to my good brother, Dr. Woods, which does not affect the sense in perspicacity, precision, and force or point. I perceive that in looking the proof over he has penciled the places where I speak expressly against moral taste or instinct, etc., and where I put in voluntary to qualify sin, etc., and in one place proposes wickedness, I believe. Now I can not consent to be silent or equivocal on those points. I might as well not write as not to speak out.

"I must add that, while I confide in the general friendship and candor of my good brother, I am fully persuaded that he, and Porter, and Stewart had rather pay for the whole expense of setting the types than to have it printed just now. I read the sermon at New Haven, and they advised its publication with sufficient commendation. If you think it will dishonor me, after all that Dr. Woods and you can do, I shall begin to demur; but, till then, I say, Revise and publish."

To this Dr. Wisner replies, December 1, 1832: "The next day after I got home from New York I saw Dr. Woods, and he talked to me about your sermon in a way which somewhat alarmed me, indicating that he had no idea of your having given to me the right

[1] Ornam Eastman (1796–1874), agent for the Board of Foreign Missions, the American Tract Society, the Home Missionary Society for the Mississippi Valley, and for Lane Seminary. He was secretary of the Tract Society from 1832 to 1870.

of umpireship in regard to suggesting alterations from him and others. I said nothing about it, however. And when Eastman brought me the proofs from Philadelphia, I sent them up at once to Dr. Woods. * * * I gave him some extracts from your letter, * * * because I foresaw that I could not assent to certain alterations he would propose, and I wished him to know that my dissent was in conformity to your views.

"He sent back the sheet with his suggestions, with a note in which he said: 'The principle on which I have acted in all my attentions to Dr. Beecher's manuscripts, and this proof as much as any, is this, to do what I can to make what he writes as excellent and unexceptionable as possible, considered as his, not as *mine*. I have not meant to suggest the addition of a phrase or a word, or any alteration whatever, which would distort, or conceal, or in any way change any thing which he believed and wished to publish as truth. It would be wholly contrary to our plan of intercourse. My whole labor has been, as he well knows, to make *him*, *Dr. Beecher*, appear as well as possible in his own dress and with his own characteristics. And when he wrote to you as though you must take care lest I should leave in something or leave out something contrary to his sober convictions, he forgot the terms of our friendship. Accordingly, I consider *him perfectly answerable* for every thing in his sermon (as in his letters), and myself not answerable for any thing; and I shall feel just as free to remark on any thing in the sermon as though I had never seen it. My object will be secured if there is nothing in it which will *unnecessarily* occasion animadversion. Our aim has been to have as little objection to each other as possible. You will proceed with the sermon as you judge best.'

"I wrote back that the principle by which he stated he had governed himself in making suggestions was precisely the one on which I should proceed in revising the sermon, * * * and that I was happy to find that I could adopt most of his suggestions; but some of them, and they among those, probably, which he would consider most important, I must, on the same principle, reject. * * * And now I hope you will like this, and all that I have done. It cost me an immense deal of trouble especially to find and verify your quotations, to which you had left no manner of clew. Had I had the same to do for any body I loved less than my *dearly beloved* brother Dr. Beecher, my patience would have been exhausted."

In commenting on the above sermon in his third letter to Dr.

Beecher in the Spirit of the Pilgrims for January, 1833, Dr. Woods observes at the outset, "Between your views and mine on the subject of man's *ability* and *inability* there is not, so far as I can judge, any real disagreement. You do, indeed, sometimes use language different from that which I am accustomed to use; but when you come to explain your language, * * you show that you have a meaning which I can fully adopt."

"It is not my design," he adds, "to controvert any of the positions which you lay down on the subject of *ability* and *inability*. Putting a candid and fair construction on your language, and considering you as agreeing with those excellent authors to whom you refer with approbation, I am satisfied, as I have before said, that there is no material difference between your opinions and mine on this subject. My remarks, therefore, will relate chiefly, if not wholly, to *modes of expression*."

Accordingly, toward the close of the article he observes, "The free remarks which I have been making" (about twenty pages) "have, as you have seen, related *to the use of terms* where, according to the supposition, there is no real difference of opinion." *

* The sermon whose history is here given is one of those on which Dr. Wilson subsequently founded the charge of heresy.

XXVII

FIRST IMPRESSIONS

CINCINNATI was laid out when Dr. Beecher was a schoolboy of fourteen. At his settlement at East Hampton, the Queen City contained about five hundred inhabitants, which, on his removal to Litchfield, had increased to twenty-five hundred. Ohio was then, to the New England imagination, at a vast distance, and the sight of an occasional emigrant's wagon excited a feeling as for those going out of the world. How impressive the thought of a mighty city, and mightier state, growing up in a man's lifetime, to become the scene of his most arduous exertions! When Dr. Beecher first visited the city, previous to moving his family, there were two colleges, twenty-three churches, and some fifty-three common schools, besides various other public institutions. Already pioneer life was forgotten, or remembered only as a dream. The following letter describes some of the first impressions received during the visit above mentioned:

CATHARINE TO HARRIET.

"Cincinnati, April 17, 1832.

"Here we are at last at our journey's end, alive and well. We are staying with Uncle S——, whose establishment I shall try to sketch for you. It is on a height in the upper part of the city,* and commands a fine view of the whole of the lower town, the river, and the towns and hills on the opposite bank. There is a main building, occupied by Uncle S——, and two wings, by two intimate friends, one of whom is an old Litchfield acquaintance of mine, and his wife one of my early playmates. Uncle John lives two squares off, in a pleasant situation.

"The city does not impress you as being so very new. It is true every thing looks neat and clean, but it is compact, and a great number of the houses are of brick, and very handsomely built. The streets run at right angles to each other, and are quite wide and well paved.

* The city stands partly on the first and partly on the second bank of the river, the upper part being fifty feet above the lower.

"We reached here in three days from Wheeling, and soon felt ourselves at home. The next day father and I, with three gentlemen, walked out to Walnut Hills. The country around the city consists of a constant succession and variety of hills of all shapes and sizes, forming an extensive amphitheatre. The site of the seminary is very beautiful and picturesque, though I was disappointed to find that both river and city are hidden by intervening hills. I never saw a place so capable of being rendered a Paradise by the improvements of taste as the environs of this city. Walnut Hills are so elevated and cool that people have to come away to be sick and die, it is said. The seminary is located on a farm of one hundred and twenty acres of fine land, with fine groves of trees around it, about two miles from the city.

"It seems to me that every body I used to know is here, or coming here. Besides my two uncles, there is Ned. King, an old Litchfield beau, and mother's own cousin, now General King; Cousin E. Tuthill; Abraham Chittenden's family, from Guilford; Mrs. James Butler, from Litchfield; Mr. and Mrs. Brigham, with whom we used to board at Dr. Strong's, and divers others, whom I recognize as old acquaintances.

"I think a very pleasant society can be selected from the variety which is assembled here. Yesterday father preached in the morning and in the evening to crowded houses, and to great acceptance, as I should judge. * * * In regard to father's removal, I feel, as I have long done, that it will take place, and, so far as I can judge, he feels much more settled in his own mind than he did when he left. The healthiness of the location has removed the greatest cause of apprehension from his mind."

May 2. "Father, and Mary F——, and I have made divers peregrinations on horseback and on foot, and I am delighted daily with the beautiful country that environs this place. We have finally decided on the spot where our house shall stand in case we decide to come, and you can not (where running water or the sea-shore is wanting) find another more delightful spot for a residence. It is on an eminence, with a grove running up from the back to the very doors, and another grove across the street in front, and fine openings through which distant hills and the richest landscape appears. * * *

"I have become somewhat acquainted with those ladies we shall have the most to do with, and find them intelligent, New England sort of folks. Indeed, this is a New England city in all its habits, and its inhabitants are more than half from New England. The

Second Church, which is the best in the city, will give father a unanimous call to be their minister, with the understanding that he is to give them what time he can spare from the theological seminary.

"I know of no place in the world where there is so fair a prospect of finding every thing that makes social and domestic life pleasant. Uncle John and Samuel are just the intelligent, sociable, free, and hospitable sort of folk that every body likes and every body feels at home with.

"The folks here are very anxious to have a school on our plan set on foot here. * * * They have fine rooms in the city college building, which is now unoccupied, and every body ready to lend a helping hand. * * *

"As to father, I never saw such a field of usefulness and influence as is offered to him here. I see no difficulties or objections; every thing is ready, and every body gives a welcome except Dr. Wilson's folks, and they are finding that it is wisest and best to be still, and we hope that before a great while they will be *friendly*. Father is determined to get acquainted with Dr. Wilson, and to be *friendly* with him, and I think he will succeed."

XXVIII

THE DECISION

Dr. Beecher, as has already been seen, never left a Church without arguing the case thoroughly. In the present instance his argument to his people was unusually elaborate, from the magnitude of the interests involved. Before, however, addressing the Church and society, there was a higher and more solemn appeal to be made, which, we are thankful to find, has been preserved, and is as follows:

"And now, O Lord my God, whom I have served from my youth in the ministry of Thy Son, and whose favor, given to me in the eyes of men, with opportunities to do good, and success in the attempt, has been as undeserved as it was unexpected; since Thou who didst give me being, and call me to the ministry, and hast in times past summoned me from one station to another of increasing responsibility, through all of which Thou hast sustained me, and granted me the desire of my heart beyond what I asked or thought, dost now call me to undertake duties still more responsible and difficult, what am I that I should distrust Thy sufficiency, or fear to confide in Thy protection and support, or withhold from Thy cause whatever may remain of my more experienced and matured powers? I give them all, O my glorious God and Savior, unto Thee in this great work, for which Thou, and only Thou, canst strengthen me.

"Thou knowest the burning desire of my heart for the West long before Thy voice said to me, Go and fulfill thy desires, and the burden of my soul for the millions of my perishing countrymen are not hid from Thee. To my tears Thou hast been a witness; and my great heaviness and continual sorrow, which can not be uttered, for my country and for this whole most miserable world, Thou, Lord, knowest.

"And now, if there be any thing which by living I can do, or by dying I can do, to mitigate on earth the miseries of sin, and to save my country, and to save the world, then speak, Lord, for Thy servant heareth.

"I do, therefore, now consecrate myself to Thee, O Lord, my Savior and my God, in the service to which Thou hast called me, to assist in raising up the foundations of Thy kingdom in the West. I *accept* in Thy sight, and for Thy sake and Thy kingdom, the call to the Lane Seminary and the call to the Church in Cincinnati, which Thou hast purchased by Thy blood; and I resign to Thee the Church and people which Thou hast given me, who are ineffably dear to me; and this city, the scene of arduous conflicts in high places, where Thou hast guided, sustained, and defended me; and this vicinity, more and more distant, to which it has been Thy good pleasure that my influence should extend; all these churches, the care of which I have felt, and some of which have arisen by my instrumentality; and all those ministers whom I have loved, and who have loved and aided me; and especially my most dearly beloved brethren in the ministry with whom I have seen eye to eye, and with whom so often in such perils, and difficulties, and conflicts, and labors, I have been engaged; and all the great interests of Thy kingdom which Thou hast committed to us, and for the time maintained by us — Lord, at Thy bidding, I resign them all to Thy care and keeping.

"Thou knowest that I would willingly stay and finish here the work Thou gavest me to do, and Thou knowest I am willing to leave all and serve thee at the West, if it be Thy will. If I have misunderstood Thy voice and my duty, Thou seest my honest, earnest desire to know and willingness to do Thy will, and wilt, I can not doubt, forgive my mistake. And if Thou hast called me to resign a field of such deep interest and high promise, Thou, Savior, Thou wilt not permit Thy cause to be injured here by my removal, and wilt not send me unaided and unblessed to my new field of labor.

"And now, most dear of all, I resign up to Thee, and commit to Thee, from the fullness of a heart overflowing with love, one of the most affectionate and desirable churches and congregations with which it has pleased Thee to bless an unworthy servant of Thine, who have been to me, and are, next to Thyself, and Thy great, dear cause, and my own family, dearer than all which I possess on the earth. O save them, build them up, prosper them, and magnify still in them and by them the riches of Thy grace! Amen."

EXTRACT FROM AN ADDRESS TO THE BOWDOIN STREET CHURCH AND SOCIETY, JULY 5, 1832.

"* * * I regard my acceptance as securing the establishment and endowment of a theological seminary bearing the same relation of priority and eminence at the West which Andover holds at the East. Its location on the skirts of the central city of the West will better unite the city and seminary influence than the location of Andover has enabled it to do, though the mutual action here of the city and seminary has been great and glorious. It is a location sufficiently central and accessible for the States and four millions of population, and is connected with forty thousand miles of steam-boat navigation on the various rivers of the West.

"Though the doctrines of the Reformation and the creeds of the evangelical churches embrace, I have no doubt, all the great elementary principles of the Word of God, experience abroad and at home shows that they may be inculcated in such a manner as to be attended by no revivals and few conversions, with cold and feeble churches of Antinomian tendencies, and throwing out among them, by their repulsion, Arminianism, and heresy, and infidelity—causing error to flourish and truth to decline.

"The exigencies of our country demand seminaries, and exposition of doctrine, and preachers of such zeal and activity as guarantee, by the grace of God, the increasing effusion of his Spirit. And the question whether the first and leading seminary of the West shall be one which inculcates orthodoxy with or without revivals, is a question, in my view, of as great importance as was ever permitted a single human mind to decide. If I accept I consider the question settled that a revival seminary takes the lead, and so much and so powerfully as inevitably to give a complexion probably forever to the doctrine and revivals of that great world.

"If I look at the leadings of Providence in the direction and discipline of my own mind, I can not but perceive what seems to be some providential preparation and action for such a work. It is true that preaching has been almost my sole employment, but it has been preaching in circumstances somewhat peculiar: for the first ten years to a congregation of implicit believers in the doctrines and in revivals with which they had been greatly blessed, but in the presence of a crafty, caviling infidelity, which had led away nearly the whole youthful generation of young men, the greater portion of whom I left members of the Church, and nearly every one rescued from infidelity and settled in the doctrines of the Gospel; the next sixteen years in a field where my predecessor had pushed the points of unexplained hyper-Calvinism to the confines of Antinomianism, and had thrown off some to Arminianism, and embodied others in a band of half doubting, half believing chafed murmurers and complainers, all of whom became convinced of the truth — most of whom, during my ministry or since, have become members of the Church; and the last six in explaining and vindicating the same system, where, to a fearful extent, all definite belief in the Bible and its doctrines had ceased, and where all the great elements of moral government and all efficient sense of accountability had passed away, and, if I may trust my own observation or the testimony of others, not without some marked indications of a public sentiment formed and forming, and returning, with a decided movement, to the Bible, and its doctrines and institutions.

"The result has been that although I have never been immured with books in my study, or occupied as a disputant in theological controversy, my mind has been constantly employed and disciplined in the exposition, for popular apprehension, vindication, and application for saving purposes, of the great doctrines of the Reformation; and when I look back and perceive that one third of my public ministry has been occupied in the labors of revivals among my own people, I have dared to hope that in my mode of explaining and applying the doctrines of the Bible I have not been unguided by the Spirit, and so confess that the call now made upon me in providence to attempt to write upon the mind and heart of a generation of ministers the results of my somewhat extended experience, which in no other form can be embodied and left for use, leads me to inquire seriously whether He who sees the end from the beginning may not have been preparing me for the self-same thing by the unusual vicissitudes of my ministry.

"Whether I am qualified to do it or not, I am well convinced that the peace and power of the Church demands nothing so imperiously as a ministry inspired with *zeal*, enlarged by comprehensive views, blessed with a discriminating intellect, and an acute but animated and popular argumentation, untrammeled by reading written polished sermons, and able, with a clear mind and full heart, to look saint and sinner in the face with an eye that speaks, and a hand that energizes, and a heart that overflows, and words that burn; competent and disposed, under the guidance of the wisdom which is from above, to convince gainsayers, allay fears, soothe prejudice, inspire confidence and co-operation in revivals and public charities, and all good things on the part of all, of every name, who substantially hold fast the truth, and love our Lord Jesus Christ in sincerity. * * *

"You are not to suppose that I have come to a conclusion without a minute, extensive, and careful examination of the arguments against a removal, pursued with a deep sense of their importance, and with great anxiety, and uncertainty, and suspense, and distress of mind in respect to the path of duty, as being undiscernible and shut up. * * *

"The appearance of a controversial division which threatens New England has not escaped my observation or failed to alarm my fears, and there have been times when it has almost decided my mind that I must stay, and here contend earnestly for the faith once delivered to the saints. But I have come to the conclusion fully that, though there are shades of difference among ministers, they respect circumstantials and not fundamentals, are amplified by misapprehension and alarm, are not inconsistent with the blessing of God in revivals on either side, respect rather the order and proportion of truth than any material difference in practice, which time, and patience, and public sentiment, and, if need be, the Associations, by careful examinations in individual cases, will rectify; while a petulant, exasperating controversy would serve only to drive excess to greater excess, and disproportions to more hurtful extremes.

"And when I see the cause of temperance, and missions, and revivals all moving the right way, and such dark clouds dispelled as just now threatened earthquake, fire, and storm over a large portion of the Church, and see the tears flow, and hear the song, 'Blest be the tie that binds,' sung at the close of the most stormy session of a great ecclesiastical body ever experienced, I can not believe that God intends to give the ministers of New England up to the infatuated madness and folly of rushing into an angry controversy; and if they should do it, I could not perceive it to be my duty to remain and wear out my strength and spirit in contending with good men after the Holy Spirit had left us, and the voice from the West still rose above the din of battle crying Come over and help us.

"Against the enemies of the Lord I can lift up the spear with good will, but with the friends of Jesus Christ I can not find it in my heart to enter into controversy. No, I can not, I can not do it!"

XXIX

THE JOURNEY

HARRIET TO MRS. P——.

"October 6, 1832.

"WELL, my dear, the great sheet is out and the letter is begun. All our family are here (in New York), and in good health. The only noticeable event to-day was a call from Zillah (of East Hampton memory). She looks quite as usual; voice soft as ever; is keeping house with Violet, in very comfortable circumstances. I should be very glad if I were quite sure that I filled up my chink in this mortal life as well as she does.

"I forgot to tell you that we are staying at Mr. Henry Tallmadge's, son of our good colonel. Mother and her tribe are at Mr. T——'s. Father is to perform to-night in the Chatham Theatre, 'positively for the *last* time this season.' I don't know, I'm sure, as we shall ever get to Pittsburg. Father is staying here begging money for the Biblical Literature professorship; the incumbent is to be C. Stowe. He called yesterday on S. Van Rensselaer,[1] and made such representations as induced him to subscribe a thousand dollars on the spot. They had really quite an affecting time, by all accounts; but, as I can not tell you as father told us, you must lose it. How long we are to stay here nobody knows. Father says we are in the hands of Providence; but mother and Aunt Esther seem to demur, and think they should rather trust Providence by the way.

"*Monday morning*. Last night we had a call from Arthur Tappan and Mr. Eastman. Father begged $2000 yesterday, and now the good people are praying him to abide certain days, as he succeeds so well. They are talking of sending us off and keeping him here. I really dare not go and see Aunt Esther and mother now; they were in the depths of tribulation before at staying so long, and now

"In the lowest depth, *another* deep!

[1] Stephen Van Rensselaer (1764–1839), landowner, reformer, member of Congress (1822–1829).

Father has been this morning in high spirits. He is all in his own element — dipping into books — consulting authorities for his oration — going around here, there, and every where — begging, borrowing, and spoiling the Egyptians — delighted with past success, and confident for the future."

"*Philadelphia, October* 18. Well, we did get away from New York at last, but it was through much tribulation. The truckman carried all the family baggage to the wrong wharf, and, after waiting and waiting on board the boat, we were obliged to start without it, George remaining to look it up. Arrived here late Saturday evening — dull, drizzling weather — poor Aunt Esther in dismay — not a clean cap to put on — mother in like state — all of us destitute. We went half to Dr. Skinner's and half to Mrs. Elmes's — mother, Aunt Esther, father, and James to the former; Kate, Bella, and myself to Mr. Elmes's. They are rich, hospitable folks, and act the part of Gaius in apostolic times.

"Our trunks came this morning. Father stood and saw them all brought into Dr. Skinner's entry, and then he swung his hat and gave a 'hurrah,' as any man would whose wife had not had a clean cap or ruffle for a week. Father does not succeed very well in opening purses here. Mr. Eastman says, however, that this is not of much consequence. I saw to-day a notice in the Philadelphian about father, setting forth how 'this distinguished brother, with his large family, having torn themselves from the endearing scenes of their home,' etc., etc., 'were going, like Jacob,' etc. — a very scriptural and appropriate flourish. I do hate this way of speaking of *Christian* people. It is too much after the manner of men, or, as Paul says, speaking 'as a fool.' A number of the pious people of this city are coming here this evening to hold a prayer-meeting with reference to the journey and its object — for *this* I thank them."

"*Downingtown, Pa., October* 19. Here we all are — Noah, and his wife, and his sons, and his daughters, with the cattle and creeping things, all dropped down in the front parlor of this tavern, about thirty miles from Philadelphia. If to-day is a fair specimen of our journey, it will be very pleasant — obliging driver, good roads, good spirits, good dinner, fine scenery, and now and then some 'psalms, and hymns, and spiritual songs,' for with George on board you may be sure of music of some kind. Moreover, George has provided himself with a quantity of tracts, and he and the children have kept up a regular discharge at all the wayfaring people we encountered. I tell him he is *peppering* the land with moral influence."

"*Harrisburg, Sunday evening.* Mother, Aunt Esther, George, and the little folks have just gathered into Kate's room, and we have just been singing. Father has gone to preach for Mr. De Witt. To-morrow we expect to travel sixty-two miles, and in two more days shall reach Wheeling; there we shall take the steam-boat to Cincinnati."

(*From a letter by George.*) "We had poor horses in crossing the mountains. Our average rate for the last four days to Wheeling was forty-four miles. The journey which takes the mail-stage forty-eight hours, took us eight days. At Wheeling we deliberated long whether to go on board a boat for Cincinnati, but the prevalence of the cholera there at last decided us to remain. While at Wheeling father preached eleven times — nearly every evening — and gave them the Taylorite heresy on sin and decrees to the highest notch; and what amused me most was to hear him establish it from the Confession of Faith. It went high and dry, however, above all objections, and they were delighted with it, even the strong Old School men, since it had not been christened heresy in their hearing. After remaining in Wheeling eight days, we chartered a stage for Cincinnati, and started next morning. At Granville, Ohio, we were invited to stop and attend a protracted meeting. Being in no great hurry to enter Cincinnati till the cholera had left, we consented. We spent the remainder of the week there, and I preached five times and father four. The interest was increasingly deep and solemn each day, and when we left there were forty-five cases of conversion in the town, besides those from the surrounding towns. The people were astonished at the doctrine; said they never saw the truth so plain in their lives.

"One young man, an Andover student, preached on the Sabbath, and his sermon was all confusion — sometimes directing to repent, and sometimes to read and pray, in order to prepare for repentance. After meeting father undertook to set him right, and show him how God could be sincere in his offers, and desire men all to comply with them. He said he had noticed that I spoke with a degree of strength and confidence of God's sincerity which he could not use, though he desired to do so. When he had the way pointed out it seemed like letting in light on a blind eye. He took the fundamental principles of moral government and free agency, and will, I trust, work his way out. Father said it was a shame that Dr. Woods should send out a young man with his mind bewildered and dark, and that he should have to come out into the midst of Ohio to set him right.

"From Granville we went to Columbus over corduroy roads, made of logs laid crosswise, for the benefit of dyspeptics.

"We arrived safely at Cincinnati November 14th, and found our furniture had arrived the day before, so we were soon settled in our new habitation."

XXX

SKIRMISHING

AUTOBIOGRAPHY.

When Vail went back to Cincinnati after seeing me the first time, he gave a favorable report, that I would probably come after the Bowdoin Street Church was finished. He was sanguine, and knew how to elaborate a thing and make it look grand. There happened to be a camp-meeting somewhere in the neighborhood, and Dr. Wilson was attending it. Wilson had been a good camp-meeting man, and was to all intents a good New School man enough; had revivals, in which many were brought in. He looked at the seminary at first as a local matter; he did not think or care about its relations to the great ecclesiastical campaign. If I could have got there a little sooner I should have got hold of him, I have no doubt, and they could not have influenced him.

Well, when Vail got home, he went out to camp-meeting, and told Wilson, in his way, that I should probably come. Wilson clapped his hands and shouted "Glory to God in the highest!"

But before I left Boston I found he had veered about. There had been some talk in the General Assembly some years before about a theological seminary at the West. Some wanted it at Cincinnati, and some up river near Pittsburg. The Assembly favored the latter site, and disappointed Cincinnati, and they had not swallowed it comfortably. The Pittsburg concern was a small affair, and a little too near Princeton; they had rather kept it down. I suppose the Princeton men had always *meant* to have one at Cincinnati when they got ready; but now, when they found it was going to be a New School affair, they vowed it should never be. All their plans would be blown up, and a mighty power exerted against them. I heard what they said. Dr. Alexander, a noble good man, saw at once that their chance was lost as to taking the ground they had supposed reserved for them, and that it would be bringing forward a system different from theirs, viz., a Congregationalized Presbyterianism.

So they wrote to Wilson a flattering letter, explaining the whole campaign, and predicting what the results would be, and attacking us as New England men, and sent a man out on purpose. I had it from Wilson's own mouth in the General Assembly that he had been accustomed to consult his particular friends at Princeton and in the Pittsburg Synod, and as it was their wish he should take back his invitation to me, he did so. (By the way, they made him next moderator after he was beat. That was a scampy concern, that Old School General Assembly, and is still; they always pay their folks when they do their business for them.)

Well, Wilson turned square round. He was the leading man in the region, and had some influence in the Second Church. It was understood I was to be called there, though the call was not formally made out till I arrived there. Through Wilson's influence, two of the elders wrote me a letter, saying that if I came there would be "a considerable secession from the Church." * Wilson thought it would scare me and break up the plan; but I sent a copy of the letter to the Session, and they wrote back that it was all moonshine, and I took no notice of it.

Besides that, Wilson fired off a forty-four pounder in the New York papers, warning brethren to take heed; had it read on trial. I replied by publishing parts of his own letters to me. After I reached Cincinnati and presented my credentials to the Presbytery, Wilson objected to my reception, and said he had no confidence in my doctrines. I rose and said that I was sure Dr. Wilson did not understand, and was laboring under a mistake; that I had not altered my views since he saw me years ago; and that if Presbytery would take recess and have a free conversation in the vestry, I could explain.

We all went into the vestry, and I began to speak kindly (I felt kindly) and solemnly. I saw Wilson *felt*. Something was said about prayer, when he said, with a gentle face, waving his hand to me, "You pray;" and I did so, and we had a good season. Just then the devil in a good man jumped up and said that there had never been a man of sufficient calibre to excite Dr. Wilson's jealousy but that he opposed and drove him away. Then the fat was in the fire. I was sure I should win him. I never was more chagrined. We went up, and it was pitched battle after that.

---

* The letter is dated June 16, 1832. The writers say, "Your opinions respecting many of the radical things of Jesus Christ, and your modes of philosophizing about these things, are so variant from our solemn convictions of what the *truth* as it is in Jesus is, that we must, in all good conscience before God, enter our deliberate and prayerful dissent to your ministry among us."

The following extract of a letter to Dr. Wisner, dated January 8, 1833, takes up the narrative at this point:

"Dr. Wilson has met me with gauntlet and glaive in *limine*. Dr. Spring, you know, obtained a censure by Synod of the Third Presbytery for receiving me by letter. Of this Dr. Wilson had been apprised, but not in authenticated ecclesiastical form. He was moderator, and therefore could not speak; and there was no minority, and therefore there was no one to protest and to complain of my irregular reception. Last week, at another meeting of Presbytery, he brought forward a resolution to appoint a committee to investigate the reports of my unsoundness in the faith, which, as he said, were long, and loud, and uncontradicted.

"This was on Friday evening, when his preparatory lecture was appointed; but just as we were about to adjourn, so eager was he in the chase of the heretic that he gave up the lecture, and yet too late to prevent the assembling of his congregation and many others who had heard the rumor of what was going on. Several of my friends did me ample justice, to whom at length Dr. Wilson replied, on a motion for indefinite postponement.

"Peaceable as you know me to be, and reluctant to contend, yet, finding myself taken by the horns, I began to think it time to take care of myself, and of the cause as assailed through me; and, though with short notice, was able to arrange my defense and argument to my mind. I denied that there was any evidence of common fame against me, and insisted that there was just the contrary. I showed that common fame did not mean the representations of theological parties and partisan editors; if it did, the whole Church was liable to a process of inquiry. As to public sentiment in my favor, I referred to my credentials from Suffolk North, from the Third Presbytery of New York, Dr. Woods's approbation of my creed, Dr. Miller's letter, Dr. Green, who said that doubtless I belonged to one department of the Calvinistic denomination; the Second Church here, who were competent judges; and last, not least, I referred to Dr. Wilson himself, who united in giving me a call, and an argument and urgent entreaty that I would accept.

"By this I cut him down to the evidence he had since discovered. I insisted, however, that the entire course of appealing to *fame*, through partisan papers, was uncourtly, unauthorized, and unchristian, when I was myself on the ground, and had offered and sought opportunities more than once for explanation. I again offered to answer him any question he wished to ask; gave him and any member of Presbytery liberty to catechise me as much as they pleased; told them my heresy was of more than thirty years standing, and of common use in all the revivals I had witnessed, and of constant Sabbath-day occurrence; let those who are jealous come and hear. I am preaching heresy, if I am a heretic, three times a day every Sabbath, and two or three times a week, and teaching it twice a week at the seminary. Why appoint a committee of inquiry? You might as well appoint a committee to ladle up water from the Ohio to water the earth when showers are falling in torrents.

"I was able to keep down all improper feeling; treated him politely and kindly; gave him credit for honesty; but every concession contrasted with his treatment of me burnt like coals of juniper. In closing I expostulated with Dr. Wilson affectionately; stated the rising prospects of a revival in the churches, and conjured him to desist till I had furnished some better evidence of heresy than rumor, or afforded him conclusive evidence of my orthodoxy, which I had not a single doubt I should ere long be able to do.

"I spoke an hour about as well as I could desire, and the verdict of public sentiment is as adverse to him and favorable to me as I could wish. He has appealed to Synod, including items, thus giving me a more extended opportunity to defend myself and put down rumor and slang."

The result of the appeal is thus described by Dr. Beecher in conversation:

"As it happened, Synod met at Cincinnati the very day my society had appointed to visit me in expression of welcome. I, of course, was occupied, and did not think of Synod, till suddenly I was sent for by a messenger. I had no time to prepare. Wilson was speaking when I got there, and I heard the main part of his argument. I rose and made an offhand reply, as keen as ever I did, as good as I wanted. Synod decided in my favor by a large majority.

"From Synod Wilson appealed to General Assembly; but they sent him back with a flea in his ear; told him if he had any case to take it up himself. He had tried to make Presbytery take it up first on common fame, and next to appoint a committee to examine my printed sermons and report. He wanted *them* to prosecute. He did not want to assume the responsibility of tabling charges himself. But that Assembly (1834) happened to be very strong New School, and they would have nothing to do with him." *

---

* The judicial committee cast out the appeal because Dr. Wilson was not one of the original parties.

The following account of the examination of a son of Dr. Beecher before Presbytery about this time was written by Miss Harriet E. Beecher:

"Well, you see, there has been a Presbytery holden in our good city, and all ministerial nature in 'ordinary generation,' as the Confession of Faith says, have been coming to our house; therefore we are in a state of — of — what shall I say? Not fighting, because *we* don't fight; but the Old School, headed by Dr. Wilson, have made a dead set this Presbytery, and are defeated — entirely so. I am glad to say, too, that, so far as I have seen, there has been very little exhibition of any unchristian or ungentlemanly conduct, at least on the New School side.

"You never went to a Presbytery? Well, put on your bonnet, and go with me and Mrs. Stowe * this afternoon. First, though, let me introduce you to Mrs. Stowe — a delicate, pretty little woman, with hazel eyes, auburn hair, fair complexion, fine color, a pretty little mouth, fine teeth, and a most interesting simplicity and timidity of manner; I fell in love with her directly. However, let us walk on to the Second Church.

"We will go into the side aisle; all the body pews are engaged by the Presbytery. Do you see them all seated *en masse*, each one with the 'Confession of Faith' by him, to turn to at a moment's warning?

"That handsome, modest, amiable-looking young man in the chair in front of the pulpit is 'Brother Rankin,'[1] the moderator. He was an Old School man once; for a long time lately he has been wavering; this Presbytery he was nominated and appointed by the New School party, and this, together with the abuse received from the other side, has fixed him, and he is now counted on as a vote. At a table sits Brother Graves,[2] the recording secretary, with paper, pen, and ink. The meeting is not begun. Some are walking about, some talking, some reading, etc., etc.

"At last the moderator calls the meeting to order. They proceed to business. They are to examine a candidate. The candidate is Mr. George Beecher, a *New School man;* but that is not the worst — a *Taylorite!!*

* Professor Stowe first married a daughter of Dr. Tyler, whose untimely death, soon after, saddened the whole Walnut Hills circle, to which she was greatly endeared.

---

[1] Probably John Rankin (1793–1886), New School pastor in Ohio and abolitionist.

[2] Probably Frederick Graves (1806–1864), New School itinerant revivalist, who defended Lovejoy's press.

"Do you see, in the front pew, a tall, grave-looking man, of strong and rather harsh features, very pale, with a severe seriousness of face, and with great formality and precision in every turn and motion? Well, if you see him, that man is Dr. Wilson. His great ivory-headed cane leans on the side of the pew by him, and in his hand he holds the Confession of Faith.

"The candidate sits on the pulpit stairs, so that he may face the Presbytery, and the examining committee are called on: 'Dr. Wilson, in Philosophy.' Here follows, 'Mr. Beecher, what is matter and what is mind, and what is the difference 'twixt and 'tween, and what is Mechanics, and Optics, and Hydrostatics, and what is Mental Philosophy, and what is Moral Philosophy, and what is right and wrong, and what is truth, and what is virtue, and what are the powers of the mind, and what is intellect, susceptibilities, and will, and conscience'—and every thing else, world without end, amen! After this the doctor's grave face gradually relaxes into a smile, which seems like the melting of a snow-drift as he says that 'he has pursued this branch of the examination as far as might be deemed expedient.'

" 'Mr. Moderator,' says one, 'I move that the examination be sustained.' 'I second it,' says another.

"The moderator then says, 'Those who sustain this examination say Ay.'

"Now hark—'Ay! ay! ay!'

" 'Those of contrary mind, No.' No answer. So this is over.

"Next topic is now announced: 'Theology!' Now you may see the brethren bending forward, and shuffling, and looking wise. Over in the pew opposite to us are the students of the Lane Seminary, with attentive eyes. There is Theodore Weld,[3] all awake, nodding from side to side, and scarce keeping still a minute together.

" 'The examiner in Theology, Brother Gallagher.' This is the tall son of Anak whom I have written of aforetime—the great Goliath, whose awful brows and camp-meeting hymns used so to awe and edify me. He rises very leisurely, and gives a lunge forward, precipitating his unwieldy size into a chair without much regard to graceful disposition, and with a deep, deliberate voice begins.

"The beauty of it all is that Gallagher is a warm friend to George, and of similar sentiments. The appointing him to examine

[3] Theodore Weld (1803–1895), converted by Finney, became a leader of evangelical abolitionism. He was influential in persuading Tappan to endow Lane and supplied most of its first students, who were largely Finney converts.

was a friendly motion of the moderator. I wish I could give you an idea of the mingled coarseness, shrewdness, humor, and the occasional real poetic and enthusiastic feeling which are all combined in this man. When he rises to speak we all fix our mouths to laugh, as a matter of course; yet he always speaks to the purpose, though you would not think he was going to when he begins. It amused me to hear his leisurely questions on a subject where the whole house was awake. He confined his examination merely to the broad and obvious truths of Christianity, and then sat down.

"But now comes the fiery trial. The moderator announces, 'Any of the brethren have a right to question the candidate.' You must have seen before now some of them fidgeting on their seats, and waiting their turn. Then such a storm of questions rains in:

" 'Mr. Beecher, do you believe in the doctrine of election? Will you please to state your views on that subject?' 'Mr. Beecher, do you believe in the imputation of Adam's sin?' 'Mr. Beecher, do you believe infants are sinners as soon as they are born?' 'Do you believe that infants have unholy natures?' 'Do you believe that men are *able* of themselves to obey the commandments of God?' 'Mr. Beecher, do you believe men are active or passive in regeneration?' 'Mr. Beecher, do you make any distinction between regeneration and conversion?' 'Mr. Beecher, do you think that men are punished for the guilt of Adam's first sin?' 'Do you believe in imputed righteousness?'

"There was George — eyes flashing and hands going, turning first to right and then to left — 'If I understand your question, sir —' 'I do not understand your terms, sir.' 'Do you mean by *nature* thus and so? or so?' 'In what sense do you use the word imputation?' 'I don't exactly understand you, sir.' 'Yes, sir' (to right). 'No, sir' (to left). 'I should think so, sir' (in front).

"So far I wrote when I heard George, and father, and Edward coming in from meeting; for Edward is with us — poked in like a ghost upon us one day just after George's examination. The first that father knew of the matter was seeing him go by the window, and exclaiming, 'There's a man looks like Edward!' and the next minute we were all electrified by seeing him standing among us. To-night, Edward, and Professor Sturtevant,[4] father, and George, have been holding a long chat. At last father and Edward went

[4] Julien Sturtevant (1805–1896), student of Taylor, member of the Illinois Yale Band, which was a group (formed in 1828) of Yale students who pledged themselves to devote their lives to furthering religion and education in the West. He opposed sectarianism and advocated the New Divinity. He taught in Illinois College, of which Edward Beecher was president, and became president himself in 1844.

down cellar to saw wood. Don't that seem natural! I heard the word 'foreordination' through the parlor floor, so I knew what they were talking about. I have come up and left them. Our hearts are warmed and comforted to see dear Edward again, seeming so well and happy too. Oh, it seems like old times, and I am really happy — only a little tired. But, oh dear! he is going away. I wish he could stay a month. I'll tell you more about all to-morrow.

"Now to finish the account of Presbytery. The examination lasted nearly two hours and a half, after which the farther consideration of that subject was postponed till examination had taken place in other branches. The next day the Presbytery were called upon to see if they had any remarks to make upon the examination thus far. Then such a war of words!

"The way of proceeding is to call over the names of the whole Presbytery in order, and each one, when his name is called, has the liberty of rising and speaking as long as he will. The whole day was taken up in this way. I went only in the afternoon, and what I heard was (apart from *moral* considerations) sufficiently diverting.

"There are men — one or two, I mean — whose minds have been brought up in a catechetical tread-mill — who never say 'Confession of Faith' without taking off their hats, and who have altogether the appearance of thinking that the Bible is the *next best book* to the Catechism. These men are, of course, mortally afraid of heresy — or '*hear say*,' as an old woman very pertinently pronounced it — and their remarks on this subject were truly lucid.

"One of them got up, and, in the course of his objections, said, with a peculiar solemnity of manner, that 'he did not wish to prejudice any one against the candidate, but, sir, if I understand him, he holds that God has no right to require men to do what they are not able to do. Now, sir, this is an awful error. If God had not a right to require things of men which they have no ability whatever to perform, what dreadful consequences would ensue! Oh,' said he, rolling up his eyes, 'they are awful! I will not even name them!'

"Here I met Aunt Esther's eye, and we, I am afraid, indulged in a very unsuitable degree of merriment. This gentleman spoke an hour in a style of remark equally edifying. For my part, as I am philosophical in my taste, and like to see every kind of mental development, I was not sorry to hear and see personally so strange a phenomenon. But my Beecher blood *boiled* when I was told that he and one or two others in the Presbytery had actually been preaching such broad nonsense for many years. I really did not think that any human mind could be so ground down — at least I never realized it before.

"The discussion, as I have said, lasted all day. In the evening we came, and they went at it again. There was quite an audience in the house, as preaching had been expected. All the Presbytery had finished their remarks except father and Dr. Wilson, who, as the oldest, came last on the list. Father, as first called on, rose, and went through a regular statement of what he conceived to be the views expressed by the candidate, and a regular argument to show that they were in agreement with the Confession of Faith. He spoke well, clearly, and persuasively, and was occasionally a little humorous. He began by saying that it was his belief that, however they might differ in points of opinion, they were all honest, well-intentioned men. 'We are honest!' (bringing down his fist). But then he said that there were some dangers in this meeting together in Presbytery; that ministers were so much accustomed to command the *whole ship* at home that they did not always feel exactly tractable in a Presbytery; 'and I hope,' said he, 'that, for the future, our elders will take better care of us' (here a general smile went round among the elders).

"Toward the close of the speech he said that, if the case should be carried up to the Synod, he should be prepared to prove even more fully many points; 'and in that case,' said he, bringing down his forefinger, 'I shall think myself *happy*, King Agrippa, to speak more fully of this matter.' He also insinuated that if Presbyteries, and Synods, and all the legislative bodies should turn out and reject all who held those sentiments, that they could not stop their progress. 'No,' said he, 'we shall still live; we shall stand on God's earth, and breathe his air, and preach his Gospel as *we* believe it.'

"When father sat down Dr. Wilson rose up, and made a speech of about half an hour, in which he stated that he believed that the candidate was not a Christian, and knew nothing experimentally about Christianity, and that he firmly believed that he, and all those who held the same sentiments with him, 'would never see the gates of eternal bliss.'

"This was abundantly courteous for Dr. Wilson, since he merely shut us out of heaven this time without pronouncing sentence any more definitely. Many people say that it is altogether the mildest and most temperate speech they ever heard him make.

After this speech the question was taken, though with much difficulty and opposition; and on calling the roll, the examination was sustained by a majority of twenty-three. About twelve o'clock at night we found ourselves once more at home and in a state of high excitement, and sat up about half an hour longer to fight over the battle to Catharine, who had not been able to go out."

XXXI

GETTING UNDER WAY

Dr. Beecher was inducted into office as Professor of Theology, December 26, 1832. At first he resided in the city, the house designed for him not having been yet built. He was thus obliged to ride out from time to time, to deliver lectures in the seminary. His installation as pastor of the Second Church took place in the spring of 1833.

Of this earlier phase of his Western life our best impressions are derived from his correspondence. To Dr. Wisner, January 8, 1833, he writes as follows: "It would require a volume to describe all the points which I have been called to reconnoitre and secure, one after another, in that process of taking possession of the public mind by the right handle which every man, with whatever age and acquired character, must study and regard.

" * * * By my people of the Second Church my reception has been, in the way of cordiality and kindness, all I could desire, not excepting those two elders, who wrote to me in Boston, threatening that they and some sixty members would leave the Church if I should come. These are now my right-hand men, and are going round with me to introduce me to the families of the congregation. Both good men, contented and cordial. They concluded to hear for themselves before they went, and, 'ere they were aware of it,' as Dr. Spring wrote to Dr. Green, 'the artful man had brought them over.' The congregation is also filling up, like the Bowdoin Street Church, with young men, and the intellectual class of persons, who, disgusted alike with Old Calvinism and Methodism, were going to the Unitarian Church or nowhere. * * *

"Every thing here confirms the justice of my opinion as to the necessity of some one to lay foundations and organize. Good materials are plenty, but no efficiency, from utter unacquaintance with systematic action. It is but two weeks since I got a pastoral meeting, in which we accomplished, I doubt not, results which years had not reached without, and the second was like unto it. One thing we resolved on was a united monthly concert of the three churches, Second, Third, and Sixth.

"There have been good appearances in my Church, and Gallagher's, and Mahan's for some time, but yesterday was among the most precious. The feeling commenced auspiciously, and rose all day. The monthly concert, the first public united concert ever held in Cincinnati, was full, solemn, and deeply interesting. I gave a history of the origin, progress, character, and success of the society, and wound the thing up to as high a point of interest as I have ever been able to do. The ministers, I rejoiced to perceive, were all electrified with double zeal, and predicted the happiest results, saying with astonishment, as they looked over the house well filled, 'We never saw it thus in Cincinnati.' Until now I have been tugging hard to get the wave in motion. Now I am just beginning to feel its power and be helped by it.

"Things in my society could not be more pleasant and promising than they are. They have given up a little vestry which did not use to be half full, and are finishing off, in good style, a spacious one, which will hold five hundred persons. Every Thursday night it has been filling up, and is now nearly full, and the preaching of the closest revival cast, and the meetings, in appearance, are revival meetings, though no results have broken out as yet. * * *

"I rejoice in your returning health and establishment, in the settlement of Linsley,[1] and in what I hear of Pine Street and my own dear people as being prosperous, there being nothing in the wide world I could not better endure than their calamity, and decline, and imbecility. Were it necessary to avert *that*, it seems to me I should tear myself up by the roots once more and fly back to save them."

Among his reminiscences of this period are the following: "I considered that to take a man out of the ministry to make him a professor, without a congregation to keep him up by revival work he would run down spiritually, as they do here * and every where else. It would have been so with me if I had had nothing to do but to con over my lectures, so I took up the full responsibility of pastoral duty, as if I had had nothing else to do. But, living three miles out, it was a natural impossibility to have those close and intimate relations that exist when a pastor lives among his flock. A number of the members of my congregation were men of wealth and capacity. Judge Burnet [2] was one of the prominent actors in

* These reminiscences were collected at Andover.

[1] John Linsley (1790–1868), pastor at the Park St. Church (1832–1835), was later president of Marietta College, Ohio.

[2] Jacob Burnet (1770–1853), head of the legislative council for the Northwest Territory in 1798, became a judge of the Supreme Court of Ohio in 1821.

the early history of the West. Then there was N. Wright, Henry Starr, Timothy Goodman, Mr. Groesbeck, Dr. Mussey — able men in all respects, property, intelligence, and influence.[3]

"I began to preach as I would in any other place that was new. Never preached more carefully and thoroughly. Did all a man could, and not in vain. The house filled up rapidly. I preached for a revival. Fifteen were converted early. There were signs of a work; I expected a great revival; but, after a few conversions, it faltered and stopped. I did not know what was the matter. The fact was, there were none in the Church who knew how to lead out, and watch, and follow up the work; and, as I was living so far out, the work languished."

In a letter dated June, 1834, allusion is made to this fact, as follows: "This has been the most difficult and slowest point of attainment. But God, blessed be his name! has granted it to me. About sixty, and among them the most influential of the congregation or in the city, and including among them a band of invaluable young men and females, have been added to the Church; and, since the revival, the whole Church are baptized with a revival spirit, and united happily in revival enterprises; so that now, as in Boston, I am beginning to be surrounded by a host of discreet and able auxiliaries in bringing souls to Christ. The congregation have also felt the power and are now under a strong pressure of evangelical influence which promises most hopeful results; so that in the Second Church, both for revivals and missions, I count that from this time to the millennium the point is gained — a citadel established and manned to last through all time."

Under date of January 28, 1833, Dr. Beecher writes to Dr. Wisner as follows: "Last evening I received my long-expected sermon.* It is all I could wish. After a long absence from my mind, I feared there might be some words or phrases which, in reference to the West, I might have preferred to alter, but I find not one. Not a word have I to add or to subtract. I am ready, as it stands, both to defend it before men and to give account of it to God.

"I know it is true and all-important, and I call upon, and exhort, and entreat you all there in Boston and New England not

* On Dependence and Free Agency.

[3] Nathaniel Wright (1817–1875) was a lawyer. Henry Starr (1790–1851), after studying theology, attended Litchfield Law School and practised law in Cincinnati, where he was noted for his frugality and benevolence. Timothy Goodman was a banker. John Groesbeck was a grocer. R. D. Mussey (1780–1866) taught surgery in Dartmouth Medical School, the Medical College of Ohio, and Miami University, and was made president of the American Medical Association in 1850.

to wrap the Sun of righteousness again in sackcloth, and bring on a suspension of divine influence, and declension of religion, and irruption of error, for some other Edwards, and Whitfield, and Tennant [4] to turn back, by yielding tamely, basely to the attempt to make the Taste scheme dominant and Old Calvinism triumphant.

"If every where in and out of New England the friends of free agency and moral government stand firm, and act with meekness, patience, and firmness, the present onset will soon be over, and probably will be the last which the devil will ever be able to make by the instrumentality of pious and orthodox ministers of Christ. I have had some fear that in Connecticut, some of the more prudent, wearied with noise, and tempted by the delusive hopes of peace, might consent to the removal of Taylor for some one less offensive, but that must not be done. Whether perfect or not in all his speculations, or most wise and prudent or not, he has done too much for the cause of truth and suffered too much to be abandoned, and is too deeply identified with truth and revivals to be given up as an instructor. It would be a victory of Old Schoolism, even though a moderate New School man should succeed, and Connecticut had better contend half a century than to strike in respect to the point in controversy and flinch. It would be the signal of new demands, and innovations, and contentions, and defeats.

"You may show these thoughts to any to whom it is safe, and to none other. But you must keep your eye and ear open; and though openly you need not act, yet you must not cease to feel the responsibility of consultation with Skinner and others, and keeping the right plans of action in train and efficient execution. *You* must, as I did, keep a general eye open, and act upon all movements, and touch the springs requisite to produce consultation and action.

"We are all better except George, who is gaining, after a temporary indisposition. My own health, which only faltered, is becoming good. For four Sabbaths in succession I have preached three times a day, and things here are all apparently moving the right way. If you see the Standard, it is needless to say that I did not say, as there represented, that every man has a right to his own explanation of the Confession of Faith. I said, We do not swallow the Confession without any knowledge of its contents, or hang it about our neck as a charm. Every man attaches to it, and

[4] Gilbert Tennant (1703–1764), revivalist in the middle colonies during the Great Awakening.

must, his *own* understanding, and no other man is a pope authorized to pronounce the exposition of his neighbor heretical. That belongs to the higher judicatories. It belongs to the General Assembly, as the ultimate resort, to expound the Confession."

From Dr. Hawes, of Hartford, Dr. Beecher was advised (September 26) of the establishment of a new seminary at East Windsor.

"Oh these angry times, these angry times! The days of peace for the Connecticut churches I fear are over. * * Week before last a meeting of ministers was held at East Windsor for the purpose of forming what is called the Pastoral Union, to be composed of those ministers in the state who will subscribe to a particular creed which is thought to be *orthodox* — in other words, opposed to New Haven divinity.

"At that meeting, as I understand, about sixty ministers were expected to be present, and thirty-six or seven actually attended. Among other things, it was determined to establish a new theological school. Trustees were appointed, and committees to carry the plan into effect. Thirteen hundred dollars were subscribed by the ministers present, five hundred of which, I am sorry to say, were subscribed by Mr. Nettleton. What this will come to I can not tell. I have been disappointed that so large a number of ministers could be found in the state who were prepared to favor such a measure.

"But, whether it succeeds or fails, the consequences will be nearly the same. A blow has been struck; a line has been drawn. By public acts it is declared by these brethren that the house is so infested with heresy that they must flee out of it. * * * I have, as you know, been anxious from the first to maintain peace with both parties; but there is no peace, and every man, for aught I see, has got to take sides."

The following extracts are from a letter of Dr. S. H. Cox,[5] April 7, 1834:

"Slavery is one of the *quæstiones vexatæ et vexantes* of the day with us — much more furiously with the people of British Europe. I am glad you are taking hold of it in your seminary, and with such light and zeal. My foreign tutoring and observation have much influenced me in all my estimates of the subject at present. I consider, since my return, the nolition of the free colored people, almost universal, to be a virtual nullification of the colonization system, if there were no other mighty objections to it. I believe

[5] Samuel Cox (1793–1881), New School pastor, active on behalf of abolition, temperance, colonization, and the Evangelical Alliance.

that God is leading the minds of millions to change *in melius* on this absorbing topic of human interests.

"Our heresy-phobia in this region is, I think, exhausting itself. Morbid in its original elements, it grows not to increasing strength, as healthy parts improve, but wanes toward extinction; or, like smouldering fire, is seen only in the smoke it sends toward heaven. I view it as little better than wickedness in its painstaking and its malignity. 'They make a man an offender for a word, and lay a snare for him that reproveth in the gate, and turn aside the just for a thing of naught.' But the time is coming, I think, when we may say, 'The terrible one is brought to naught, and the scorner is consumed, and all that watch for iniquity are cut off;' but how near, I know not, in our Church! We expect the next General Assembly to be an arena of fire; but I hope God will frustrate the purposes of the fiery, and order things obviously for the fitting peace of our Zion."

During the prevalence of cholera, Dr. Beecher writes (July 22) to Dr. Wisner: "Have rewritten and revised eight of my lectures on Political Atheism, and got six of them stereotyped. There will be some defects, I can not doubt, which your friendly aid would obviate; but standing, as I feel myself to do, on the confines of eternity, and amid the shafts of death, I thought it better to do what I could immediately than risk doing nothing by waiting to do it better. * * *

"I see Brother Rand has gathered up and poured out after me in one stream, like the water from the mouth of the dragon, all the gall and bile which he so ceaselessly spread out around me while I was in Boston. It is best to let it roll unimpeded till it enters the Styx and mingles with congenial dark waters. Brother Thatcher will get, I conclude, a streak of fat therefrom, and some dozen or more hyper-tasters and exercisers. If there is any necessity of touching it, you will let me know.

"The statement in the Standard of my disavowal of New Haven and Finney, though it contains some things I said, omits others, and is colored and distorted, and in its impression false. * * * I need not say how much my head and heart feel here the want of such a one as you to confide in and lean upon, and commune with; but most of our communion, dear brother, must be reserved for heaven."

Dr. Wisner replies: "I have seen and read Mr. Rand's letter to you, ending off his volunteer by pouring out a flood of venom after you when a thousand miles away! I don't think it will reach the mountains and rise till it pours over them and overwhelms you. I have heard many speak of it as a contemptible ebullition of spleen. It needs no answer.

"As to your statement in Presbytery about not being responsible for all Taylor has said and Finney has done, of which Mr. Rand and others have *wickedly* made so much (I say wickedly, because they must have known, as well as I did, what it amounted to), I never supposed that you said any thing more than that you were not to be held responsible for every thing they said and did; that in some things you differed from Taylor, and some things you disapproved in Finney, though in the main you agreed with the former, and thought the latter a good and useful man; and so most persons whom I have heard speak on the subject have interpreted the remark as reported by Dr. Wilson and published by his copyists. Yet some have attempted and still attempt to make a great deal of it; perhaps it may be best to deprive them of the pleasure."

XXXII

WALNUT HILLS

Dr. Beecher's residence on Walnut Hills was in many respects peculiarly pleasant. It was a two-story brick edifice of moderate dimensions, fronting the west, with a long L running back into the primeval forest, or grove, as it was familiarly called, which here came up to the very door. Immense trees — beech, black oak, and others — spread their broad arms over the back yard, affording in summer an almost impenetrable shade.

An airy veranda was built in the angle formed by the L along the entire inner surface of the house, from which, during the fierce gales of autumn and winter, we used to watch the tossing of the spectral branches, and listen to the roaring of the wind through the forest. Two or three large beeches and elms had been with difficulty saved from the inexorable woodman's axe by the intercessions of the doctor's daughter Catharine, on the visit already described, and, though often menaced as endangering the safety of the house from their great height, they still flourish in beauty.

Through that beautiful grove the doctor and two of his sons, during the three years 1834–'7, passed daily to and from the seminary buildings. A rustic gate was hung between the back yard and the grove, and the path crossed a *run* or gulley, where, for a season, an old carpenter's bench supplied the place of bridge.

In this old grove were some immense tulip-trees, so large, in some instances, that two men could scarce clasp hands around the trunk. How often has that grove echoed to the morning and evening song of the children or the students! We can hear yet, in imagination, the fine soprano of James, then a boy, executing with the precision of an instrument solfeggios and favorite melodies till the forest rang again.

In that grove, too, was a delightful resort of the young people from the city of Dr. Beecher's flock, who often came out to spend a social hour or enjoy a picnic in the woods.

The doctor's study, whose door appears in the vignette, was decidedly the best room in the house. No longer, as at Litchfield, in the attic, but on the ground floor, and the first entrance to which you came on arriving from the city. Here, from its cheerful outlook, its convenience of access, and other inviting properties, soon was established the general rendezvous. Here came the students for consultation with the president, here faculty meetings were held, and here friends from the city spent many a social hour.

On one side of the room the windows looked westward on an extensive landscape; on the opposite side, a double window, coming down to the floor, opened upon the veranda, serving in summer the double purpose of window and door; between these, on the back side, were the bookcases and sundry boxes and receptacles of MSS.; while opposite was the fireplace, with the door on the left, and a window on the right.

From said door you looked forth across the carriage-drive into a garden situated between the road and the grove, where the doctor extracted stumps and solved knotty problems in divinity at the same time, and whence the table was supplied with excellent vegetables.

A little barn was ensconced in the back part of the yard, just beyond the end of the L, under the shade of the big beech-trees, in which Charley (a most important member of the doctor's establishment) had his stable. This Charley was a white horse with chocolate-colored spots, strong, high-spirited, quick, yet gentle, kind, and intelligent, able to appreciate his master's moods, and make all due allowances for sudden jerks of the reins when the doctor was jerking an imaginary opponent, and cuts of the lash evidently bestowed on some form of error or wrong.

Like his master, too, Charley was decidedly progressive, and believed in going ahead, whether up hill or down hill, over smooth roads, or over rough pavements and through mud-holes. He thought nothing of cantering down the long hill, and, after thundering through the streets of Cincinnati on various errands, cantering gayly up again, with the old carryall swinging, and rocking, and cracking behind him.

Joint occupant with him of the little barn was a cow, of whom a little anecdote is worth relating. She had been purchased of a farmer residing two or three miles distant, and being rather wild, had led the doctor, mounted on Charley, quite a steeple-chase, twice swimming the Ohio and back again, and performing sundry other exploits of an exasperating nature. But, by infinite perseverance, the doctor had succeeded in getting her home and safely fastened in the stable, and was reposing victorious in the house. Just at this time, Henry Ward, who had been absent, and knew nothing of the new acquisition, chanced to visit the barn for some purpose, and finding, as he supposed, a strange cow, was seized with indignation.

"Why here," said he, "here's a strange cow in our barn! Get out! go along! whey!" and, suiting actions to words, he seized a whip and drove the astonished brute out into the street. "There!" said he, coming in, panting, where the doctor was lying stretched upon the sofa, "there! I guess that cow will not get in our barn again in a hurry!"

"*What* cow?" says the doctor. "What do you mean?"

"Why, I found an old cow out in our barn, and drove her out in the street, and chased her till I was tired out, and gave her a good beating."

"Well, *there!*" exclaimed the doctor, in despair; "you have done it! Here I have been chasing half the day to get that cow in, and you have gone and chased her out again!"

Other occupants of the back-yard were the poultry, who used frequently to roost in the trees, where they were occasionally subjected to nocturnal alarms, being thrown into consternation by the visit of weasel or pole-cat.

But the choir of birds, which made the grove resound, were the most favorite tenants of its leafy shelter. The richness, variety, and beauty of their song was, to a New England ear, a constant source of wonder and delight. Aunt Esther, especially, who was always fond of pets of every kind, whether furred or feathered, was never weary with listening to their concert.

The square formed by the veranda and the door-yard fence was devoted to flowers and shrubs. Roses and honeysuckles were trained up toward the upper portico, and a tall ailanthus shot up at the corner of the wing.

Of the subordinate members of the household, the department of hired help, we can not speak except to pass a momentary tribute to the mirth-provoking qualities of Dutch Charley — Charley man, who had the charge of Charley horse, and the Dutch boy John, whose jargon, mixed with that of the hired girls, one Welsh, the other Irish, afforded daily food for merriment.

During the first year of Dr. Beecher's Walnut Hills life, the care of the family was shared between Mrs. Beecher and Aunt Esther, though, as the health of the former declined, the burden of responsibility fell more and more upon the latter. The family was large, comprising, including servants, thirteen in all, besides occasional visitors.

The house was full. There was a constant high-tide of life and

RESIDENCE ON WALNUT HILLS.

RESIDENCE ON BROOKLYN HEIGHTS.

animation. The old carryall was perpetually vibrating between home and the city, and the excitement of going and coming rendered any thing like stagnation an impossibility. And if we take into account the constant occurrence of matters for consultation respecting the seminary and the students, or respecting the Church and congregation in the city, or respecting Presbytery, Synod, and General Assembly, as well as the numberless details of shopping, marketing, and mending which must be done in the city, it will be seen that at no period of his life was Dr. Beecher's mind more constantly on the stretch, exerted to the utmost tension of every fibre, and never, to use an expressive figure of Professor Stowe, did he wheel a greater number of heavily-laden wheel-barrows all at one and the same time. Had he husbanded his energies and turned them in a single channel, the mental fire might have burned steadily on till long after threescore years and ten. But this was an impossibility. Circumstances and his own constitutional temperament united to spur him on, and for more than twenty of his best years he worked under a high pressure, to use his favorite expression, to the *ne plus* — that is, to the utmost limit of physical and moral endurance.

It was an exuberant and glorious life while it lasted. The atmosphere of his household was replete with moral oxygen — full charged with intellectual electricity. Nowhere else have we felt any thing resembling or equaling it. It was a kind of moral heaven, the purity, vivacity, inspiration, and enthusiasm of which those only can appreciate who have lost it, and feel that in this world there is, there can be "no place like home."

XXXIII

STUDENT REMINISCENCES

We have seen how Lane Seminary obtained its president and professors. It remains to see how it obtained its students, and what manner of men, or "boys," as the doctor affectionately called them, they were. The following is a very imperfect and meagre outline of the narrative of one of them (Theodore D. Weld), written down soon after hearing it from his own lips:

"When I was seventeen years old, being at Phillips Academy, I endeavored to overtake the class ahead of me, which I liked better than my own, and studied so intensely that I lost the use of my eyes, and was threatened with blindness. After many weeks and months of suffering, bodily and mental, my hopes all cut off, I recollected some lectures I had heard on the science of Mnemonics, and determined to try to support myself by lecturing on that subject. I traveled through Connecticut, New York, Maryland, Virginia, and North Carolina, in this work, during the years 1822, 1823, and 1824.

"On this tour I saw slavery at home, and became a radical abolitionist. On my return, my eyes remaining almost useless, I fell in with Kirkland, of Hamilton College, New York, near Utica, where I had an uncle residing. Kirkland had suffered much himself from weak eyes, and told me he could tell me how I could manage to study some, and invited me to come and room in the college.

"Some time in the spring of 1826 my uncle died, and I went to Utica to see my aunt. Mr. Finney was at that time preaching in Utica, and I had heard of his 'frightening' my cousin Sophia, to whom I was much attached, by his terrific Jupiter Tonans sort of style, and was enraged at him.

" 'My father,' I said, 'was a real minister of the Gospel, grave and courteous, and an honor to the profession. This man is not a minister, and I will never acknowledge him as such.'

"Accordingly, I talked against him in the college, and opposed the revival with all my might. Well, when I went to see Aunt

Clark (she was a great friend of Finney, and lived next door to Aikin's, where he stopped), she tried to get me to go and hear him. No, I would not. At last she said, 'Mr. Finney never preaches in the morning; go with me in the forenoon.' So I consented. What does she do but slip over and tell Mr. Aikin. I mistrusted nothing, and went. When we came to the pew door she motioned me to go in, and followed with several ladies, and shut me in.

"Aikin took the introductory services. But by-and-by Mr. Finney rose, with those great staring eyes of his (never was a man whose soul looked out through his face as his did), and took for his text, 'One sinner destroyeth much good.' I stooped down and took hold of my hat; but just as I rose, Aunt Clark put her mouth close to my ear and whispered, 'Theodore, *you'll break my heart* if you go!' I gave it up, and resigned myself to my fate; and then, for an hour, he just held me up on his toasting-fork before that audience.

"You see, they all knew; they had heard about me. And finally he wound up, 'And yes! you'll go to college, and use all your influence against the Lord's work,' and described all the different methods of destroying good.

"I went home, and on the way aunt said, 'Why, Mr. Finney *never* preached in the forenoon before, but *always* in the afternoon.' So I suspected nothing. Next day I was sitting in a store. One of the partners was in the revival, and he slipped out and told Finney. In he came, and began to talk. I was greatly exasperated, and all the vocabulary of abuse the language afforded I used pretty thoroughly upon him. The store was crowded, and out in the street about the door. He took it all meekly; not a word of anger or of harshness; only he would every now and then just take my feeling and show it to me — take it and show it to me.

"At last I saw I was acting meanly, and quit and went home. I was so ashamed I could not live. Finally, I made up my mind I'd go and ask his pardon. I went, and rung at Aikin's door. A girl came. I stood in the entry, and she called Mr. Finney. He came down stairs. It was rather dim light, so he put his hand up over his eyes to see. Did not recognize me till just as he reached the bottom of the stairs. 'Ah!' said he, 'is it not enough? Have you followed a minister of the Lord Jesus to his own door to abuse him?'

" 'Mr. Finney,' said I, 'I have come for a very different purpose. I —'

"But I hadn't time to finish my sentence. He saw in an instant what it was, and opened his arms, threw them round my neck, and dragged me into the parlor, and down on his knees, sobbing and praying, and sobbing and praying.

"That put an end to my studying. I was with him in his meetings, speaking and laboring, all that summer.

"In the winter I went to Labrador with my brother, who was out of health, and, on my return, spent two or three weeks in Boston. I had several conversations with your father, and remember going with him to see the missionaries Judd and others sail, and coming back in the pilot-boat.

"After this I went out to the Oneida Institute, New York, partly in the capacity of agent and partly as student. It was a Manual Labor institution, but not well endowed, and I spent about half my time soliciting funds. When at the Institute I was monitor of the milking class, for we milked some thirty cows, and had to get up in the morning in time to get the milk off in wagons to Utica by daybreak. I remember we wanted a barn for our stock, and did not know how to get one. A farmer in the neighborhood, who did not think much of students' work, told me he would give us all the timber we would cut with our own hands, and, what was more, he would haul it to the canal. I went and organized the boys with axes, and we cut down the timber, made a raft, and built a large barn, with sheds.

"In July, 1831, a National Manual Labor Society was formed, and I became general agent, and traveled and lectured, visiting most of the Manual Labor institutions in Ohio, Indiana, Illinois, Missouri, Kentucky, Tennessee, and Alabama. I also lectured from time to time on Temperance, and conversed freely, wherever I had a chance, with young men on the subject of slavery. The Liberator had just been established then, and had not become known, and there was entire freedom to converse on the subject every where, provided we kept out of hearing of the slaves.

"At Huntsville, Alabama, I became acquainted with Dr. Allen, the leading Presbyterian minister of the state, a slave-holder, and with his son, who had recently graduated. J. G. Birney [1] was one of his elders, and it was owing to my discussion with Dr. Allen that he was led to think on the subject and became an abolitionist. During this tour I found several young men who resolved to come to Lane — among others, the son of Dr. Allen. By-the-by, on my

[1] James G. Birney (1792–1857), lawyer and member of the Ala. legislature. In the early 1830's Birney advocated gradual emancipation, but later he became an abolitionist. In his *Philanthropist* during 1836–1837 he attacked the Whig and Democratic positions on slavery. In 1840 he ran as presidential candidate of the Liberty Party and published *The American Churches, the Bulwark of Slavery.*

way down South I lectured in Cincinnati ten evenings in succession on Temperance, and several evenings on Manual Labor—part of the time in the Second Church, part in Dr. Wilson's Church, and then, the crowd was so great, in the Methodist Episcopal Chapel.

"At that time the seminary was not in operation. On my return from the South, in the fall, I lectured at the seminary on Manual Labor. Vail was there, and Mr. Lane, from whom the institution was named, though he only gave about $4000. Your father was not there at that time.

"I went on to New York, and made my report in January, 1833, and, while in New York, had several conversations with the Tappans and others interested in anti-slavery. I made a statement of the results of my observation. I remember telling them I knew of a number who were coming from the Southern States to Lane, besides many of the Oneida Institute boys; for we had heard of your father's appointment, and had spoken some of going to Lane. At that time I was planning to establish a great Manual Labor institution somewhere, and liberal offers had been made by gentlemen at Rochester. I had been on the ground, and spent some days looking at sites in the vicinity. Beman and Kirk [2] were talked of as professors.

"But when I went through the West and South, and saw the situation of Lane Seminary, I was satisfied that was the place for us. I developed, in conversation with the Tappans, my views on slavery, and my intention to improve the excellent opportunity to introduce anti-slavery sentiments, and have the whole subject thoroughly discussed.

"After a brief visit to my father, who then resided near Oneida, some time in May, '34, H. B. Stanton, Samuel Wells, Ezra A. Poole, and I, bought a boat for six dollars, and went down French Creek and the Alleghany River to Pittsburg. We had good times, discussing anti-slavery, and stopping occasionally to get supplies, hold prayer-meetings, or find a place to sleep; if we could not, we got along in our boat. At Pittsburg we took deck passage to Cincinnati. You know deck passengers pay nothing, find themselves, sleep on the deck, and help 'wood.' I believe there were some other of the Oneida boys that hired on board of flat-boats, and earned some money to begin their studies."

---

[2] Edward Kirk (1802–1874) was a New School revivalist active in the missionary movement. Dismissed from his fashionable Albany church, in 1829 he took charge of a newly organized church, also in Albany. In 1842 the Mt. Vernon Church was established for him in Boston.

It was not long after their arrival that the cholera broke out in the seminary. A letter written by Mr. Weld at the time gives so vivid a picture of the scene, and illustrates so forcibly the character of the writer, and of the first class of students, that we insert it here.

"The first case occurred in the room next my own. The student was taken in the morning, about daybreak, and, in spite of the most efficient means, was in a state of collapse by eleven o'clock, but, by the most incessant efforts, was brought out of it and lived. I was with him from the time he was taken until midnight, when the disease yielded.

"The next case occurred the next morning at eight o'clock — Brother Burr, of Virginia; one of the first students for mind, scholarship, and piety. I had the great privilege of being with him from the first moment of his attack until his death, which occurred in just twenty hours. His last words were, addressing me as I was bending over him, 'Brother, I feel as if I was beginning to die. Don't you think I am?'

" 'Yes, my dear brother. Your Father calls you.

" 'Yes, he calls me — yes, I am beginning to die. Oh, blessed be God through Jesus Christ, I am beginning to live!'

"From the first he expected to die, and, while we were plying him with various external applications to aid the operation of medicine, he was continually exhorting us to prayer, great personal holiness, and ceaseless efforts to save sinners. The *Cross* — the *Cross* was his theme, even when racked with bodily agony.

"In the brief intervals between the dreadful spasms, which for the last four hours contorted his frame, he would speak to us in language of the utmost tenderness. '*My dear brethren*, pray that this may be sanctified to the seminary; my dear brethren, you must be exhausted.' * * * I could fill this sheet with the heavenly breathings of this dying saint, but must pause. When I closed his eyes I could not refrain from crying aloud, 'Blessed — blessed! oh, blessed are the dead that die in the Lord!'

"Five or six of the students were taken with the disease on the morning of the day Brother Burr died, one of whom died the same afternoon, exclaiming, with a look of transport, 'The face of the Lord! the face of the Lord!'

"Within a few hours another young man died, after an illness of only eight hours. His spasms were almost without intermission, and the spectacle of his last hours was fearful and appalling. His mind wandered so much that we could not ascertain his feelings for some hours before he died. His hope *did not* sustain him when first taken.

"By the close of the third day there were about thirty of the students confined to their rooms, mostly with premonitory symptoms, but some six or eight cases of malignant cholera, with all its peculiar horrors. Ten or fifteen, though able to be about, were rather indisposed, and could not assist in taking care of the sick and dying; some twenty others could not aid much on account of utter inexperience; add to this, the steward's family were seized, help could not be procured, and a number of students were called into the kitchen to provide food, heat water, prepare poultices, etc., so that the burden of the toil, watching, responsibility of dealing out medicine, etc., etc., devolved upon about twenty of the students.

"For ten days I did not go to my room but once to change my clothes, but can not particularize. The Lord sustained me throughout. I never seemed to myself to possess more energy of body or mind. I had not, during the whole time, scarcely a single sensation of fatigue, or the least disposition to sleep, though in more than one instance I was without sleep forty-eight hours in succession. Perhaps you will say this was presumption. Extraordinary providences demand extraordinary labors, and the God of providence provides *extraordinary* supplies always adequate to the demand.

"There was another death among us two days after the last mentioned, which made upon us all an impression which can never be effaced. The individual was George ——, the youngest brother of my dear friend ——. He came on with his brother and myself when we came down the river in the spring. George was one of the youngest members of the seminary, about eighteen years old, a young man of most extraordinary powers. I have never seen his superior. He had been religiously educated, had passed through three or four powerful revivals, had been convicted deeply and often, asked prayers, attended meetings of inquiry, etc., but still resisted the Spirit, caviled, criticised, and started skeptical queries, until the last revival passed away with such a flood of light upon his understanding that he could paralyze his conscience only by a desperate rush into infidelity.

"He devoured infidel books, and thought, wrote, and discussed, and hardened his heart with fearful rapidity and to an appalling extent. His principles were known to but few of us. I had frequently talked with him, and in our last conversation, only a day before he was taken, he acknowledged himself in a difficulty from which he could not *then* extricate himself, but said, 'I'll think of it, and, rely on it, I'll give you a satisfactory answer, and sustain all my positions in a day or two.'

"The next day he tested the strength of his principles in conflict with *Death*. He was taken in the afternoon, and died the same night, or rather at three o'clock in the morning. I was with him all the time, and such a scene! After all had been done that could be done by the medical faculty, and we saw him beyond recovery, we looked in each other's faces in speechless agony — he was an infidel! But we knew God could save *to the uttermost*. We consulted with the physician. He said he had never in all his life seen a case of disease so desperate; it was impossible — *impossible* to save him; he probably would live two hours. After mutual consultation, it was agreed I should tell him that it was certain *he must die soon*, and urge on his soul *the great salvation* provided for the chief of sinners.

"From the commencement he had possessed perfectly all the powers of his rare mind. I told him we had done all we could for him; *he must die;* and pressed on his soul repentance and faith in Christ.

" 'My mind is made up on that subject,' said he; 'let me alone. Infidelity is right, after all; let me alone, I say. I am *determined* to try *my* experiment.'

"He was in a rage — thrust me from him with violence: 'Let me die in peace,' said he.

"I endeavored, with the utmost gentleness and tenderness, to press the subject at intervals for an hour and a half, but, the more affectionate the approach, the fiercer did he repel it, till at last he screamed to drown my voice.

"His brother threw himself in tears upon his neck, and, with a bursting heart, cried, 'Oh, George! dear George, won't you listen to your brother?'

" 'No — no,' said he; 'let me alone.'

" 'What shall I tell your poor mother, George?'

" 'Let me alone,' he repeated.

"I stepped out to call a brother in the fourth story. While going, I heard George calling my name with frightful energy. I hastened down. When he saw me approaching his bed he reached out both hands, grasped me convulsively, and cried out, 'Dear — dear Mr. Weld, *now I'll hear you! now I'll hear you!* Oh, tell me, *is there* an eternal hell? Convince me by sure arguments. Oh, to be damned! to be damned! Oh, for a light! for a light! Bring me a light — the light of my salvation! No, never, never, never!'

"This word he repeated as many as twelve or fifteen times, all the while tossing his body from side to side with an energy which nothing could inspire but the death-struggle. He stopped, and, with a phrensied look of horror, died! * * *

"I have been afflicted with sore eyes; was obliged to get my lessons through my ears entirely for about three days, but can now use my eyes about three hours a day. Seminary going on well. I have a fine class, and have never been placed in circumstances by any means so *imposing*. When I came here matters were getting at loose ends. The Lord has ordered every thing in great mercy. System and efficacy are the stability of our times."

XXXIV

ANTI-SLAVERY IMBROGLIO

THERE are some expressions toward the close of the letter given in the last chapter that have a singular appearance, coming from a student in a seminary class. One would naturally suppose them to have been written by one of the faculty. This, however, is not entirely unaccountable, in view of the previous career of the writer, his executive talents, habits of control, experience as public lecturer and teacher, and the encouragements held out to him by the agent of the institution.

At the time when, as already mentioned, he was planning the establishment of a grand national Manual Labor institution, Mr. F. Y. Vail writes to him (November, 1831) as follows: "Brethren W—— and T——, finding I possessed a spirit congenial with yours and their own on the subject of a great model Manual Labor institution for the nation, have confidentially and fully made me acquainted with your plans and prospects in reference to such a seminary. Brother W—— will write you fully on this subject, and express his full conviction that you ought not to fix upon your location for this institution until you have paid a visit to this great valley, and have conferred with some brethren who have been looking over the rising millions of the West with a view of raising up just such an institution as you wish. * *

"Now, as we already have New England identified with this enterprise, we only need to have your plan and efforts identified with our own, in order to secure the influence of New York, and make it strictly a national, model institution. * * * We want now, my dear brother, just such a man as you are (I do not flatter you) to be the mainspring in the whole concern. We want the funds promised you exceedingly for buildings for 500 or 600 students, for more land if necessary, for workshops, tools," etc., etc.

Again, in August, 1832, he writes: "I wish, my dear brother, you could join us this fall, and aid us in getting this great seminary of the West into successful operation; * * * and remember that, by God's blessing, you are yet perhaps to bear one of the four corners of our institution by occupying the chair of Sacred Rhetoric and Oratory."

The sentiments of the students toward their gifted companion and leader may be gathered from the following testimony by Professor Fairchild,[1] in his Address to the Alumni of Oberlin: "Among these students was Theodore D. Weld, a young man of surpassing eloquence and logical powers, and of a personal influence even more fascinating than his eloquence. I state the impression which I had of him as a boy, and it may seem extravagant, but I have seen crowds of bearded men held spell-bound by his power for hours together, and for twenty evenings in succession."

In his reminiscences of that period Dr. Beecher observed: "Weld was a genius. First-rate natural capacity, but uneducated. Would have made a first-rate man in the Church of God if his education had been thorough. In the estimation of the class, he was president. He took the lead of the whole institution. The young men had, many of them, been under his care, and they thought he was a god. We never quarreled, however."

It was a noble class of young men, uncommonly strong, a little uncivilized, entirely radical, and terribly in earnest. Penetrated as they were with admiration and love for their brilliant leader, they constituted a kind of *imperium in imperio*, to govern which by ordinary college law might prove difficult.

An illustration was soon found. At first they recited daily to the professor of Ecclesiastical History, a most amiable and excellent man, but not possessed of all the elements of character necessary to bridle these fiery and unbroken steeds, or to inspire them with sufficient interest in the lectures of his department. At length there was a species of *emeute*. The class informed Dr. Beecher that they could not and would not attend the obnoxious lectures any longer, and implored relief.

After consultation, the doctor replied, in his vivacious way, "Boys, I'll tell you the best we can do for you. You must attend Professor ——'s lecture once a week, and *behave*, and Stowe and I will take care of you the rest of the time." This was before the regular course of study had been matured. With this arrangement the young malcontents were, of course, highly delighted, and all things moved on smoothly and pleasantly.

All this time, however, the great subject of emancipation was not forgotten. "A great work," observes Mr. Weld, "was to be

[1] James Fairchild (1817–1902), graduate (1834), professor (1841–1866), and president (1866–1889) of Oberlin.

done in preparing the way for an open discussion. We early began to inculcate our views, by conversation, upon our fellow-students. Those of us who sympathized together in our abhorrence of slavery selected each his man to instruct, convince, and enlist in the cause. Thus we carried one after another, and, before ever we came to public debate, knew pretty well where we stood."

Dr. Beecher's position on the slavery question, before the discussion was held, is sufficiently clear from the following reply to Arthur Tappan, who had written to inquire whether the trustees had taken any action in reference to admitting students of color to the institution. "We have taken," he says, April 23, 1833, "no order on the subject, as none is needed, and I trust never will be. Our only qualifications for admission to the seminary are *qualifications* intellectual, moral, and religious, without reference to color, which I have no reason to think would have any influence here, certainly never with my consent.

"I am not apprised of the ground of controversy between the Colonizationists [2] and the Abolitionists. I am myself both, without perceiving in myself any inconsistency. Were it in my power to put an end to slavery immediately, I would do it; but it is not. I can only pursue the measures best calculated, in my judgment, to get the slaves out of bondage in the shortest time and best manner; and this, as I view the subject, is to make emancipation easy instead of difficult; to make use of the current of human fears, and passions, and interests, when they may be made to set in our favor, instead of attempting to row up stream against them.

"I would press the consciences, so far as they have any, of the Southerners, and shake their fears, and press their interests, as the Abolitionists are doing; but then, that the pressure might avail, I would not hermetically seal their hearts by cutting off the facilities of emancipation, and tempt them to delay it till insurrection might do the work, but offer them an easy, practicable way of doing their duty, as the Colonizationists are doing; and I can perceive no need that the two classes of philanthropists should fall out by the way, though, if they do, perhaps they may provoke one another to do more than they might otherwise accomplish. I trust God has begun, by the instrumentality of both, a great work, which will not stop until not only the oppressed here are free, but Africa

[2] Colonizationists worked to establish colonies in Africa for freed Negroes; the abolitionists advocated immediate recognition of the sin of slavery and consequent emancipation.

herself shall have rest in the Lord along her extended coast and deep interior."

A practical answer to the question of admitting colored students was given by the presence in the first class of James Bradley, once a slave, and his cordial welcome to go wherever his classmates went. On one occasion, the class having been invited to a levee at the president's, James was absent through timidity. When the doctor discovered the fact, he expressed to Mr. Weld and others his great regret; "if he had thought of his feeling so, he would have gone to him personally, and told him he *must* come."

When the idea of a debate was first mentioned to Dr. Beecher in conversation, so far was he from deprecating free discussion, that he offered to attend and take part in the argument. It was the result of more cautious counsels from some of the trustees that led him and the other members of the faculty to advise postponement. The reasons assigned were the absorbing nature of the discussion, its divisive tendency, the risk of exciting popular prejudice, and the probability that at a later period discussion might be either needless or safe.

As the students, however, insisted on being allowed to go on, the faculty would not refuse them. The result was a nine evenings' annihilative onset upon slavery, followed by a unanimous vote in favor of immediate emancipation. Nine evenings more devoted to the colonization scheme resulted in its rejection, with but a single solitary vote in its favor. Anti-slavery and colonization societies were immediately organized, and active efforts commenced to elevate the colored population of the city.

"We have formed," writes Mr. Weld to Arthur Tappan, April 12, "a large and efficient organization for elevating the colored people in Cincinnati; have established a Lyceum among them, and lecture three or four evenings a week on Grammar, Geography, Arithmetic, Natural Philosophy, etc. Besides this, an evening free school, for teaching them to read, is in operation every week-day evening, and we are about establishing one or two more. * * * We have three large Sabbath-schools and Bible-classes. By sections in rotation, and teaching the evening reading-schools in the same way, we can perform an immense amount of labor among them without interruption to our studies. * * *

"I visited this week about thirty families, and found that some members of more than half these families were in bondage. May God make us more humble, fearless, unflinching, full of faith and of the Holy Ghost, full of sympathy for suffering humanity, and rejoicing that we are counted worthy to suffer shame for his name."

Perceiving the momentum of their motion, and well aware how easy it was in those days to rouse the slumbering demon of pro-slavery fanaticism, Dr. Beecher endeavored to caution them, particularly with reference to putting in practice their principle of "social intercourse according to character, irrespective of color" — a principle as dangerous as it is just.

"When they founded colored schools," said Dr. Beecher, "I conversed with Weld repeatedly, and pointed out these things. Said I, you are taking just the course to defeat your own object, and prevent yourself from doing good. If you want to teach colored schools, I can fill your pockets with money; but if you will visit in colored families, and walk with them in the streets, you will be overwhelmed."

The young men, however, thought they saw the danger, and really tried to guard against it. Their opinion was, and probably still is, that no amount of prudence, nothing short of surrender of the enterprise altogether, would have availed.

Dr. Beecher thought differently. He felt decidedly that the students had not, in all respects, shown a proper spirit in their treatment of their instructors. Still, his letters show that, before leaving for the East during the summer vacation, he anticipated no such serious results as actually ensued.

As late as June, 1834, he writes: "Our first class is forty, and the large majority of it composed of men of matured age, powerful mind, and ardent and devoted piety. I have never known such power for intelligent and strong action condensed in a single class. Their progress in study is highly satisfactory to the faculty, and we are quite willing that their attainments should be the first specimens to represent the seminary.

"The only inconvenience we encounter as the offset to so much good is from the independence inseparable from such mature age and power of mind, unaccustomed to the discipline and restraints of college life. But this has not occasioned the slightest trouble except in one instance: we allude to a few particulars in respect to the Abolition Society, in which, as a matter of conscience, mistaken we suppose, but real, they have not regarded our advice as we hoped they would, and think they ought to have done.

"But, after having said and done all which we consider proper, and waited for the teachings of experience and wisdom from above, we are united in the conclusion that, *if we and our friends do not amplify the evil by too much alarm, impatience, and attempt at regulation,* the evil will subside and pass away."

Some time previously a committee had been appointed by the trustees on this subject, but the recommendation of strenuous measures was resisted by the faculty. After the departure of Dr. Beecher, Professor Stowe, and Professor Morgan,[3] however, this committee, in connection with the Professor of Ecclesiastical History, proceeded to consider the subject.

The result was, Dr. Beecher was informed by letter that on the 20th of August the executive committee adopted a resolution "declaring that rules ought to be adopted prohibiting any societies or associations in the seminary, any public meetings or discussions among the students, any public addresses by the students in the seminary or elsewhere, or appeals or communications to the students at their meals or when assembled on other ordinary occasions, without the approbation of the faculty; and requiring that the Anti-slavery Society and Colonization Society of the seminary should be abolished; and providing that students not complying with these, as with other rules, should be dismissed. * * *

"It was decided to postpone the enactment of these rules until the faculty should be reassembled; and in the mean time, in order that the students might not remain in ignorance of the contemplated regulations, and that the public impressions on the subject might be rectified, it was ordered that the proceedings should be published, which will be done in a week or two."

A few days later the following letter was received from the same writer (September 13, 1834), still farther unfolding the state of affairs: "We have acted with great deliberation, and great reluctance in the absence of the faculty. If we could have felt any reasonable confidence that even the existence of the seminary could have been preserved, we should have postponed every thing till the faculty were reassembled. Many of our best citizens were looking upon the seminary as a nuisance, more to be dreaded than cholera or plague.

"The spirit of insubordination, resistance to law, and of civil commotion, which they regarded it as fostering, was deprecated in a tone to make one shudder. The scenes of France and of Hayti recur to their imaginations, and it is impossible to make them calm or even reasonable. It is impossible for persons not well conversant

[3] John Morgan (1805?–1883), Williams graduate, self-educated minister, was professor at Lane until 1835, when he went to Oberlin, where he taught until his death.

in the slave states, and the part of the country on their borders, to realize the state of the public mind on these subjects. If once excited, we may as well tamper with the whirlwinds and the lightning."

These resolutions of the trustees, having been published, were denounced by the anti-slavery press as an attack on freedom of speech. "In what age do we live?" asks the New York Evangelist, "and in what country? and who are the persons thus restrained? and with whose endowments was the seminary founded? and who is its president? * * Nor do we see how such men as Dr. Beecher, and Professor Stowe, and Professor Morgan could consistently remain, nor how those subscribers to the funds of the seminary who expected to make it an institution of elevated character, could make any farther payments to trustees so incompetent to appreciate the wants of the age. But let us hope the trustees will pause before they take the final step."

Unquestionably, but for this hope, Dr. Beecher might have been justified in resigning. But the laws were not yet passed, nor did the absent professors consider themselves compromised by what the trustees had done. "We, of course," writes Professor Stowe, September 20, to Dr. Beecher, "are not responsible for the doings of the committee, especially as we tried with all our might to prevent the passage and publication of the resolutions referred to." Nor would Dr. Beecher's sanguine temperament permit him to leave his post without an effort to avert the threatened rupture.

In this, however, he was destined to be disappointed. The hope had been cherished by some of the students — so it was stated publicly at the time in the Emancipator, of New York — that Dr. Beecher, on his return, would be able to arrest the execution of these laws. This hope, however, proved vain. The trustees declined to await Dr. Beecher's return; the laws were formally promulgated; and as things had gone too far to afford much prospect of a change, the students, with one consent almost, resolved on retiring from the institution.

"When I got back," said Dr. Beecher, "I found all in a flurry. If I had arrived a little sooner I should have saved them; but it was too late." An attempt was made, indeed, to expound the obnoxious resolutions and orders as containing "nothing which is not common law in all well-regulated institutions, since they merely commit the whole management of the internal concerns of the seminary to the discretion of the faculty," but this the students regarded as indorsing the despotic enactments in all their extent.

After the departure of the students, and during their residence at Cummingsville, a final attempt was made at an agreement. "I determined," said Dr. Beecher, "to make one more effort. I went to the trustees, and told them that the manner of reformation in my absence was untimely, and the phraseology of the resolutions and orders not the most felicitous, and that they must let us offer terms. They consented. The laws were revised, and the objectionable features struck out.* We then called a meeting of a number of the most discreet and sober among them, telling them I had a confidential communication to make to them.

" 'The fact is,' said I, 'there are some things you don't know, and you have ignorantly done just what others meant you should. Professor ——, though an excellent man, has not been popular with you, nor you with him, and, in fact, it was either you or he must leave. So, when he saw the tide of public excitement rising against you, and a mob threatening, he felt his time had come, and used all his influence with the trustees to do what they did, hoping you would bolt, and he has succeeded. He has ousted you, and you have helped him: If we had been here it would not have been done. We can not say it openly, but he has led the trustees, who know nothing about such matters.'

" 'Well,' said they, 'what can be done?'

"I said, 'That is for you to determine. It is sad for us; it will be apt to be sad for you. You are excellent men, but I am afraid it will wreck you, some of you. You may tell the rest what I have told you, on condition that you do not divulge it publicly.' They worked like beavers to form a reaction, but said they could not do it."

Our limits do not allow us to insert extracts from the statements published by the students and faculty respectively, setting forth the reasons of their course.

Viewed at this distance of time, we find much to commend and something to condemn on either side in this most painful affair. That the rules as passed by the trustees are indefensible, we do not deny; that the first "declaration" of the faculty was equally so, we frankly concede; but that the final revision of the laws was perfectly unobjectionable, and such as ought to have been accepted by

* By this revision the laws were restored nearly to the same form in which they were before the discussion, the only difference bearing upon this subject being the following:

Original Laws (before the discussion).

No student shall be absent from the premises of the institution during study the students as a ground of reconciliation, we see not how any candid mind can question. As to the statement of the Liberator that "Lane Seminary was now to be regarded as strictly a Bastile of oppression — a spiritual Inquisition," time has shown how to estimate its real value. Certainly the two sons of the president, who entered in the very next class, found no shackles imposed on their minds, and have not been generally regarded as graduates of a school of tyranny, nor have the professors and their families impressed the world as keepers of a spiritual Bastile.

In our judgment, nay, to our certain knowledge, those young men might have kept their place and their principles, and accomplished all their noble aims, if they had consented to adopt Dr. Beecher for their leader. They made the mistake, common to ardent minds, that to submit to an unjust law is as sinful as to enforce it. They forgot that men may waive their rights voluntarily, even to the laying down of life. They abandoned too easily their noble design of stamping an anti-slavery character upon this central seminary of the West. Without the least concession of principle, they might have calmly and quietly gone on with their studies, trusting to time and to Dr. Beecher, whose heart they knew beat for liberty with a pulse as high as their own, to bring things right again.

But it was overruled for good. The seminary suffered, being "obliged to bear up under a load of prejudice as a pro-slavery institution;" but it was not a pro-slavery institution, and God would not permit it to go down.

At the same time, the students were taken care of. Providence stirred up friends to their support. Arthur Tappan exhibited a princely liberality in their behalf. A theological department was projected and endowed at Oberlin; and although the welcome to students "irrespective of color" was ungracious in appearance, it proved cordial in effect.*

---

hours without permission from the instructor of his class for the time, or from the president.

REVISED LAWS (November, 1834.)

"No student shall be absent in term time without permission from the instructor of his class, or from the president. General meetings of the students, and public addresses or lectures by them, and societies formed among them in the seminary, shall be with the consent and subject to the direction of the faculty."

Rather a slender foundation, one would think, for so painful a measure as rending away a whole class, and threatening to wreck the institution.

* It was with great difficulty, and only in the prospect of rich endowments and of securing a large class of students, that the principle of admission irrespective of color, already in practice at Lane, received from the trustees of Oberlin a cold and ambiguous sanction.

Thus, though by a way he knew not, was Dr. Beecher's removal to the West directly or indirectly instrumental in the establishment of two theological schools instead of one; and we can almost imagine we hear the seminary on Walnut Hills exclaiming, as she gazes on the numerous alumni of Oberlin, "Who hath begotten me these, seeing I have lost my children and been desolate? Who hath brought up these? Behold, I was left alone; these, where have they been?"

XXXV

PLEA FOR THE WEST

During the summer in which these unpropitious events were taking place at the West, Dr. Beecher was successfully pleading the cause of the seminary at the East. In so doing, he was led to speak of the character, wants, and dangers of the great valley as they appeared to the eye of comprehensive benevolence, and as would be adapted to kindle the interest of the churches and draw forth their liberality.

Invidious misrepresentations of his statements having been reported at the West, and the "reporter's mouth being sharp," as Dr. Beecher expressed it, he was led to revise and publish his address under the title at the head of our chapter.

In stating the wants of the seminary, he had said, "What we now need is a chapel for the accommodation of students and fast-increasing community, with a place of worship, the endowment of a professorship of Rhetoric, and a library. For the first we have dared to rely on our friends in Boston and its vicinity; the library we hope to receive from our friends in New York; and for the professorship of Sacred Rhetoric *we look up*, hoping and believing that God will put into the hearts of one or more individuals to endow it."

On the margin of the copy in our possession is written in pencil, "All these were secured in an agency of six or seven weeks; and the one for which I *looked up*, $7000 in Boston by one individual, an equal sum in Worcester by four, and the remainder in Hartford." *

In a letter written shortly after his return, he says, "My reception by my people (in Boston) was all that affection could desire. I met the Church first in their vestry prayer-meeting, was expected, and the room was full. As I entered the gas-lights were dim, but as I passed up I could note well-known faces, and see the expression pass across them as the light moves over the standing corn. As I

* It may be comprehensively stated here that, in the three years following the spring of 1833, Mr. Vail, aided by Dr. Beecher, raised at the East subscriptions to the amount of about $40,000 for a fourth professorship, and for the erection of a chapel and professor's house.

entered the stand, and turned round to face the audience, the light flashed into vivid illumination, and presented as suddenly every countenance brightened into a smile. It was a touching moment."

The Bowdoin Street people subscribed about $4000, showing that, in pleading the cause of the West, there were cords that would vibrate, and that whatever was really needed could be obtained.

It was during this visit that the Catholic nunnery at Charlestown was destroyed by a mob, and the city of Boston thrown into a state of great excitement. This circumstance, in connection with the fact that, in his Plea for the West, he laid bare the despotic character and hostile designs of popery upon our country, led to the charge of having incited the mob to that act of violence.

Referring to this, he says, "The late violence done to Catholic property at Charlestown is regarded with regret and abhorrence by Protestants and patriots throughout the land, though the excitement which produced it had no relation whatever to religious opinions, and no connection with any denomination of Christians."

On the margin is penciled, in the doctor's handwriting, the following words: "The sermon of mine to which the mob was ascribed was preached before my presence in the city of Boston was generally known, and on the very evening in which the riot took place, two or three miles distant from the scene, and not an individual of the mob, probably, heard the sermon or knew of its delivery."

The following paragraph illustrates the condition of things at the time:

"For what was the city of Boston for five nights under arms — her military upon the alert — her citizens enrolled, and a body of five hundred men constantly patroling the streets? Why were the accustomed lectures for public worship, and other public secular meetings, suspended? Why were the citizens, at sound of bell, convened at midday in Faneuil Hall? — to hear Catholicism eulogized, and thanksgivings offered to his reverence the bishop for his merciful protection of the children of the Pilgrims! And why by the cradle of liberty, and under the shadow of Bunker's Hill, did men turn pale, and whisper, and look over their shoulders and around to ascertain whether it were safe to speak aloud, or meet to worship God? Has it come to this, that the capital of New England has been thrown into consternation by the threats of a Catholic mob, and that her temples and mansions stand only through the forbearance of a Catholic bishop? There can be no liberty in the presence of such masses of dark mind, and of such despotic power over it in a single man. Safety on such terms is not the protection of law, but of single-handed despotism. Will our great cities consent to receive protection from the Catholic priesthood, dependent on the Catholic powers of Europe, and favored by his Holiness, who is himself governed by the bayonets of Austria?"

In the letter already quoted he says, "The Catholic effervescence, though it obstructed for the moment, aided us on the whole. It was a favorable providence, which called me back to speak in undaunted tones, when, without some one to explain, and take correct ground, and inspire courage, all were likely to quail and be carried away. Before I left the tide turned, and Catholicism forever in New England must row up stream, carefully watched, and increasingly understood and obstructed by public sentiment."

We well remember the time when Dr. Beecher was getting this Plea through the press. One or two very influential men had rather taken a hostile attitude, under the influence of distorted rumors and reports; but, after the publication of the Plea, which quickly passed through several editions, the opposition died away. The influence of this little volume in deciding the character of the West is believed to have been extensive and salutary to a degree at present not easily to be estimated, when institutions are firmly rooted, and social character established and mature. "I have just read," writes Dr. Blagden, "your lectures on Skepticism and Plea for the West, and I have risen from both with a deeper conviction than ever before that you are a good man, and that the motto of your heart is 'All for God.' * * * Oh, my dear friend, keep humble! I never feared any thing so much in relation to you as that, in the consciousness of power, you might become vain."

Dr. N. Adams,[1] also, who was preparing to review the volume, writes, "If I could only throw into the review but a small portion of my feelings toward you, Judge —— would not wish for, nor you demand another for some time."

We believe that it was in getting this Plea through the press that the little incident occurred narrated by Professor Stowe, with which we close the chapter. "One day, after the printers had been on tenter-hooks forty-eight hours for some copy, he hastily finished his manuscript in his study, crushed it into the crown of the hat

[1] Nehemiah Adams (1806–1871), Trinitarian, was called in 1829 to be a colleague of the liberal Abiel Holmes at the Shepard Church, Cambridge, Mass., where in 1831 he became sole pastor. In 1834 he accepted a call to Union Church, Boston.

that lay nearest him, clapped another hat on his head, drove down to the city, rushed up to the printing-office, and snatched off his hat.

" 'Here's your copy — h'm — h'm. Well, if it isn't here it is somewhere else!'

"The copy was still in the hat that was left at home. But who could be angry with so much good-nature, even if it were a plague?"

XXXVI

CORRESPONDENCE, 1834–1835

PROFESSOR C. A. GOODRICH TO DR. BEECHER.

"New Haven, August 3, 1834.

"COULD we have known that you were to pass through town, we should have waited on the wharf for an opportunity to welcome your return to Connecticut, and to have seen you for a single moment. As it is, let me say, the affections of past days are cherished with increasing strength as years pass over us. I hope you will give us a number of days before you leave New England. Brother Taylor, I suppose, will feel that he has the prior claim, but none would welcome you more cordially to his home and heart than myself.

"I am particularly desirous, however, that Brother Taylor should enjoy as much as possible of your society, because he is unwell, and cast down in mind from the influence of disease. Still, he goes on lecturing with his accustomed power and clearness. But the unkind treatment and gross misrepresentations which he has to encounter have perhaps a greater effect on his feelings now than at any former period, and demand from his friends peculiar exhibitions of attention and sympathy. I do believe, with Brother Skinner, that 'there is not in this country a man who has been so shamefully ill-treated.' I only wonder that he is alive under the continual pressure of care and responsibility.

"There is one subject on which I could have wished to say a word on your coming back to Connecticut; I mean, the use which has been, and will, perhaps, again be made of your name and influence in our theological concerns. Last winter Brother Hawes said to me, 'There is a great deal of Jesuitism at work to procure subscriptions for the East Windsor scheme.[1] They say, among other things, Governor Smith tells us *go on;* Dr. Beecher tells us *go on.*'

"Governor Smith soon after took pains to inform Judge Dag-

[1] East Windsor Seminary was established in 1834 as a citadel of orthodoxy to counteract heretical Yale.

gett that, so far from this, 'he had given formal notice to the secretary of his rejection of his appointment as a member of the board at East Windsor, stating his reasons at length, and saying that he considered the new institution as hazardous to the peace of the churches, deeply injurious to Yale College, totally uncalled for, and on every view to be deplored.' Still, his name was, after all this, given to the public as one of the trustees, and used as Brother Hawes represented.

"Your own was used in the same way; and we now see, from Brother Nettleton's extracts from letters sent down to Virginia, how a mere remark of yours, that good would come out of the new scheme, connected as it was with matters hostile to Brother Taylor, was made to leave the impression that you sympathized with the friends of the new school in their feelings, and entered into their designs. It is highly probable that any thing you may say on this visit which *can* be turned to the same purpose will be. You can hardly be aware how every thing is now changing from *argument* into the array of *names and influence* to consolidate a party.

"All I wish is that you may know how things stand. Had you remained in the state, our ecclesiastical concerns, I am persuaded, would have been totally different; but it is the will of God. A new institution I care nothing about, but the *principle* on which it is founded — *charges* against brethren which are utterly unfounded — charges which apply to Brothers Skinner, and Hawes, and Porter, and yourself, just as truly, in their full extent, as to Brother Taylor. While this is the foundation of the scheme, can it do good?

"My earnest prayer is, dear brother, that you may act as a peacemaker. There are many brethren who have been brought by misrepresentation into a state of alarm, which needs only the restoration of confidence to dissipate. One thing is particularly to be considered. The whole attack is now turned into this: 'There is a *tendency* to a fatal error in the New Haven views.' This is the most delusive of all modes of '*agitating*.' Every error, however small, if really *followed out*, would lead to heresy, for truth is one. Dr. Dwight thought the tendency of Arminianism was to Pantheism. Dr. Mason expelled Loring Dewey [2] from his school for maintaining general atonement, because this *tended* to Universalism; and it did, in Mason's scheme of theology. Tendency is always controlled by other and counteracting principles. If, on Brother Tyler's scheme, our views lead to heresy, they do not on ours; and

[2] Loring Dewey (1791–1867) worked for the American Colonization Society, acted as a schoolteacher, and eventually entered business.

the proof is, they have had a trial of twenty years, and nothing of the kind has occurred. It is *wrong*, therefore, against such evidence, to reiterate such charges.

"You are out of the way of this contest, and you may therefore do something, on returning, to promote peace. But your words will be watched closely, for the sake of turning them against your old and tried friends."

REV. ALBERT BARNES[3] TO DR. BEECHER.

"Philadelphia, March 20, 1835.

"I yesterday received a communication from the Rev. Dr. Junkin,[4] of Easton, informing me that he felt it to be his solemn duty to prefer charges against me before my Presbytery for my Notes on the Romans. He asked me to 'waive my constitutional right of ten days, etc., in order that the trial might proceed with as little delay as possible.' It has been known to us here that a caucus was held in Philadelphia more than a month ago on the subject, but the exact plan which it was intended to pursue was not developed until Dr. Junkin informed me of it yesterday. It is evident now that the design is to bring this matter before the next General Assembly. They can have no doubt about the result of a trial before my Presbytery; and the intention is, I doubt not, to make this a pre-eminent matter in the 'Convention' and in the next Assembly.

"The matter concerning which I need the advice of my friends is whether it is *best* that this case should come before the next General Assembly. It is in my power, undoubtedly, to keep off the trial and the decision in Presbytery until *after* the Assembly, and thus to prevent the agitating of the subject at Pittsburg this year; or it can be *hastened* through the Presbytery here, and brought up there. I should add that Dr. Junkin informs me that it is the *design* to have the *doctrines* in my book, and which have been so long agitated, brought up unconnected with ecclesiastical questions, etc., *for a fair and full decision.* Will the cause of truth, and peace, and

[3] Albert Barnes (1798–1870), pastor of the First Presbyterian Church in Philadelphia (1830–1870). From 1830 until the General Assembly sustained him in 1836, he was under attack for New School heresies, particularly for his contention that sin consisted in voluntary action and was not imputed.

[4] George Junkin (1790–1869), Pa. minister, president of Lafayette College, Pa. (1832–1841, 1844–1848), of Miami University, Ohio (1841–1844), and of Washington College, Va. (1848–1861). Advocate of temperance and of the compensated emancipation of slaves, he led the opposition to Barnes and to Taylor's New Divinity.

love be promoted by suffering this matter *this year* to come before the Assembly?

"You feel an interest in me, and in the cause, and in my perplexity. I have felt it to be a privilege to ask your advice. May I ask the favor of you to drop me a line on the subject as soon as convenient, expressing your views, and giving me the advice which I need? If you will, you will relieve my embarrassment, and do me a kindness which I know you will love to render."

DR. BEECHER'S REPLY.

"Cincinnati, March 31, 1835.

"Yours of March 20 was duly received. I supposed that you had passed the ordeal, and that the charges brought against me by Dr. Wilson were only the violence of his individual obstinacy, but I now perceive it to be a part of a systematic plan to press into the next Assembly as many causes as possible of inflammatory action. I had made up my mind *instanter*, on his presentation of the charges at the last Presbytery, to have them laid over, without being put into my hands, till the next Presbytery, which is next week, that I might have time for consultation. I have conferred with all my brethren here — with Brother Wisner, of Boston, now in heaven, and many others; the unvarying advice has been, defer, and keep it out of the General Assembly.

"I read your letter to our pastoral meeting. They are *all* true men, and the advice in respect to your course was the same. Several thought that the whole Old School act and testimony insurrection would be so crushed and put down that it might be best for us both to have our heresies wiped away and the whole business done up; but a decided majority of the meeting regarded the result at Pittsburg as an experiment, not so certain in its results as needlessly to commit hastily an important interest; that time to *you*, whose book is popular, and whose character is rising and extending in the Church and at the West, and to me also, and to the cause generally, is gain.

"Every year of our action is telling powerfully in contrast with their accusations and growling. We wish also to avoid, if possible, what they so much desire, any doctrinal authoritative exposition of the Confession, either Old School or New, and should therefore keep ourselves out of the Assembly as long as we can. But,

"Finally, though I have never intended to meddle with the Presbyterian squabble, yet if I must, and you also are compelled to do it, it may not be amiss that we should both stand for the truth at the same time. I shall be tried about the 1st of August probably, and I intend to make an explanation and defense which, while it maintains every principle I hold, shall afford as little occasion of alarm and offense as may be to candid Old School men. The ultras nothing will satisfy but drumming their ears with a certain set of words which they don't understand, and for one good reason, that they are words without sense or reason, but under which their fears subside and their people go to sleep. The Lord have mercy on them!

"I trust we shall get through without difficulty to ourselves or schism to the Church, unless there is so much of popery in the Presbyterian system of settling doctrines — by majorities — that God intends to let loose the principles of free inquiry by taking out of the way, by convulsion and revolution, whatever 'letteth,' whether pope, or Presbytery, or Assembly. We can spare any fragments which will fly off, because our doctrines are not condemned; but any decision which should go to condemn us, and exclude all who believe as we do, would make the Church a wreck.

"Such a result I do not anticipate; but, to avert it, it is of immense importance that the South, and the East, and New York send a copious delegation of faithful men, and especially that a great effort be made to send *elders*. They hope to regain a majority at Pittsburg by crowding in an uncommon number of elders, which, if the East should not take care to balance with the same material, may produce mischief. We shall look to it here as far as able, and trust our friends will do the same every where on the other side the mountains. The best way to settle the Church is to produce at Pittsburg a decided and powerful majority of calm, decided men. The subject has given me no anxiety, and I do not intend it shall. I mean to press on in duty, defend myself when I must, and commit the event to God, and I hope you will do the same."

DR. BEECHER TO DR. TAYLOR.

"Cincinnati, April 25, 1835.

"I have long wished to sit down and pour out my heart in a long train of reminiscences and miscellaneous remarks on all the way in which God has led us — our early Episcopal controversy; the religious tracts; Nettleton's revivals and inquiry meetings; the Christian Spectator, which broke my back and almost broke yours;

the beginning of the schism; Hewitt, Harvey, Pinneo,[5] Hooker, Nettleton, Woods, Tyler; with the controversy through which you have passed, not without great provocation, abuse, and trial — through which the Lord has sustained you, and by which he has, I trust, purified both yourself and the truth.

"I did not think the controversy necessary, and should have preferred the purification of the truth by an unrepulsive peaceable process. But God saw that the error which lay at the bottom of the New England philosophy of free agency, depravity, and regeneration, both the Taste and the Exercise schemes, demanded a convulsion to root them up, and cast them out of the vineyard as plants not of his own planting.

"It was the doctrine of a physical execution of God's decrees and of physical regeneration — in short, of moral government by direct omnipotence, which lay at the foundation of revolt in Woods, and Tyler, and Nettleton. This philosophy I suppose they hold and teach still, and are probably in danger of giving up New England divinity, and going back to the natural inability of Old Calvinism in the Emmons and Burton form.

"This must not be permitted. You must, all of you, on this point, watch and be strong, and quit yourselves like men; for when it is made prominent and preached clearly, it produces Antinomian formality and spiritual pride in the Church, and Methodism, Unitarianism, Universalism, and infidelity out of it. But in doing this you must watch the opposite extreme of a free agency which avails to save by its own actual sufficiency without the Holy Ghost — which will run headlong into Arminianism in the opposite direction, and meet Old School error on the common ground of infidelity. You know with what intense affection I have loved you, and the steadfastness with which I have rejected the charge of heresy or dangerous error preferred against you, and the indefatigable efforts I made to prevent a rupture and then to restore peace. I love Tyler and Nettleton, but I have disapproved of and deeply regretted many things they have done, especially Nettleton."

DR. BEECHER TO WILLIAM.

"Seminary, July 15, 1835.

"As to abolition, I am still of opinion that you ought not, and need not, and will not commit yourself as a partisan on either side.

[5] Bezahiel Pinneo (1769–1849), Conn. revivalist pastor, trained in New England Divinity.

The cause is moving on in Providence, and by the American Union, and by colonization, and by Lundy[6] in Texas, which is a grand thing, and will succeed, as I believe; and I hope and believe that the Abolitionists as a body will become more calm and less denunciatory, with the exception of the few he-goat men, who think they do God service by butting every thing in the line of their march which does not fall in or get out of the way. They are the offspring of the Oneida denunciatory revivals, and are made up of vinegar, aqua fortis, and oil of vitriol, with brimstone, saltpetre, and charcoal, to explode and scatter the corrosive matter."

[6] Benjamin Lundy (1788–1839) published the weekly *Genius of Universal Emancipation* (1821–1834) and supported Negro emancipation and colonization.

XXXVII

THE TRIAL

It is difficult to state in few words the precise difference between the Old School and New School churches, in whose conflicts Dr. Beecher was so prominently involved. It is our impression, which his history tends to confirm, that one principal cause of the controversy was the want of comprehensiveness in the views of both the great contending parties.

Two great truths underlie the Christian system — original sin and the freedom of the will — the fact of native ill desert, and the principle that ill desert is impossible without voluntary transgression of known law. These great truths, though often supposed to contradict each other, are evenly blended in the Bible, and in the experimental and devotional language of God's people.

In the Confession of Faith they are blended, though less evenly. "God hath endued the will of man," we read, "with that natural liberty that it is neither forced, nor by any absolute necessity of nature determined to good or evil." Nothing can be more satisfactory than this. But "man, by his fall into a state of sin, hath wholly lost all ability of will to any spiritual good accompanying salvation; so as a natural man, being altogether averse from that which is good and dead in sin, is not able, by his own strength, to convert himself or prepare himself thereunto."

Here the freedom of the will is at least shaded with doubt. Here there is room for a party to rise and say that, though the will was free by creation, its freedom has been annihilated by the fall. True, there is also room for another party to contend that the only inability here asserted as the consequence of the fall is *moral*, consisting in aversion only, "so AS a natural man, BEING altogether AVERSE," etc.

But the other interpretation can never be deprived of the power of making a formidable stand, so that we say the grand truth of the freedom of the will is at least shaded. But the grand co-ordinate truth of inborn blameworthiness is so clearly stated as much less easily to admit of two opinions. It is far easier to justify the fact of inborn blameworthiness by the Confession than the freedom of the will. Therefore, though these two foundation-truths are blended in the Confession, they are not evenly blended. The truth of man's innate and just exposure to divine wrath is far more prominent that the truth that a righteous God can really censure nothing but the free transgression of known law.

This unbalanced statement by the Confession of truths so eminently harmonious is itself the effect, not the cause, of a tendency in the minds of Christians to give undue prominence to one or the other of these great truths. Either because the human mind had not room enough to receive them both in their utmost latitude, or for some other reason, there has been in every age a tendency to exaggerate one at the expense of the other. The first three centuries exhibit a tendency to enhance free will at the expense of deep views of native depravity, resulting at length in Pelagianism. The age of Augustine reacted to an opposite extreme, asserting original sin at the sacrifice of free agency. The Tridentine theologians swung back toward the former extreme, the Reformers reacted again toward the latter.

Yet the germs of a more salutary reaction in the direction of human freedom were not wanting in the systems of the Reformers themselves. The Westminster Confession was to some extent a compromise between the two opposite tendencies of absolutism and moral government. We use the term absolutism in no invidious sense, to denote a system where the freedom of the will is practically annihilated, and the divine agency virtually absolute. By moral government we mean a system where the divine agency is related to, and limited by, the freedom of the creature will.

That there is a compromise between absolutism thus defined, and moral government in the Confession, is plain from such passages as the following:

"God from all eternity did, by the most wise and holy counsel of his own will, freely and unchangeably ordain whatsoever comes to pass, YET so as thereby neither is God the author of sin, nor is violence offered to the will of the creatures, nor is the liberty or contingency of second causes taken away, but rather established."

In that "YET so" the absolutism of the former sentence is forever tamed down and chained to the governmentalism (if we may coin a word) of the second.

A union of opposite tendencies appears in the earliest history of the Presbyterian Church in this country, during the quarter of a century previous to the adoption of the Confession in 1729. The Scotch and Irish Presbyterians united with the Congregationalists of New England on the Bible as their only creed. When the Confession was adopted, it was avowedly in a spirit of concession, and for substance of doctrine.

The great awakening under Whitefield and Edwards quickened the nascent reaction from absolutism, until, in the struggle between Old Side and New Side, the Church was rent asunder. In 1740 the compromise was renewed, and the two tendencies, modified but essentially unchanged, were transmitted under the auspices of the General Assembly. As the vast regions of the West were thrown open, and emigration began to pour onward, missionary enterprise was developed as a matter of course.

But nowhere is the genius of the two tendencies more strikingly exemplified than in relation to the organized forms of benevolent effort. Absolutism naturally tends to hierarchal authority, free agency to voluntary associations. The one predisposes to operate by Assembly's boards and ecclesiastical machinery, the other by popular societies and revivals. In the plan of union of 1801 we see a sort of compromise between the two, under the practical operation of which the great reaction from absolutism reached its height, and a counter reaction set in.

"Three fourths of the churches formed under this plan," said Dr. Beecher, "became Presbyterian. New England ministers looked on and approved. Dr. Dwight did, and I did. But it was in this way that the New School element increased in the Presbyterian Church. Wholly, wholly. Now, as long as the Old School had the sails and tiller to manage, they never grumbled, but were hugely tickled; for Presbyterianism grew so fast that the Methodists used to complain of a combination to run them down. But when, without any previous manœuvring (for we never had any of that foolish feeling about it), we chose the moderator in General Assembly five years out of seven, there began to be uneasiness."

The truth was, that when Dr. Beecher went to Lane Seminary there was in the New School mind of the country a buoyant and jubilant anticipation that their theology, which asserted free agency at the expense of profound views of innate ill desert, was moving on to take possession of the country. The Old School theology — that which asserted innate ill desert at the expense of the eternal principles of accountability and moral government — took the alarm, and rose up to battle. Then, for a time, the compromise became as tow, and the makers thereof as a spark, and none could quench them.

Now, inasmuch as the denial of either of these co-ordinate

truths — innate ill desert and accountable free agency — subverts Christianity and ends in infidelity — in the one case by the door of naturalism, in the other by that of fatalism — it was inevitable that the two parties should, with nearly equal justice, charge each other with tendencies to undermine the Gospel, and bring in a flood of error upon the churches, and should conscientiously put forth the greatest efforts to destroy each other's power.

While doing this, however, they would be, with nearly equal justice, grieved and offended at the accusations brought against them as uncharitable, unkind, and unchristian. In this state of mind, other motives incidental to partially-sanctified humanity would come in to embitter the strife — personal pique, resentment, rivalry, ambition, and the like. Thus, though neither party could succeed in destroying the other — both being right in what they affirmed, wrong in what they denied — they would exhaust each other's strength, quench each other's piety, grieve away the Spirit, and convulse the Church at last as by an earthquake.

That the baser motives alone, without the nobler, could have led to the mournful catastrophe, is incredible. The nobler motives were undoubtedly in many minds, if not in most, decidedly predominant. Alas! that they should have been stained and defiled, as they were, by admixtures of the baser. But men are not angels, and it is impossible that the shock of battle between two grand schemes of thought contesting the dominion of a continent should occur without lamentable exhibitions of human frailty, even in the best of men.

The trial of Dr. Beecher, together with those of Drs. Barnes and Duffield,[1] constituted the first shock of absolutistic theology thoroughly aroused and reacting against the theology of moral government. We can not, in this connection, go into the details of the trial, nor is it necessary. We shall content ourselves with such side glimpses as may be afforded by Dr. Beecher's recollections or correspondence.

"About a year after Dr. Wilson tried and failed to have a committee appointed to examine my writings," said Dr. Beecher, "toward the close of a session of Presbytery (November, 1834), he rose and preferred charges against me. My elder had gone, and there were two or three who had leave of absence and were just

[1] George Duffield (1794–1868), Pa. pastor, was found guilty of New School heresies (1832). Dismissed in 1835 from a Presbyterian church in Carlisle, Pa., in 1838 he took a church in Detroit, where he continued to lead New School reforms.

going. I laughed in my sleeve, and said to myself, 'You think you know more of Presbyterian management than I do; but I have as much common sense as you have, and have attended several ecclesiastical trials in my day, and all those councils and consociations in Connecticut were not for nothing.' I went to those that had leave, and told them to stay, and sent messengers after those that had left, and thus secured a majority to postpone the trial till after General Assembly, so that I should have time to prepare.

"When the trial came on (June, 1835), I took all my books and references, and sat down on the second stair of the pulpit. It was in my church. I looked so quiet and meek, my students were almost afraid I shouldn't come up to the mark. I had every thing just then to weigh me down. My wife was lying at home on her dying bed. She did not live a fortnight after that. Then there was all the wear and tear of the seminary and of my congregation. But when I had all my references, and had nothing to do but extemporize, I felt easy. I had as much lawyer about me as Wilson, and more. I never got into a corner, and he never got out; though the fact is he made as good a case as could be made on the wrong side.

"Morse, who was fond of me, hearing I was on trial, sent Stansbury, his best reporter, from Pittsburg, to take report. So we got it, every word of it. We had a good working majority, and the atmosphere was congenial and cordial, every thing safe and smiling. In those days we had to count noses every time there was a meeting of Presbytery or Synod, and keep a sharp look-out about absentees.

"Wilson attacked me for abandoning the standards. I said no, and gave what I deemed the right exposition, subject to the revision of General Assembly, which must be the final interpreter. Soon after, in his speech, he said I claimed a right to adopt the Creeds, and put my own construction on them. I corrected him, putting in the statement respecting General Assembly. Five minutes after he repeated it again, and I corrected him again. A third time the same thing over, and I corrected him as before. At this he scolded, and said he did not wish to be interrupted so, as it hindered him.

" 'Dr. Wilson,' said I, 'this is the third time you have misrepresented me, and I shall correct you until you put it right. You shall not go ahead from this point till you do it;' and he quailed, notwithstanding his hardihood.

"He did not know what he undertook. I knew to a hair's breadth every point between Old School and New School, and knew all their difficulties, and how to puzzle them with them. In Presbytery he had only inferior men on his side. He knew they were fools. Two of them had been sitting all their lives on goose-eggs * till they rotted under them. There was not another man equal to Wilson on his side, nor any where near it. On our side the trial was as strong as possible, and every body exulted with great exultation. So they laughed at him, even some Old Schoolish folks, and called him a dead man. Presbytery acquitted me, and he appealed to Synod."

In a letter dated July 15, 1835, Dr. Beecher thus writes: "My trial was the greatest blessing I have had happen to me this many a day, and the prospect is fine of two more opportunities of expounding the Confession, and defending and propagating all I believe and teach under its auspices, which I believe will, by the blessing of God, do much to tranquillize both the East and the West, and is a manner of defense much better than in the way of assault. You will see my defense. It was done *instanter*, most of it, and yet, under the momentum of the occasion, better than I could have prepared it in my study. The effect on the community here was good, and almost universally satisfactory. You will see what ground I take, and what you can take and maintain under the banner of the Confession, and it is best to study and rally round the Confession, for it contains the elements of all we need."

The following humorous account of Dr. Beecher's setting forth to attend Synod was written by his son Henry Ward, who accompanied him, and is dated Canal-boat, Wednesday morning, October 14, 1835.

"You who live remote from Walnut Hills have, notwithstanding, heard something of one of our stars, *Lyman Beecher*. But, though of note as a public character, he is not less famous and interesting in private life. Indeed, we, who see him daily, imagine that he exhibits more unequivocal marks of genius in the domestic than in a wider sphere; for in the pulpit (thanks to the attention of Aunt Esther) he wears whole stockings, has decent handkerchiefs and cravats, a tidy coat, and never wears one boot and one shoe together; and in his published works, who can see, through the type, either the manuscript or the writer?

"But in his family, and unmolested by feminine pertinacity of neatness, his genius peeps forth in various negligences of apparel, particularly his shirt sleeves, open bosom, and ample display of flannel. As if to put the broadest seal upon his genius, Nature seems to have ordained that he shall study half undressed.

"But if we admire these marks of innate abilities which appear

* That is, preaching imputation, inability, and limited atonement to the full extent.

on the exterior, no less are we surprised at those which he exhibits as a business man. Let me give you a sketch of our departure for Dayton.

"Having several weeks for preparation, he felt secure, and made no attempt at a beginning until the day before. Then, while cutting up stumps in the garden, he fell upon a *plan* for his defense, which was indicated to us by his precipitate retreat from his stump to his study. In the afternoon he dragged me away six miles, in an excess of patriotism, to deposit his *vote*. Before going to bed, he charged me to be up early, for he must get ready, and the boat was to start at nine.

"The morning opened on a striking scene. As I emerged from my room, the doctor was standing in his study doorway, a book under each arm, with a third in his hands, in which he was searching for quotations. In an hour and a half all his papers were to be collected (and from whence!), books assorted, breakfast eaten, clothes packed, and horse harnessed.

"After a hasty meal, whew! he goes up stairs, opens every drawer, and paws over all the papers, leaving them in confusion, and down stairs again to the drawers in his study, which are treated in like manner. He fills his arms with books, and papers, and sermons, and straightway seems to forget what he wanted them for, for he falls to assorting them vigorously *de novo*.

"Eight o'clock, and not half ready. Boat starts at nine.

" 'Where's my Burton?'

" 'Father, I have found the Spirit of the Pilgrims.'

" 'Don't want it. Where did I put that paper of extracts? Can't you make out another? Where did I lay my opening notes? Here, Henry, put this book in the carriage. Stop! give it to me. Let's see — run up stairs for my Register. No, no! I've brought it down.'

"Half past eight. Not ready. Three miles to go. Horse not up.

"At length the doctor completes his assortment of books and papers, packs, or rather stuffs his clothes into a carpet bag — no key to lock it — ties the handles, and leaves it gaping.

"At length we are ready to start. A trunk tumbles out of one side as Thomas [2] tumbles in the other. I reverse the order — tumble Tom out, the trunk in. At length all are aboard, and father drives out of the yard, holding the reins in one hand, shaking hands with

[2] Thomas K. Beecher (1824–1900) had such marked scientific interests that his father almost gave up his "favorite purpose" of the ministry for this son. But after graduating from Illinois College and acting as principal of schools in Philadelphia and Hartford, Thomas studied theology under his father, and in 1854 became pastor of an anti-slavery Independent Church in Elmira, N. Y. He equipped this church with pool and billiard tables and with a free library. Though

a student with the other, giving Charles directions with his mouth — at least that part not occupied with an apple; for, since apples were plenty, he has made it a practice to drive with one rein in the right hand and the other in the left, with an apple in each, biting them alternately, thus raising and lowering the reins like threads on a loom. Away we go, Charley horse on the full canter down the long hill, the carriage bouncing and bounding over the stones, father alternately telling Tom how to get the harness mended, and showing me the true doctrine of original sin. Hurra! We thunder alongside the boat just in time."

Dayton, Friday morning, October 16. "Yesterday the Synod was 'constituted.' Old School moderator by a majority of seven. Under his administration the system is beginning to receive form, and becomes apparent. All the committees are one way, and the whole aspect of affairs shows you that there is a deep-laid, regular plan, and the elders are all *drilled in.* The committee on leave of absence grant leave to all New School men, and refuse all others, so that they may increase, and we decrease.

"It is Friday morning, and every body is talking, planning, plotting — all bustle — heads together — knots at every corner — hands going up and down, and faces approaching earnestly or drawing back in doubt — one taking hold of the other's coat, leading off into one corner for a *particular argument* — elders receiving drill, some bolting the collar. Here, in my room, is father, George, and Mr. Rankin. They are looking over the ground, prognosticating, arranging for the onset, or for the reception of an onset. Abolitionists are standing on one foot, doubtful where to put the other down; with Dr. Wilson as a new-fledged Abolitionist,[3] or with father as a New School man.

"Nothing can give you such an idea of matters during this morning before nine o'clock as to imagine the preparation for a military battle — overhauling knapsacks, fixing flints, picking locks, fixing ammunition, cleaning muskets, arranging regimentals; then aids-de-camp riding to captain and corporal, from tent to tent, from man to man. It's all fever, all expectation — a bracing up the

---

he was expelled from the Ministerial Union for his billiard-playing and beer-drinking, he built a new Home Church in 1873–1875, which included a gym, a playroom, dancing room, theater, pool and billiard tables, and rooms where poor members might entertain their friends, and which was one of the first "Institutional Churches" in the country. To his large congregation, he stressed Jesus' ethical teachings. A moody man, he satisfied his mechanical interests by keeping the town clock in order. He contributed a weekly column to the Elmira *Advertiser.*

[3] Wilson in 1837 actually urged that Southerners should be free to "manage their concerns in their own way."

mind to meet all things — a determination to do all things — an expectation of all things.

"You know that the members of Synod are distributed among the families. Peter Kemper [4] was sent to Judge Holt's, where father had been invited. When, yesterday noon, we returned to dinner, there sat Sir Peter, with his huge round spectacles mounted on his nose, behind which his whole face seemed striving to come to a focus and peep through the glasses. Father came in to him laughing. 'Well, Mr. Kemper, we come together, I suppose, by the principle of *elective affinity*, do we not?' Mr. Kemper sprawled his legs, wriggled his hands, and drew down his mouth to the proper pitch of gravity and discretion, and then, with a most ominous monotony, he says, 'No — no — I suppose — it was what we — call — in common conversation — a cas — cas-u-al-i-ty.'

"I never saw so many faces of clergymen and so few of them intellectual faces. The predominant expression is that of firmness (in many cases deepening into obstinacy), kind-heartedness, and honesty. As for deep thought seen in the eye or lineaments — for lofty expression — for the enthusiasm of genius — for that expression which comes from communion with great thoughts, with the higher feelings of poetry and religion, and even of speculation, there is an utter want of it. There is very little dignity of expression: it is homespun, sensible integrity which characterizes them; and the elders are just what forty or fifty common farmers would be supposed to be, except that *for eldership the soberest men are chosen, and as stupidity is usually graced with more gravity than great good sense*, the body of elders are not quite so acute in look as the higher class of working men."

"When I got there," said Dr. Beecher, "and looked around, I thought the vote would run very close. My Presbytery, being appealed from, could not vote. The Old School had raked and scraped all the old dead churches where they could get an elder, and thought they might carry the day. It looked squally.

"When Wilson got up and made his speech — the best he ever did make, as he misrepresented things — it made the issue look dubious. The house grew dark; it didn't look dark to me; I knew what artillery I had got; I had some letters of his as a kind of masked battery. But there was an Old School majority, and his speech made a *sensation*.

[4] The Kemper family, who had given lands and funds to Lane, were divided by the Presbyterian schism. After 1832 the Old School Kempers withdrew their support, but Elnathan joined the New School.

"There was one time, though, he came near getting overset; it came near terminating the trials. In his argument before Presbytery he had said that man has *no ability of any kind* to obey God's commands. I told him then he was the first man I ever knew to march boldly up to that without flinching, and I praised him for his courage.

"But the fact was, that did not set well on Princeton. They wrote to him. Dr. Miller wrote — tutored him — hints, you know. He found he had gone too far; it was too rank. He undertook to change front. He went on, and changed his phraseology, and stated what he did hold. I jumped up and said, 'Dr. Wilson, that is precisely what I believe; let's have no more trials; give me your hand!' He was astounded — hung back. We adjourned till afternoon, and it lacked but a hair's breadth of his giving up the case.

"When my turn came, I went on from one point to another, and by-and-by the tide turned; and when the time came to vote, there was a majority against him of ten to one.*

* *Extract from the Minutes of Synod.*

"After recess the roll was called, that the members might express their opinions on the appeal of Dr. Wilson; after which it was, on motion, resolved that the appeal be sustained:

"1st. Because the Synod see nothing in the conduct of J. L. Wilson, in preferring and prosecuting charges against Lyman Beecher, which ought to infer censure.

"2d. Because, although the charges of slander and hypocrisy are not proved, and although Synod see nothing in his views, as explained by himself, to justify any suspicion of unsoundness in the faith, yet, on the subject of the depraved nature of man, and of total depravity, and the work of the Holy Spirit in effectual calling, and the subject of ability, they are of the opinion that Dr. Beecher has indulged a disposition to philosophize, instead of exhibiting in simplicity and plainness these doctrines as taught in the Scriptures; and has employed terms and phrases, and modes of illustration calculated to convey ideas inconsistent with the Word of God and our Confession of Faith, and that he ought to be, and he is hereby admonished to be more guarded in future.

"*Friday morning.* The parties in the case of J. L. Wilson's appeal being called in, L. Beecher declared his ready acquiescence in the decision of the Synod, and his determination to act conformably to their admonition. Whereupon it was resolved,

"1st. That the Synod express their satisfaction with the aforementioned acquiescence and determination of Dr. Beecher, and are happy in believing that nothing insuperable remains to prevent his usefulness or impair our confidence in him as a minister of the Gospel in the Presbyterian Church.

"2d. That Lyman Beecher be, as he hereby is, requested to have published, at as early a day as possible, in pamphlet form, a concise statement of the argument and design of his sermon, Native Character, and of his views of Total Depravity, Original Sin, Regeneration, and Natural and Moral Ability, agreeably to his declarations and explanations made before Synod.

"J. L. Wilson gave notice that he would appeal from the decision of Synod to the next General Assembly."

"They came round me like bees, some that had been on his side, as cordial as could be. The next day, when Wilson came in in the morning, he was as pale as a ghost — first time I ever saw him look *down*. Dr. Bishop [5] told him that they had been merciful to him, but that, if he ever put himself in such circumstances again, he must look out.

"He said he did not know what course he should take — whether to appeal to General Assembly or not; but finally he grew stronger, and appealed.

"Well, just before the appeal came on at Pittsburg (May, 1836), I sent two or three dozens of the report of my trial up to be distributed in the Pittsburg Synod. When I got there they flocked round me. 'Why, your doctrine is just that of our great favorite, Dr. ——, and we are not going to see you hung.' The third day of the session, Dr. Wilson rose and said he was prepared to prosecute the appeal, but that his friends had told him they could not sustain him, and he was willing to withdraw.

"That, however, depended on my consent. He could not give it up unless I chose. Dr. Miller, in high glee, hoped I would not object.

"I rose and said meekly that I was ready for trial, but that if Dr. Wilson wanted to cease, I supposed that, according to the Book, after being dragged through all the Church courts, I had a right to claim that my prosecutor ought to be treated as I should have been if condemned.*

"Dr. Wilson bounded from his seat and blazed out — he had no concessions or confessions to make. Others begged of me not to make difficulty; and such a great flustration as they were in I never saw. I did not know the reason then, but I know it now. You see, in my trial, I had taken the New School doctrines, and expounded and proved them under the Confession, and now, if the trial went on, those doctrines would be sustained by the General Assembly. The fact was, that in the discussion between New Haven and Princeton, conducted in the Christan Spectator and the Repertory, New Haven had pushed them so, and they had made such

* The prosecutor of a minister shall be previously warned that if he fail to prove the charge, he must himself be censured as a slanderer of the Gospel ministry, in proportion to the malignancy or rashness that shall appear in the prosecution. — *Book of Discipline,* ch. v., § vii.

---

[5] Robert Bishop (1777–1853), editor of the *Evangelical Record and Western Review,* after pastorates in Ky. and Conn., became president of Miami University, Ohio (1825–1841).

concessions and distinctions, that some of my strongest testimonies were drawn from their own documents.

"Now this would make trouble among themselves. Many of the Old School would be scandalized to find Princeton had been on New School ground, and to have New School doctrine sustained by General Assembly through their aid. Well, I never knew how much they were troubled about that till afterward. So, after enjoying their consternation for a moment or two, I said I should make no objection, and the thing was dropped."

XXXVIII

A FAMILY MEETING

In the same class with the doctor's two sons, Henry Ward and Charles, and very intimate with them, was a young man named George Hastings, a graduate of Harvard, of fine qualities, sparkling wit, full of fun, and rather distinguished for literary and linguistic acquirements. He gradually came to be regarded almost as one of the family, and when the following scene occurred, was present during much of the time. Being in habits of constant correspondence with a friend in Boston, he sent the following description, with no thought of its publication. His friend, however, thinking it would prove interesting to the doctor's numerous friends, inserted it in one of the papers of the day. As a vivid reproduction of a striking scene in the doctor's life, we insert it here.

"Long before Edward came out here the doctor tried to have a family meeting, but did not succeed. The children were too scattered. Two were in Connecticut, some in Massachusetts, and one in Rhode Island. That, I believe, was five years ago. But — now just think of it! — there has been a family meeting in Ohio! When Edward returned, he brought on Mary from Hartford; William came down from Putnam, Ohio; George from Batavia, Ohio; Catharine and Harriet were here already; Henry and Charles at home too, besides Isabella, Thomas, and James.[1] These eleven! The first time they all ever met together! Mary had never seen James, and she had seen Thomas but once.

"Such a time as they had! The old doctor was almost transported with joy. The affair had been under negotiation for some time. He returned from Dayton late one Saturday evening. The next morning they, for the first time, assembled in the parlor. There were

[1] James Beecher (1828–1886) was drawn to the sea, but early accepted that he would be a minister. "Father will pray me into it." He graduated from Dartmouth and studied at Andover. After some years in the East India trade as sailor and officer, he became chaplain of the Seamen's Bethel in Hongkong. During the Civil War he was a chaplain and then colonel of the First Company of Colored Volunteers. He held churches in N. Y., but became increasingly troubled in mind. From 1881–1882 he served in the Bethel Mission of Henry Ward's church. In the last years of his life he suffered periods of insanity. When the "water cure" treatment failed, he committed suicide.

more tears than words. The doctor attempted to pray, but could scarcely speak. His full heart poured itself out in a flood of weeping. He could not go on. Edward continued, and each one, in his turn, uttered some sentences of thanksgiving. They then began at the head and related their fortunes. After special prayer, all joined hands, and sang Old Hundred in these words:

" 'From all who dwell below the skies.'

Edward preached in his father's pulpit in the morning, William in the afternoon, and George in the evening. The family occupied the three front pews on the broad aisle. Monday morning they assembled, and, after reading and prayers, in which all joined, they formed a circle. The doctor stood in the middle, and gave them a thrilling speech. He then went round, and gave them each a kiss. They had a happy dinner.

"Presents flowed in from all quarters. During the afternoon the house was filled with company, each bringing an offering. When left alone at evening they had a general examination of all their characters. The shafts of wit flew amain, the doctor being struck in several places; he was, however, expert enough to hit most of them in turn. From the uproar of the general battle, all must have been wounded. Tuesday morning saw them together again, drawn up in a straight line for the inspection of the king of happy men. After receiving particular instructions, they formed into a circle. The doctor made a long and affecting speech. He felt that he stood for the last time in the midst of all his children, and each word fell with the weight of a patriarch's. He embraced them once more in all the tenderness of his big heart. Each took of all a farewell kiss. With joined hands they joined in a hymn. A prayer was offered; and, finally, the parting blessing was spoken. Thus ended a meeting which can only be rivaled in that blessed home where the ransomed of the Lord, after weary pilgrimage, shall join in the praise of the Lamb. May they all be there!

"Truly the crown of old men is their children."

XXXIX

BROKEN TIES

WHILE pursuing the thread of ecclesiastical narrative in a former chapter, a passing allusion was made to scenes of deep interest transpiring in Dr. Beecher's household. For several years the health of Mrs. Beecher had been gradually failing, and now, under the combined influences of change of climate, the fatigues of removal, increased responsibility, and anxiety, her constitution sunk under the power of disease, and while Dr. Beecher was defending himself before Presbytery, she was slowly passing away from life.

Constitutionally less inclined than some to look on the bright side of things, her mind had been gradually losing that elasticity and brilliancy which was the charm of her early youth, and faith and hope were for a season dimmed by a melancholy depression of spirit. She had witnessed the awful ravages of cholera in the city and in the institution, and had felt its strange, depressing effect upon her own nervous and physical system — an ordeal, to those in the most robust health, never encountered without horror nor remembered without awe. She had watched by the bedside of a young and lovely friend, whose untimely death spread a veil of sadness over all the families connected with the institution.*

With morbid facility, her mind had received and retained the sombre hues of grief, and she shivered as she entered amid the clouds of the dark valley of the shadow of death; nor could she at first find her Savior there. Yet, as her end drew nigh, amid acute and protracted sufferings, she was enabled to say, "Thou art with

* The following is an extract from one of her letters describing the death-bed scene: "Esther was with her that day constantly. The next morning we found no hope of recovery left. She was struggling with death when I entered: her brows were knit, and a deadly paleness was gathering fast, with distressing movements and convulsive throes. I thought, 'O Lord God! can we go through this?' Mr. Stowe said, 'Oh, my love, remember, remember, "The Lord is my Shepherd, I shall not want; he leads me in green pastures, beside the still waters: these comforts have delighted my soul."' She broke out, 'Oh how delightful!' Her whole countenance brightened and gleamed. She waved her hands with joy, saying, 'Oh how delightful! Did you ever see any thing like it? Joy unspeakable and full of glory! There is not room enough to receive it!' She continued in this state until she sunk into a sleep-like state, from which I suppose she had no more consciousness."

me; Thy rod and Thy staff, they comfort me." In her last moments the veil was lifted, and the glories of the celestial city seemed to meet her view, and the sounds of celestial minstrelsy to strike her ear.

"Music!" she exclaimed, "music! Can you not hear it? Beautiful music! Oh sing! sing!"

Thus the darkest hour was just before dawn; and though her weeping endured for a night, joy came in the morning. She fell asleep in Jesus. And now her dust rests in the beautiful cemetery on Walnut Hills, with the dust of many another loved form deposited there in tears till the archangel trump. The bright, the beautiful, the accomplished of Eastern circles of refinement slumbers on the banks of the far Ohio, to wake on the banks of the river of life, that proceedeth out of the throne of God.

The Christian character of Mrs. Beecher was unusually deep, earnest, and solemn. Her prayers for her children were agonizing, her solicitude for their spiritual welfare overwhelming, and her instructions all that such maternal emotions and a naturally fine intellect could prompt. In the holy yearnings of this truly devoted mother the whole family were included, nor could the older children perceive any less fervency in her desires for their true welfare than for that of her own flesh and blood. To her superior character in this respect is undoubtedly owing, in large measure, that unbroken unity that continued to characterize so large a band of brothers and sisters — a unity of perfect love, that could admit no distinctions.

From the correspondence of that period a few extracts are here presented, in which affectionate reference is made to her departed worth. August 30, 1835, Edward writes as follows:

"My dear Father, — Since I heard of the death of mother, I have been waiting to obtain some particulars concerning her last hours before writing to you; but as I was not in New York after the news of her death arrived, I could not expect to hear directly from you. It is not until now that I have been able to ascertain any of the facts of the case. I am glad to find, from your note to Mary, and from what is said by Catharine and Henry, that God was with her in her closing days, and that the light of his countenance cheered her passage to the tomb so long as reason remained. * * *

"God so ordered, in his mercy, that nothing should remain to prevent, in the minds of any of her children and friends, unmingled emotions of love, respect for her character, a full sense of her worth, and sincere sorrow for her loss. As far as I am concerned, though I never was with her as with my own mother, and though I could never feel for her that peculiar attachment for a mother which can, as I suppose, be felt but once, yet my feelings toward her were ever those of unmingled respect and affection, and not one thing now occurs to my memory of an unpleasant kind that ever took place between us, and with deep and filial sorrow I mourn her loss. I only regret that it never was in my power to do more than I did to manifest my love for her, and to promote her happiness. But her scenes of trial are over; her hours of depression and gloom shall never more return; but her tears God has forever wiped away, and I look forward with joyful anticipations to the time when I shall join her and my own dear mother in heaven.

"I have just been to Guilford and Litchfield, and have been endeavoring to recall the recollections of other days. Never have I felt more vividly the shortness of life, and the rapidity with which all whom we have known and loved are passing into eternity; and the thought is not depressing. Soon our work will be done, and we shall be there.

"I can assure you, my dear father, that I have felt the deepest sympathy for you in all your cares and trials. It would have been but a painful sympathy had I not felt an assurance that you are engaged for God in a great work, and that he will sustain you in all your trials. So far as your public cares are concerned, I feel confident that you were never laboring to greater effect than now."

"Your mother's death," writes Dr. Beecher to Edward, in December, 1835, "sits heavily on my spirits. I feel her absence and am solitary. My affection for her was sincere and unfailing. But her mental sufferings, the result of constitution, habit, and disease, during her decline, which I could not possibly alleviate, connect sadness with every reminiscence. She, I am satisfied, is at rest; but I can not stay my sorrow at the remembrance of her great sufferings. I do not yield to it, nor permit the subject to prey upon my health or spirits; but I disclose to you my secret sorrows, that you may know how to sympathize with me and pray for me.

"Write a letter to me for my own particular satisfaction, as, having lived in and with you so many years, I do not like our growing non-intercourse and non-communion. So, if you have no time or strength, please do as I have done, and dash off a letter instanter without any. * * * I send you my Oxford address, called 'Plea for Colleges.' I trust it may do good in these ultra days of flippant genius and insubordination. I am now preparing my Views on Theology by request of Synod, in which I have got on so far as to feel persuaded that I shall satisfy myself, which is the most difficult thing, and most laborious, you know, for me. All the signs of the times indicate that our Church will not go the Philadelphia gate, but will bolt from the central leading-strings."

From the many expressions of sympathy at this time received by Dr. Beecher, the following will be read with interest. Dr. Skinner writes, Sept. 17, 1835:

"If the face of things, as far as they are publicly known respecting you, is not deceptive, you must be in a frame of spirit, in the midst of your deep and various afflictions, too calm and triumphant to be dependent on human sympathy for comfort; yet your brethren would not deserve your affection or respect if they could refrain from feelings of condolence, or from praising God for the grace whereby he has enabled you to endure and quench the violence of the fire which has been kindled by the adversary for your destruction. I can not tell you how great joy I have had in contemplating the power of the Gospel as lately illustrated in your history.

"When I remember that God's hand was heavy upon you in your family at the very time that his providence called you to exercise a strength and a patience in defense of the truth to which there has been no parallel in our land, I can not avoid exclaiming, in view of the result, What hath God wrought? The saints, dear brother, are refreshed by the exhibitions which you have made of your mind and heart in the conflict through which you are passing, and I doubt not that when you are dead they will continue to be edified and blessed by the same exhibitions. God meant your trial for greater good than could have been anticipated by yourself or any creature. The happy consequences of it begin to develop themselves, but will not end, until the Valley of the Mississippi, and the American continent, and the world, are full of the glory of God as the waters cover the seas. The press will give perpetuity to your defense of the Gospel, and God, I can not doubt, will follow it with an abundant blessing in coming ages.

"Why talk we of hoping to be in heaven? Are we not in heaven already while thus surrounded by the unequivocal marks of the divine presence and smiles? What is this joy but the beginning of that which will exhaust the promise? Let us retain our confidence, and we shall assuredly continue to advance in blessedness until we join the company of the saints and angels above. I suppose that nothing is now to be watched against more than vain elation and pride. Ought we not to have a concert of prayer, that we may be delivered perfectly from that spirit which has caused all our ecclesiastical strife, and be robed in humility?"

XL

CORRESPONDENCE, 1836–1837

In the present chapter a few extracts will be presented from the correspondence of 1836–7, part of which period has been already gone over.

February 19, 1836, Rev. W. A. Stearns,[1] of Cambridgeport, Massachusetts, writes as follows: "Inclosed is a bank-note of one hundred dollars, which you will please accept, for your own use, from your friends in Cambridgeport. It is a feeble expression of gratitude for favors which we can never repay — an acknowledgment of obligations which we can never cancel. Not more than seven or eight years ago you went to war in this place at your own charges. You fought a hard battle, and, through the blessing of God, gained a great victory. We enjoy, in consequence, peace and plenty."

April 9, 1836, Dr. Pond, of Bangor, writes: " * * * In Maine we do not sympathize very deeply in your Presbyterian squabbles, except to look on, and laugh at you all. The silencing of Barnes, however, was a pretty serious matter, about which but one opinion is entertained in this quarter. We all regard it as a stretch of power which must, and ought to be, followed by a reaction and retribution. The theology of Maine is almost entirely the old New England theology. We have a few *Tasters*, but a great majority hold the doctrines of depravity and regeneration as taught by yourself.

"Our ministers are serious, able, godly men, and the Lord blesses their labors. Many precious revivals of religion are in progress at the present time. Some twenty or twenty-five of our ministers are *anti-slavery*, but not boisterous nor overbearing. My views on that subject remain much as they were, and very much, I have reason to believe, in harmony with your own. The business of instructing in theology is very much to my taste. I have one difficulty, however, which I will state. I early wrote out a course of theological lectures, hoping that they would stand by me from year to year; but I find, on recurring to them, that they do not *keep well*. They need rewriting almost every year. If you can sug-

[1] William A. Stearns (1805–1876) became president of Amherst College in 1854.

gest a remedy for so great an evil, I shall be very much obliged."

At this time Professor Stowe was authorized by the trustees of the institution to proceed to Europe for the purchase of books, to lay the foundation of a library. From New York he writes, May 30, to Dr. Beecher, then attending the session of General Assembly at Pittsburg, as follows:

"We have just heard of poor old Dr. Wilson's misfortune and retreat. I suppose you will stay to see the Assembly through, and on that supposition I direct to you at Pittsburg. I have engaged passage in the ship Montreal, which will sail day after to-morrow. Mr. Stevenson, our embassador to London, to whom I have a letter from Mr. Rives, of Virginia, goes out in the same vessel.

"We have had no success in attempting to raise money, and have not been able to collect all the subscriptions already due, such is the pressure; but people hope it will be better in a few weeks. I am obliged to set out with less than $5000, trusting to you and Brother Vail to raise more in the summer, and send it on to me. *You* can get the money. Brother Adams said the Boston people would give to you liberally if you would ask them, and I am sure the New York people will also. The money market will be easier then, and if you do not take hold our whole library effort will be a failure. I shall employ the money I take out in purchasing complete sets of the fathers and reformers, for these must be the cornerstone of a theological library, and I do hope that $5000 at least will be added. * * *

"I think, also, you can do much in New England toward allaying the theological disputes. Every body appears to feel kindly toward you, and to have confidence that you are not far from right. Do, by all means, go to East Windsor and see Father Tyler. He is *longing* for you to come."

October 16, Professor Stowe writes from London: " * * I am grieved, but not surprised, at the wrong-headedness of the old party in our Church. It is all in vain. Their day has gone by, never to return. Their philosophy is exploded — blown sky-high; and their theology is a dead letter, for which there is no resuscitation. Keep good order at the seminary; let things go on like clockwork, and you have nothing to fear. I shall endeavor to lay out the additional £700 to the best possible advantage.

"There is so much that I wish to say to you about matters here in Europe that I hardly know where to begin. Dr. J. P. Smith,[2]

[2] John P. Smith (1774–1851), nonconformist, held the theological tutorship at Homerton College, wrote a two volume defense of Trinitarianism (1818–1821),

by many degrees the best theologian in England, is much pleased with your book, and indorses cordially its principal sentiments. The evangelical men in Germany to whom I have shown it concur with great pleasure in your statements of the doctrines, but express their regret that, with your *fine mind* and *stirring logic*, you should still be in bondage to the *empiric, utilitarian philosophy;* [3] and I can not deny that I think them more than three quarters in the right. They appreciate your powers a great deal better than I thought they would, and think very highly of your *theology* separated from your *philosophy*, of which they can not speak with the least patience, any more than you can of theirs."

---

and in 1839 attempted to present an exegesis of *Genesis* in harmony with geological evidences.

[3] At Yale Beecher had been trained in British empiricism, which taught that most of our knowledge was ultimately derived from sensations. Kant's critique of empiricism had influenced German theologians, but there is no evidence that Beecher investigated or pondered theories of knowledge after he left college.

XLI

PERILS

THE failure of Absolutism to crush Moral Government by ecclesiastical trials led to the adoption of more strenuous measures. A combination was formed between certain New England theologians and the Old School Presbyterian leaders for the summary ejection not only of the New Haven theology, but of all those who refused to pronounce it heretical.

In the course of conversation on the subject, Dr. Beecher was asked, "Father, is it a fact that Taylor's opponents in New England were co-operating with the Old School leaders in the Presbyterian Church?"

"Expressly and entirely," he replied; "and because I would not denounce Taylor, they did every thing they could to help my assailants. At first they tried to bring me over. They wrote letters, which were shown to me, designed to exert an urgent influence in that direction. They held on with tenacity; they wanted to draw me in; they hated to give me up. They said, 'We have got to fight this great battle with Taylorism, and Dr. Beecher refuses to help us; he stands in our way; we must either win him over or put him down.' Their whole strength was put forth, first in one and then in the other attempt. I must either denounce Taylor or share his fate."

The voluminous correspondence in our possession enables us to verify and illustrate the above statement. Immediately after Dr. Beecher's trial before Presbytery, Dr. Tyler writes to his son-in-law, Professor Stowe, now also Dr. Beecher's son-in-law, and thus admirably situated to mediate between the two, a letter seriously yet kindly reflecting on Dr. Beecher's course.

He deeply regrets that Dr. Beecher should have fallen into trouble, the more that there was no necessity for it. If he "had pursued a perfectly straight course the Old School men would never have thought of prosecuting him." Dr. Wilson has risen in the writer's good opinion both as to talents and piety. Dr. Beecher "has given too much occasion for the charge which Dr. Wilson brings against him in his closing plea of aiming at popular effect."

His defense "is ingenious and able, and his reasoning, for the most part, conclusive, *particularly on the subject of ability*." His views of the Spirit's agency in regeneration the writer does not entirely approve.

He is surprised at Dr. Beecher's indorsement of the Confession, especially after Mrs. ——, of Andover, heard him say, in a stage-coach, that Old Calvinism, as taught by Dwight, Bellamy, and Edwards, must go down.* He thinks "what Dr. Beecher has said about Dr. Taylor will be to his discredit among all those who are dissatisfied with New Haven theology," both in New England and in the Presbyterian Church; also, that "it would have been better for him not to have said any thing about Mr. Finney."

His course in reference to these two men "has lowered him in the esteem of many of the best men in New England. The feelings of Dr. Porter were very much hurt, and very many sympathized with him." Mr. Rand's letter is disapproved, yet "the facts stated are generally true." The statements of "Edwardean" are unquestioned.† On the whole, those who are opposed to the New Haven theology feel that Dr. Beecher "has needlessly plunged himself into the fire."

In December (24th) Dr. Tyler writes again:

"When I said in my former letter that Dr. Beecher had needlessly plunged himself into this difficulty, I referred entirely to his course in New England before he went to the West. The time was when he had the confidence of the Old School Presbyterians, as is evident from letters which he exhibited on his trial, and from other facts which might be mentioned. And yet he was then supposed to entertain the views of doctrine which prevail in New England. And what is it which impaired that confidence? It was the countenance which he gave Dr. Taylor and Mr. Finney. Had it not been for his connection with these men, and the fact that he was supposed to sympathize with them in their theological views,

* Here Dr. Beecher interlines: "Mrs. ——'s representation is utterly false; I said no such thing."

† Reference is made to an anonymous pamphlet published in 1832 by Dr. Harvey, of which Crocker remarks: "This pamphlet, with all its misrepresentations of the views of Dr. Taylor and his friends, and with all its bitterness and denunciation, was not without its effect. It increased jealousies and suspicions at home, and gave currency abroad to the widely-circulated rumors of heresy, and an extensive and lamentable defection among the ministry and churches of Connecticut. Though it was without any responsible name, and none except those in the secret could tell whence it issued (the letter wanting even the name of the printer or place of publication), yet it was adduced in a far distant Church judicatory as evidence against a distinguished minister, whose character it aspersed."

he never would have been the object of such jealousy and suspicion. Had he been understood to sympathize with such men as Dr. Porter, Dr. Woods, Dr. Humphrey,[1] etc., in relation to the New Haven speculations, he might have gone to the West and taught the New England divinity, as it was taught by our standard divines, without molestation. * * *

"One thing, however, is certain — the New Haven men and their satellites do consider Dr. Beecher as on their side. They proclaim it upon the house-top that he has assured them that he agrees with them in sentiment. His name is made use of from Dan to Beersheba to give currency to their views, and they rely on him to sustain their cause more than any other man. If he does not intend that his influence shall be thrown into that scale, he ought not to suffer his name to be thus used, and I do hope that when he shall publish his views he will set the matter right.

"I can assure you that many in New England are waiting with anxiety to see what course he will take. A good opportunity is now afforded him to wipe off the suspicions which he has excited: such another opportunity he will probably never have while he lives. I do hope he will come out fully and frankly, and speak with such plainness that it can be seen by every body on what ground he intends to stand. * * *

"I wish you to understand that I was highly gratified with the decision of your Synod. So also was Brother Nettleton, and all whom I have heard speak of it. If you suppose that I, or any who sympathize with me, should have been glad to see Dr. Beecher condemned as a heretic, you are greatly mistaken. I have ever felt that he ought to be acquitted. And yet I think the admonition of Synod was merited, and I was happy to witness the spirit with which it was received. I love the man. I have confidence in his piety. I shall ever cherish with warm affection my long and intimate acquaintance with him.

"But much as I love and venerate him, and painful as it would be to do aught to circumscribe his influence, yet, if he lends his influence to promote what I believe to be dangerous error, I shall feel it to be my duty to oppose him. * *

"Now for your question, 'Do you, or those who think with you in New England, intend or desire, for the sake of putting down New Haven, to make common cause with the Old School Presby-

[1] Heman Humphrey (1779–1861), New England pastor, active in the temperance movement, became president of Amherst in 1823. Though sympathetic to revivals, he opposed Finney's New Measures.

terians against your own brothers and sons in the Gospel at the South and West?' I can answer, for myself, that such a thought never entered my mind, nor did I ever hear any such desire or intention expressed by others. * * * If there is any plan in New England to form such an alliance as you speak of, it has not yet come to my knowledge.

"But your letter has suggested to me the inquiry whether there ought not to be a better understanding between those who mean to stand on old New England ground in the Presbyterian Church and their brethren here, that they may act in council, and not seem to oppose one another. We have one *ism* to contend with, you another. If you wish us to sympathize with you, you must sympathize with us. If you wish us not to enter into an alliance with your opponents, you must not enter into an alliance with ours. If Dr. Beecher wishes for our influence to hold him up at the West, he must not lend his influence to put us down at the East. Let those who think alike understand one another and act in concert.

"It is my decided opinion that if the New School men in the Presbyterian Church will take decided ground, and let it be known that they disapprove the new *isms,* the moderate Old School men will co-operate with them in opposition to the measures of the ultras, and thus keep the Presbyterian Church straight. But if they temporize, and attempt to stand on the fence, and suffer their influence to be thrown into the scale of the new isms, not only the Old School men, but their more decided brethren of the New School, will be suspicious of them, and every thing will go wrong.

"I see not why your seminary should not have a good understanding with Princeton. Dr. Beecher held the confidence of the Princeton professors till he was *supposed* to favor the New Haven theology; but now, I am told, they really believe that not only he, but even you, intend to give all your influence to countenance the New Haven errors. Let this suspicion be wiped away, and confidence will be again restored, and the two seminaries may co-operate in promoting the common interests of the Church."

"Meanwhile," says Dr. Beecher, "Nettleton was down at Richmond, Virginia, staying with Dr. Plummer,[2] a leading Old School Presbyterian, and suggesting to him all that the party in New England could furnish to push me deeper into difficulty."

[2] William Plummer (1802–1880), famous as a preacher, was pastor in Richmond, Va. As editor of the *Watchman of the South,* he exposed New School heresies and in 1837 led in the exclusion of New School synods from the General Assembly.

From Petersburg Dr. Nettleton writes to Dr. Tyler, January 21, 1836: "When I was at Richmond the other day, Dr. Plummer put the question to me seriously, 'Did Dr. Beecher say to you, at such a time and place, "Taylor and I have made you what you are, and if you do not behave yourself we will hew you down?"' I did not know what answer to make but 'Who told you?' 'Dr. Taylor himself, when I was at his house last summer.'"

On this Dr. Tyler immediately writes to Professor Stowe, January 26, 1836: " * * * This fact Brother Nettleton never mentioned to me before, and he assures me that he has never before mentioned it to any one. You can judge of his surprise, therefore, when this question was put to him by Mr. Plummer. The threat I understand was made by Dr. Beecher at his own house in Boston in 1829. It would never have been known to any one but himself and Brother Nettleton had he not communicated it to Dr. Taylor, but would have suffered it to pass like many other improper things which are said in secret. But it has come to light through Dr. Beecher's own agency, and, it would seem, was regarded by him as a *bonâ fide threat.*

"And is it so? Is there a league between Dr. Beecher and Dr. Taylor to 'hew down' Brother Nettleton? the man of whom Dr. Beecher said in 1827, 'Mr. Nettleton has served God and his generation with more self-denial, and constancy, and wisdom, and success, than any man living?' * * * And what is the misbehavior of Mr. Nettleton for which he is to be '*hewn down?*' The occasion on which the threat was uttered I understand to be the following:

"In October, 1829, Brother Nettleton met several of the orthodox ministers of Boston in Dr. Beecher's study; and being about to leave New England for the South, in company with Dr. Porter, he said to them that * * * he was opposed to the New Haven speculations, and should feel it his duty, wherever he went, to bear his testimony against them. It was this which called forth the threat from Dr. Beecher after the ministers had retired. * * * This is the crime for which he is to be *hewn down;* and Dr. Taylor and his friends have begun in earnest to *hew him down.* * * * Now I feel constrained to ask, Do Dr. Beecher, and those who act with him, for the sake of putting down 'Old Calvinism,' intend to make common cause with the Taylorites, and *hew down* their own flesh and blood in New England? The facts which I have named demand an explanation, and they must be explained before we can believe that Dr. Beecher does not intend to throw the whole weight of his influence into the scale of the New Haven school. I will thank you to show this letter to Dr. Beecher, and inform him that there is yet 'one man in New England who will consider that in defending Mr. Nettleton he defends the cause (of Christ) in one of its most vital points.' "

On this letter is endorsed, in Dr. Beecher's handwriting, as follows, March, 1837: "The transaction called a threat was a mere playful act of humor, and was so understood by Nettleton. In cutting wood, with a look and tone he understood, I shook my axe at him, and said playfully something of the kind repeated, at which we both laughed, and it passed away in that form. That same evening I read him my sermon on Infant Character, which I supposed crossed Taylor's track, and with which he was pleased. I mentioned it to Taylor as a piece of playfulness, and so he understood it and stated it to Plummer. Nettleton's affecting to have taken it seriously, and kept it secret, and permitting this impression to be made on Plummer and Tyler, is one of the inexplicables of one who was then a friend and brother, and who has no right to pretend now that he thought the threat real at the time."

Next came a letter from Dr. Plummer, of Richmond, Virginia, dated January 30, 1836, informing Dr. Beecher that "for some two or three years there have been things said respecting you in all the line of our Atlantic States where I have traveled, which were of a distressing nature, * * * and they are gaining rather than losing strength." If Dr. Beecher will answer a few questions, Dr. Plummer will take great pleasure in publishing his reply in Richmond. The questions were such as the following:

Did Dr. Beecher ever say that the attempt to invigorate the Assembly's Board of Missions was the dying kick of Presbyterianism? Does Dr. Beecher hold the same sentiments about creeds as he expressed in New York in 1829? Did Dr. Porter ever have any correspondence with Dr. Beecher to try and change his theological views? Did Dr. Beecher ever say in a public stage that Old Calvinism must go down? What did Dr. Beecher mean by what he said of Dr. Taylor and Mr. Finney in his recent trial? Is Lane Seminary to be an engine for opposing Old Calvinism and sound Presbyterianism? etc., etc. "A frank avowal on these points," it is stated in conclusion, "would make many friends to Lane Seminary."

On this letter Dr. Beecher remarks at the time in a letter to one of his sons: "The war in Connecticut between New Haven and East Windsor is becoming more intense in feeling, and is working up to an eruption. Nettleton is in Virginia operating, and the plan is to form an alliance, offensive and defensive, against New Haven, permitting all other heretics to live who will consent to abjure that school. I have received a letter from Plummer, raking up all old things and new ever reported by Old School or others about me? It gives me an opportunity to kill a brood of vipers at once. There are Old School men who have made deliberate and indefatigable efforts to undermine confidence in me in the South, and in this way to choke the seminary."

Shortly after, February 20, 1836, Dr. Tyler writes to Professor Stowe a very long and elaborate letter, of which the following is a condensed outline. The writer is glad that Professor Stowe is perfectly aware "that the New Haven speculations are the real cause of the convulsions in the Presbyterian Church." He is pleased with the course marked out for Lane Seminary to pursue, and has "no wish that it should assume a belligerent attitude against New Haven men or any body else." But he adds, "Some things in Dr. Beecher's course have awakened suspicions which ought in some prudent way to be removed. I sent a copy of my letter of December 24 to Brother Nettleton, which, he informs me, he sent to Dr. Miller (of Princeton). The following is an extract of Dr. Miller's letter in reply."

DR. MILLER TO DR. NETTLETON.

"I feel particularly indebted to your kindness in communicating a copy of Dr. Tyler's letter. Every word of it is weighty, and worthy of the most serious consideration. I rejoice that he takes such clear and just views of almost all the subjects which he undertakes to discuss, and that the estimates which he forms of the real state of things, both in our Church and in New England, are so correct. I can not but hope that such a letter, being shown to Dr. Beecher, as it doubtless was, may have been useful to him.

"Yet, to say the truth, I was much discouraged with one thing in Dr. Beecher's trial; I mean, that he should, after making such explanations and declarations as really placed him upon pretty thorough Old School ground, have spoken as he did of Dr. Taylor and Mr. Finney. Is it possible to reconcile that man's whole course with a sound, honest, straightforward purpose? It would give me more pleasure than I can express to see him come out *bright*, and *entirely consistent*. But I fear there has been somewhere such a tampering with conscience as will be found to eat like a canker both into character and usefulness.

"I was struck with your (Mr. Nettleton's) just remark that

'attempts are now made to account for all the opposition to Dr. Beecher and Dr. Taylor on the ground of sheer prejudice against the New England divines as a body.' I am aware of this fact. Those who wish to make this impression, after presenting a dishonest caricature of Old Calvinism, in real verity dressing it up 'in bears' skins,' try to persuade their disciples that none but such as adopt this *ultra orthodoxy* have any objection to the New Haven opinions. There can not be a more unjust statement; nor can any one who is acquainted with facts believe it.

"For, on the one hand, it is well known that a large number of divines resident in New England, most eminent for talents, learning, and piety, are as thoroughly opposed to the New Haven opinions as any of us, and these venerated brethren enjoy the affectionate confidence of the ministers of the Presbyterian Church.

"On the other hand, it is equally well known that a number of revered and beloved ministers of our own Church, originally from New England, and still possessing no small share of New England feeling, such as Dr. Richards, Dr. Spring, Dr. J. Woodbridge, Dr. Fisher, Dr. Hillier, and a number more like them, while they enjoy the intimate confidence of the brethren, think as unfavorably of the New Haven speculations as any of our number."

"I trust," continues Dr. Tyler, "you will not impute it to vanity that I have copied this extract. My sole object is to let you know the views of Dr. Miller."

Dr. Tyler then quotes from a letter of Mr. Nettleton, dated Petersburg, Virginia, February 4, 1836, in which he attempts to fasten the charge of inconsistency on Dr. Beecher in his treatment of Dr. Taylor, and closing, "From that day (1830) to this I have not felt at liberty to say yes or no to the question which has hundreds of times been asked by ministers, 'Where does Dr. Beecher stand?' My answer is, 'You must ask him.' "

"We have certainly no disposition," continues Dr. Tyler, "to molest Dr. Beecher, unless we are compelled to do it in self-defense. But we do not like to have his influence made to bear against us. Those who are doing their utmost to put us down do insist upon it that he is with them, and he is not willing, as appears from what he said to Mr. Nettleton in 1830, that we should contradict them. Besides, in his eulogy of Dr. Taylor and Mr. Finney, he did not take any exceptions to their doctrinal views; consequently, the impression was made that he did intend to defend them in the gross, and to lend his influence to sustain them. If such is his intention, so be it; let us understand it. If such is not his intention, he must do something to remove this impression. Just look at it. The testimony of Dr. Woods and myself is made use of to sustain him at the West, and yet his influence is made use of to strengthen the hands of those who accuse us of maintaining sentiments which involve the most blasphemous errors. Now I appeal to you whether this is as it should be."

Dr. Tyler then enters into a warm and lengthy defense of Mr. Nettleton from certain reflections that had been made upon his course. "It may be," he says, "that he talks more than is expedient, but I am persuaded that an impression has gone abroad in regard to him that is entirely erroneous. I am equally sure that he is most egregiously slandered and persecuted. * * * He does honestly believe that the New Haven speculations do tend to sap the foundations of evangelical truth, and to destroy the character of revivals of religion; and he has seen more of their influence, probably, than any other man. Such being his convictions, how can he be silent? and has he not a right to express his opinion of writings which have been published * * * for the purpose of * * * changing the faith of the churches?

"He set his face from the first against the new divinity and the new measures, and he has maintained his ground against flatteries and frowns, in the midst of obloquy and reproach. He has never shuffled nor fallen in with what his conscience condemns, for the sake of gratifying friends or foes, and it is for this that he is now the object of unrelenting persecution. When you speak of him as 'originating and propagating mere religious gossip,' I know not how to understand you. * * * I regard it as an unfortunate thing that his letter to P——, of Georgia, got into the papers, but for this he is not responsible; he had no idea of its being published, nor does he know to this day how P——'s letter to him got into the papers. It was published by somebody without his knowledge or consent.

"He committed an error in suffering that extract from your letter and some others to be published two years ago, but it is the only error of the kind which I have known him to commit. * * *

"I hope you will not infer that I have lost any of my affection for Dr. Beecher. I think in some things he has erred. But I can not cease to love him. Wherein he has erred I hope he will see his error, and do what he can to correct any wrong impressions which he may have been instrumental in making."

This letter was before the publication of Dr. Beecher's Views in Theology, and, of course, before the session of the General

Assembly at which Dr. Miller and the Princeton leaders so cordially urged him not to make objection to Dr. Wilson's retreat. Between the time of his correspondence with Mr. Nettleton, therefore, and that session of the Assembly, it would appear that Dr. Miller had discovered that it was "possible to reconcile that man's course with a sound, honest, straightforward purpose," and had enjoyed the inexpressible pleasure of seeing him "come out *bright* and *entirely consistent*."

We now proceed to notice the progress and results of the Plummer correspondence. Among Dr. Beecher's MSS. was found the following paper, entitled,

Prayer before signing, sealing, and sending the Letter to Plummer.

"O Lord, my Savior and my God, Thou seest the entire course of my ministry, and all the reasons and motives which have dictated my conduct in all my public life, and in all the trials and difficulties I have been called to encounter; and though in respect to the relations of my heart to Thee, compared with Thy holy law, or with Thy glorious Gospel, I have only to make confession of shortcomings, and in many things offending altogether, yet, relying only on Thy blood, and righteousness, and intercession for pardon, and Thy free rich grace for my sanctification and meetness for heaven, I may humbly appeal to Thy searching eye for the general rectitude of my purpose, and the integrity and honesty of my motives in all my public actions.

"Thou seest, as I can not but hope and believe, that my great and all-absorbing desire has been to promote Thy cause and kingdom in this world, and that in all the circumstances in which I have been misunderstood, I have acted in Thy fear, and in good faith with my friends and Thy friends, and my fellow-men.

"And till now I have supposed that I have followed the guidance of Thy wisdom from above in waiving, for the most part, all public explanations of my course and conduct, which, having been determined by local circumstances and existing reasons which could not be explained to the world or appreciated, I have committed to Thy faithful, providential care, confiding in my own rectitude of life, and Thy preservation of me, to obviate the evil.

"But, in the present case, though I have hesitated at departing from my general course by a public reply to rumors and mistakes, I have supposed that the condition of Thy Church is now such as affords me not sufficient time for private explanations, and that evils may come upon it from a misdirection of public sentiment in respect to me. I have come to the conclusion, therefore, that it is Thy will that I should forego my personal reluctance, and give to Thy ministers and friends these explanations which may prevent the mischief to Thy cause of their misdirection by mistake. But I do it humbly confiding in Thy approbation, and I do now most affectionately commit to Thy providential care this letter and all its consequences."

The following is an outline of Dr. Beecher's letter to Dr. Plummer:

"You are not insensible of the difficult task your interrogatory letter imposes on me, extending over some six or eight years, and demanding ay or no concerning words which may easily be forgotten or misunderstood — words which, interpreted by the occasion, and attendant circumstances of intonation, look, or gesture, may mean one thing, and, stripped of these aids of exposition, quite another. Metaphors or hyperboles, for example, put down as literal matter, or a burst of emphatic displacency, as Edwards would call it, transient as lightning, set down as a solemn, settled purpose of evil, would make sad havoc both of truth and reputation.

"Such habits of frank, earnest, and unpremeditated expression in times of peace, or while the enemies of truth assailed and my friends defended me, have occasioned me very little inconvenience; but, since confidential friends have fallen out by the way, and I, in my unavailing efforts to prevent division, have tried their patience on both sides, and the whole Church is shaking with fear, though I have learned henceforth to measure my words or bridle my tongue, I can not tell exactly how I may succeed in reducing to intelligible order those vagrant words, the offspring of unsuspecting confidence in days of peace which have passed away."

He then proceeds to answer the questions in detail, in every instance entirely refuting the injurious construction placed upon his words and actions, or denying the allegations altogether. As to the charge of having said that Old Calvinism, as taught by Dwight, Bellamy, and Edwards, must be put down, he says:

"Dwight was my theological instructor and father, most beloved and revered of all the men to whom this heart of mine was ever drawn, and I am not aware that there is now, or ever was, any discrepancy between his doctrinal opinions and mine. The last interview I ever had with him I recollect explaining my views on a point where he had apprehended there might be some difference, to which, as I moved on, he said, with his peculiar smile of heavenly benignity, 'Very well, very well, very well.' While Edwards, and Bellamy, and Fuller, and Witherspoon [3] have constituted the bone and sinew, and heart and life of my theology, I have been steeped, as Brother Stuart once said of me, in Jonathan Edwards for more than forty years; and when the theology of Edwards, and Bellamy, and Witherspoon, and Dwight goes down, I expect that the Bible itself and Christianity will go down."

As to Dr. Taylor and Mr. Finney, he says: "I intended the public to understand that in a trial of such serious moment to my character and usefulness I would not be identified with *any* man — that I would be answerable for no opinions but my own, and would make no declarations of concurrence or disavowal."

The following is a brief extract from the closing portion of the letter:

" * * * For more than three years, various injurious and unfounded rumors concerning me have been put in circulation, and I have held my peace, as the only alternative of avoiding a newspaper controversy, which would have inflamed inflammation itself. My trial before Presbytery and Synod, and your letter, have given me favorable opportunities of vindicating myself and disabusing the community; the result of which, I hope, will be the dissipation of the *mists* which have gathered about our institution, and commending it, with its resources, to the confidence of the Presbyterian Church, for whom it has been endowed, and to whom, in all its united and unperverted influence, it is offered and will be faithfully devoted. * * *

"But there never has been so solemn a crisis in all the Church's history. If her ministers and members can check their jealousies, and drop their bickerings, and bury their animosities, and all cultivate the meekness and gentleness of Christ, a glorious destiny is before her. But let dissension prevail, and actual division and subdivision ensue, and it will be a wreck over which angels might weep. Every valuable interest throughout the land, throughout the world, and perhaps for generations to come, must sympathize in the sad catastrophe."

In speaking of the effect of this letter, Dr. Beecher remarked: "I sent him my answer, requesting him to publish it; but he wrote

[3] John Witherspoon (1723–1794), Scottish-American Presbyterian clergyman, stressed that ministers should preach orthodox doctrine. In 1768 he became president of the College of New Jersey, and was a member of the Continental Congress.

back, asking another string of questions; whereupon I wrote back, answering his questions briefly, and referring him to my Views in Theology." The following is an extract of the second reply:

" * * * I have endeavored to render myself intelligible in my Views of Theology. I have read the extracts from the Spectator (to which you refer), and regret that I can not meet your desire by an unqualified yes or no, and that I have neither time nor strength to perform the work of a critical discrimination. * * * That I may not, however, even seem to avoid the frank exposition of my own opinions, I shall not hesitate to answer your questions in my own language, and without any particular reference to the extracts.

"*Quest.* 1. Do you believe that all sin consists in the voluntary transgression of known law? *Ans.* I believe in original sin as existing anterior to actual sin or any knowledge of law.

"*Quest.* 2. Is there any sense in which infants are depraved and sinful besides the fact of a constitutional bias to evil, an effectual tendency to sin? (I give the substance.) *Ans.* Yes; yet not in the substance of the material body — it would be Gnosticism [4]; not in the created substance of the mind — it would be Manicheism [5]; nothing, either, that forces the will to actual sin by an absolute necessity of nature — it is contrary to the Confession. And yet it is something more than the Pelagian bias or tendency, by the premature ascendency of appetite and passion over reason and conscience; and something more than a constitutional tendency, which renders actual sin certain. *Before the era of known law and actual sin, infants manifest a depraved action of mind, voluntary and sinful in its character or qualities. Selfishness, self-will, malignant anger, envy, and revenge indicate clearly their existence and action in infant minds anterior to the knowledge of God's law. Apparently,* ALL the prominent embryo outlines of sinful character which are developed in adults are clearly manifest in infants — developments inconsistent with *innocency*, that is, exemption from evil tendency or meetness for heaven, and such as unfallen beings can not be supposed to inherit. They are actions of mind, and feeling, and will, in their nature unbenevolent and malignant; and, compared with those benevolent movements of mind which the law requires, they are, in themselves considered, *ανομια*; not subject to the law, and contrary to the law and the elementary principles

[4] Gnosticism: the doctrine that the believer by the worship of wisdom might free himself from bondage to matter.

[5] Manichaeism: the doctrine that the world is engaged in a struggle between good (light) and evil (darkness). Adam and Eve were under the power of darkness, which may explain Beecher's interpretation.

of the carnal mind, which, as capacity and knowledge are developed, become in the adult enmity against God, and that total depravity which makes regeneration by the Holy Spirit indispensable. For these reasons infants can not properly be denominated innocent, or be saved without an atonement and regeneration, and are correctly and in an eminent sense denominated *sinners* and *children of wrath.*

"All this, however, which is anterior to knowledge, and personal accountability, and *actual sin,* comes upon them in consequence of their federal alliance with Adam, and as the curse of the law brought on them by his sin imputed to them."

On this letter, at a later period, Dr. Beecher indorsed the following:

"The sentiments contained in the answer to Question 2, though never published, are known by not a few to have been my opinions from the very outbreak of the modern controversy about original sin."

Copies of these letters were carried to the East by Professor Stowe, in the earnest hope, to which Dr. Beecher clung so steadfastly to the very last, of assuaging or averting open rupture between brethren once tenderly united, to be submitted, if opportunity offered, to the brethren at Andover, East Windsor, and Princeton. In reference to the latter, Professor Stowe writes, May 2, 1836: "I have been providentially prevented from going to Princeton. Mr. Barnes said, if it was his case, he would not have me go on any account. He said it was of no use to pay court to Princeton; matters had come to such a pass that Princeton must be resisted and humbled rather than conciliated. I shall be at New York during the anniversaries. In all probability the Princeton professors will be there. I shall take advice of Peters, Skinner, and others, and, if they think best, I will there read the letters to such a circle as they shall advise me to call together for the purpose. It will look less like 'courting Princeton,' as Barnes says. I shall read it to Dr. Tyler while I am at East Windsor.

"*May* 7. I laid the correspondence before Dr. Woods, and his feelings are freely expressed in his letter, a copy of which I send you. I have also read it to Dr. Tracy,[6] of the Recorder. He feels as Dr. Woods does. * * * A copy of Dr. Porter's *suspicion* letter to you was found after his death. It was taken in two or three

[6] Joseph Tracy (1793–1874), author of *The Great Awakening* (1842), director of the American Colonization Society, editor of the *Boston Recorder* and the N. Y. *Observer.*

transcripts, and repeated attempts were made to get it into the newspapers. It was prevented by Dr. Woods's earnest interference, and now all the copies are called in and in Mrs. Porter's possession, and all is safe in this quarter."

The following is an extract from the letter of Dr. Woods above mentioned:

May 6th, 1836.

"I have read the letters with great satisfaction. Dr. Beecher's frankness and honesty, and the piety and orthodoxy which he brings out more and more clearly, must secure to him the confidence as well as love of all sober, enlightened, candid men. The farther I proceed with his 'Views in Theology,' the better I am pleased. The Lord be praised for raising up such a man, and keeping him right while so many are going wrong. It is really well for ministers and churches to be pretty jealous over us, and I would thank God for the degree of wakefulness which shows itself in regard to the doctrines we hold, for there is no end to the erratic speculations of the times; the very atmosphere we breathe is tainted with them. I am quite desirous of having a copy of these papers, and my object is to use them in particular cases, in a private, confidential way, to remove suspicions, and bring about a happy state of feeling toward Dr. Beecher."

In his letter to Dr. Plummer, as well as in his "Views in Theology," Dr. Beecher had gone as far as was possible to him in avowing his belief of the great truth of innate ill-desert. Few men then living could have gone farther; certainly not either Drs. Woods, Tyler, or Hodge. The General Assembly indorsed his position as entirely satisfactory. Dr. Wilson retired baffled and disconcerted, with the assurance that his Princeton brethren could not sustain his appeal. Dr. Woods was delighted, as his letter shows, and thankful to God for "raising up such a man, and keeping him right, when so many were going wrong."

One thing, however, Dr. Beecher yet lacked. He must not only assert native ill-desert, but deny that ill-desert is conditioned upon voluntary transgression of known law. He must not only deny this, but denounce it as heretical. In short, he must not only be orthodox, but he must denounce Dr. Taylor.

Two impossibilities stood in the way of this: first, his love of Taylor, and, second, his love of truth. This his Old School brethren could not understand. They really thought that, to be sincere, he must do what they desired; for how could he, or any other man in his senses, hold two great fundamental propositions which they were accustomed to consider contradictory? The idea that both were true, that both could be held in equal prominence by the same mind, had never occurred to them. They would have scouted the notion as a self-evident absurdity.

Hence, finding Dr. Beecher refusing to abandon Taylor and the principles of Moral Government, they began to doubt him. They fell back upon the same kind of suspicions Dr. Miller had expressed before, in his letter to Dr. Nettleton, There must have been somewhere a fatal "tampering with conscience" — some latent, inexplicable obliquity, rendering it impossible to reconcile "that man's whole course with a sound, honest, straightforward purpose."

Those doubts had been somewhat allayed in course of the correspondence of which an outline has been given. He had been unexpectedly full in his assertion of innate depravity; so much the more necessary for him to go farther, and become a thorough-going, zealous, one-sided partisan, or they would be compelled to doubt his sincerity or his sanity; and, in either case, he must be sacrificed on the altar of truth.

The tendency of the doctrine that ill-desert results only from voluntary transgression of known law they honestly believed to be subversive of the Gospel. And, indeed, if this doctrine be held, without being counterbalanced by the doctrine of native ill-desert, they were right. It is impossible to deny native ill-desert without logically *tending* to undermine the Gospel. But they conscientiously denied the possibility of thus counterbalancing the one great doctrine by the other. Hence their unwavering conviction that to encourage New Haven speculations was to become responsible for heresy; hence the painful necessity of sacrificing Dr. Beecher, if he would not denounce Dr. Taylor.

It was a painful sacrifice. They really loved Dr. Beecher. Dr. Tyler was an old friend, and in the old Litchfield days their love had been that of brethren indeed. Dr. Miller and the Princeton professors really liked him. Notwithstanding his want of that "cold prudence" of metaphysical subtlety in which they especially gloried, "there was no one whose white plume they would more willingly see leading the van" of God's embattled hosts. Dr. Woods really loved him. His farewell note, written just as Dr. Beecher was leaving for the West, breathes a tenderness that must be genuine. "My dear brother," he exclaims, "my heart melts to think of parting with you! The blessing of the God of Jacob be upon you and upon your dear family."

But what are personal preferences or natural affections, however pure and deep, in comparison with the great interests of the Redeemer's kingdom? Convinced, as these excellent brethren were, that their moiety of truth was *the* Gospel, and Dr. Taylor's moiety another Gospel, they had no option; they must not confer with flesh and blood. Dr. Beecher must be plucked as a brand from the New Haven fire, or be overwhelmed with the devoted city; and the crisis was now come when forbearance must cease, and he himself accept the alternative of peace or war.

This may seem a trivial alternative to those uninitiated in the secrets of ecclesiastical administration, and unaware of the tremendous pressure that can be brought to bear on a given point when once the vast system of ecclesiastical machinery, with all its countless concealed springs, and bands, and wheels, is set in motion with full momentum, with the public sentiment of a continent to turn the dark water-wheel.

But let them remember that nothing so terrifies men who can be terrified as the loss of professional reputation, especially when that reputation is bright, and felt to be, in the evening of life, on the point of being swept away; let them remember how bitterer than gall and wormwood is defeat, the failure of an enterprise like that in which Dr. Beecher was embarked, the crushing out of a theological institution, the disappointment of hopes so high raised, benevolent plans so comprehensive — let them reflect that such a wreck would involve both reputation and support, and then let them try to judge whether it was a slight and trivial thing for Dr. Beecher to resist the pressure, velvet in touch, Alpine in weight, that came to hurl him in, like a rock from a catapult, against New Haven. The velvet touch was that of Dr. Woods; the Alpine weight was that of Andover, East Windsor, and Princeton combined, by private correspondence, in full co-operation and concert.

It was immediately after his triumphant acquittal by the General Assembly at Pittsburg in 1836, and the letter of Dr. Woods on the Plummer correspondence, that the final attempt to bring Dr. Beecher over was made, and made in vain.

"While I was at the East," says Dr. Beecher, "the summer after my trial, Dr. Woods called on me and asked me to walk with him. He said, hesitatingly, that the brethren were satisfied in the main, and yet there were some things not quite so clear. They *wanted* to be satisfied, and have things as they used to be between them and me; and finally he wanted to know if it might not be in my power to make such concessions in regard to Dr. Taylor as would be satisfactory. I turned round and said, 'Dr. Woods, I know what these gentlemen and you want. They want me to say what will go to implicate Taylor as heretical, and I never will do it; and you may tell them so.' "

This was a thunder-clap. Dr. Beecher's household inmates in those days can well imagine the look and tone with which these decisive words were spoken. Often, in the long course of efforts to involve him in the crusade against New Haven, had they heard him exclaim, "I'll never denounce Taylor. To reach Taylor they must pass over my dead body. My bones shall whiten on the battle-field beside Taylor's."

The consequence was immediate. The same attack that had been hitherto made on Dr. Taylor now burst in all its fury on Dr. Beecher.

The confidential letter of Dr. Porter was published in the Hartford Watchman. A volume was published by Dr. Harvey, containing, in the language of the Princeton Review, "a detailed refutation of the errors of" Dr. Beecher's Views in Theology. It also contained the above-mentioned letter, together with portions of one of Dr. Beecher's private letters to the editor of the Christian Spectator in regard to New Measures, written just before the truce signed with Mr. Finney's friends at Philadelphia, as already mentioned.

In that transaction Dr. Beecher was declared to have manifested an "utter incompetency for the station of leader and guide." He was "either outwitted by his crafty antagonists, and made to believe that the general interests of religion would be promoted by tying his own hands and sealing his own lips, or he betrayed the cause which he had professed to defend through cowardice or something worse, and without assigning a reason."

Dr. Beecher's reply to Dr. Porter was persistently ignored, and the evidence, furnished in abundance, of Dr. Porter's entire satisfaction, was suppressed. Diligent efforts were made in various ways to array against Dr. Beecher the names of his dearest departed friends, such as Evarts, Cornelius, and others, as having sympathized in the suspicions of Dr. Porter.

A series of letters was addressed by Dr. Tyler to Dr. Witherspoon,[7] of South Carolina, and published by him anonymously in the Southern Christian Herald, from which they were copied into all the Old School papers in the country and in the Hartford Watchman. They profess to give an impartial account of the New

[7] John Witherspoon (1772–1853), first a lawyer, became a Presbyterian minister in N. C. and later S. C.

Haven controversy. They were indorsed by Dr. Woods as "written ably and justly." The impression they were adapted to produce, however, on the minds of readers at a distance of five hundred or a thousand miles was, that Dr. Taylor and his friends were Arminians, Pelagians, and Unitarians.

"I have just received," writes Dr. Beecher, "the tenth letter of the anonymous history of the origin and progress of Arminianism in New England, from near East Windsor, as I suppose, *via* South Carolina. The letter can hardly have been delayed by bad roads and negligent postmasters so as to fall in by accident just at the climax of the concentrated assault on me, to have its influence on the Convention and Assembly. It is written, apparently, in answer to Dr. Hoge's request for the publication of more confidential letters and *ex parte* anonymous testimony to do good with, and to give information what has been Dr. Beecher's course in relation to the recent controversies in New England. The letter seems to be a regular manifesto attendant upon the open declaration of war against me which for years had been carried on secretly.

"It affirms that my published Views in Theology certainly do not agree with New Haven theology. That I have spoken freely to those opposed to Dr. Taylor in terms of strong disapprobation of Dr. Taylor's writings, and yet that I am responsible for the spread of Dr. Taylor's opinions more than any other man; have not sympathized with those who were distressed about them; have frowned on every expression of alarm; have said they must prevail every where; that Old Calvinism must go down, etc., etc.

"This is anonymous evidence volunteered by persons of another communion to affect, contrary to the recognized laws of Church discipline, an individual, and, through him, half the Church. The obvious design is to produce on me, and on all associated interests, the EFFECT OF A TRIAL WITHOUT A TRIAL, and by such evidence as would not for a moment be tolerated in an ecclesiastical court. The justification of this course by influential men on the plea of necessity — the plea of despotism — is to tear up foundations and let in the tide of anarchy and revolution. The end sanctifies the means. The consequence is, that laws disappear before lawless combinations.

"The publication of a history made up of confidential conversations of friends, to bear on subsequent party contentions, is a violation of the sanctities of friendship, compelling a man always to treat his friends as possible future enemies, or risk the assassination of character by their volunteer testimony. It is, in effect, a system of desolating falsehood under the guise and semblance of truth. *Ex parte memoriter* statements of insulated words which, interpreted by accompanying look, tone, and gesture, may be harmless, but, stripped of these, are treason and heresy, is false witness. One wholesale manufactory of published private letters and private conversations for the nation is enough to blast innocence in the minds of thousands, and is as perilous to character as brigands are to life and property.

"It is the testimony of parties interested in sustaining an institution in rivalry with New Haven, brought into being in opposition to the advice of Andover professors and others, their annual income depending on sustaining the panic which gave it birth. My reputation for orthodoxy, freshly vindicated by Presbyterian courts and uncommitted against New Haven, might be too powerful a neutralizer of fear to be permitted to stand in unbroken power.

"To this I am pained to be obliged to add the indication of such a state of feeling in some who manage affairs as must abate the force of their testimony. I allude to those who published Dr. Humphreys' letter, expressing his views of New Haven, contrary to his expectation and without his consent; who published Professor Stowe's most confidential letter to Dr. Tyler, his father-in-law, without the permission of either, and to the regret of the latter, who is yet, I believe, an honorable man; to those who counseled and procured the publication of Dr. Porter's letter, and attempted to defend it as done with his permission, and refused to publish the testimony to the contrary; and, above all, the publication, in this tenth letter to Dr. Witherspoon, of extracts from a private friendly letter to Dr. Tyler, taking out of their connection such expressions as go against me, while in their connection they convey no such implication.

"I do not accuse these brethren of intentional violation of truth; but history has abundantly shown that the high, continuous fanaticism of party spirit can not absorb the feeling and engross the attention on one theme day and night for years, and not destroy the finer sensibilities of the soul to the claims of propriety and honor, and render the memory unfaithful, and the moral sense obtuse in its discriminations between right and wrong.

"The testimony itself can not bear the ordeal of a careful analysis. Either the facts are not as stated, or they are colored by the omission of explanatory circumstances. This is painful, because the chief materials of the principal accuser are such as his position as a very confidential friend and frequent inmate in my family for years gave him access to, and which now he has volunteered to throw over into the Presbyterian Church; and the pungency of my sorrow is increased by the recollection that twice, when his character was assailed, I hastened to his defense, and received thickly in my own bosom the shafts which were aimed at him.

"When Mr. Evarts expressed to me his fears that I was not preaching as I used to do, though not on account of any thing he had heard himself, but through impressions received from sources which I well understood, I wrote the sermon on Dependence and Free Agency, in fulfillment of what is called my promise to Dr. Porter, and also for the satisfaction of my friends who for many of the last months of the controversy in Boston sat under my ministry.

"The morning after hearing it, Evarts met me with a smile, and said, 'That will do; that is the genuine old-fashioned New England divinity;' and though he heard me every Sabbath for months, and I saw him in the most familiar and open-hearted communion daily till he left, never to return, he never breathed a whisper of disapproval of my doctrines, and our friendship was never more perfect than during this period."

In conversation on this subject, looking back from the close of life upon the whole campaign, Dr. Beecher exclaimed, with profound emotion, "They took burning arrows dipped in gall, and shot them over into the Presbyterian camp. They rifled the graves of my dead friends, out of their ashes to evoke spectral accusations against me." Those "burning arrows" were caught up by the Princeton Review — the most powerful organ in the land — and hurled, with deadly aim and increased momentum, at their mark.*

His Views in Theology were reviewed in the remorseless style of partisan criticism, and the resources of rhetoric exhausted in sustaining the charge of contradiction between his earlier and later writings. The animus of the reviewer is manifest in every line. His purpose is to make an end of Dr. Beecher once and forever.

"There are statements in these writings," he says, "which no ingenuity of explanation can reconcile — discrepancies which no sophistry can bridge over. * * *

"Here he teaches that infants are guilty before they rise to personal accountability, and deserving God's wrath and curse; in his letter he tells us that there is no depravity or guilt but that which arises from the transgression of the law under such circumstances as constitute accountability and desert of punishment.

* Repertory for April and July, 1837, art. Beecher's Views in Theology.

"Here is contradiction palpable and broad. The two views presented by Dr. Beecher in his earlier and his later publications belong to two entirely different — two opposite systems. They have no common points of resemblance, and the same man can no more hold the two simultaneously than he can believe both in the Ptolemaic and the Copernican systems of the universe."

Happily for Dr. Beecher, the reviewer was entirely deceived, and his assertion destitute of the least foundation in truth. The two propositions which he declares to be contradictory are not contradictory; the two systems which he denies to have aught in common are the twin hemispheres of rounded and completed divinity. The impossibility of both being held simultaneously by the same mind is purely imaginary, the hallucination of his own unsuspected but habitual one-sidedness.

Thus absurd to minds dwarfed by narrow, partisan contemplations must needs appear that truly catholic comprehensiveness which can accept apparently conflicting truths, each on its own independent evidence, and patiently wait for the reconciliation.

With no misgivings, however, confident of having annihilated his victim, the reviewer moves on, his face alternately wreathed with smiles and bedewed with tears. "We have heard it said," he remarks, "that after the publication of his Views in Theology, Dr. Beecher, as if doubtful of his own identity, sought to assure himself by going on to New Haven and ascertaining whether Dr. Taylor would recognize him. It is added that the result of the experiment was entirely satisfactory. But this story must be apocryphal. We can readily conceive that Dr. Beecher might feel himself in the predicament of Amphitryon when he exclaimed,

" 'Num formam perdidi? Mirum quin me norit Sosia
Scrutabor: eho dic mihi, quis videor? Num satis Amphitruo?'

But the incredible part of the story is that Sosia recognized Amphitryon."

A page or two farther he weeps: "We regret most sincerely and deeply the result of our examination into Dr. Beecher's opinions."

Still farther on he smiles again: "A German author has recently obtained two prizes, one for an essay in defense of the medical theory of homœopathy, the other for an essay against the same theory. This exploit, however, is by no means equal to that which Dr. Beecher aims to accomplish. The German did not aspire to obtain a favorable verdict upon both his essays from the same body of men." The reviewer ought to have enhanced the superiority of

Dr. Beecher by stating that he actually succeeded in his aspiring aim, the General Assembly, including the Princeton professors, having unanimously awarded him full permission to believe in the alleged contradictory propositions.

The tendency of these and kindred measures to precipitate the catastrophe of the Presbyterian Church is manifest. No man, after the event, could be more fully aware than Dr. Tyler was beforehand that "the New Haven speculations are the real cause of the convulsions in the Presbyterian Church." It is not our object, however, to trace those results any farther than necessarily connected with the fortunes of Lane Seminary and its president.

In themselves considered, it seems incredible that such charges could seriously affect the character of a man so long successfully engaged in revival labors, and the instrument of leading so many lost sinners to Christ. But the power of a theological panic surpasses calculation. When once the storm bursts in full violence across the ocean, the fairest reputations, the stanchest characters go down in a moment.

When Dr. Wilson brought the charge of hypocrisy against Dr. Beecher, every body smiled at it as the mere extravagance of partisan prejudice; but when the charge was taken up by New England men, Dr. Beecher's own former associates, and in some instances his intimate friends and associates, and systematically blazed abroad with ostentatious display of circumstantial evidence, it is not strange that the minds of some excellent persons should be distressed, and that letters should be received making serious inquiries in respect to these things.

To some of these letters his children claimed the privilege of replying. An extract from one of their epistles may suffice to indicate the aspect of the onset from their point of vision:

"I need not say that I feel deeply the baseness and malignity of an attack upon my father's honesty and Christian character, because his opponents find it impossible to refute or answer his published statements; or that I regard it as deeply humiliating for a man like him, so long engaged with great simplicity of purpose in the great work of saving souls, and so often honored by God by signal aid in the work, to be called on to prove his own honesty, or for his son to attempt to do the same.

"Were I writing to any but a friend I would not do it; for of what use are declarations of truth in reply to assaults on veracity? But, assuming what I have no doubt is true, that your confidence in my father remains unshaken, and that you will believe concerning me, at least until you have proof to the contrary, that I abhor a lie as I do the devil its father, though I am ready both to pity and forgive the liar, I will proceed to say,

"That, to my certain knowledge, the theological opinions of my father for at least the last twenty years have, in all the great fundamentals of truth, remained identical and unchanged. I have no doubt that the same is true of the whole course of his ministry, but I speak particularly of the last twenty years, because during that time I have thought intelligently and with deep interest on the subject, and have had every possible opportunity of knowing his views. I have heard him preach, studied with him, been with him in revivals, corresponded with him, argued with him on every point, and known the inmost recesses of his soul, and I need not say that I know him to be incapable of deceit, and that his published writings are a fair exposition of his most mature and deliberate convictions, and accord with his constant strain of preaching at all times, and with his most private thoughts. The controversy that now rages began when I was in college, and from the outset I have studied it and the course of all engaged in it with the deepest interest, and as it regards some I must say that the measures they have adopted have filled me with the most unmingled surprise and abhorrence. I have no disposition to speak in anger; but there are emotions of holy abhorrence at what is polluted and vile that are essential to the maintenance of the moral purity and soundness of our own minds, and to the enjoyment of communion with Him who hateth iniquity in all its forms.

"And though I freely forgive and pray for the authors of the wrong, yet I must say that, for a combination of meanness, and guilt, and demoralizing power in equal degrees of intensity, I have never known any thing to exceed the conspiracy in New England and in the Presbyterian Church to crush, by open falsehood and secret whisperings, my father and others whom they have in vain tried to silence by argument or to condemn in the courts of the Church.

"But I doubt not that a day of reckoning will come, and God himself will vindicate all who trust in him. Therefore let us not be disquieted, or return evil for evil, but commit our cause to Him who judgeth righteously, and all will be well."

If such were the effects on minds friendly to Dr. Beecher — if the question of his honesty was forced upon those desirous to view every thing in the most favorable light until they were compelled to write and ask relief, what must have been the effect on minds predisposed in precisely the opposite direction, and how formidable the blow thus aimed at the prosperity of the seminary and the usefulness of its president! If there had been no other cause, this alone was enough to stagger the just commencing enterprise. But there were other causes. The anti-slavery excitement, resulting in the loss of a large class and the alienation of Abolitionists throughout the country, had weakened the institution. The failure of Mr. Tappan in 1837, and the loss of the endowment of the theological professorship weakened it still more. Added to these, this onset on personal character shed blasting and mildew on every prospect. All these causes together proved well-nigh fatal.

The classes from 1836 to 1840 averaged only five. The professors were discouraged. The only man who did not for an instant lose hope, and admit the conviction that the enterprise must be abandoned, was Dr. Beecher himself.

"He worked," says Professor Stowe, "during all these difficulties like a Hercules, and never lost courage or hope. Disappointment followed disappointment, and obstacle was heaped on obstacle. Ossa was piled on Pelion, and then Olympus on Ossa; friends fell off and foes multiplied; endowments diminished and salaries ceased; prejudices were inflamed and students were kept away. Still he was hopeful and jovial, always good-natured, and never irritated. If students would not offer themselves, he would go after them even to the highways and hedges, and compel them to come in; if the regular income failed, he would beg; if he could not clamber over an obstacle, he would go round it or dig through it; if he was disappointed in one thing, he would hope for another that would be surely better when he got it. Nothing ever really hurt him but the supposed treachery of trusted friends; this would go to his heart and make him sigh.

"In every tight place he would say, 'Come, let us get by this pinch, and then we'll have plain sailing.' I never believed him, and sometimes expressed my dissent in terms rather emphatic than befitting. I was so often right in my apprehensions that after a few years he changed his mode of address to me, and would say, 'Come, Stowe, let us get by this pinch, and then we'll get ready for the next,' but always with the same good-humored hopefulness."

"There was one time," said Dr. Beecher — "(it was the year of the dry time: they waded across the Ohio River) — there were no students offering for our next class. Stowe was discouraged; Dickinson[8] had a call at Auburn; Biggs[9] had a chance at Woodward College. I went up to Marietta College, born after us, and saw the faculty and students. There I secured four or five. Had an invitation to lecture at Jacksonville. Went down to Louisville on my way, and spent a Sabbath. Got one student there. He was a member of my Church in Boston; he was in business. I told him to study, and he did. Then I went to Jacksonville, and there I found six. One of them was expecting to be a teacher. I got hold of him — excited his interest. I told him, 'Come on, and bring these young men, and I'll support ye;' and I saw it done.

"Well, when I got back to the seminary I found Stowe sick abed, and all discouraged. Said 'twas all over — of no use — might just as well leave, and go back East first as last. 'Stowe,' said I, 'I've brought ye twelve students. You've got no faith, and I've got nothing but faith. Get up and wash, and eat bread, and prepare to have a good class.' The consequence was a class of thirteen, and the next year thirty-five."

Having thus exhibited at one glance the main features of this crisis in his life, we shall return upon our track to introduce the correspondence of the period, with some additional details of his personal history.

[8] Baxter Dickinson (1793–1875), Andover graduate, had held pastorates in Mass. and N. J. before coming to Lane, where he taught from 1835 to 1839. From 1839 to 1847, he taught in Auburn Seminary; later he was an officer in the American Board of Missions and taught at Andover. From 1859 to 1868 he was head of a girls' school in Ill.

[9] Thomas J. Biggs (1787–1864), Princeton graduate, was at Lane from 1832 to 1839. Later he was president of the University of Cincinnati and pastor of the Fifth Presbyterian Church, also in Cincinnati.

XLII

FAMILY HISTORY

DURING the summer of 1836 Dr. Beecher married Mrs. Lydia Jackson, of Boston, a widow with several daughters, two of whom were married, and one son, nearly of the same age with the doctor's youngest son, James. In the support of her family, as well as in the various benevolent movements in which the ladies of the orthodox churches of Boston were organized, Mrs. Jackson had shown that energy and executive talent which fitted her for the wider sphere of active usefulness into which she was introduced at the West.

Her two younger children, Joseph and Margaret, accompanied her, and formed thenceforward a part of the household, somewhat reduced by the departure of the older children to various fields of labor. In the care of the family, in visiting among the families of the congregation, and in promoting good enterprises, she displayed untiring zeal, supplying in part the lack of pastoral labors necessarily incident to Dr. Beecher's position as head of the seminary, proving, in these respects, an invaluable auxiliary.

Between the widely-scattered children and their home a constant intercourse was maintained by means of correspondence; and, to insure a greater regularity, a system of "circulars" was devised. A large folio sheet was taken at the eastern end of the line and sent to the next westward, each one adding something, till the full sheet reached the western extreme, and was returned to its starting-point, and *vice versa*. We have before us one of these interesting letters missive, with the following postmarks and directions upon it: New Orleans, La.; Jacksonville, Ill.; Walnut Hills, Ohio; Indianapolis, Ind.; Chilicothe, Ohio; Zanesville, Ohio; Batavia, N. Y.; Hartford, Ct. One direction, Rev. Mr. Beecher, served for all except the two extremes. Merely as a specimen of the method, we insert a paragraph or two from each locality.

CHARLES.

"Brother George's perfectionism is a curious matter, and lies in a nut-shell. That a Christian can be perfect is evident, else God commands impossibilities. Whether they ever are or not, who can decide? Does a man think himself perfect? Amen. I hope he is not mistaken. So long as he behaves well, let him pass for immaculate. If he does not behave properly, he deceives himself. If you ask, 'Have I attained?' I say, Ask God. The more you try to decide, and the nearer you come to an affirmative, the more probable is it you are deceived. The heart is deceitful: who can know it?"

MRS. EDWARD BEECHER.

"We received this yesterday, and I hasten to add my say and pass it along. I suppose that we are to pour our sorrows as well as our joys into each other's bosoms through the medium of these circulars, for we should sympathize with each other in affliction as well as in blessings. Our little daughter (you know she is the only daughter that we have ever had, and therefore *very* dear to us) we have had much anxiety about, because she was a crying child; but she had improved so much in this respect, and appeared generally so well, that we had dismissed most of our fears till a few weeks ago, when she was a little over seven months. I was dressing her in the morning, when I perceived all at once that she was in a convulsion fit. The pang that shot through my heart I can not describe to you. No one can understand it who has not watched for days, and weeks, and months, day and night, the writhings, distortions, and agonies of a beloved object, hoping all the time that death would terminate its sufferings, and fearing that something worse than death would be the result; and then, by degrees, to have every hope extinguished, and that being, which promised so fair to be a comfort and a blessing, prove a constant source of trouble, care, and perplexity. We have lost, or more than lost, three of our six children, and what the Lord means to do with this fourth we know not."

HENRY WARD.

"There are some signs of better things among my people; more feeling in Church and congregation, and more solemn meetings, and some cases of incipient anxiety — just that state of things that encourages, yet makes me feel most powerless.

"I wish, George, you could be here a while and help me. I would, if you were here, have continuous preaching, and believe immense good could be done. I thought it possible you might be able to come. Besides, we have grown almost strangers to each other since you groped off to Rochester, and I would fain have some of our long talks again. As to perfectionism, I am not greatly troubled with the fact of it in myself, or the doctrine of it in you; for I feel sure that if you give yourself time and prayer you will settle down right, whatever the right may be; and I rejoice, on this account, that your judgment has led you to forbear publishing, because, after we have *published*, if we do not hit exactly right, there is a vehement temptation *not* to advance, but rather to nurse and defend our published views. The treatises which have had influence in this world from generation to generation are those which have been matured, re-thought, re-cast, delayed. Apples that ripen early are apt to be worm-eaten, and decay early, at any rate; late fruit always keeps best. * * * I have seen men by an injudicious effort run so high up aground that there never was a tide high enough to float them again. They dried, shrunk, and rattled. May God never let you run ashore until it is upon the shores of that land of peace where perplexities shall cease their tormenting flight, and all be joy!"

MRS. STOWE.

"Well, George, it seems to be the fashion of the day to address you firstly and prime; and I, setting apart metaphysics, will enter only that interesting department of physics which your gift of flower-seeds brings to mind. Many thanks for them, hoping that you and S—— will be here to see them in all their glory. I have a fine place laid out for them, and shall proceed with them *secundum artem*. What is your experience about dahlias? for I was never more puzzled in my life than with the contradictory directions I hear about soil, etc. Some say the richest you can find — can't be too rich; and the other day a celebrated gardener of New York advocated dry gravel. What do you think? If you don't write pretty soon it will be too late. I have some roots which might be handsome if they only would be; but last year they brought forth little besides stalks and buds, and some of them run out into single flowers."

CATHARINE.

"Where is the eastern circular that started from Hartford, or ought to have started, two months since? I shall recommend that any one that delays a circular over a week shall lose the reading of the return one, as a penalty to make them remember. I shall flit about here this summer till I find where it is best to settle next. Love to you all."

DR. BEECHER.

"William, why do you not write to your father? Are you not my first-born son? Did I not carry you over bogs a-fishing, a-straddle of my neck, on my shoulders, and, besides clothing and feeding, whip you often to make a man of you as you are, and would not have been without? and have I not always loved you, and borne you on my heart, as the claims and trials of a first-born demand? Don't you remember studying theology with your father while sawing and splitting wood in that wood-house in Green Street, Boston, near by where you found your wife?

"Little do those know who have rented that tenement since how much orthodoxy was developed and imbodied there; and now why should all this fruit of my labors be kept to yourself? Nothing would give me more pleasure, so long have your interests and mine been identified, than to hear often what and how you are, and how things go on all around you. Our prospects at the seminary are good. I am obliged to work too hard; still, my health is good, and we shall certainly get along now, as I fully believe. Let me hear from you soon — a letter to me in particular, which shall soon be repaid in kind."

PROFESSOR STOWE.

"DEAR BROTHER GEORGE, — As to perfectionism, Brother Charles ''spresses my mind 'xactly,' and I trust you will duly appreciate the patriarchal, paternal, grandfatherly, and most judicious counsel of Brother Henry. Brother Charles's advice as to *faith*, and Brother Henry's as to *works*, on this perfection matter, are just the thing, according to the best judgment of your dutiful brother."

GEORGE.

"I am quite amused with the sympathy of all my brothers, and their fatherly advice touching perfectionism, as if I were on the verge of a great precipice; but I trust in Him that is able to keep me from falling."

WILLIAM.

"We received the circular, and forward it to-day. The Lord has been with us, and there is now a great amount of labor to be done, and great difficulties yet to be overcome. We expect to build a vestry and repair to the amount of $1000."

Perhaps these extracts may fail to interest a general reader; and, it must be confessed, they convey a very inadequate conception of the variety of subjects, interests, emotions, shades of thought, and flashes of wit and humor which make these circulars a kind of moral kaleidoscope — ever changing, ever beautiful. By them, many families, wide asunder in locality, of independent and often antagonistic views, were bound together, year after year, in a more than patriarchal unity.

XLIII

CORRESPONDENCE, 1837–1838

MARCH 3, 1837, Dr. Taylor writes to Dr. Beecher:

" * * * I have been glad to see your reply to Dr. Porter's letter. It will fully answer its purpose in respect to all except the willful and perverse. The Watchman * is determined to put you in the wrong; misrepresents the matter grievously; pretends to believe, and to be able to prove that Dr. Porter never expressed himself satisfied in regard to your soundness in the faith. I suppose you see that paper. The controversy is no longer one of truth and evidence, but an attempt to put down by odium, and by authority which is no authority.

"What if Dr. Porter was alarmed; so do many *living* doctors profess to be; and why is the opinion or forebodings of a dead doctor of so much infallibility? * * *

* * * And then, what was the ground of his alarm, according to his own showing? Why, if all he says in his letter be true, it is the merest nothing; it is rather a criticism on your supposed mode of preaching, as that by which certain impressions, as he thought, would be made, '*in direct contravention of your own meaning!*' Now away with Dr. Beecher! Burn him! at least, let every theological dog in the land bark at him, for the Professor of Rhetoric has found a blemish in Dr. Beecher's preaching! I do think such ridiculous attempts at the *odium theologicum* should be exposed.

"The fact, however, is, that all that is now doing by these men is helping onward the cause of truth with more efficient influence than any we could use in the way of argument. All discerning men and women see what the matter is. Who does not know who is wrong when abuse and reproach are the only weapons of assault? I am as patient under it all as the love of truth and of its progress can be well supposed to make me. Theirs is the trouble and the

* Of Hartford, Conn., edited by Dr. Harvey.

expense of this work, and no doubt they belong to them. We here have, I think, only to go on, without contending in this unholy warfare of personal abuse, imparting light and truth to the people from the pulpit, and other forms of upright and clear argumentation. God blesses us at every step. Revivals are now all around us in this county. In New Haven the work is now powerful. It began in the Free Church, where I have been preaching since November. It has extended to other churches, and is most auspiciously beginning in the college. In its form and type just such a revival as I love and desire. In the city, I suppose, eighty or one hundred conversions, with crowded meetings of inquirers; in college, twelve or fifteen conversions within a few days, and several inquiring. I expect to begin to preach in the college on Saturday evening.

"And now what I long to see in the Presbyterian Church is a thorough separation of Old School and New School, brought about in the right way. I am fully convinced that the errors of Old School are calamitous, and too much so to seem to be countenanced by New School in that *manner and degree* in which they have been by union. The Old School men will never rest; and the question is, How much time and strength shall be expended in conflict? God means to effect a division ultimately — on the ground of essentials I do not say, but on the ground of expediency; and if I were king, I should say to the next General Assembly, Divide — not on the ground of heresy, and with mutual hate and denunciation, but divide for peace's sake, with mutual toleration, as sects differing so much, and with such conscience of the *speculative* importance of the differences that the cause of God will be better promoted. To the New School I should say, show your magnanimity by giving up Princeton Seminary and all Old School funds to the Old School party, and begin anew for yourselves. In five years and less you will have more funds, more seminaries, more power for God and his cause than the whole Presbyterian Church now possesses, and have it unclogged and unencumbered by that incubus which has so long made her strength weakness. I wish you could think as I do on this subject."

May 25, Professor Dickinson writes from the General Assembly: "The Old School has a majority of about fifteen or twenty; but we are embarrassing them amazingly in their action on the Memorial. You can hardly conceive of the headlong spirit that reigns among them, and of the intense interest and sometimes excitement in the house. They have obtained one vote, which is, to abrogate the plan of union with the Congregational churches adopted in 1801. This division, however, can not affect the representation in the next General Assembly. Such as are Presbyterian will, of course, continue to be so. They next took up the doctrinal errors, as reported in the paper I send you. One of our men moved an amendment, adding to the list four others, the first of which is, 'That man has no ability of any kind to obey God or do his duty.' The others are closely allied to this.

"It has troubled them amazingly for one whole day, and we have done nothing but talk on a motion indefinitely to postpone the amendment. Last night we adjourned on this motion. To meet the emergency, and get rid of discussion on the amendment, they brought in this morning a resolution to amend the rule relating to the previous question — which, as it stood, admitted of one speech — so as to cut off all debate when a majority call for the previous question. We have been all the forenoon debating that. They have carried the alteration, so that hereafter we are to have 'gag-law' in abundance.

"Next followed a motion and vote to let the doctrinal report, with the amendment, lie on the table, to take up another high-handed measure that will make the public stare. They seem really afraid to meet the doctrinal discussion. But the measure — to cite such Synods and *Presbyteries!* as are suspected of heresy, and appoint a committee to report what bodies they are; also to decide that the ministers and elders of all such Synods and Presbyteries as may be cited shall be excluded from a seat in the next General Assembly! We are now just starting with this monstrous proposal. We have good men on our side. We are united and firm, and determined to contest the ground inch by inch; but they will probably carry about all their plans except the favorite one relating to the Home Missionary and American Education Societies, which I think the committee on the Memorial are afraid to report to the house, and will not do.

"We think we shall have, before we get through, abundant materials for protests, and, if I am not mistaken, we shall speak out in a manner to be heard and felt through the Church, and rouse a spirit that will bring up to the next Assembly a phalanx of the friends of liberty, and good Presbyterian order.

July, 1837, Doctor Beecher entered the following memorandum in one of his commonplace books:

"I have this morning received a letter from New York, informing me that my draft on Mr. Tappan has been dishonored, on account of his suspension of payments.

"Thus has the ground of my support failed, and the considerations which brought on me a sense of duty to leave Boston and my people have, in a degree, failed also. But my confidence that it was the will of God that I should come, so signified in his providence as to make it my duty, has not failed; and my confidence that the end of my coming would be the establishment of Lane Seminary has not failed; and my confidence that God was well pleased with my coming, approved of my motives, and will sustain me as through my life of dependence on him he has done, has not failed. And though one half of a needed income has suddenly stopped, and I know not precisely in what manner my wants are to be supplied, I desire to praise Him who has clothed and fed me and mine to this day that I do not distrust him, and am not anxious, but cheerful and happy in my confidence in Him whose I am and whom I serve. I shall reduce my family expenses to the lowest practicable amount, and, taking counsel of God, and my friends and family, take such measures as may seem advisable."

In a tremulous hand, under date of December 4, 1852, the following lines are added: "This morning I fell accidentally upon the above record in my waste day-book. The following narrative records the result. My first movement was to request by letter from George, my son, and Sarah, his wife, for my immediate necessity, $200, which they immediately advanced. My people, then, of the Second Church, added, unasked, $200 to my salary annually, and the rest was raised among my friends in Cincinnati, in contributions to Lane Seminary for my special support. When at the East I made solicitations myself for funds for this object with success. For several years Mr. Tappan's payments were resumed, but soon stopped permanently.

"I then was sustained by contributions in Cincinnati, Boston, and New York, as before, until the organization of the Society for Western Colleges was established, and then by that, until the funds of the institution superseded the necessity. I felt no delicacy in making the above-mentioned solicitations, having secured the primary endowments by my acceptance of the presidency, and having, by personal labors as an agent with Mr. Vail, erected the buildings, founded the library, and endowed two professorships; yet such was the condition of the seminary, that the failure of my support would have disheartened the trustees, disbanded the faculty, and for a long time paralyzed, if not finally suspended the institution."

XLIV

REVOLUTION

The Presbyterian Church in the United States at the time of which we are now writing presents to the mind a truly imposing subject of contemplation. Its form of government is that which was fashioned by the Westminster Assembly (A.D. 1643–'9) to replace the Episcopal hierarchy, which had just been swept away. Parliament, which had abolished that form of Church government, desired to set up another. The Assembly was convened for the purpose.

The Independents, by the genius of their system, could furnish nothing of the kind desired by Parliament. They were only in the way of the Presbyterians, who had no such scruples, and wanted nothing better than to set up a framework less gorgeous and expensive, though no less powerful than that which had vanished, they thought, forever.

To this great work of ecclesiastical architecture, during their five years' session, their chief energies were directed. The Confession of Faith was a secondary consideration, the marked antagonisms of subsequent schools being as yet latent and undeveloped. It was on questions of hierarchal law and the machinery of Church courts that the antagonism between Presbyterian, Independent, and Erastian [1] came out. Half a dozen Independents held the whole Assembly at bay, hampered all its movements, and proved ultimately, as Hetherington complains, "the main cause why it failed to accomplish all the good which had been expected from its important deliberations," *i. e.*, the nationalization of Presbytery.

But, though a handful of Congregationalists prevented the nationalization of the Presbyterian system, it did not prevent its subsequent voluntary adoption over the broad plains of America, and the erection there of a more imposing structure than ever could have been realized in Great Britain by act of Parliament.

According to the radical principle of the system that "the sev-

[1] Subordination of the church to the state.

eral different congregations of believers, taken collectively, constitute one Church of Christ, called emphatically the Church — that a larger part of the Church should govern a smaller, and that appeals may be carried from lower to higher judicatories, till finally decided by the collective wisdom and united voice of THE WHOLE CHURCH," the General Assembly was one of the most impressive as well as powerful bodies in the world. On its floor were some of the ablest, wisest, most enterprising, and influential men from almost every state in the Union.

In its relation to educational, charitable, and missionary enterprises, in the appellate jurisdiction of hundreds of local churches, it swayed a power rivaling, if not really surpassing, that of Congress, and affecting not merely the religious, but the civil interests of the nation; opening an arena on which discussions of the most momentous questions were debated by practiced speakers, animated by the highest motives, temporal and spiritual, that can lend fire to oratory or enthusiasm to controversy.

In the eyes of multitudes of Christians, its symmetrical structure from Session to Presbytery, Presbytery to Synod, Synod to General Assembly, was the ideal of representative government, perfect in every detail, free from the defects of civil organizations, scriptural, spiritual, a kingdom of Christ, "clear as the sun, fair as the moon, and terrible as an army with banners."

What power should suffice, then, to shatter the mighty edifice from turret to foundation, opening in the midst a chasm as by earthquake? Could a handful of Congregationalists wield that power, greater beyond comparison than that of their prototypes in the parent Assembly? Could a half dozen plain New Englanders with a puff of their lips wreck the stanch vessel as if smitten by a sudden tornado?

So it seems, if Dr. Tyler is admitted to be qualified to judge. "The New Haven speculations are the real cause of the convulsions in the Presbyterian Church." Undoubtedly Dr. Tyler is right in part. The full development of those grand principles which eternally underlie God's moral government, and are the natural antagonists of absolutism in every form (a development unbalanced, to some extent, and not sufficiently conservative of the grand truth of native ill-desert), was probably the most effective cause of the disruption. The statement of errors by the Philadelphia Convention, on which the abrogation of the plan of union and exscinding acts of 1837 were predicated, reads as much like an indictment of New Haven as if it had been drawn up at East Windsor.

Mr. Crocker,[2] speaking of the letters of Tyler to Witherspoon, says: "For whatever purpose they were written, there can be no doubt that they exerted a considerable influence in causing the violent proceedings of the Assembly which immediately followed their publication. They assisted the members of the Philadelphia Convention to make out so accurate a list of errors as to need, perhaps, no correction from their friends in New England. They emboldened the Assembly to adopt measures which could never have been carried but for their belief in the existence of wide-spread and prevailing heresy in the Congregational churches."

The abrogation of the plan of union was shutting the gate against streams of New Haven influence in future. The excision of four Synods was a summary ejection of the mass of churches formed under that influence in the past.*

But there was another cause of the great catastrophe — we refer to the slavery question, which yet is not another. The first number of the Liberator was issued January, 1831, a few months after Dr. Beecher received his call to Lane Seminary. Confessing himself to have been till September, 1829, the advocate of gradual emancipation, the editor defines his present and future position by the emphatic menace, "Let Southern oppressors tremble! Let their secret abettors tremble! Let all the enemies of the persecuted blacks tremble!"

The interval between this challenge and 1837, while gradually destroying Mr. Garrison's[3] original sympathy with the theology of revivals and its kindred developments, added constantly to the intensity and power of his appeals. Yet the fact of this divergence of the Liberator from the theology of the Puritans does not nullify the fact that it was itself the child of that theology, albeit a wayward child. Its first numbers speak the dialect of Canaan — the

* The nature of these celebrated exscinding acts will be understood by the common people if we say that of two nearly equal parties in THE CHURCH, one put a large part of the other under discipline, and, on the ground that parties under discipline can not vote, proceeded to expel them. By this method, four Synods, covering two thirds of New York and part of Ohio, were disfranchised, and 599 churches, with 57,000 members, excommunicated at a stroke.

---

[2] Zebulon Crocker, author of *The Catastrophe of the Presbyterian Church in 1837* (New Haven, 1838).

[3] William L. Garrison (1805–1879), for a time attended Beecher's church, but became disgusted at Beecher's caution on the slavery issue. Apostle of temperance, women's suffrage, and abolition, he demanded immediate abolition in his *Liberator* in 1831. Though mauled by a well-dressed Boston mob in 1835 and alienated from other anti-slavery reformers by his rejection of political action, he continued his intransigent attacks on slavery and other evils.

dialect of faith, and prayer, and evangelical sympathy. "Take away the Bible," it exclaims (April 2, 1831), "and our warfare with oppression, and infidelity, and intemperance, and impurity, and crime is at an end; our weapons are wrested away, our foundation is removed; we have no authority to speak, and no courage to act."

Religious revivals, it says, "are scriptural occurrences; without them the promises of God would fail, and the earth be flooded with iniquity. If the kingdoms of this world are to become the kingdoms of our Lord and of his Christ, the event can never come to pass independent of great revivals."

The jargon of Ashdod was later learned, taught by impatience under tribulation, and exasperation at the sins of good men.

It was really the power of the Puritan theology, whose impetus remained long after its distinctive spirit was lost, beneath which the guilty nation was heaving and surging like the ocean before the impending tempest of divine judgment. "I regard," writes Dr. Beecher, March, 1838, "the whole abolition movement, under its most influential leaders, with its distinctive maxims and modes of feeling, and also the whole temper, principles, and action of the South in the justification of slavery, as signal instances of infatuation permitted by Heaven for purposes of national retribution. God never raised up such men as Garrison, and others like him, as the ministers of his mercy for purposes of peaceful reform, but only as the fit and fearful ministers of his vengeance upon a people incorrigibly wicked."

Instinctively the guilty region now expiating its crimes in terrible fulfillment of this augury betrays its consciousness of the source of its punishment by desperate reaction against New England Puritanism. It is against Puritan ideas that the rebellion proclaims itself to be waging internecine war. In so doing it does not mean that conservative Puritanism, so called, which is absolutistic and in sympathy with traitors, nor that destructive Puritanism which is naturalistic and in sympathy with infidelity; but it means that Puritanism which coincides with the progressive theology of common sense, accountability, and moral government — the natural foe of despotism in every form.

Accordingly, it was the Synods most imbued with this theology — Utica, Genesee, Western Reserve, Cincinnati, and others, which were foremost in urging the General Assembly to disfellowship slaveholders, while the president of the Old School Convention which indicted the New Haven theology was an infatuated defender of slavery as a Bible institution.

The discussion of the slavery question in the Assembly of 1836, at which Dr. Beecher was acquitted, as also of preceding Assemblies, was exciting. Dr. Witherspoon, of South Carolina, subsequently writes to Dr. Beecher:

"*Division* I do most sincerely and deeply deplore; and *if* it must, as a dernier resort, come to this, I am strongly inclined to the opinion that Mason and Dixon's line must be the *ridge*. It needs but the *lifting a finger to bring this to pass;* and if it will promote the peace of the Church, it shall be done as speedily as the most violent Abolitionist could desire. And what will be the effect of this? Southern ministers will be utterly excluded from Northern pulpits and churches — Northern ministers driven from the South, or conducted to the '*lamp-post à la mode de Paris*' — a pretty state of things in Christian America, the *nest* of the eagle, home of the stranger, asylum of the oppressed.

"Yet *so it will be* if the Abolitionists rule. Our land must be deluged in blood by a contest fiercer and more bloody and unrelenting than even *Tory* warfare during the revolutionary struggle. When men contend for *liberty* — an *opinion* — they will *fight like men;* but when they contend for *property*, they will fight *like devils. This cause* will arm son against father, daughter against mother, and prostrate the strongest and most tender ties of life. I have been a slaveholder from my youth, and yet I detest it as the *political and domestic curse* of our Southern country; and *yet I would contend to the death* against Northern interference with *Southern rights*, and would follow *Dr. Beman to the scaffold on Charleston Neck* if he continued to hold the sentiments he expressed at Pittsburg in 1835. I give you, Brother Beecher, my honest, undisguised sentiments. They may be *wrong*, but I think them *right*.

"Abolitionism leads to *murder*, *rapine*, and every vile crime that an enthusiastic ignorant slave could commit, and therefore I *abhor* abolitionism and *detest the Abolitionist*. It was *well* that I was not on the *floor* of the *last Assembly;* but, if God spare me, I shall be on the floor of the *next;* and let *Lovejoy*,[4] or *Patterson*,[5] or Dickey,[6]

[4] Elijah Lovejoy (1802–1837), editor of a Presbyterian weekly, was opposed to slavery and eventually advocated immediate abolition. Edward Beecher helped him defend his press against an Illinois mob. Lovejoy was shot while defending his press.

[5] James Patterson (1779–1837), Philadelphia pastor (1813–1837), denounced the rich, and supported temperance, revivals, and New School Divinity.

[6] James M. Dickey (1789–1849), New School divine, after acting as pastor of several Ind. churches, did missionary work in the Wabash Valley, and wrote anti-slavery articles in the Cincinnati *Journal*.

or any like them, *dare* to advance the opinions I have heard expressed, and — the consequences be *theirs*."

Southern Presbyteries and Synods were expressing themselves emphatically in the same direction. The Princeton Review had already, as early as 1832, recommended a plan of reorganization, by which "the churches in the slaveholding states will be separated from those in the Northern States."

"The South," said Dr. Beecher, conversing on the subject, "had generally stood neutral. They had opposed going to extremes in theology either way. Rice,[7] of Virginia, was a noble fellow, and held all steady. It was Rice who said, after my trial, that I ought to be tried once in five years, to keep up the orthodoxy of the Church. He was full of good humor, and did so much good. But they got scared about abolition. Rice got his head full of that thing, and others. John C. Calhoun was at the bottom of it. I know of his doing things — writing to ministers, and telling them to do this and do that. The South finally took the Old School side. It was a cruel thing — it was a cursed thing, and 'twas slavery that did it."

So the great and imposing fabric was shattered in fragments, and the rebellion now raging was a not distant consequence. And it was ideas that did it. It was ideas concerning God and man — ideas concerning the divine administration, the government of the universe, the origin of evil — that convulsed the Church and convulsed the nation; and why should they not? Theology and politics are next of kin. Their study is but the study, in different relations and connections, of the fundamental principles, and historical facts, and moving powers of the universal government of God.

We know of no more striking and even awful picture than that casually thrown off in a private letter of a Lane Seminary student, writing from Philadelphia at the time of the great ecclesiastical earthquake:

"*Philadelphia, May* 17, 1838. The Assembly convened this morning at 11 o'clock. After the sermon Dr. Elliot proceeded to organize. Before the calling of the roll, Dr. Patton[8] attempted to introduce a resolution with reference to the exscinded Synods. The moderator pronounced him out of order, and told the clerk

[7] Benjamin Rice (1782–1856), Andover graduate, pastor in Hampden Sydney, Va.

[8] Probably William Patton (1796–1879), who was pastor of several N. Y. C. churches, active in reforms and education, and sided with the New School in the 1837 schism.

to proceed. The roll was called, and the names of the four Synods and third Presbytery omitted.

"One of the proscribed offered his commission and demanded an explanation. 'It is out of order,' was the reply; 'proceed to business.' Mr. Cleaveland,[9] of Detroit, then requested permission to read a paper. 'It can not be heard,' says the moderator. Cleaveland commenced reading. Moderator turns pale; pounds the desk, crying 'Order!' Cleaveland reads on, amid cries of order, and hissing less and less vociferous, as they see him determined to read: 'Whereas these Synods, contrary to law, are denied a seat, we proceed forthwith to organize THE *General Assembly* of the Presbyterian Church of the United States of America, with as little disturbance as possible, at the opposite end of the house.'

"Dr. Beman was elected moderator. The Old School looked aghast. Mason and Gilbert [10] elected clerks. The New School then proclaimed at the doors of the Seventh Church, crowded to excess, that THE GENERAL ASSEMBLY of the Presbyterian Church of the United States of America would proceed forthwith to the First Presbyterian Church. The New School marched down the aisle, the greater part of the throng following them.

"Both parties have been in secret conclave for two days. The New School anticipated the course of the other side, kept a lawyer at their side, and, when the time for action came, were prompt and self-possessed, for they had looked ahead, and correct too, to the *letter of law*, for their counsel was at their ear.

"*Afternoon.* THE General Assembly directed their clerk, Mr. Mason, to obtain their books, papers, etc., from Mr. Krebs,[11] clerk of the other body. Mason had not returned when the Assembly adjourned. The remaining time was occupied in reading the minutes of the last year. Your father and brother distinguished themselves in the Convention on Monday and Tuesday. I did not hear them — did not reach Philadelphia till yesterday evening.

[9] John P. Cleaveland (1799–1873), pastor in Salem, Mass. (1827–1834), and Detroit, Mich. (1835–1838), agent and president elect of Marshall College, Mich. (1838–1843), pastor in Cincinnati (1844–1846), served several churches in the last twenty years of his life. Baird's *History of the New School* (1868) claimed that Beecher and Taylor egged on the hesitant Cleaveland.

[10] Eliphalet Gilbert (1793–1853), New School pastor in Wilmington, Del., formed another church there because of a schism in his congregation. President of Newark College (1840–1843) and Delaware College (1843–1847), he was called to a Philadelphia church in 1847.

[11] John Krebs (1804–1867), graduate of Princeton Seminary, Old School pastor of Rutgers St. Church, N. Y. C. (1830–1867), moderator of the General Assembly (1845).

"The Assembly is by no means, however, the most exciting matter at present to the citizens. The heavens at this moment are lighted up by the flames of the Abolition or Liberty Hall in Sixth Street. The mob have set it on fire. It was dedicated two weeks ago: cost $40,000. The Anti-slavery Society are holding a Convention in it. Miss Grimké,[12] or rather Mrs. Weld (she was married on Tuesday), spoke there last night. The mob broke the windows. Dr. Parish told them not to hold night-meetings, but they would. The ladies walk arm-in-arm with the blacks. I was there this afternoon: the women were holding a Convention. The streets were thronged by the mob watching the door. So long as the Abolitionists kept off from the negroes, the street was still as the grave — the mob looked only; but when they saw a huge negro darken the door arm-in-arm with a fair Quaker girl, they screamed and swore vengeance. The mayor and sheriff were on the ground. The fire raged with great violence. The engines refused to play upon the building.

"*18th.* THE ASSEMBLY met at 11 o'clock this morning again. Rescinded the resolutions of the last Assembly against the Boards of Education and Missions, and passed others commendatory.

"The bell of the State House is tolling again — there are cries of fire! The mob were seen this afternoon *en masse* parading the streets, rioting over the ruins of the last night's conflagration, and threatening another.

"The heavens are lighted up. The African Hall, in Thirteenth Street, is on fire. The mob is cutting the hose, that no water may reach it. Such is the state of things in the city at present. The police are on the ground, but do nothing but talk; in fact, they are not able; in heart, they do not wish to restrain the rioters.

"That the Convention have been imprudent there is no doubt, but that the rabble in the midst of an enlightened and powerful community should be permitted to trample on all law is shameful."

[12] Angelina Grimké (1805–1879), Southern Quakeress, battled for immediate abolition and women's rights. In her letters to Catharine Beecher in 1838 she denounced gradual emancipation.

XLV

CONSEQUENCES

The first consequence of the organization of the Constitutional Assembly was the adoption by the revolutionary body of measures to carry with them, or to divide, all inferior judicatories. The next consequence was the adoption, by the constitutional body and its leading members, of counter measures in self-defense.

The interest felt by Dr. Beecher in these painful scenes, and the active part he took therein, will appear from the following extracts of letters written during the years 1838–9:

May 18, 1838: "The organization of the General Assembly was accomplished yesterday without violence, and in accordance with the directions of the ablest jurists, so that, unless legal science err, we are The General Assembly, and once more enjoy the protection of our civil and religious rites. It is the Lord's doing, and we give him the praise. Great efforts had been made the past year to divide our counsels, and we knew, as the result of different locality and independent thought, discrepant opinions had been formed, and were not without fear that God might give us up to divided counsels; but his presence was signally manifest with us from the beginning in a spirit of deep solemnity, of humble reliance on God and meek submission to his will, and of brotherly love.

"In this frame, all our conferences and discussions resulted in the progressive disappearance of diverse opinion until yesterday, when we passed, with but two dissenting votes, the resolution to organize as The General Assembly.

"In accordance with this vote, arrangements were made for the reading of three papers by three persons appointed for the purpose at the proper moment. The other body had made arrangements to defeat us, but were wholly taken by surprise in respect to the time and nature of our movement, and, in a state of utter paralysis, sat the amazed spectators of the event."

A few days later he writes: "Our own Assembly goes on decently and in order; the other, like Jehu, full drive and furiously. But perhaps the worse the better, though no one can tell what will come from the cool, deliberate determination of one half the Presbyterian Church to inflict upon the other half all the injury possible. But enough. The Lord will take care of them and of us."

From New York he writes again still later: "The Rubicon is passed, never to be repassed. Twice, now, the amalgamation of American and foreign Presbyterianism and Congregationalism has produced a violent expulsion. We are now divided, I hope forever, till grace shall put an end to ambition, selfishness, envy, and the lust of dominion. Our organization, guided by the best legal counsel, was determined on with wonderful unanimity and good feeling, and executed with wonderful alacrity according to the legal pattern. Our meetings were spiritual, devout, kind, and harmonious — almost all our votes unanimous. If our Presbyteries sustain what we have done, it is a noble band charged with the liberties of untold millions. The others are adopting acts to drive the plowshare of desolation through every Synod, Presbytery, Church, and family, excluding all who will not sustain the doings of the Old School Assembly of 1837, and declaring minorities who do the true Presbyteries.

"We advise that, in respect to the plan of union, it have no retrospective action, and that in time to come Presbyteries and Synods, in the exercise of their own evangelical liberty, pursue the things that make for peace and general edification. In respect to minorities, you will have to stand for your rights, and, if unconstitutionally exscinded, organize, and send commissioners to the next Assembly; *i. e.*, I suppose it will come to this, for they are driving so over the Constitution that no force will appertain to their doings."

Still later in May he writes: "They have consolidated their General Assembly into an irresponsible despotism, and intend to compel in or force out every Synod, Presbytery, and Church who will not succumb."

The following letter from Dr. Bishop, President of Oxford College, Ohio, to Henry Ward Beecher, then preaching as a licentiate at Lawrenceburg, Indiana, was transmitted to Dr. Beecher in October, 1838:

"It is no inconsiderable matter in these days that Dr. Beecher has at least one son, who, after a full and free examination before the Oxford Presbytery, has been pronounced to be orthodox and sound in the faith; and that, in order to exclude the son of the *arch-heretic*, *a new term* of ministerial communion had to be introduced.

"I hope you will, as I do this morning, thank God and take courage. The Presbyterian Church, if it is to be saved, is to be saved by those who have not yet taken their stand with either Assembly, but have taken *new* and independent ground, anathematizing neither.

"I hope you will not think of applying for ordination to any other Presbytery, but continue your application to Oxford. A change, I am confident, will be produced before the next meeting."

The following letter was written by Dr. Beecher about this time to a young convert on difficulties of an experimental nature:

"You complain that you are not perfect, and do not feel satisfied at making no approximation. This describes exactly the experience of every living spiritual Christian. 'I count not myself to have attained, but this one thing I do: forgetting the things that are behind, I press forward to the mark;' and 'when I would do good, evil is present with me.' 'The good that I would I do not.' 'Oh wretched man that I am, who shall deliver me from the body of this death?'

"The law is the rule of duty, but perfect conformity never the ground of justification or the required evidence of pardon. The law is our schoolmaster to bring us to Christ. The effect of sanctification is never to make us seem to ourselves to be growing better. The increase of light and of moral sensibility to evil serves to make what remains of sin the occasion of humiliation, strife, and prayer. But it is in this view the text applies: 'If any man sin, we have an advocate with the Father, Jesus Christ the righteous.'

"It is no uncommon thing for Christians to have a marked variety in respect to the prominent outlines of Christian character. Some admire especially the law of God; some his decrees and sovereignty; some think much of God the Father, while others are absorbed in affectionate thoughts of Christ. But, though comprehensive and well-proportioned views of the great revealed system are desirable, they are not indispensable to evidence, or comfort, or acceptableness with God. 'He will not break the bruised reed.' Nor is this attainment to be expected immediately as the result of conversion. It is 'first the blade, then the ear, then the ripe corn in the ear.' Cultivate an acquaintance with Christ. It will constitute the best and happiest form of Christian character; but, if you can love, and obey, and worship the Father, you do approach him in the name of Christ so long as you regard what he has done, and the place he occupies as the ground of your acceptance. You may pray, therefore, as you find most easy and edifying, though I would, if practicable, pray to Christ as God, for he is God as truly as the Father, as is also the Holy Spirit — three persons possessing the same voluntary, intelligent social powers, one in nature, one in sameness of personal attributes, plan, affection, and concordant action, so that whoever loves one loves all; so be quiet, and pray to either person as you can."

In February, 1839, we find Dr. Beecher at Columbus: "I arrived here Thursday. Called, with others, to advise and assist in organizing a Church of forty members, who have come out from Dr. Hoge's.[1]

"They had invited three other ministers, but all failed to come. I immediately sent eight letters to different ministers in my own name, but in behalf of the Church, urging them to come by some very cogent motives, which, if they have the breath of life in them, will bring some of them on." Among these "letters missive," one was addressed to his son William, then settled at Putnam, Ohio.

"No event at this moment can be more important to the Church in Ohio than the formation in her capital of an efficient Presbyterian Church. But I can not do it alone, and must have help; and am requested, therefore, by the brethren, to request you to come immediately, without fail. I have left the seminary and a pleasant incipient revival, and it is outrageous that those so much nearer should not be here. It is too bad that this little Church, with all her fortitude and decision in coming out, should be subjected to disappointment. I have preached every evening since I came (Thursday), and thrice yesterday, and expect to preach every night till help.

"So, dear son, make haste, and come on as fast as your horse can bring you, to help your father and do good, besides all the comfort it will give me to see you. I know you so well that I have confidence that you will come if possible — a true chip of the old block — to do the Lord's work, at all events."

The results of these vigorous measures were auspicious, and the new Church duly launched.

In March he receives intelligence from Professor Dickinson respecting the progress of the lawsuit in the Supreme Court of Pennsylvania, in which the trustees of the New School General

[1] James Hoge (1784–1863), pastor in Columbus after 1810, leader in temperance, anti-slavery, and benevolent reforms, founder of the Ohio Bible Society.

Assembly were plaintiffs and those of the Old School defendants.

"The judge (Rogers) has repeatedly to-day given evidence of a determination to allow a fair trial. The opposite counsel have two or three times objected to evidence offered, and in every instance been overruled by the court. They made a desperate effort to keep out the exscinding acts of 1837. This was their strong fort. They do not, I judge, pretend to justify those acts — they can not to any purpose. They were willing almost to admit that they were wrong.

"After hearing their objections, however, and without time for argument from our counsel, the court just told them he did not see how we could understand the proceedings of 1838 without a view of those of 1837. Their counsel have evidently injured their cause materially by the effort to suppress light, and every thing now will have to be exposed in all its deformity. Thus far every thing is encouraging. It seems hardly possible for us to lose the case."

In May, 1839, Dr. Beecher visited Oxford, Ohio, and, while there, was blessed with a revival. "I accompanied your father," writes Mrs. Beecher, "to Oxford on the occasion alluded to in his letter. He went, at the earnest solicitation of Dr. Bishop, to spend a single Sabbath. The evening we arrived it was proposed that your father lecture in the college chapel. The students and others used their best endeavors to break up the meeting. Sunday, Mr. Thomas and your father preached, the latter the second service, at the close of which a young man went up to the pulpit requesting your father to invite to remain any present who would like to converse upon the interests of their souls. Seven or eight remained.

"It being late, your father requested as many as would like to see him again to call the next morning at Dr. Bishop's. By eight o'clock the next morning they commenced to come, and continued through the day. So great was the interest, that instead of leaving that day, as he expected, his stay was prolonged a fortnight, and I left him there the following Wednesday. It was estimated that there were over one hundred conversions — eighty from the college."

The following letter was written to Mrs. Beecher after her return, as above-mentioned:

"*May* 26, 1839. I snatch a moment immediately after breakfast to write, before the young men begin to call upon me for personal conversation, which for two or three days past has occupied all my forenoons, and yesterday nearly all day. It is a delightful employment, and generally they are young men of excellent minds, gentlemanly manners, skeptical feelings, not well informed, but yet, for the most part, candid, and in some degree startled and uneasy.

"Some, who began early to call, have got through their doubts and are rejoicing in hope. A number of them are from the South, five or six from Mississippi, others from Kentucky, and some from Ohio. A dozen or more are in the different stages of inquiry — some just begun, others almost through.

"I have never been placed in more interesting circumstances — so accordant with my desires — so calculated to task my powers, and in the best manner to bring out all the resources of my mind, and all my knowledge of human nature, and all my experience and wisdom in removing objections, conciliating confidence, inspiring candor, and reaching at length the conscience through hosts of difficulties. It is delightful. My intellect is invigorated by heaven and by use, and my heart rejoices, and my health rises, while I preach every night, and thrice on the Sabbath, attend morning prayer-meeting at five and talk, and four o'clock prayer-meeting and talk, and inquiry meeting after preaching every night, and converse with forty or more, and talk with young men from eight till twelve A.M. besides.

"With good appetite, unexhausted spirits, and as fine sleep and firm health as I ever have — so you see the promise is fulfilled, 'As thy day, so shall thy strength be.' Perhaps the secret of my faltering health for some time past may be the want of employment, or rather want of concentration in one channel, with a single object, and that the noblest and most delightful in which men or angels can engage — the restoration of disordered minds.

"The Lord has permitted the accumulation upon me, for the last two years, in domestic and public cares, and anxieties, and labors, a greater pressure of responsibility and suspense, and baffled plans and hopes, than ever before in my life; and, withal, in a state far distant, among strangers, and remote from the cheering sympathy and affectionate confidence of that host of friends who in one part of the Church had grown up around me, and on whom the slanders and misrepresentations of alienated friends and the conspiracy of religious party spirit could have no influence to embarrass my success. In the mean time, my mind and body were taxed and tasked by responsibilities sufficient for the time and resources of two men; and yet, with such providential hinderances and discouragements as, while they did not preclude success which cheered my heart and demanded gratitude, yet did press upon a heart sickened by hope deferred, and a body so sympathetic with the mind's anxieties and sorrows that no strength of will could hold firm its muscular powers against the tremulous action of the nervous system under the heavy hand of unceasing anxiety, suspense, and sorrow.

"If He had not, through a long life of relative infirmity, taught me the habit of mental abstraction, and silent, and sometimes, when nature is exhausted, unfeeling endurance; if, with unerring wisdom, He had not seen how much my frame could endure, and laid upon me just as much, but no more than it could sustain; indeed, if an unseen hand had not held up a mind and body of strong, enduring powers, and elastic, self-restoring energies, I should long since have been a wreck or in the grave.

"Often has been the time when I thought that the cord was broken and that my last work on earth was done; and now, if any man can say it I can, 'Having obtained help of God, I continue to this day.' My brain, pressed almost to paralysis, returns to its cheerful elastic action under the removal of the pressure of His hand; my stomach, the seat of torture, and cause of dark forebodings and heart-sickness when the mind suffers, is relieved by the alleviations of the heart, and sends out through my soul the elastic and buoyant feelings once more of my light and prosperous days, the return of joys departed which I did sometimes fear might never come back.

"But the tidings from Philadelphia of a holy and meek decision, and regular and harmonious organization of the Constitutional General Assembly, with so large a representation, and such determined courage and reliance on God; the movement of such a needed public sentiment against the exscinding acts; the confidence of life to our seminaries and Church property, both in and out of Pennsylvania; the movement at Indianapolis to give Henry a call; the noble promise, and Christian decision, and better prospects of the students in the seminary; the obliteration of so much prejudice in this college, and establishment of so much influence, all tend to inspire the cheering hope that in me God may be fulfilling his promise that no temptations or trials shall be permitted but what his grace will enable me to bear, and withal make a way of escape. Psalms cxliv., cxxv., and cxxvi., may be beginning to find their fulfillment in me, and all the concerns of the Church of God, which comprehend all my heart and all my desire.

"That 'the rod of the wicked shall not be upon the lot of the righteous, lest he put forth his hand unto iniquity;' that 'the Lord has turned again our own, and the captivity of Zion;' and that 'they that go forth weeping, bearing precious seed, shall doubtless come again rejoicing, bringing their sheaves with them.' So, indeed, it seems now; conversions are coming to pass every day, and new cases of committed seriousness and inquiry. Since I commenced this letter, Mr. L——, a man of business, who has accumulated great wealth, has come in to converse with me; he had attended two inquiry meetings before, and is now 'clothed and in his right mind' — a clear, strong mind, brought under the power of the love of Christ, and converted as a little child.

"I wish my conversations with the young men who call on me could fall on paper; the dialogue would be immensely interesting, I am sure, and I believe more efficacious, as produced by the constantly recurring exigencies, arguments, and necessities of a diseased mind, than any thing that can be written beforehand for use.

"But the wish is vain, and I am comforted that if it can not be written with pen and ink, it is written, I trust, indelibly and savingly on the fleshly tables of many hearts. It was the sermon last night which brought Mr. L——, by the grace of God, to a state of happy, affectionate reconciliation to God. It was upon 'the *sincerity* of God in his invitations and expostulations with sinners.'

"Mr. T—— has not arrived, nor Henry, and there are between thirty and forty who now have hope, and as many more in a critical and interesting state, and a larger number to whom we are beginning to have access as the tide of mercy rolls on. Until help arrives I dare not leave. If you have any reason to think Henry may not come, send this letter to him, and tell him to let nothing but two or three impossibilities prevent him from coming right up. Much can be done now in a week to secure this college to Christ by those whom Christ has owned in the extension of free inquiry, and Christian liberty, and revivals, and missions, and the movements immediately preparatory to the latter day. But I know he will come if he can, who feels so deeply that we have got to work for our lives, and is so willing to work, and so like-minded with his father.

"I believe now I have opened my heart and let out thoughts and feelings which have never escaped before, and to utter which while the pressure was on, and the darkness visible, would only have added to their weight and gloom, without increasing strength to bear. I trust God is preparing for me at the West a more open door, with less distraction from adversaries, and preparing my mind for an atmosphere where my character needs no establishment, and where the co-operation of cordial friends will afford me opportunities of cheerful and efficient action. But, at any rate, so sudden and signal a change as now every day greets my eyes and cheers my heart is not for nothing, and is to be received by us, as it is, with unutterable gratitude, deep humility, and vehement desire to make returns according to benefits received."

XLVI

CORRESPONDENCE, 1840–1842

THE most perilous part of the Seminary's history was now well-nigh passed by; still, Dr. Beecher was destined for some time to struggle with embarrassments arising from the loss of the endowment of his professorship, and those resulting from the agitation in the New School Church of the slavery question. Some idea of his situation in these respects may be gained from the following letter, January 6, 1840, to his son George, then settled at Rochester, New York:

"I am at length so entirely and distantly separated from my sons as I have never before been since the birth of my first-born, having always had one or more with me, and others so near as to secure frequent intercourse and aid in public action, but having now not one within two, four, and eight hundred miles. I am lonesome, and am stirred in spirit to bring my dear sons around me by correspondence, by which our sympathy and co-operation may be sustained, otherwise my quiver full of them may not avail me to speak with the enemy in the gate.

"The seminary is in more favorable circumstances, on many accounts, than it has been at any time, though there are yet some adversaries and difficulties to be encountered. Our students between thirty and forty, and a better class of young men in *talent, study, attainment, and contented, kind feeling* than we have ever had, and they come to us, too, through two ranks of opposition — Old School and ultra Abolitionists, though the conservatives among the latter confide in and patronize us, and most of our students are conservative Abolitionists.

"The lines, too, are drawn between Old School and New, and the conflict which absorbed so much time and feeling is gone by, and the churches begin to have rest, and the Presbyteries and Synods to assume consistency, and are increasing in numbers and spirituality; and, through the power of the Holy Spirit, revivals attend their sessions, and are spreading once more in our churches.

"The importance of Lane Seminary is now also more clearly seen and deeply felt by the entire constitutional body, and we are beginning to enjoy what we have lacked through manifold conflicts, an all-pervading sympathy and efficient co-operation by the whole Church. The young colleges of the West, also, are with us — Jacksonville, Marietta, Crawfordsville, and Oxford — and are beginning to yield a yearly augmenting patronage, so that our prospects East and West are brightening.

"Henry, though so recently established at Indianapolis, is beginning to be felt not only at home in the power of the Holy Spirit which attends his labors, but abroad as a man of piety, talents, and power, in the churches and in the capital of his state.

"Of our difficulties I may say, the resignation of Professor Dickinson, in some respects to be deprecated, may be, in the end, a benefit, without any disparagement to him.

"——[1] has resigned, but is malignant; will join the Old School; and he and —— are planning to break down the seminary and deliver it over into the hands of the Old School. —— says that Stowe shall go at any rate, and if he refuses we both shall go. They have, however, in the board but six to twelve, and we intend to elect such and so many additional trustees as shall give them a stern chase without hope forever.

"But, in the midst of our joy in tribulation, Tappan has again stopped payment. My people are kind, but, as I give them but half my time, I can not rely on them to meet my exigencies, and shall need, imperiously, temporary aid till Tappan resumes or the times change. If I stop now and leave the seminary, it would go into the hands of the Old School infallibly and immediately. Dr. Bishop writes that he knows they intend to leave no stone unturned to get it into their own hands, and that they are sanguine, and no doubt in correspondence with —— and ——, and are talking of Breckinridge[2] as my successor.

"Now the seminary, though thus pressed just now, possesses a more ample endowment than any other in the land but Andover, valued at $130,000, and needing only $5000 as a lien to make us easy. And if I am sustained through the present panic, it will go down auspiciously through all time; but I can not stand without

[1] Probably George Beckwith (1801–1870), Mass. pastor, professor at Lane from 1820 to 1830, when he joined the faculty at Andover. Later he held a church in Me. and was agent of the American Peace Society.

[2] Robert Breckinridge (1797–1841), graduate of Princeton Theological Seminary, Baltimore pastor (1826–1831), agent of Presbyterian Board of Education (1831–1836), professor at Princeton Seminary (1836–1838), agent of the Presbyterian Board of Missions (1838–1841).

my salary. Poverty and debt, added to all that is on me, will break me down and end my life.

"I hoped and intended to get through life without being obliged to call on any of my children for help, even temporary; though, if need be, none are more naturally to be looked to, and I fully believe none are more willing to come to my aid than my children, and of these none more than you. But at present I need $200 to save me from distressing perplexities. You may loan it to me if you prefer to do so, though I wish you to do it *for me*, and also as a gift to the Lord if any thing should prevent a return. * * * My health is good, never better, under accumulating cares and responsibilities. The old ship, you know, has always seemed to go best with ample ballast and a stiff gale; so may it be now, for she has enough just at present of both."

February 28, he writes to the same as follows: "The very prompt and filial manner in which you responded to my request rendered me so happy as almost to compensate for the deprivation which occasioned it; and to know that S——'s heart moved with such affection in unison with yours, and that it is with her the free-will offering of love, doubles the pleasure.

"The revivals in our city are great and powerful, and the Methodists, Baptists, Presbyterians, and Episcopalians share in them. Soon after the receipt of your letter, I had commenced a course of sermons every evening, with morning prayer-meetings and favorable prospects; but on Thursday evening, as I was going down with wife, Catharine, and Miss M—— in the dusk of evening, I was met by a train of six or eight wagons in the worst part of the long hill, and crowded off, and rolled over and over down a steep declivity of some thirty feet to the bottom, without a bone broken, or any deep vital injury. * * *

"Myself was handled the worst, though, in great mercy, only a rib slightly cracked on the right side, and left arm deeply and badly bruised. I laid by two Sabbaths as a matter of prudence; on the third preached once, on the next expect to preach twice."

It was on this occasion that an amusing instance of his quaint dry humor took place. The stupid teamsters who had crowded him off, on hearing his cries for help, came to the edge of the road, and, peering over into the darkness, inquired, "How shall we get down there?" "Easy enough," was the reply; "come as I did."

Early in March he received from Professor Goodrich the cheering intelligence of revivals in Yale College, Hartford, and other places. "The whole length of the Connecticut River," said the letter, "on one side or the other, from its mouth to the borders of Massachusetts, is lined with revivals. Saybrook, Westbrook, Essex, Chester, Deep River, Haddam, Wethersfield, Rocky Hill, Glastonbury, East Hartford, Windsor, Ellington, and, I believe, Suffield, together with New Britain, Worthington, and part of Woodbridge, are at this moment visited. * * * *You* will not misunderstand my feelings when I remind you that in all the places above-mentioned, except one or two, the pastors and laborers in the work are New School men, or at least men who have no hostility to New Haven sentiments. We can not be too thankful that God, notwithstanding our weakness and deficiency, does not leave us without witnesses. * * * And now, dear brother," the letter concludes, "farewell. My heart cleaves to you and Brother Taylor more and more as I advance in years. We are associated in the best of causes, and have been called to suffer what we little expected when we entered life. But ours is a blessed service. Thanks be to God for permission to suffer for him. Oh, dear brother, let our hearts be much in heaven, where we shall meet when the labors of life are over, to be together forever in the Lord."

In the latter part of 1841, appeals were made by letter at the East to meet the wants of the seminary and of the beneficiaries among the students. In one of these, December 23, he says, "Our seminary has helped already into the ministry between eighty and ninety young men. With few exceptions, they settle at the West, in feeble churches, on small salaries, work hard, and have revivals, and are soon surrounded by large churches, and blessed with a competent support, and act as missionaries to organize and multiply new churches around them."

In helping these students in the seminary, Mrs. Beecher, with the ladies of the Second Church, rendered constant and invaluable aid, thus effectually helping Dr. Beecher in the great work of "laying the foundations of many generations."

Among the many encouraging responses from Eastern friends was one from Dr. Brainerd,[3] of Philadelphia, March 29, 1842, from which we extract the following: "You have stood at your post through the hardest-fought ecclesiastical conflict ever waged in this land, and though something has been lost by the timidity or

[3] Thomas Brainerd (1804–1866), agent for the Home Missionary Society, became pastor of the Fourth Presbyterian Church, Cincinnati, in 1832. Editor of the Cincinnati *Journal* and the *Presbyterian Quarterly Review,* he supported Beecher and the New School. After 1837 he held a Philadelphia pastorate.

desertion of old friends, I think we all have reason to bless God that it is no worse. But for your timely translation to Cincinnati, New England principles would by this time have had no lodgment in Southern Ohio, Indiana, and Old Kentucky. Such a combination of local prejudice and personal jealousy, with ecclesiastical and abolition denunciation, no other man could have sustained without discomfiture. I believe with you that the crisis has come and gone — that the question is decided that Lane Seminary shall be the ecclesiastical helm of the Great Valley."

At this point in the letter the following comment is thrown in by Dr. Beecher: "This is true. In revivals, before I left the West, in the Old School churches they did not dare preach limited atonement, but preached *the Gospel*, as we do."

Dr. Brainerd closes as follows: "I may be permitted to say that I have found here no substitute for your friendship and countenance. In all my acquaintance with men, I have known but one to whom I could be subordinate with pride, and with and for whom I could cheerfully suffer persecution. Doctor, you have had many bitter assailants; it will do you no harm to receive these assurances of love and veneration from one who knows your private character as well as your public services."

The following letter to Dr. Pond will be read with interest: "*Lane, April* 14, 1842. I have just read your review of the History of Harvard College, and what a flood of remembrances rolled in of conflicts and successes achieved together, and of joys departed, in which we alike sympathize, and mutual friends now gone — Evarts, Wisner, Greene, Cornelius! Through what toils and cares we have been called to pass in kindred employments in such distant parts of the Church! You, for the most part, cheered and sustained by friends, I environed by adversaries, once my special friends, whose lowest aim was to obstruct my success and ruin my character. But the Lord has delivered and prospered, so that I look back on all as the ship looks back on squalls and head winds passed, when favoring gales give her a prosperous course, regretting no suffering for the great enterprise, and giving thus early and thus needed a well-endowed evangelical theological seminary so near in influence to the mart of the West. Though the times are hard, our prospects, on the whole, are good, for which we give to God fervent praise.

"In your review you have made a new development of what the much-boasted Unitarian liberality is, *viz.*, to subvert and monopolize the institutions and funds of orthodox generations, and to libel their illustrious dead with a malignity unknown to living hate, and augmented by the lapse of time and the supposed impunity of misrepresentation. God bless you for your victorious defense of the dead, and for the disciplinary justice administered to their living calumniator, as also for a new edition, revised and enlarged, of the shameless perversions of a noble state institution by a 'little sect which thirty years ago had not courage or honesty enough to admit they had a living.' Your account of what the state has done, and the evidence of their sectarian bigotry and meanness in the exclusion of Dr. Griffin, etc., will be one of the links of the chain of causes which will draw on a mighty change in public sentiment, as will also now the revivals in Boston and the shameless infidel fanaticism of the transcendental party.

"My chief object, however, in writing at this time is to suggest to you the importance of a well-written ecclesiastical history of New England by one so well qualified as yourself, and so well situated for collecting and arranging the necessary information — one, too, who comprehends the grand design of Providence in the establishment of the Pilgrims in New England, and so well understands their principles, policy, and deeds as to be able to do justice to them and to the doctrine of Church policy which they introduced.

"There is no chapter in English history so important as that which preceded and led to the exile of the Pilgrims, including the Commonwealth, the Restoration, and the revolutions which followed. It was the struggle for evangelical truth and for civil and religious liberty which eventuated in the planting of the institutions of liberty in the New World, to throw back an influence upon the Old World till the earthquake of revolution shall prepare the way every where for Him to reign whose right it is. It is not too early, and it will soon be too late, to write to the best advantage a complete history of the grand experiment of primitive orthodoxy and strict conditions of Church membership, contrasted with the Half-way Covenant and Stoddardean communion [4] as a converting ordinance, followed by declension and suspension of revivals, till the tide was turned by Edwards.

"This is a chapter of history that should be soon recorded for the instruction of all coming time. It was my intention that Wisner

[4] Solomon Stoddard (1644–1729), minister in Northampton, Mass., maintained that all baptized people of respectable conduct might partake of Communion, even though they were unconverted, as the sacrament could be the means of their conversion.

should do it; but God has called him to other employments, and I know of no one who in interest, and preparation, and capacity is so well qualified to execute such a work as yourself.

"Let me hear from you soon; and do not say you can not command time, for nobody ever did or will do any thing who is not pressed for time. We who have time enough are always lazy; for men who are willing to work and do work will always have their hands full. I am satisfied that my judgment of your fitness will be corroborated by your clerical brethren in New England. My greatest deprivation here is coming away from the scenes, and minds, and interests of New England, with which I can never cease to sympathize."

XLVII

WESTERN COLLEGES

At this time, the efforts made to obtain aid for the seminary and its beneficiaries at the East culminated in the organization of a distinct society, whose object should be to foster this and other rising institutions of the West. Dr. Beecher addressed, July 11, 1842, a long and eloquent appeal to Dr. Albert Barnes, commencing as follows:

"The time has come in which we must unite our counsels and our forces for the West, as all we have done will be impotent to exert the controlling influence of Christian science, civilization, and holiness over the infinitude of depraved mind here bursting forth, and rolling in from abroad upon us like a flood."

After a masterly argument in support of this proposition, he concludes: "No human means can so certainly meet and repel this invasion of Catholic Europe as a competent evangelical ministry and revivals of religion. These speedily will throw all mischief into the distance, and render our salvation like the waves of the sea, and our glory like the unsetting sun. Oh, my brother, could the ministers and churches of the East see and feel the unutterable demand for ministers as I see and feel it, and the cheapness with which we could fit young men for the ministry by their aid, and the ease with which we could settle them, whatever they might think of the Education Society having fulfilled its destiny at the East, they would see that never was the call for its aid for the destitute millions here so imperious as now, and the consequences of neglect so certain and so dreadful; therefore the streams of Christian emigration from the East must flow again, the prayers of Christians for the West must go up day and night, and the hand of benevolence must open wide.

"Though approaching the confines of threescore and ten, my heart burns anew with the fire that glowed in it when I left New England and came here; and when I see what one seminary has done and may yet do, by Eastern and Western munificence, to fill the West with a holy ministry, and revivals of religion, and millennial liberty, I exult in the sacrifices I have made, in the conflicts and buffetings I have passed through, and in the far-reaching providence of God that hath lifted up a standard here, where the enemy cometh in like a flood. May God, my brother, guide your understanding and fire your heart to act immediately and efficaciously in behalf of the West; to blow the trumpet around you, and rally the sacramental host for the onset that is coming on here; for if we fail to hold our own in our own land, how shall we lead in the aggressive movement for the conversion of the world? I am on the field. The battle is begun. We give notice of it to our fathers, and mothers, and brothers, and sisters, and children at the East, and call for help. Who is on the Lord's side — who?"

The results of this letter will be alluded to farther on in this chapter. Meanwhile we find him at Crawfordsville, Indiana, delivering a Commencement address "on the elements of the power of the Catholic system, and the means of subverting it over our country."

Owing to the combined effects of traveling over corduroy railroads, coffee, green tea, and Western fare generally, followed by insurrectionary stomach and blue pill, he says, "I was very much incapacitated, and felt, when I rose to speak, as if the chances were that I should fail; but, though I did not satisfy myself, I escaped breaking my neck, and made a safe, and salutary, and pretty strong impression."

Next we find him assisting Henry Ward in a revival at Terre Haute, Indiana. "The revival here under Henry's administration and preaching was, in the adaptation of means and happy results, one of the most perfectly conducted and delightful that I have ever known."

In May, 1843, we find him at the East, engaged in organizing the society before alluded to. From Philadelphia he writes, May 19: "Our prospect of success in organizing an efficient society to superintend and co-operate with us in the support of Lane and our colleges is cheering, and, my belief is, will go into permanent operation. * * * We shall secure Philadelphia for the organization, which after this year will be the main thing, and without so much personal effort of our own."

August 14 he writes from Williamstown, Massachusetts: "Our cause commends itself to favor and patronage wherever we go. If Edward and myself could spend a year together in the field we could do up the business."

Under date of July 7 he writes from Boston: "This is the first move I have made to solicit funds in old-fashioned style. It was, as to all interest in us at the West, gone almost out of mind. Edward's year of conversing with ministers, and preaching and taking up collections, had got the thing ready to be pushed. By consultations in New York, Philadelphia, New Haven, Hartford, and Boston, we had secured the full conviction of the ministers and influential laymen that the Western institutions must be sustained, and that to this end a society is indispensable.

"Though there was so much cold water thrown in Boston from the Puritan newspaper folks and a few others that it took us three weeks and eight or ten discussions to carry the point, yet it was all so much the better, for we got out all their objections to be answered, which threw all possible lights on the subject, and produced silence on the one side and augmented decision on the other. With this exception here from a quarter to be expected, all every where was cordial and even joyful that a practicable way was discovered to help the West."

August 24 he writes from Boston an account of his journey to Lowell, and thence to Nashua, to meet the General Association of New Hampshire: "Edward beat himself; I did the same, as near as I could. * * * Am quite well and in good spirits to-day. Have seen Palmer, Stone, Noyes, Crocket, and White, and shall see Deacon Proctor where I am writing. My friends here mean to make up my salary out of the first part of the subscriptions, being given and designated for that purpose. That will make it sure, and I feel at rest about it. I start with William and Edward at four for Norwich, to take the boat for East Hampton, which if I do not now, I may never see again. This excursion to Long Island is the first hour of recreation I have had, and I hope it will be pleasant and salutary."

"I had a blessed time," he writes afterward, "at East Hampton, where all old and middle-aged persons that I left thirty-three years ago were gone, and those I left youth of twenty, found up to fifty-three; about half a dozen at ninety-three, and the rest all the way back to fifty. We preached and prayed, exhorted and wept. It was a solemn and joyful time. I never had a visit of such thrilling interest."

On surveying the summer's operations after his return to the West, he writes: "Nothing could have been more auspicious than the results, both in respect to public sentiment, propitious organization, and getting Baldwin [1] for our agent and secretary. I hear from Edward and from Baldwin that things are going well. But for this aid just now we should have all been blown up."

[1] Burr Baldwin (1789–1880), ordained evangelist, did missionary work in the Ohio valley, N.Y., and N.J. until 1824. After 1833, he served as agent for benevolent and missionary societies.

XLVIII

THE BROKEN LINK

WHILE at the East, as already mentioned, during the summer of 1843, Dr. Beecher was suddenly informed of the death of his son George. He thus speaks of the effect of the sad news in a letter to the afflicted widow:

"I have almost this moment received the news of the death of our dear George, now no more on earth, but with his mother, the glorified in heaven. A friend met me at a corner of the street, and said, 'Have you heard the dreadful news which has come into the city this morning?' I said 'No.' He said, 'Your son George is dead,' and handed me the paper containing the account. The shock was like that of a blow across my breast which almost suspended respiration, and left to me only the power of articulating at intervals, Oh! oh! oh! Tears soon came to my relief, but they were not the tears of the father which flowed first, but the tears of disappointed hope for so much and so needed usefulness in the cause of Christ cut off. But soon busy memory flashed upon me its thousand tender recollections of feature, and person, and affection, and co-operation, and his life's history in rapid succession, and then a father's heart paid the debt of nature in a flood of tears. I went to my place of letters immediately, and met Catharine's letter, which opened deeper the sluices of sorrow as I sympathized with you and yours in that overwhelming scene. I returned to my room through the streets of the city sighing and bathed in tears, subsiding and anon bursting out again.

"I have just reached my room and am alone, and becoming more composed. I do not murmur — I do not faint. I am grateful and joyful that God gave me such a son to consecrate to his service. I thank him for his early conversion; his consistent, Christian life; his great affection for me, and co-operation with me during my conflicts and trials at the West; for the great amount of good he has done — some of it in sermons which, I think, will not perish, and much more written on the fleshly tables of sanctified hearts, to be known and read in heaven. And yet, while Faith submits, Nature feels the chasm of disappointed hopes. I have long seen that

George was ripening fast in holiness, which I thought was to qualify him for more esteemed usefulness on earth.

"The event shows that God was preparing him for more esteemed usefulness in a higher, nobler sphere; and, though we see not exactly what it is, we may confide in him who reigns above that there is no mistake, and that God will not promote his cause above by injuring his cause on earth, but that our usefulness in eternity shall be as much greater than on earth as our blessedness is greater; for there is the vision of our God, of Jesus who died for us, and the Spirit who sanctified, and the general assembly of the first-born. The reunion of friends and families, so dear on earth and unforgotten in heaven, and then the rapid flight of time, and the nearness of the glory to be revealed in us, are all themes of thought so full of consolation, that while we look at these glorious, unseen, eternal things, our light and momentary affliction shall work out for us a far more exceeding and eternal weight of glory."

The circumstances attending this afflictive event were described in the "family circular," in which the deceased had just written the following, which proved his last greeting to earthly friends:

"Dear Brothers and Sisters, all hail! — I only wish I had you all here, and every room in my house stowed full. When, think you, Henry and Charles, shall I see your faces here? Can you not come, one or both, this summer? Our house is completed, except a little painting, and will be ready for every body that will come in two weeks, so do make haste!"

Then followed an enumeration of his fruits and flowers, in great variety and abundance, which he had just set out, and in which he took great delight.

Immediately after this, on the same page, followed the account of his death, written by his sister Catharine, then visiting there. He was found in his garden lifeless, with the gun, by whose accidental discharge he had fallen, lying at his side.

"And so it is at last," writes Mrs. Stowe, in the same letter; "there must come a time when all that the most heartbroken, idolizing love can give us is a coffin and a grave! All that could be done for our brother, with all his means, and all the affection of his people and friends, was just this — no more! After all, the deepest and most powerful argument for the religion of Christ is its power in times like this. Take from us Christ and what he taught, and what have we here? What confusion, what agony, what dismay, what wreck and waste! But give Him to us, and even the most stricken heart can rise under the blow, yea, even triumph. 'Thy brother shall rise again,' saith Jesus; and to us who weep he speaks, 'Rejoice, inasmuch as ye are made partakers of Christ's sufferings, that when his glory shall be revealed, ye also may be glad with exceeding joy!' Deeper than all sophisms, and all mazes of crooked reasonings, is the heart's triumphant *knowledge*, when in its utmost strait and agony it casts itself on Christ, and finds 'He is here!'

"Oh my brothers all, let this first blood shed baptize you as soldiers of Christ, to fight manfully in the steps of him who has fallen, but who also has triumphed. Then at last

> " 'We all shall meet at Jesus's feet;
> Shall meet to part no more!' "

XLIX

THE LOST FOUND

According to the apostolic injunction, "Count it all joy when ye fall into divers tribulations," Dr. Beecher, during the earlier half of his Western life, ought to have been a very joyful man, for seldom does hero of romance encounter troubles more numerous or severe than seemed to combine from every quarter against his peace. In addition to the suffering attendant upon the anti-slavery imbroglio, the assault upon his orthodoxy, the death of his wife, and sudden failure of his support, he was obliged to witness the descent of one of his sons and pupils into the midnight of fatalism, and to find his favorite author, President Edwards, the occasion of the disastrous change.

In his senior year in college this son read the "Inquiry respecting the Freedom of the Will," in the first part of which the author apparently annihilates free agency, while in the second part he proves from Scripture that men are subjects of moral obligation notwithstanding.

Now, as Isaac Taylor well observes, "just as these conclusions (of the second part) may be, they commanded no respect beyond the Christian community; nay, they excited the scorn of those who naturally said, 'If these principles of piety could have been established by abstract argument, a thinker so profound as Edwards, and so fond of this method, would not have gone about to prove them by the Bible.' Deistical and atheistical writers, availing themselves eagerly of the abstract portions of the 'Inquiry,' and contemning its Biblical conclusions, carried on the unfinished reasoning in their own manner." *

This describes precisely the course pursued by this son of Dr. Beecher. A more patient study of the treatise, especially taken in connection with that on the Nature of True Virtue, might have shown him that in the definition of holiness as love to being in general, Edwards had laid the foundation for a system of perfect

* Logic in Theology, p. 13.

accountability. Taking this premiss, his disciples deduced what Dr. Alexander characterized as "a system of false theology, which, under its first phase as Hopkinsianism, and under its second as Taylorism, has been to our Church the '*fons et origo malorum.*'" It is true that in his earlier treatise on the Affections, President Edwards gives a different definition of true virtue as a love or relish for holiness, and that thus he is the father of "the Taste scheme," so called, as well as of "the Exercise scheme."

But, though his writings really contain the germs of two different and often antagonistic schools, it is his latest and maturest works in which the germs of a system of moral government are found, a careful study of which might have proved the antidote of fatalism. But young Beecher was neither a patient nor thorough student of Edwards at that time.

"Availing himself eagerly," as Isaac Taylor says, "of the abstract portions of the 'Inquiry,' and contemning its Biblical conclusions," he pushed the logic of causation out to its most consistent and disastrous extremes of fatalism; and yet, in doing this, his arguments were strikingly similar to those employed by standard Old School theologians against their New School brethren. "No one," it is said, "has ever given an intelligible account of any active power that man can exert save to move the muscles of his body or to direct the attention of his mind, and that only within certain limits. This beggarly power is strangely glorified when clothed in the princely habiliments of semi-omnipotence."

The power to choose in given circumstances, otherwise than a man does in fact choose, is represented as "the most disastrous power that can well be conceived of, and, if any man possesses it, he ought to make it his daily prayer to be delivered from it. No man, while cursed with such a self-determining power as this, could be safe for a moment. With his whole soul bent in one direction, he might be borne, and that, too, by his own will, in another. With the most anxious desire to escape from danger, he might be carried immediately into it. He could form no plans for his own conduct, nor would others be able to anticipate, in the least degree, what they might expect from him." *

These reasonings are specious, but, unless there is some flaw in them, they conduct to fatalism. The will is but "a beggarly power," limited to the control of the muscles and of the attention; and when "the whole soul is bent," by overmastering temptation,

* Princeton Review, July, 1837, p. 392.

from inflamed desire, in a given direction, however unlawful, the power to will in the contrary direction "is the most disastrous power that can well be conceived of."

It was by just such reasonings, consistently carried out, that Dr. Beecher's son made shipwreck of the faith, and became, for a season, a confirmed fatalist. Dr. Beecher did all that could be done under the circumstances, but his influence over his son's mind was from the first impaired by the fact of his well-known admiration of President Edwards. Time only, and experience, could work a cure, and reveal the error of such reasoners, namely, as Isaac Taylor expresses it, "that of mingling what is purely abstract with facts belonging to the physiology of the human mind." This, he observes, produces "a vague dissatisfaction or latent suspicion that some fallacy has passed into the train of reasoning, although the linking of propositions seems perfect. This suspicion increases in strength, and at length condenses itself in the form of a protest against certain conclusions, notwithstanding their necessary connection with the premises." This suspicion, this protest, was produced in time, partly by suffering, and partly by the power of God in answer to a father's prayers.

No one can know Dr. Beecher's mind and heart, in some of their deepest, richest beauties, so well as does that son, as he recalls the amazing developments of wisdom, patience, logical power, and love then made, and made apparently in vain. Never can he forget the impression of those encounters, in which all a father's influences were thrown back like waves from a rock. Never will memory cease to recall the look, the tone, the attitude with which that father bade him farewell on his departure to New Orleans.

"My son," he said, with quivering lip, "eternity is long!" and, with a glance of anguish and a grasp of the hand, he turned away.

But even then he did not abandon hope. Well he knew that time, and the inevitable unhappiness produced by fatalism on any mind of Christian nurture, were stern teachers. He fell back on Providence and prayer. The whole family were combined in a weekly concert of supplication for the wanderer; and, amid all his multiplied cares, through a period stretching from 1834 to 1840, Dr. Beecher's own supplications were incessant and importunate.

For the purpose of introducing a letter in which his feelings on this subject are expressed, the following stanzas, composed and published in New Orleans, though of little intrinsic merit, are inserted here:

"Oh, must I live a lonely one,
Unloved upon the thronged earth,
Without a home beneath the sun,
Far from the land that gave me birth?

"Alone — alone I wander on,
An exile in a dreary land;
The friends that knew me once are gone;
Not one is left of all their band.

"I look upon the boiling tide
Of traffic fierce, that ebbs and flows,
With chill disgust and shrinking pride,
That heartfelt misery only knows.

"Where is the buoyancy of youth,
The high, indomitable will,
The vision keen, the thirst for truth,
The passions wild, unearthly thrill?

"Oh, where are all the bounding hopes
And visions bright, that were my own
When Fancy at her will could ope
The golden doors to Beauty's throne?

"My mother! whither art thou fled?
Seest thou these tears that for thee flow?
Or, in the realms of shadowy dead,
Knowest thou no more of mortal woe?

"In that still realm of twilight gloom
Hast thou reserved no place for me?
Haste — haste, oh mother, give me room;
I come — I come at length to thee!"

On reading these lines, Dr. Beecher addressed his son as follows:

"Dear Charles, you will perceive by my last letter, if received, the trembling solicitude of a father's love, which the slightest danger alarms. Since writing it, I have seen the report of yellow fever contradicted in the papers, and have also conversed with Mr. Findley; so that, though I should prefer your returning home, yet, so long as New Orleans remains healthy, and your friends think it safe, I would not interpose my fears. I only desire you to maintain the living recollection of my inextinguishable interest in you, and my love and tender solicitude for your life, health, and happiness, and that, though our opinions may differ, this circumstance produces, instead of alienation, only a more intense interest, solicitude, and sympathy, which makes your sufferings mine, and my joys, if you may but return, more than for the 'ninety and nine that went not astray.'

"Oh, my dear Charles — the last child of my angel wife, your blessed mother — you can never know the place you fill in your father's heart, and the daily solicitude and prayers of his soul for your protection and restoration to equanimity, satisfaction, and joy of heart in communion with God.

"Since dinner to-day Henry has put into my hands the stanzas in the New Orleans paper, which have distressed and alarmed me not a little, especially the lines beginning

" 'The friends that knew me once are gone.'

Now I can perceive, in your passing out of the circle of family sympathy in respect to opinions, how you may feel a conscious *loneliness;* but that it should distress you that we are not associated with you in a change of opinions which has brought to your bosom so little that is cheering and sound — which has brought you into such close communion with suffering, I can not believe, though I may comprehend, perhaps, how the loneliness of your departure from us should create the deceptive and unfounded feeling that we have placed you beyond the pale of our warm affections and tenderness. I hope the retrospect of our unwavering and constant love, and tender interests, and efforts to hold and restore you, and to mitigate your sorrows, and to minister consolation and aid in your embarrassments, will chase from your candid and affectionate mind apprehensions so unlike yourself, and so unjust and painful to us.

"I have never known a case of aberration in sentiment from parental instruction and family belief, environed by such constancy of unwavering affection, such perseverance of hope, and such importunity of fervent, and, I trust, effectual prayer; so that, amid your melancholy complainings and despondencies, and my own tremulous susceptibilities, I seem to hear the reply of the Bishop of Hippo to the mother of Augustine, who came beseeching him to pray for her skeptical son — 'Depart, good woman,' said he, 'the child of so many prayers can not be lost!' And when I know and remember how by your sainted mother you were borne and nurtured, while she lived, amid supplications and most entire consecration of you to God, sealed by both our vows at your baptism, I can not, will not despair of your passing from this dark cloud into the glorious light and liberty of the Gospel.

"Whenever the temptation comes over you to feel that you are friendless, remember, I pray you, that your father lives, that Aunt Esther lives almost only to suffer and pray for you, and that every one of your brothers and sisters are united in a weekly concert of prayer for your preservation and restoration to joy and peace in believing.

"Your address to your mother is overwhelming to me. That you should address her *in doubt* whether she now adores as an angel amid the resplendent joys and glories of heaven, or is bereft of consciousness amid the shadowy dead by annihilation, and that you should implore her personified dust to give you quickly a place in her realms of twilight gloom, as if resolved to follow her — did I not regard it as a poetical amplification, I should be terrified — petrified. Oh, my dear Charles, would to God that this blessed mother could look upon you as in life, and in my dreams since her death, she has looked and smiled on me in my despondencies and sorrows — that she might speak to your troubled soul as she was wont to speak to mine, in the language of wisdom, and meek submission, and unutterable kindness — it would stay your maladies, revive your spirit, fill up your dreary void of desolation, and make your life, as she did mine, as full of enjoyment as can appertain to the lot of mortals.

"But, though she can not smile on you, her suffering son, and can not speak alleviation to your wounded spirit, there is One who can do it, more kind and gentle, more compassionate and even more sympathizing than even she ever was — who every day beholds your solicitude, and is every day saying, 'Come unto me, thou weary and heavy laden, and I will give thee rest.' And I trust that He who never rejected an applicant for bodily alleviation, or the petition of friend or parent for help, will hear our supplications for you, and make us the partakers of your common joy on earth and a peaceful heaven at last."

To this same son, restored through the mercy of a covenant-keeping God, after a thorough experience of the desolating effects of fatalism, and engaged as a licentiate in proclaiming the unsearchable riches of Christ, yet still to some extent perplexed by the deeper problems of redemption, he writes, July 16, 1844:

"Your letter to Harriet has come under my eye, and that extract from your sermon required two pocket-handkerchiefs to keep my eyes and face dry. It is now three or four days since, and I have read it three or four times, else my enthusiastic admiration might have broken out in terms unsafe for one so young in preaching as yourself. It is the evidence of resources in powerful writing evangelized, which may make sermons of the first class of literary merit, and yet be read with the interest of wicked novels, preserving the unbroken power of revival sermons.

"Let me say, by the way, that too long, quite too long has the devil held in his exclusive possession the fine arts, and what is called fine writing, classical writing, etc., quenching in sermons the power of the imagination and taste, and condemning the most sublime and soul-stirring truths in the universe, which are the themes of saints and angels, to the dry technicalities and endless formal divisions of leaden prose sermons, offering no chance for the soul of the ministry untrammeled to take fire and cry like the Tyrolese, 'In the name of the Holy Trinity of heaven, let all loose.'

"Your 'jaded, overwearied sense of inability' reminds me of my own experience after a bilious fever, September, 1801, with suspended labor until September, 1802, a dozen Sabbaths excepted, with protracted debility through 1803, only just able to revise and bring out of my treasury things new and old. But I did not think it was best to die, and I was as hungry to live and labor as a fish out of water is to get into his own element again. And I do not believe that I should have done more good 'in a tight bark, sailing with propitious breezes over the peaceful ocean of heaven,' than God has been pleased to secure by my labors here. My early days were very much checkered with despondency, and shamefacedness, and jealous feeling, as if every body saw my emptiness and vanity; but I resisted it as a physical, lying disease, representing things that are not as though they were; and I said to such feelings, 'Get thee behind me, Satan, for thou savorest not the things that be of God.'

" * * * In respect to your objections to systematic divinity, why should a topic in theology be exceedingly distrusted the more it becomes systematic? Are not all the works of God in the natural world systematic — the orrery of the universe, the anatomy of bodies, planets, and trees, and the chemical laws of matter? and is matter methodized, the mere footstool of immortal mind, while law, and motive, and moral government, and the remedial influence of the atonement, and redemption, are thrown heap upon heap in immethodical masses? and is all approximation to system in subjects which angels desire to look into, and which, in their eternal unfoldings, are destined to make forever, by the Church, to principalities and powers, the brightest manifestation of the wisdom and the riches of the goodness of God, without foundation, revealing only immethodical indiscrimination?

"Because some men adopt false theories in natural science, is there then no true system of natural science? and because some men blunder in their expositions of the light of nature and the science of God's revealed remedial government, is there no correct system of mental philosophy and doctrinal revelation? I admit that we ought to systematize with great carefulness, and include no *à priori* theories, and build only with the unquestioned principles of the moral divine government and matters of fact. Perhaps, however, all you mean may be only that, while the great revealed system of God discloses the general and obvious skeleton of systematized relations, it is dangerous to give way to the lust of systemization throughout all the ramifications, and to make the hair veins as fundamental as the jugular, and the heart, and the arteries.

"No doubt the desire of systematizing the minutiæ of things appertains more or less to our creeds and theologizing, which ought not to be imitated; and yet original investigation, by the tracing of relations, and dependencies, and symmetrical analogies, and nature of things, with the desire of progress, is not to be inhibited. It maintains the vigor, and acumen, and wakeful interest of mind, and probably will constitute no small part of its exhilaration and untiring occupancy through eternity; for God is manifested as delightfully and wonderfully in the minute beauties and delicacies of his works — in the endless kaleidoscopic tints of beauty in flowers and shrubs, etc., as, in the sublime majesty of the conformation of suns and worlds.

"The following are the rules which I have prescribed for myself upon this subject, and rigidly adhered to from early life:

"1. I will not push my own theories and reasonings against the just interpretation of revelation on subjects that lie beyond the range of the senses, or of intuition and reason; nor,

"2. Will I urge the minutiæ of a system against its obvious skeleton truths, nor set aside that which I know certainly for that which is less certain, substituting ignorance or uncertainty as my guide instead of knowledge and fact.

"3. If I find myself going off the track of the general philosophizings and Biblical expositions of the generations of the great, and learned, and good who have gone before me, I assume that there is such presumptive evidence that I may be wrong as demands great circumspection in coming to an opposite conclusion; still, I do not abandon immediately what seems to me to be true, but examine all its perceptible relations to what are admitted to be the laws of mind and moral government, and God's revealed system; and if it repels no acknowledged revealed truth, and demands no unnatural violence to come into its place in the system, as if it were made for it, I begin to believe it to be true, but suspend my full assent till long-continued time, and thought, and revision confirm my judgment; and now there are many important truths which I believe and preach which I held for many years *sub judice*.

"4. And even when convinced myself, before I publish any thing contrary to received opinion, I inquire whether it is a truth of such fundamental importance that I am bound in conscience to preach it immediately, or whether, as Christ did with his disciples in respect to some truths, I may regard time and circumstances in respect to the preparation of the Church to receive it. When convinced of the truth and the propriety of its communication, I present it in its own light and relations, without sounding the trumpet of a discovery, or that I am preaching in opposition to received opinions.

"If I anticipate that it will be regarded as new, I say that 'I am aware that others, whose judgment is deserving of great deference, have thought differently, but, after long and careful investigation, I have not been able to come to any other conclusion.' Here I stop in the early development; never attack the opposite opinion, or amplify its absurdity or mischief, or stigmatize it by hard names. I generally prefer to present it first in the way of answering objections, in which, if it be seen to work well, by relieving the difficulty which error always makes somewhere, and truth always relieves, many that might contend against it may silently acquiesce when they see how well it works in stopping the mouths of gainsayers. But then even I avoid the too frequent repetition of it, lest it should attract needless notice, or produce in my own mind a paternal favoritism, and become a cosset or a hobby-horse, or create a fever of nervous affection, or exalt my pride as the discoverer of some new thing. It is enough if we may be allowed to think and speak freely, and to push noiselessly, and with unprovoking, meek modesty, a new truth amid the prescriptive rights of error. It is difficult enough to push our little steam-boat up to the landing, amid swamps of other preoccupants, if we treat them with all possible courtesy; but if we jostle for a place with invidious epithets and harsh denunciation, or offensive caricature, we shall hardly gain or keep it without many hard blows and great damage. I endeavor, therefore, to find out intelligible and acceptable words, which shall afford the least possible occasion of mistake or offense, and the least tangible surface to any return fire.

"In respect to the atonement, I remark that it is made up of facts more or less systematic, and may be pushed to extremities of minute theorizings, which, the farther it progresses, the less may be our ground of confidence of perfect accuracy; and yet, so far as our positions are symmetrical and analogical with the facts already known, we are not likely to be wrong, and only so when we substitute *feelings* or *theories* of our own, which either are not implied in the fundamental elements, or are assumed without evidence against them — recusant theories which will not go with the stream.

"It is true that the evangelical system, including the atonement, is pervaded more or less by the doctrines of necessity and free agency, if by necessity be meant the *certainty* of human sinful character and action, without the interposition and reforming influence of the Spirit, and the certainty of perseverance with it; but if by necessity be meant that the volitions and actions of sinful mind are produced by a necessity as irresistible as that which controls the planets and unites physical effects to their causes, then *both* can not pervade God's system, for they are intuitive contradictions — not a mystery, but a known, certain impossibility.

"It is true, then, that the doctrine of the atonement assumes a class of facts without explaining minutely their *modus operandi;* and yet these facts are symmetrical, and do indicate a powerful adaptation to their designed results. The facts assumed, and the principles implied or expressly taught in the atonement, constitute an encyclopædia of knowledge, of which that doctrine is the radiating, central point touching them all.

"One of these implications goes back to God's eternal purpose to create a universe of mind voluntary, intelligent, social, immortal; to gratify and manifest his benevolence in the production of the greatest amount of created good. Another, to the moral law as the guiding and conservatory power of mind — the permanent mode of maintaining the happiness of the universe; it touches the entrance and consequences of transgression, eventuating in permanent, incorrigible alienation from God and his government; the impossibility of reformation and pardon on principles of law whose rewards are suspended by disobedience, and whose penalties, self-inflicted and accumulating, chafe and exasperate selfish mind; and the impossibility of giving up the law to save the guilty.

"It would not save them were it given up; for sin would still be what it is, and to be carnally minded would be death, and the anarchy of ungoverned mind would be a hell. To interpose by omnipotence to make sinners happy, and maintain the efficacy of law in the neglect of its principles, would be to give up moral government, and change the perfect system for one without moral excellence — a mere physical result of animal enjoyment. But to do this would be unjust to himself — unjust to the loyal subjects of his government, destroying in their behalf the conservatory power of law, and their own character and immortal happiness as rational, accountable subjects of the government of God.

"If it should be said that the universe of mind is not affected by what God does in our little world, the answer is, that all the capabilities of disembodied mind indicate ample adaptations for a universal communion with God and his intelligent government as the common property of the universe, and all the implications of the Bible carry us strongly to that result."

In October this same son writes, proposing some inquiries in respect to the import of the adopting act in presbyterial ordination, whether it implied an unqualified acceptance of every article of the Confession, or whether the Confession was to be taken for substance. "I can accept it," he said, "*yet so* that my liberty of differing therewith, in all cases where there is question of agreement with Scripture, be not diminished, but rather established."

He also stated that while, to his mind, in some respects the Confession, according to the present popular understanding of its language, failed to give an entirely just expression of the spirit of the Bible, nevertheless he admitted that it plainly recognized all the fundamental facts necessary to salvation.

To this Dr. Beecher replies, October 25, 1844: "Your qualification in your first answer you need not make and will not feel the need of, when you see that the Confession itself makes the same condition, chap. i., § x: 'The supreme judge, by whom all controversies of religion are to be determined, and all decrees of councils, opinions of ancient writers, doctrines of men, and private spirits are to be examined, and in whose sentence we are to rest, can be no other but the Holy Spirit speaking in the Scripture.'

"This provision was intended to meet just such difficulties as you feel about some things. As to your other remark, I understand you to mean that the language of the Confession, read continuously, does not make the same impression on the popular mind that reading the Bible does. This I have always supposed and said, and still say so to my classes, though you might easily state it in the presence of uncandid and hostile minds so as to be misunderstood. In accepting the Confession, you do not profess to believe that it contains all that the Bible contains, or that it is as unerring as the Bible is, but that it does comprehend the system of fundamental doctrines taught in the Bible.

"There have always been two different expositions of the meaning of the Confession on some doctrinal points from the beginning, in respect to which both parties appeal to the Bible and have been allowed to differ, as holding substantially the fundamental doctrines of the system taught in the Holy Scriptures. But do not worry. If I come, you are sound enough to make all safe. Nothing will prevent me but dangerous sickness from setting out on Monday next. Be of good cheer, and leave off pulling up the roots of things all at once just now; provide no mark for the enemy to fire at, and all, with diligence and spirituality, will go well.'

To this excellent advice Henry Ward adds the following: "Preach little doctrine except what is of mouldy orthodoxy; keep all your improved breeds, your short-horned Durhams, your Berkshires, etc., away off to pasture. They will get fatter, and nobody will be scared. Take hold of the most practical subjects; popularize your sermons. I do not ask you to change yourself; but, for a time, while captious critics are lurking, adapt your mode so as to insure that you shall be rightly understood."

These letters indicate the occasion of that horseback journey of seventy miles through "the black swamp," from St. Mary's, Ohio, to Fort Wayne, Indiana, an account of which, at the time, went the rounds of the papers. One well remembers the doctor's appearance as, besplashed and bespattered, with smoking steed and saddle-bags crusted with mud, he rode, in the dusk of evening, up to the back gate of Judge M'Culloch's residence, and alighted, weary and stiff, but still hale and hearty, as though horseback rides of seventy miles were every-day occurrences. A hearty welcome, a heartier supper, and a thorough washing, before going to bed, of the whole body in cold water, brought him out the next morning sound as a nut, and with a step as light and springy as a young man.

When the Presbytery of Fort Wayne was constituted, with the

doctor and his son Henry Ward present as members of a sister Presbytery, the examination of the candidate began. As the conversation proceeded, and especially while the candidate rehearsed his experimental history and read his trial sermon (on Faith), the doctor was repeatedly detected in the act of wiping his eyes. When the time came for the services of ordination, after the sermon by Henry Ward, the doctor, whose duty it was to deliver the charge, spoke as follows:

"My son, this day, much longed for and waited for, has come. The consummation of many prayers is realized this day. You are now a minister of the Lord Jesus Christ, and the pastor of a Church of Christ.

"Scriptural example and the designation of my brethren call me to give intensity to exhortation in the form of a solemn charge that you fulfill the duties of your high calling. Remember, then, the gift that is in thee, as an ambassador of Jesus Christ to negotiate peace between God and men — the mightiest power God delegates to mortals.

"Remember that this power is to be used in a period of high conflict and glorious history, and yet of persecution and blood. The stress of the conflict and the intensity of effort will be great. In view of the coming struggle, I charge thee, before God and the Lord Jesus Christ —

"1. Be strong in thy determined purpose, for no ordinary decision will avail.

"2. Count the cost, and give thyself *wholly* to thy work. One calling is enough in such a war, and half a minister is almost worse than none, for the devoted half *is never but little better than a quarter*.

"3. Preach the Gospel. Not human philosophy, not your own imaginings, but the GOSPEL — the law violated, man depraved, the atonement made, the law honored, the rebel reconciled. Reprove, where reproof is needed, with benevolence, meekness, and power. Rebuke presumptuous wickedness with all long-suffering and doctrine.

"4. Take heed to thyself — to thy body, in which thy spirit dwells, and whose abuse will cripple and eclipse thy soul; give it food without excess, and exercise sufficient for digestion — to thy mind, to have it exercised by reason of use. The mind without discipline will not maintain its power, but decline to premature impotency.

"Take heed to thy heart; keep it with all diligence, by meditation, by prayer, and by habitual communion with God. The power of the heart set on fire by love is the greatest created power in the universe — more powerful than electricity, for that can only rend and melt matter; but LOVE can, by God's appointment, carry the truth quick and powerful through the soul, and will, in a few generations, subdue and tranquillize the world.

"Take heed to thy doctrine; understand it clearly; believe it cordially, and preach in demonstration of the Spirit and with power. I do not mean an everlasting thrumming over of a few cut and dried truths; but let your congregation be fully indoctrinated, and then, like food or ammunition, you can keep the system for use, rightly dividing to every man his portion in due season, with an application.

"But, while much must be done for your Church and congregation, much must be done for the general cause. To plant Christianity in the West is as grand an undertaking as to plant it in the Roman empire, with unspeakably greater permanence and power."

The following letter from Mrs. Stowe, immediately after the ordination, will be read with interest:

"DEAR CHARLEY, — I have thought of you all much during father's visit to Fort Wayne, and how you, and Henry, and he must be enjoying yourselves together, and have prayed that Christ would strengthen your heart and encourage your hands by it. In truth, such family visits are small specimens of Eden yet unwithered. Father has come home well and refreshed by his journey.

"Charley, you must not be discouraged if no immediate and powerful results follow your preaching, since He who spake as never man spake often preached in vain as to immediate results. 'How long shall I be with you? how long shall I suffer you?' he once exclaimed, when he perceived how little effect instructions most earnestly reiterated had upon his disciples. How, in his hours of midnight prayer, must he have longed to finish his work, as he says, 'I have a baptism to be baptized with, and how am I straitened till it be accomplished!'

"I have been considering lately the subject of Christ's *pre*-appearances in the Old Testament, and if you see the Evangelist, you will perhaps see some remarks I have written on one of them in your style of descriptive filling out. Also, I have sent to the same paper a piece of poetry on the words, 'Now there stood by the cross of Jesus *his mother*,' many of the ideas of which were suggested by your lectures, or by the state of feeling consequent on them. I wish you could see them both, because I think you would enter into the strain of feeling in them.

"It is exceedingly interesting to my mind, and produces a wild poetic thrill to look far back into the Old Testament, and read of those interviews of the yet veiled WORD with Abraham, Isaac, Jacob, Moses, and onward. How gently he led them! how he condescended to each peculiarity of character, and made physical and outward blessings the means of attaching them to himself, and thus creating a tie which should result in spiritual elevation. The skeptic may smile at the idea of God entering into all the little plans of a shepherd's life, as he did with Jacob, but God no more feels it a little thing to attend to the undignified mortal wants of his child than the mother to attend to those of her infant or the father to plan toys for his child.

"Jacob's history especially encourages me. He was essentially a desponding, timid man, though, as we see by full proofs, just such a man as is always beloved in a family. Now to this timid, desponding, yet affectionate man, how admirably did the divine WORD adapt himself; how he upheld him at every step with dreams and visions, and whispers of presence and comfort, and thus, in the absence of any written word — any previous history, or sacraments, or outward means, he won the heart of Jacob just as a mother wins the heart of her child. 'The God who fed me all my life long — the *angel* that redeemed me from all evil' — so Jacob calls him in dying.

"And this WORD, thus walking and communing with man, guides the Jewish nation like a flock, and in all their afflictions till the fullness of time, and then 'The Lord whom they seek comes suddenly to his temple, even the *messenger of the covenant* whom they delight in.' How sublimely mournful now sounds the passage in John, 'He came unto his *own*, and his own received him not!'"

L

RECOLLECTIONS OF NETTLETON

THE memoir of Dr. Nettleton was published in 1844. On reading it, Dr. Beecher's heart was stirred and the memories of former days revived. He went back to the time when they labored together in revivals, preaching the same doctrines and aiming at the same glorious results.

Calling up before his mind the Nettleton that was, before sickness had shattered his constitution and party spirit supplanted brotherly love, he threw off the following hasty notes, so singularly free from the least traces of resentment that from them no one would ever suspect that any alienation had ever existed.

"Nettleton's personal attention to the critical state of individuals in the progress of a revival was wonderful. This is a field in which the greatness of his vigilance, and wisdom, and promptness, and efficacy lay, the wonders of which, though much may be told, can never be recorded. His eye was open on every side so far as to see if any danger betided, and his solicitude was intense and his adaptations wonderful and efficacious. He no doubt, by timely special interpositions to avert danger and continue the unbroken associations of seriousness, has been the means of plucking thousands as brands from the burning and bringing them into the kingdom of God.

"When cases of this kind multiplied beyond the power of personal attention, he selected and associated with himself instrumental agents with great sagacity and precision of judgment in sending the person adapted to do the specific thing to be done.

"While I was once laboring with him in New Haven in a revival, there occurred a wedding ball, of which the parties availed themselves to draw in by invitation three young ladies whose minds had been tenderly impressed. The effort to enlist the judicious parents, and to call the attention of the young ladies personally to the danger which threatened them, filled his soul. On the morning of the day preceding the ball he went himself to one of the three, to another he deputed some one else, and the third he gave to me, and in the evening preached one of his most powerful sermons from 'To whom I now send thee, to turn them from darkness to light, and from the power of Satan unto God.'

"It was an eloquent and successful assault, as if he had rushed into a circle of enemies to liberate captives destined to a hopeless bondage, where the whole energy of his soul and strength were bestowed in the desperate onset. He fought it out as if the devil had come to take them and he stood there to defend them.

"The power of his preaching included many things. It was highly intellectual as opposed to declamation, or oratorical, pathetic appeals to imagination or the emotions. It was discriminatingly doctrinal, giving a clear and strong exhibition of doctrines denominated Calvinistic, explained, defined, proved, and applied, and objections stated and answered. It was deeply experimental in the graphic development of the experience of saint and sinner. It was powerful beyond measure in stating and demolishing objections, and at times terrible and overwhelming in close, pungent, and direct application to the particular circumstances of sinners.

"But, with all this intellectualization and discriminating argument, there was in some of his sermons unsurpassed power of description, which made the subject a matter of present reality. Such was his sermon on the Deluge one evening, in a village a few miles north of Albany. It was in a very large and crowded hall, and the house was filled with consternation, as if they heard the falling of the rain, the roaring of the waves, the cries of the drowning, the bellowing of cattle, and neighing of horses, amid the darkness and desolation. The emotion rose to such a pitch that the floor seemed to tremble under the tones of his deep voice. He would say, pointing with his finger, 'Will you take up the subject immediately?' and each would reply, 'Yes, sir!' 'Yes, sir!' as if Christ was speaking and the day of judgment had come.

"But there was another thing which gave accumulating power to his sermons. They were adapted to every state and stage of a revival, and condition of individual experience. His revivals usually commenced with the Church in confessions of sin and reformation. He introduced the doctrine of depravity, and made direct assaults on the conscience of sinners, explained regeneration, and cut off self-righteousness, and enforced immediate repentance and faith, and pressed to immediate submission in the earlier stages. Toward the close he had a set of sermons to guard sinners against dropping the subject, such as 'Putting the Hand to the Plow,' 'Quenching the Spirit,' 'When the unclean spirit is gone out of a man,' etc. To this was added whatever was necessary on the signs of self-deception and the evidences of true religion, with sermons to young converts.

"But these all would have been comparatively feeble but for the ubiquity and power of his personal attention where exigencies called for it, and the little *circles* which he met daily, when many were interested, to instruct and guide, and often to press submission with a success unsurpassed any where.

"To these were added a meeting of inquiry for all who were willing to attend and receive exhortation and personal instruction, and of young converts to tell their experience, sing and pray, and a circle initiated in the singing of hymns and spiritual songs.

"On the whole, taken together, it was one great movement upon the intellect, conscience, and heart, guarding against obstructions, and augmented in power by continuity of attention, and impressions, and all sorts of co-operating auxiliary influences, with less of defect and more of moral power than I have ever known or ever expect to see again.

"He commenced when the fear of revivals, from past mistakes, had not wholly subsided, and when infidelity and opposition made carefulness necessary; and he fairly introduced a series of revivals conducted in a manner so unexceptionable, and with such power of argument, and attended with such glorious results, as put an end to opposition to revivals, and gave them an honored and unquestioned place in the Church of God, and generally in respectable society."

LI

CORRESPONDENCE, 1845

THE following extract of a letter, March 27, 1845, to his son Henry Ward, illustrates the tenacity of Dr. Beecher's purpose that all his sons should become preachers of the Gospel:

"Ever since your letter to Thomas, speaking of your preaching and the prospect of a revival, he began to speak about going to Indianapolis. Harriet thinks, and the same occurred to me, that he was moved to do so with the hope of becoming a true Christian; and, though I could employ him just now in assisting me, I have preferred that he should be with you. He said, when he first read your letter, 'Well, I think I had better go and help Henry.'

"His bent of mind is so strong for the natural sciences, and his originality, and power of mind, and mechanical execution, and his attained qualifications are so distinguished for a professor of chemistry and natural philosophy, that my heart had let go of its favorite purpose that he should preach; and yet I feel reproved almost in giving it up, as if my faith had failed, though, as in the case of Charles, I do not give it up, and only yield to an irresistible Providence, still hoping and desiring yet he may be a minister.

"But, whether he preach or not, I can not think without pain and fear of his character being formed as a man of talents and celebrity without religion, every year adding to the chances that he may spend his life and die without holiness. His usefulness in a professional college life will be greatly augmented by religion. * * *

"He has earned a high reputation in his year's labor and study with Dr. Lock, of the Medical College of Ohio, whose reputation you know, and who says:

" 'My laboratory is peculiarly arranged, having a complete work-shop for the manufacture and repair of instruments appended to it. In this shop, myself, Mr. Beecher, and my son have labored as much as circumstances would permit, and I am now surrounded by beautiful and efficient instruments, the result of our labors, some of which have been made solely by Mr. Beecher. He has become familiar with the general circle of instructions and experiments in the public course of lectures in this institution, embracing much that is original and peculiar.'

"Dr. Lock said to me lately that there were few professors in the United States that understood chemistry better, or could excel him in dexterity of experimentation; and that, give to some men a well-furnished apparatus, and in five years it will be run down, whereas in that time Thomas would create one around him."

The following letter was at this time written by Mrs. Stowe to her brother Thomas, and is inserted here as having an indirect but powerful bearing on the happiness of Dr. Beecher in this period of his life.

"*June* 2, 1845. Your letter satisfied me that yours is not a mind unperceptive of its own moral wants — so far I have hopes. The most hopeless class of minds to me are those self-satisfied ones whom a few favorite ideas and theories of their own seem capable of contenting, and who have no conception of the deep, immortal longing which pursues spirits of another order — a longing which, whether developed in diseased action, as in superstition and fanaticism, or in intense, never-satisfied worldly fore-reaching, or haunting the mind amid floods of accomplished wish and successful effort like an unlaid ghost, is yet, in all these forms, a high and sacred relic of a better nature.

"But some minds, from a natural overestimate of themselves, and a certain shallowness of their emotions, a want of deep feeling, never know this except by the presence of some crushing outward agony; others, of more sensitive construction, more earnest and craving desire, find it momently in the discrepancy of the outward with the exigent demands of the inward — the burning *inward* of a deep, unsaid dissatisfaction. True, what is called common sense, worldly wisdom, lays its stern hand upon it, hushes its mouth, as some vagrant gipsy who would degrade a high-born child to unwonted and disgusting servitude, repressing its cries for father and mother, and grinding it down to outward service by stern assurances that such, and such only, are its portion; and yet, though the child learns to be still, and to labor in uncomplaining despair in its bondage — nay, though it becomes so habituated to it that it can scarce conceive of living any other way, and though all its physical habits may have become so reversed and unadapted that a return to that home and father may neither be desired nor attempted, still, deep within, the perverse longing groans, and sighs, and bleeds, and murmurs — all in vain.

"But that repressed and crushed longing, useless, unreasonable, without end or purpose, is all that remains to the captive of a noble lineage and high inheritance; and even though it become mania or moroseness, or though it unfit him for the office of a patient drudge without fitting him for any thing else, 'tis all one, there it is, a mournful fragment of something divine.

"Now here is my creed. God made man to be happy — not by himself, but happy only in a deep, absorbing, sympathizing union with his Maker; such a union as makes His will the soul's will, His joy the soul's joy, His aversion the soul's aversion. Now, if He made the soul expressly to exist in this way, and *no other*, so far as the soul tries to live in any other it is going against the laws of its being — against the inexorable and inevitable limits of things that are, and can not be otherwise. Man — you — I — we all have a desperate determination to live an independent life, by our own will, impulse, and choice, apart from God; hence the eternal wound, forever bleeding, over which we only draw the robe of outward things; hence involuntary fear, perplexity, doubt, remorse, uncertainty, and endless conflict, flashes of truth, fragments of effort, yearnings of desire unutterable, untold.

"Now this, to my apprehension, is perceived by Satan more distinctly than by us. Were he to come into our pulpits and lecture on the mind's need of God — its agonies without him, and the utter uselessness of all the treasures of eternity to satisfy its hunger, who could, with such splendid, heart-burning eloquence, unfold? Good heavens! what a preacher! with what outcry and agony of reality, what fearful, bitter intensity, could he wring, and rive, and wither his audience! He, too, could beautifully portray the remedy. Yes, he could say, 'Return, ye children of men; nothing is easier. Love the All-Lovely till ye have no will nor desire apart from his, and then ye will never have a will or desire that meets not its full result. All God's power will then move as certainly in the direction of your wishes as of his own; all God's wishes will be yours — his knowledge yours; and as he is infinite, so shall be your joy. Put away, then, mortals,' he would say, 'put away this *sin;* turn your will instantly and thoroughly into the will of God; have not a thought, a feeling, a hope, or wish, or pulsation except in sweet accord with him, and ye shall have peace, deep, strong, broad as God's eternal being.' And as he thus exhorts, you may see the fierce, derisive smile of bitter irony. 'Try it! only try it!' he pleads; 'see what a simple and beautiful contrivance to secure your happiness! Nothing but this: become exact in your natures *like*

God, and what you want in physical and mental power shall become yours by the common property of love!'

"Ah! vain mockery! How well he knows it! Well does he know the strength of rebellious will — the loud uproar of passion which such an effort for liberty will awaken in the soul. Does *he* not know that Omnipotence has no power that could possibly pain him, were his will indissolubly one with God's? He knows, as well as St. John, that '*perfect love casteth out fear*' by an inevitable necessity, and that he has only to turn, repent, perfectly love, and perfectly harmonize with God, to come within limits where happiness is unavoidable.

"You must see yourself that if the whole universe were in every part inevitably governed by a will which was exactly your own, that, of necessity, you could have no ungratified wish in any portion of your being. Now that will in many points conflicts with yours; for yours, if not a diametrically opposite, is at least a separate and unconsulting will, exposed, therefore, continually to cross the divine one. In those places where it happens accidentally to harmonize, and you stumble for a short time into the orbit for which you were made, you have happiness — for example, when you indulge your social feelings, love of knowledge, sense of honor, probity, etc.; but when you carry any of these, or others, beyond that orbit, as when you place your friend or your knowledge in God's stead, you then conflict with his will, and suffer as necessarily as a man who puts his hand into the fire, or otherwise acts out of the line of his being.

"Now the problem of happiness is this: There is a fixed, inflexible WILL, armed with almighty power, that, say, or do, or feel what we can, still governs, and will govern. We see it in nature, moving with iron, inflexible certainty through all the vain struggles, resistance, and agony of those who stand in its way. It is hopeless to contend with it; we can only hope by falling in with it. So much natural religion teaches us; but it only shows us the necessity of submission, without a word of conciliation. Before a fixed, marble, inflexible will, she commands us to bow or break — no matter which. The wave must bear us on, or sweep above us, and all our outcry and despair are but the futile curses and struggles of the drowning man. Old ocean lifts one scornful, hissing wave, stops every sense, strangles, bears him off, and dashes him like a weed upon the strand.

"But the Bible draws aside the veil, and shows us in the mighty central power a Father, who says to each individual, 'Even the hairs of your head are all numbered.' 'Fear not! the great inevitable movement beats with a Father's heart, and the happiness of each individual is as minutely cared for as that of the sublime whole.' 'Love me, and I will love thee; choose with me, sympathize with me, and all my power, and all my wealth, and my glory, are thine!' Hence, through the whole Bible, the full union of the soul to God is called marriage; the whole of two minds becomes one, and all the riches of the superior mind becomes that of the inferior. God is generous as rich. He lives not to admire himself — not to pursue a cold, showy, glittering scheme, that has no heart in it; but He makes a whole gift of Himself, and all that He has, to each individual, as far as they can comprehend or use it.

"Now, then, *we are* — we exist. The laws and necessities of our being are inflexible, and nothing but a perfect coincidence of our will with His brings us into the orbit of things as they are and must be. Our will must be identical with his. Well, then, can you make it so? Try it. Gaze up those hopeless heights of unattainable excellence. See Him, dazzling in spotless loveliness, the fair *Ideal* beyond all artist's dream — true, tender, sweet, self-forgetting, yet immovably right and just; willing to suffer in his own bosom, to any extent, for the wandering, yet inflexibly maintaining against their aggressions the rights and happiness of all who trust him; burning — living — dazzling with intense intelligence and life, yet stooping to the prayer of the little child, the poor slave, and 'him whom man abhorreth.' Such he stands above us, and says, 'Become ONE with me in thought and wish, and thou shalt be as I am, blessed forever.'

"Would not this perfect union make you blessed? Effect it, then. Love with perfect love; trust with perfect trust; become in heart yourself pure, tender, sweet, and self-forgetting, just and true, and that not by 'force and military subjection,' but by 'involuntary harmony.' Does saying, knowing, admitting all this restore us to God? When you have demonstrated that it is a deranged and unsubdued *will* that is the disease, are you any nearer the remedy? Methinks I see Satan mocking lost souls on the sweetness of this divine concord which he spreads before them, in contrast to their eternal unrest, fair as Elysium, sweet as the distant paradise seen through the eternal fire of rebellious passion; and pointing, he says, 'Behold how blessed! each loving, each beloved! each will the will of God, God's will the blessedness of all! And what hinders you, ye burning, self-consumed, withering spirits? Once join heartily in God's will, and I have no power — nothing has power. The great gulf is passed, and ye are in his bosom. Oh ye fools! know ye not the blessed doctrine of free-will? *Choose* life and live!' With what burning, cursing despair do they know this, and yet dare eternal anguish rather than yield!

"Ah! my dear brother, there is a deep meaning in the word eternal death — living, perpetual death, and God has shown me lately that I had it *in me*. I also know what eternal life is; it is *begun* in me. The deep unrest of this life is eternal death begun; and the deep, immovable peace of a perfect submission, perfect trust, and love, is eternal *life* — begun here, going on forever.

"Now, my dear brother, I freely admit that I may have been mistaken as to your past religious exercises, and that you may have more deeply and truly felt the powers of the world to come than I had supposed; and, to repay confidence with confidence, I will tell you also of my religious experience.

"For some three or four years past there has been in my mind a subdued under-current of perplexity and unhappiness in regard to myself in my religious experience. I have often thought, when sifting myself, why am I thus restless? why not at peace? I love God and Jesus Christ with a deep and real devotion; nay, at times I am overwhelmed, pierced to the very soul with the perfect beauty and sweetness of the Divine One, and in general I trust in him, in general I mean to conform my life to him. I am as consistent as many Christians, more so than some; then why not satisfied? Ah! I thought to myself, still I am not satisfied. Though I live, perhaps, what might be in Christian courtesy called a religious life, still there is something wrong. I can conceive of a style of Christian devotion as much higher than my present point as my present position is above that of the world. The sudden death of George shook my whole soul like an earthquake; and as in an earthquake we know not where the ground may open next, so I felt an indistinct terror as if father, brothers, husband, any or all, might be just about to sink. Such unexpected, stunning agonies show us heart secrets before undreamed of. I had written and spoken of Christ, the immovable and ever-present portion, and while I was writing my heart *exulted;* yet when I had done writing all went down, as a fire burns itself out, and I returned to grief and tears. Ah! said I to myself, is my soul fully on God, to be so shaken? I saw that my trust was partial, superficial, and that was one more element of self-discontent.

"The winter after, care and anxiety came upon me, and I often, day and night, was haunted and pursued by care that seemed to drink my life-blood. A feeble, sickly child — a passionate, irritable nurse, with whom I feared to leave it, from whom I feared to withdraw it — slowly withering in my arms, and yet I exerting my utmost care for it in vain — harassed, anxious, I often wondered why God would press my soul, longing for reunion, with a weight of cares that seemed to hold it prostrate on the earth. I felt alone, unsupported, and He whom in former times I had found very present, seemed to leave me entirely. Often thoughts like this would flash upon me: 'How much of your anxieties are caused by apprehensive fears of what this, that, and the other will think and say of you? how much by having separate purposes and plans which have no reference to Christ's will, and here and there cross it?' In short, I often saw, as by a dart of sunlight, that an entire IDENTITY of my will with God's would remove all disquiet, and give joy even to suffering, as says Paul, 'Sorrowful, yet always rejoicing.'

"Oh how I have groaned in spirit, and longed and prayed for it; but the more I strove and prayed, the more inveterate, and determined and unsubdued seemed every opposing desire. The sensitive fear of blame, the ever-living, self-conscious desire of proving to myself and others that I was right, I perceived to be stronger and more efficient in me than the love of Christ, the fear of his opinion, and the desire to do his will.

"Am I then a Christian? thought I. Since I have always heard that the *balance* or preponderance of the soul decides the character, certainly I have more thoughts of myself separate from Christ and his will, more anxieties that relate not to his plans, more agitations and distresses, in short, that are the fruit of my own separate will, than all that I feel for him, his will, his cause altogether. Then it must be that I am not a Christian. But, then, why do I — why have I loved Christ — loved him so deeply as I know I have, nay, as I know I do? I can not tell. I think I love him above all, yet certainly my will is, at best, only in a small degree subjected to his.

"Well, then, I thought, if you see that entire union and identity of your will with Christ is the thing, why don't you have it? Just submit — give up all these separate interests — unite your soul to him in a common interest — why not? Why not? ah! why not? Words of deep meaning to any one who tries that vain experiment! Every effort breaks like a wave upon a rock. We reason, reflect, resolve, and pray — weep, strive, love — love to despair, and all in vain. In vain I adjured my soul, Do you not *love* Christ? Why not, then, cut wholly loose from all these loves, and take his will alone? Is it not reasonable, since you can be blessed in no other way? What else can you do? Yet, for the same reason that the lost cling to a bitterer, more unmitigated anguish, when they know what might make them at peace, so did I. I reasoned with myself, Circumstances are against me; this pressure of outward care stands in my way: God must remove this.

"Well, the summer after, I spent some months with Henry, and was, of course, free from all pressure, and I thought *now* is the time; but now my soul seemed all to collapse; the imperious sense of *want* receded, and only a complaining, dissatisfied undertone remained. On my return this winter, again the wave of dissatisfaction rose. 'Still there! oh, dissatisfied heart,' said I to myself, 'why wilt thou never rest?' Something said to me, 'You are a Christian, perhaps, but not a full one.' 'Learn of me,' said Christ, 'and ye shall find REST.' I do not find rest, consequently I do not learn of him. I perceive that the New Testament ideal of a Christian was different from and higher than what I even tried or purposed to be; that I was only trying at parts, and allowedly in some things living below. Nor did it comfort me at all to think that other Christians did so, and even good ones too, for I remembered, 'He that shall break one of these least commandments,' etc.

"The question was distinctly proposed to me, 'Will you undertake, and make a solemn and earnest effort to realize, the full IDEAL of Christ's plan, though not one other Christian should?' The obstacles were many. 'Twill do no good to try. With a lower standard have I striven, wept, prayed, despaired, in vain, and shall I undertake this? I shall never do it. But how I prayed that by some vision, some sudden and mighty influence, God would bring me up to this conceived but not ever felt state! I felt just in your words, 'If there is a fact I know not, a truth I never saw — if there is an emotion that the Holy Spirit has never breathed into action in my soul — if there is a motive unfelt that should bring me to Christ, oh let me know it!' This was the burden of my prayers; and my discouragement was, 'How can I see God clearer than I have seen him? Can I ever be searched, and penetrated, and bowed by a deeper love than I have been, and which yet has been *transient* — has never wholly subdued me? Can I make deeper, sincerer resolutions? No. Can I have more vivid views? No. What then?

"I thought of this passage: 'I will love him, and my Father will love him, and we will come unto him and *make our abode with him.*' This is it, I thought; Christ has been with me by visits and intervals: this *permanent abode* is what I have not known. Again: 'Abide in me, and I in you' — a steady, ever-present Christ within, who should exert an influence steady as the pulse of my soul; this I *needed.* I copied that class of texts — I prayed with prayer unceasing that Christ would realize them — I despaired of bending my will — I despaired of all former and all present efforts; but at *His* word I resolved to begin and go for the whole. As James and John: 'He said unto them, Launch out now and let down the net. They say unto him, Master, *we have toiled all night and have taken nothing;* nevertheless, *at thy word* we will let down the net; and lo! the net brake with the multitude of fishes.'

"What was the result? When self-despair was final, and I merely undertook at the word of Christ, then *came* the long-expected and wished help. *All* changed. Whereas once my heart ran with a strong current to the world, now it runs with a current the other way. What once it cost an effort to remember, now it costs an effort to forget. The will of Christ seems to me the steady pulse of my being, and I go because I can not help it. Skeptical doubt can not exist. I seem to see the full blaze of the Shekinah every where. I am calm, but full — every where and in all things instructed, and find I can do all things through Christ. Now if this is, as you say, a dream, so is certainly every form of *worldly* good; but this, if it be a dream, answers the purpose entirely, and I shall never wake till I awake 'in His likeness.' "

In June, 1845, Dr. Beecher attended a convention at Chicago of Congregational and Presbyterian churches. He says: "The Convention was a great and good one, whose influence will be felt powerfully for good through all coming time. It will, I trust, avert a schism between Congregational and Presbyterian churches, and consummate and perpetuate their union. It was impossible not to feel the difference in affectionate estimation and influence among ministers chiefly from New England, Western New York, Northern Ohio, Indiana, and Illinois, and that which I encountered in Southern Ohio, in the form of Old School opposition.

"The affectionate eagerness of the younger class to hear, and the reverential respect and deference paid was new, compared with the rough-and-tumble and don't care that I have been through; and yet for the world I would not reverse the course I have taken here and its results for all the social estimation and pleasurable cooperation I left behind. I preached for the Methodists on the Sabbath on justification by faith, with great delight, and multiplied 'Amens,' and other tokens of emotion and approbation; and though my theories often swept across their track, the stream of feeling swept them along, and they still cried 'Amen!' It was a delightful time of boundless liberty, and heart-melting, and flowing onward of the copious stream of truth."

Dr. Beecher's views of the comparative merits of the Presbyterian and Congregational systems were thus set forth by himself in conversation:

"The late enmity between New School Presbyterians and Congregationalists is most unhappy. I always had the confidence of both. I went to Boston to defend the foundations of Congregationalism, and resuscitate those that had declined. In collecting funds for the seminary I collected of both. The seminary was at first named Presbyterian and Congregational, but Wilson got it changed. It ought to have been so, for the Congregationalists contributed as liberally as the Presbyterians. But there were those who said then, and have said since, that I was a Congregationalist, unfaithful to my trust, and that I used my position in the Presbyterian Church to undermine it. There never was any thing more false than that. In fact, the Congregationalists, some of them, attacked me as not faithful to them.

"But I brought all the influence of my previous extensive connections to build up the institution, and Presbyterians were very glad till the jars began, and New England was called all at once 'a suspected quarter.' But the fact is, the Presbyterian Church in this country had its beginning by sending to Boston. It was in their records, but they made away with it. Dr. Greene knows what has become of it. They wouldn't have it on record that they had been cradled in Congregationalism.

"The fact is, I was true as steel to build up the Presbyterian Church as the stream of Providence had set; and as to working to produce Congregationalism, or make Presbyterianism lax, there was no man stood stronger than I. While I was a Presbyterian I worked Presbyterianism, as every body that knows me knows.

"In Litchfield I was just as Congregational in administration as I had been Presbyterian before. I came in to Consociation by the door. I was examined, and held fellowship, and worked on that model. So in Boston I worked the independent Congregational system. I was faithful to the maintenance of their order. I've tried both ways, and I wouldn't give a snap between them, though, on the whole, where community is established and intelligent, I think Congregationalism is rather better.

"Never had a particle of sectarian partisanship for either. I can say with Pope, 'Whatever is best administered is best.' I may have erred. I see not in what respect I should have conducted differently in existing circumstances.

"I remember a time before the division of the Assembly when they began to grumble about admitting Congregational committee men to vote according to the plan of union, and do various things to vex them and make them withdraw. I went up to Western Reserve College at Commencement on purpose to head off the Old School in that thing. I took a dozen men there with whom I was acquainted, and explained the matter, and how the Old School were operating. The thing was understood. It was all safe. They stood by in all our troubles, and are there now.

"The fact is, I was as impartial in administering the system in which I was as a pair of scales. I served each and loved each; and, while I was in the same Assembly with the Old School, I loved them, and there was more than half — there were two thirds of them who would have given me heart and hand."

August 9, 1845, Dr. Beecher writes as follows to Mrs. Beecher, then absent on a visit at the East:

"How little of the history of the heart can ever be written, and, if it were, could ever be reached by language; and, if it could, the world itself could not contain the books which should be written, and one generation would have no more than time to read the history of another.

"Now what a scene was that sickness, and all but sudden death of Harriet! It was a violent attack of cholera, running for three hours without medical aid into a regular collapse, with spasms, burning, and cramps, and the stamp of death on her face. When the doctor came he was thunderstruck, and made prescriptions without any hope she would live. I did not get back till he was gone, and came into her room, and, coming to the bedside, realized her state. She was sinking. The universal languor and distress of death was upon her. I immediately took her hands in mine and began to rub them with perseverance and vigor, while the most powerful remedies were applied for an hour without any perceptible effect.

"The first indication of the reversed and healthful action of the system was the excitement produced by the stimulation of the brandy, which at first I mistook for delirium. It was terrible for a moment. Dying, as I feared, she began to sing, and called on Mary, in a wandering way, to sing. But it was soon apparent that the ebbing tide was rising, and then my heart sang also and gave thanks;

yet through the night she was so low that if a relapse should take place she would not live an hour.

"Mary stood by her all the while with a mother's solicitude and care. I could not leave her, and slept on the settee in the dining-room, hot as an oven and thronged with musquitoes, sleepless from their annoyance, and conscious of every noise and movement. The night of suspense passed safely, and she was better in the morning.

"I am not sick—never was better in my life, though last week I had to diet and abstain from corn and succotash; but this week I have studied and worked like Jehu every day, trimming up the trees, hoeing in the garden till my face was bathed and my shirt soaked, and yet I have not felt so well for a year past—so much like being young again.

"I see by your letter to Joseph that you begin to talk of coming home in September. I begin to count the days, and hold on, so you will finish your visit and fly home as swift as possible, for two pairs of pantaloons have given out, and a new pair (of summer cloth) I bought the other day were spoiled on my late journey by reading with a mutton-tallow candle, and must wait your disposal. I have not shaved for four days till to-night, but, as a penance, have done it so roughly that you never saw the like.

"Our buggy, also, has not been oiled for some weeks, nor washed top nor bottom, and looked very shabby till I myself 'slicked it up.' But, though a good overseer and executor when I get at it, I must confess that I need taking care of *some;* but don't be uneasy, for I have lectured at Mount Pleasant on Temperance with such bursts of eloquence and wit as astonished the natives and endangered their sides.

"I saw yesterday a letter from Mr. A—— to Mr. S——, saying you would be glad to hear from one L. Beecher. It was very good news, since my letters, four or five, flying about like bullets without hitting, you will have a considerable account of him in this."

The following letter to Dr. Taylor, March 17, 1846, will be read with pleasure:

"Dear Taylor,—I wish I had a son going to New Haven every month, and then I should write to you as often, and possibly get half as many letters from you, and make a beginning of talking over things old and new. You and I are the same as when we projected the Christian Spectator, and battled about the means of grace and episcopacy, and Hartford College, and Nettleton, and Tyler, and Woods, and *Harvey,* if you remember such a one. But now, like Bonaparte's battles and marshals, have all these gone through the little end of Time's telescope into the dim but not uninteresting distance; and how has our generation fallen off, and another and another pushed up behind us, and what things have come to pass which, had we lived in Connecticut, we should have written letters about, and held consultations and talked over so much, but have not talked about at all, and never shall till we have more time in another world.

"Well, our personal identity remains, and our friendships and our children, one of whom, my son Thomas, will hand you this, whom, I doubt not, you will receive gladly for my sake and his own. He is a graduate of Illinois College, and raised under the ministration of Edward. He possesses, I think, a mind not inferior to any of my sons, and quickness, depth, and comprehension of discrimination surpassing almost any mind I have come in contact with.

"Think not I am vain; I only give you the outline, to say that he would like to spend a little time in New Haven, and see and hold communion with your *literati* as one who will appreciate the society of literary men, and all your literary treasure accumulated there since the time I entered in 1792, when there was one rusty telescope, one air-pump, a prism, and one band and wheel to make the figure of the oblate spheroid, or the earth flattened at the poles.

"Our students have been greatly quickened and strengthened in faith and holiness again this winter, and we are now in the midst of a revival progressing and extending around us. I preach once on the Sabbath with great pleasure, and lecture every day with increasing satisfaction."

LII

AUTUMN LEAVES

FROM REV. THOMAS K. BEECHER.

"Dear Charley, — You are editor, I am but contributor; therefore use the pen, the scissors, or the stove for the improvement of what I write concerning my father, Lyman Beecher, now with God.

"I remember an earnestness which used to betray father into a curious repetition whenever he would bend his energy to a profitable exhortation anent my waywardness: 'This is the most important year of your life, my son; you have come to the turning-point of your history.' The first time he told me so I was a lad just turned eleven years; and by many letters and words I was certified four times a year or oftener that I was at an 'important,' 'critical,' 'decisive' turning-point in my career, until I became a teacher at Philadelphia. In 1846–7 father was sorely exercised by the severity of my work in Philadelphia. He feared a sudden break-down. His urgency could not abide the slowness of the mail; he must save me by telegraph — I suspect, his very first telegram. Aided by a daughter, he undertook his costly ten words to save a son thus:

" 'My very dear Son, — I have worked more — '

"*Daughter.* 'Father, father, you can't write so much; don't say My very dear son.

" 'Dear Son, — Trust a father's experience, and let me tell you — '

"*Daughter.* 'No, no, father, skip all that. You can't make love by telegraph. Tom knows your love.

"An hour was spent learning how to suppress his exuberant affection, till at last the message came into shape thus:

" '*Ease up. Rest — sleep — exercise. Cold water — rub. No tobacco.* — Father.

"Some books of health contain less than this telegram."

"For various reasons, I used to worship in Christ Church (Episcopal) while in Philadelphia. As a member of the choir there, I was invited to unite with the Church. Father happened to visit me just then, and as those months were truly the turning period of my religious life, we spoke often and earnestly together. 'Tom,' said he, 'your mother loved the Episcopal Church (he often counted me a son of *your* mother, Charley). She was a good woman. The Episcopal Church is as good as any. Go there, if you can do any good by going; I have no objection at all; only, whatever Church you go to, be a Christian and work.' "

"Visiting home during one of my school vacations (1847), I found father at last without a child to love or govern, and it seemed to me that his long-trained faculty was keeping itself fresh in training a very stubborn and active terrier called Trip. Trip had taken my place in the study and by the table. At every interval of rest from writing, father would talk a word or two to Trip. On the mantle-piece lay a short switch, and Trip knew where it lay. Ordinarily Trip would receive rebuke and exhortation with becoming quietness; but it was quite impossible to follow up the counsel with chastisement, for Trip had an eye ever to the mantle-piece. If father's hand tended thither, Trip tended toward the door or table, and no soothing blandishment would restore his filial confidence until father, showing both palms, would say, 'There, Trip-pee, Trip-pee, I forgive you this time, but you mustn't do so any more.' For myself, I protest that Trip, if he lives, has memories of escape and forgiveness more gratifying than I."

"Do you remember, Charley, how father in those days used to carry a comb in his pocket for Trip, much to mother's annoyance? and those frequent excursions down to the bridge in the woods which father and Trip would make, father talking to the little dog, and promising cleanliness and relief in soothing tones such as New England boys used to hear o' Saturday nights? Trip was always grateful.

"In all soberness, I declare that father, in those days, found comfort in venting upon Trip those tender emotions which he could not suppress nor his own children longer receive."

"Farther back — for I follow no chronologic order, but write as my heart incites my memory — farther back (1843–4), I remember that father's income had ceased. He was living by gifts literally. Every morning at prayer he would pray for the needed supplies, and in phrases of varied simplicity speak forth our Lord's suggestion, 'Give us this day our daily bread.' One morning, after I had brought him the mail, I came back to the study and found him tear-blind, and trying to explain a letter in his hand. 'Tom, you can get some boots now — here's some money; and your mother can get you a vest from —— (whose slightly-worn wardrobe had kept me clothed at second-hand for years); and *now* you'll stay with me.'

"He had prayed for means that morning, and he looked upon all such unexpected gifts as true and proper answers.

"This 'staying with him' was, in the time of it, trying to me, yet it enriched me with my only deep knowledge of father's loving heart.

"I was a man — graduated, and competent to work and support him; yet he insisted on my staying with him to be supported. He felt that I was unsettled in religion, and was set in his determination to keep me near him and lead me to safety. Of course, irritated by frequent reproaches from the thoughtless for 'living on my father,' I was impatient to be gone, and many a passionate discussion came up between us about the matter. I never gave up entirely until one morning, as I stood impatient on the south step of the study, in the sun. He came out suddenly, not knowing I was there. He sniffed the air, looked up into the maples, down upon me, put both hands upon my shoulders, looked me full in the face, and said, with broken utterance,

" 'Tom, I love you; you mustn't go 'way and leave me. They're all gone — Jim's at college. I want one chicken under my wing.'

"Of course I staid by until I left with a blessing."

"For more than a year I sat writing in the study with him every morning, usually copying his MSS. or reducing notes of his last sermon or lecture. He rarely wrote more than half an hour continuously. His lips moved as he wrote, and his left hand gestured, and now and then an inarticulate tone indicated doubt; another, hesitation; but, when the words and pen raced through to a satisfactory period, up went the spectacles, round came the writer, with a '*There*, Tom!' and he would read aloud his last written paragraph — 'that'll DO?'

"One day in 1841 father rushed up stairs in a great hurry, and said, 'Wife, give me five dollars' (one of the students was needing help).

"'Why, husband,' was the reply, 'that is every cent we have.'

"'I can not help it,' said he; 'the Lord will provide;' and away he went with the five dollars.

"The next day, about the same hour, he came in, holding out a wedding fee of fifty dollars before mother's face, saying, 'Didn't I tell you the Lord would provide?'

"At another time, a friend in Boston received from him the following laconic epistle: 'Dear brother, the meal in the barrel is low, the oil in the cruse has failed. Send me a hundred dollars.'—This and no more."

"One day in 1844 a family circular was received from the East, in which was a copy of a letter written at the time of Roxana Beecher's death by Mrs. Judge Reeve, of Litchfield. Father read it. When he had read a line or two the tears stood in his eyes, his lips were compressed. 'What a multitude . . . of reminiscences . . . this calls up;' and he read on with most violent emotion. 'Well,' he said at the close, 'her prayer for me and her children has been answered; her sons are all preaching, and God has blessed my labors. She consecrated them all to God, and 'tis wonderful to see how they have all been guided by strange paths until now.' He could not study for some time, and left the room."

"About the same time he had written a letter to Dr. Blanchard on the subject of prayer, which he submitted to Sister Catharine for her perusal. This led to a conversation at the dinner-table as follows:

"*C.* 'I wish you would mention one view of prayer which I have never yet seen offered by any writer, viz., that all the prayers of Christ and his apostles of which we have any record are short, calm, and utterly want all the fury which many think constitutes zeal and earnestness.'

"*Father.* 'These prayers were meant to be short; they are long enough to answer their purpose; but I don't think that they should be so considered as models as to bind us as to time, manner, or any thing else. The fact is, if any one should find fault with me because my prayers are shorter and less violent than those of some others who appear more fervent and in earnest, 'twould be just for me, in my own *defense,* to point to the Lord's Prayer; but I should not be right in quoting it as my text in reproving others because they don't pray just as I do.'

"*C.* 'But I have been accustomed to think that the deepest rivers make the least noise, and that real emotion always exhibits itself in low, firm, and calm intonations, and not in violent gesturings.'

"*Father* (*laughing*). 'I never saw the difference between real and artificial feeling better than in ——. 'Twas just after he was converted, and was on his high heels, and he had to mouth, and swing his arms when he prayed, and he always thought he couldn't pray unless he had a room big enough to swing a cat in by the tail. Well, he came through Boston just as there was beginning to be some suspicion and distrust felt about Finney and his measures, and so I thought I would disarm violent feeling by kindness, and when —— came to see me I treated him kindly, and talked, and we chatted along smoothly enough, and he was touched by my treatment of him. I saw it, and I asked him to stay over night; he did; and after breakfast we had prayers, and I asked him to pray. Well, 'twas lucky our room was large, for he got right down on his knees, and began to pray as though he would bring the ceiling down; and he kept on, and on, and swung his arms round, and clapped his hands, until he came to pray for me and my family' (here father stopped through emotion), 'and then his hands folded, and his voice sunk, and his intonations became changed, and . . . I . . . knew he was in earnest then.' "

"One evening of the same year he was preaching in the chapel, and, in conclusion, was with much power inculcating the necessity of Christian effort and attention when sinners were in particularly critical situations.

" 'Oh how I remember,' he said, 'that day when God first flashed deep conviction upon my soul, and tore away the veil from my heart, and set my sins in order before me! I was overpowered, and broken down with grief and confusion; and when I went out of my room, whom should I meet but Edward Herrick,[1] of Southampton, Long Island, who was a student with me at Yale College. How he happened to know of my feelings I can't tell, unless he saw it in my face, but he came up to me, and, kindly taking my hand, began to talk with me upon the subject of religion. Oh, he was an angel sent from heaven to my soul! You ought all to be ministering spirits too.' "

"Speaking of his sermons, he once said, 'I have tried two or three times to write a sermon upon the tears that Mary shed upon

[1] Edward Herrick (1775–1831), Conn. pastor until 1806, when he headed a school for boys.

the feet of Jesus, but I never could, for the text was so much more forcible than any thing that I could say that I couldn't do any thing until I tried it in dramatic-narrative style. I preached it at East Hampton, and it melted the whole congregation to tears, and me too.

" 'I have got another sermon, unlike any thing that was ever written before (though I never aim to be peculiar or enigmatical in my sermons), in which I labor to answer the difficulty which is often felt by Gospel-hardened sinners when they are tired of the old story about repentance and faith, repentance and faith all the time, and they want some other way of salvation; and so I wrote this sermon to give them another way — not superseding the necessity of an atonement, and repentance, and faith, but a new way of securing the attainment of the old conditions.' I suppose he referred to a sermon which he had just preached, in which the point established was that the performance of one Christian duty, and the possession of one Christian grace, will necessarily induce the whole train, by the bond of affinity that unites them all."

"One morning I was speaking of the value of the night time to me as a time of study and thought. 'Yes,' he replied, 'there is something in the entire silence of the night, particularly in places where you are accustomed to noise, that is wonderfully tranquillizing in its effect upon my mind, but I can't bear the fatigue of sitting up late. * * * But I shall never forget one scene that I once saw of this kind. 'Twas when I was settled upon Long Island. I thought I would get up early and go down to the bay, where the brook-ducks used to come up every night, hundreds of them, and I thought I would go down and get a shot into half an acre of them at once. So I got a great big double-barreled gun, and, when I had slept a while, I got up and started down. 'Twas a great deal earlier than I had supposed; but I kept on, and came down the east shore, where the surf is always foaming up on the beach, and it comes in wave after wave, rolling and roaring, as high as your head; but now, I don't know why or how, for once it was still; you couldn't hear a sound except a little softly-murmuring noise as the ripples came creeping up the beach; 'twas as still as stillness itself; I didn't want to shoot, I tell you. I laid my gun down, and sat down to hear such a silence as I never did before. I forgot the ducks.' "

"I was once speaking of times of high excitement and elation caused by little things, and instanced a successful shot at a match near Jacksonville. 'I guess you felt about as I did when I caught a trout as big as a shad in my hands. 'Twas when I was going with *your mother* — my first wife, I mean — down to New Haven, and we stopped at Baldwin's as we went down. I had my tackle with me, and I went out to the trout-brook, and soon came in with enough for supper; and we went on, and came back the same way. We got in just before dark, and I thought I would go and try my luck again; so I got out my tackle, and went and dug some bait, and started out for the brook. 'Twas a little one, and I fished for some time all along down, but didn't catch any thing, and it began to grow dusk. At last I came to where the brook ran into a dark ravine, and it was dark enough, I tell you, and pokerish too, but I thought I would go in and try a little longer.

" 'The brook ran on eight or ten rods, and then widened out into quite a little lake, and at the lower end there was a shallow, rocky place, where the water ran out. Well, I was standing fishing, and I saw a big wave coming along toward the rapids. Thinks I, that's a big one, and if you try to go down those stones I'll give you a box on the ears, if you are not pretty spry. So I broke off a stick and crossed over, and I saw that the trout had stopped under a log that was lying there, and at first I thought I would start him out and catch him as he went down the rapids; but I had heard — I didn't know whether it was so or not — that trout will let you put your hand under them without being scared, because they are accustomed to being touched by sticks and stones as they go in shallow water. Well, I thought I would try; so I took off my coat, and rolled up my sleeves, and got down on the log, and put my hand cautiously down till I could just feel the water from his fins. I slid my hand up softly along his side, up, up, till my fingers came just behind his gills, and then I clinched him and sprang to my feet, swinging him in the air, and shouting as if I was crazy. We had him for supper.' "

"Nothing used to fascinate father so much as tales of fishing and hunting. One of his most frequent wishes as to self-indulgence was, 'Oh, Tom, now if we only had a lake about forty rods long, right out the porch, and a little snug boat, just to row out into the middle, and drop your line, and pull in the fish, and come back quietly, and come in, and nobody see you, I believe I would go right off now.' From the time I was big enough to hunt, father had this standing plan, though ever unfulfilled: 'Some of these days, when I have more time, I mean to take Charley and the wagon, and go off ten or twelve miles, and have a hunt and fish. I'll give up a whole day to it.' "

"One of the seminary exercises was declamation by the students. At one of these an argument was delivered by one of the class, ably written, advocating the organization of a Western anti-slavery General Assembly:

"Father listened to it attentively and said, 'A very clear argument. I can say amen to every word of it. A wholesome exhibition of facts. Truth with good temper we need never beware of; it is always safe. True, it is vexatious to those it hits, and the stronger 'tis, the more it hurts. As to the caucus in the Assembly of 1835 and 1836 to prevent anti-slavery action, it is a case where the wisdom of man is foolishness with God. If we had split then, we could have thrown slavery all overboard, for the division would have been between the North and the South, and we should have kept the North together. They could never have done as they have if we had divided then and kept clear of slavery.

" 'But I am fast coming to the opinion — I am not quite made up yet about it, but I begin to feel that this business of a great united Church is nothing but popery, after all. There never can be strict discipline and purity of doctrine in a body that covers so much ground as we once did. I don't believe in it. For, if we had now one Church district in Ohio, as they have in New England, dependent upon no other body, but corresponding merely, just as the Associations of the East do — if we had such in Ohio, I think there would be homogeneity enough of character and community of interest to keep us quiet and unanimous. They never split in New England, nor ever came near it but once, and that was upon the doctrine of decrees, and election, and free will, just Old School and New School theology; and the reason why they did not split, at least in the single state of Connecticut, was because they had no judicial courts, and their leading men could not be brought to disunion so long as their rights were uninvaded.

" 'I never believed in the Methodist organization for this same reason: they cover so much ground that they must govern with a loose rein, and corruption must sooner or later come in. And this will prove to be the case with the Presbyterian Church too; there is too much popery in the whole plan.' " *

---

* Lest these remarks should appear somewhat radical and revolutionary, we append the following from the Princeton Quarterly for July, 1864: "Our present book of discipline is confused, contradictory, impossible. It

"One day he was talking about his East Hampton life. 'Sometimes,' he said, 'when Roxana would go home to Guilford on a visit, I used to get all the children round me and write to her about them *seriatim*, and then when she returned I would write to Grandma Foote. I wrote the image and superscription of them all as they came up along. I should like to see those letters now. I wonder who has them. Dear me! if I should sit down now and try to write out all their history, what a volume it would make! I have often thought of it, and if I did it at all, I should have to put it in the form of letters to my wife in heaven — a narrative of all that has gone on since she left us.' "

"A sermon of his — I can not now recall any of it — had been 'reported' by me with more than usual accuracy. He had criticised, interlined, and carefully perfected it. I had finally engrossed it, and tied it up neatly as a finished sermon. Going to Oxford, Ohio, he took this sermon, among others, with him. When he returned I asked him, 'Did you preach *that* sermon?'

" 'No; that sermon's spoilt; never shall preach it again.'

" 'Spoiled?' asked I, feeling a little annoyed that I should have spoiled a good sermon.

" 'Yes; it's all fixed and tight, like a new coat; I can't work in it,' said he.

"All earnest preachers can understand this, I fancy."

"But how unlike a student's his room always was, and what singular ways of studying! Do you remember the gun he used to keep loaded by the door ready for the pigeons that in those days came over by millions? (1833–5.) Father would sit in his study chair deeply occupied, and set me by the cocked gun to watch for game. But he would hear the roar of wings as soon as I, and, with remarkable jumps for a divinity doctor, would get out the door, have his shot at the birds, and then go back to his pen.

---

can not be acted upon without a consumption of time that is intolerable. In every Assembly where judicial business is to be transacted there are confusion and disorder — decisions which shock and offend first one party and then another, all because the book itself is what it is. It is no answer to this to say that our book was framed by great and good men; so was the Constitution of England the work of great men, but it must be altered or overthrown to suit the changes in men and things; and our old book, we are persuaded, must be altered, or our whole system must break down. That a Church of three thousand ministers shall be occupied, as it may be for days or even weeks, in its General Assembly in determining the merits of a petty slander case in any village of the Union, is a solecism not longer to be endured." — *Page* 515.

"His spectacles used to delay him, and I well remember his delight with a new pair which he brought home, each glass composed of a plane half and a convex half. Looking through the convex lower section, he wrote metaphysics; through the upper, he shot pigeons.

"Have you ever seen father when a fit of order and arrangement came over him? I remember five green boxes, say twenty inches square, in which the dear man again and again determined to put his disordered MSS., arranged and classified. 'There, Tom, keep my lectures all in this box, No. 1; put my revival sermons in this; and then — let's see,' and he would begin to look over his piles, and to devise a third class. He could pile them up on the floor methodically. 'Now don't let any one touch 'em, and to-morrow we'll finish up.'

"Alas! what with Trip, and father himself, in a hurry to find some dimly-remembered fragment, the piles soon became remedilessly confused, then scattered, until a distant to-morrow came to rebegin and never finish the ordering of his MSS. At one of my last visits to him in Boston he fondly embraced me, saying, 'Oh, Tom! I wish you could live with me and help me arrange my papers.' "

"One Sunday afternoon he listened to a sermon from Mr. C——, from the text 'I would not live alway,' showing the reasons of this strange feeling in all true saints. Father was deeply moved, and made a prayer beyond any thing I ever heard, as he pictured out the happiness beyond the grave. Verily he appeared to taste it already, and seemed ready to go. There was not a dry eye in the house; even Judge —— and Mr. —— were moved. When the people rose to the benediction, father gave two or three words of most moving exhortation: 'I believe *without a doubt* that I shall see many of you soon in heaven. But there are some whom I scarcely expect to see there, * * * and those I charge — now, as my last word — I charge you to prepare to meet me in heaven, before the throne of God and the Lamb.'

"Father's blessing at the supper-table was longer than usual, showing the unwonted movings of his heart: 'Almighty God! in Thee we live, and move, and have our being. We thank Thee for life, and for all Thy mercies and great goodness toward us. Grant us Thy blessing upon all our labors, that, though we shall "not live always" together in the loved fellowships and communion of earth, we may soon meet in heaven. Amen.' "

"One day (1843–4), as we sat writing in his study, he suddenly broke out, without any warning or introduction, 'Tom, I wish I could have heard Pag-(*g* soft)-a-nī-nī!' Getting up at once, and walking to his rusty, three-stringed fiddle, he took it up, thrummed the strings, tuned, sounded a tone or two unsatisfied, and said, 'If I could only play what I hear inside of me, I'd beat Pag-a-ni-ni.' He felt disquieted — unsatisfied, but gradually contented himself with 'Merrily O!' "

"Have you ever seen him, Charley, persevering in the hymn at family prayers during those years after his singing boys and girls were all gone away, leaving him and mother as boarders in their own house? I was verily moved to tears when I was present (1847 or 1848), for I remembered a choir of us at prayers. And when I saw the same old 'village hymn' books, and sat in the same room, and saw father go to the study, and fetch his fiddle, and tune it, to sing 'Joy to the World' — his voice serving him only occasionally, and mother's more persevering than strong — yet somehow the fiddle reminded me of father's old time style and expression. Yes, we went through all the verses, and when father's voice failed from the pitch, his lips kept the time and the words till his voice could master the easier tone; and so they sang with the spirit and understanding, while I dreamed and dried my eyes. Since then I've heard the fiddle bearing up the music all alone at family prayer in Boston; not a voice to join in, yet at least three of us following the words, while dear old father persevered in the music to the end. Oh, Charley, we must have a family meeting in heaven, and sing and have prayers again!"

LIII

VISIT TO ENGLAND

In June, 1846, Dr. Beecher writes, "My physicians and friends have urged me vehemently to go to England, and attend the Temperance and World's Conventions, assuring me that probably it would add five years to my life and usefulness. Until now I have never felt any desire to cross the Atlantic; but these Conventions have roused up a pretty strong desire, and if it will add to my life, there are some things undone which I should hope to accomplish."

"Early in the spring of '46," writes Mrs. Beecher, "your father, on the receipt of his newspapers one day, as he read, turned to me suddenly, and with emphasis said, 'I will go!' 'Go where?' I said. He repeated, 'I *will* go! I thank God for such a movement.' Then he read to me of the movement of a Christian Alliance [1] proposed to be held at London the following summer, where Christians of all denominations should be invited to attend.

"He added, 'I have never had the slightest wish to cross the ocean or visit other countries before, but now I must say I should be glad to go, if it is possible.' His interest increased continually in the subject, but the carrying out of his wishes seemed not to be in reach. I wrote to Dr. Patten, of New York, to inquire if there were any arrangements to send such as would go as representatives. In answer, Dr. Patten said he 'knew of no such arrangement.' I considered $700 as requisite for the emergency, at least. A few weeks afterward a gentleman called, whom your father introduced as Mr. Wilcox, of Ohio. Mr. Wilcox remarked: 'Some three years since you called on me, stating that in consequence of the failure of your professorship you had to act as agent for the seminary. At that time I did not feel prepared to do any thing of that kind, but must say it was a matter of regret to me that I refused you such aid, and have now called on you to relieve myself of that regret.'

"He then placed in your father's hands the sum of $300 and

[1] The Christian Alliance, organized in 1842 in Conn. as the Evangelical Alliance to overthrow the Papacy, was a union of evangelical Protestants. The London meeting foundered on an English resolution condemning slavery

went his way. As soon as he left, your father said, 'Now, wife, we will go. God has provided the means in twenty minutes.'

"We took passage from Boston, July 1, in the Caledonia. Edward, accompanying us to the steamer, handed his father $75 as a present from W. W. Stone, and soon we were out on the Atlantic."

The following incident is mentioned by Dr. Beecher in a letter written on board ship to the children at Hartford: "On the Sabbath it was expected Episcopal service would be celebrated, and all assembled in the cabin — about two hundred. The audience was seated as Nettleton could have desired, and I longed to preach, but had made no preparation; when lo! just as service was to begin, the captain, stimulated, I suppose, by the curiosity of the passengers, came to say he was not till recently apprised that I was a clergyman; but, as Mr. —— would read the service, he would be obliged to me to deliver a short address.

"I took for my text, 'God so loved the world that he gave his only begotten Son to die, that whosoever believeth in him might not perish, but have everlasting life,' and spoke in such a free, untrammeled, earnest, affectionate, extempore, and applicatory manner for thirty or forty minutes, that they all heard too earnestly to be accurate judges of the time; for, as old Deacon Tallmadge used to say, 'I spoke to be refreshed from the fullness of a clear head and a warm heart, and felt the better for it.' "

The letter is filled with the ordinary details of a sea voyage and a brief description of Liverpool — "a great city of brick and mortar strung along on the banks of the Mersey, bordered with 120,000 acres of docks, and a swamp of masts, and great high, clumsy warehouses, the streets, like Boston, of all widths, and angles, and wedges."

In conclusion he adds, "Please note that this is my first letter. I have crossed the t's and dotted the i's."

"We spent two days in Liverpool," continues Mrs. Beecher, "then went to Glasgow and Edinburg, visiting several distinguished clergymen, and, above all, Dr. Chalmers,[2] with whom we breakfasted, and whom we heard preach at a mission station which he had established in the midst of a destitute population.

"Your father preached, in the afternoon of the Sabbath we spent there, at a place called 'Cannon Mills,'' where the 'Free Church' resorted at the time of the separation. We visited schools

[2] Thomas Chalmers (1780–1847), leader in the organization of the Free Church of Scotland, was famous in America for his evangelical preaching and philanthropy.

and other public institutions of Edinburg by invitation. The evening before we left he delivered a Temperance address before the 'Scottish Temperance League.' On the morning of July 30th we left for London, stopping at York a few hours, where we visited the 'Minster,' the oldest cathedral in the kingdom. Arrived at London in the evening. Found several American friends at Fitz Roy Square, where we put up.

"While there we called at Baring Brothers, and visited St. Paul's. After seeing all of interest below, we ascended the tower 260 feet. Your father, not satisfied with that height, insisted upon going to the top, 404 feet, and then crept into the ball on the summit, much to the astonishment of the guide.

"The next day we went to St. John's Church to hear Baptist Noel[3] preach, and the day following took up our abode with a friend at Regent's Park.

"July 7th father prepared a speech on Temperance, to be delivered at 'Covent Garden Theatre,' where an immense crowd was gathered. August 8th he prepared 'a letter for all Christendom' upon the subject of Temperance. On the 9th he preached in the Tabernacle to a vast audience. In the evening he delivered a Temperance lecture in 'Portland Chapel.' It was said the chapel was never before so well filled.

"The 10th of August he met a committee to confer upon arrangements for the '*Alliance*.' In the afternoon he met friends at Alexander's to confer upon Abolitionism in America. He gave an account of slavery from the time that we were a colony. By cordial invitation, we made it our stay at Mr. Alexander's the remainder of the time we spent in London.

"Your father preached and lectured on Temperance repeatedly after this, and was also very much absorbed in matters pertaining to the Alliance. I remember, after he had closed his sermon at Crown Chapel, a brother of the pastor, Rev. Mr. Leifchild, said to me, 'My dear madam, go home and take care of that blessed man, for his like is not to be found.'

"On the 12th we took passage from Liverpool on the Great Western for home. Had preaching in the morning next day by Mr. Balch, of New York, and husband in the evening. On Saturday night, the 19th, a violent hurricane came on, which continued until Monday. The fierceness of the storm was beyond description. We had no expectation of being saved. Sunday noon, as many as

[3] Baptist Noel (1798–1873), popular evangelical preacher, active in missions and the Christian Alliance, became a Baptist in 1843.

could assembled in the saloon for religious services. I am told by our friend (Dr. Marsh) that after the services your father addressed himself thus to those present: 'I have seen Christ, and have the assurance that not one of us will be lost. Be of good cheer.' After this meeting it is worthy of record that the '*wrecking*' ceased, though the wind increased. We arrived in New York on the 27th. The remainder of the voyage after the storm, as you would suppose, was comfortless."

LIV

QUO WARRANTO

IN December, 1847, a case was argued in the Supreme Court of Ohio in bank, entitled "Lyman Beecher *adv.* The State of Ohio, *Quo Warranto. On the Relation of David Kemper.*" The writ was served at Dr. Beecher's residence in October, 1845. He retained as counsel S. P. Chase,[1] H. Starr, and Charles L. Telford.[2] The following extracts from the argument in Dr. Beecher's defense may be of interest:

"In the case at bar, if we may follow the general interpretation of the act already given by this court, the complaint must have been made within three years after the cause for the ouster of Dr. Beecher arose.

"The cause of ouster, in this case, must be contemporaneous with the inauguration of Dr. Beecher into his office, or else it must have arisen at some time subsequent to that. Either his entry into office was an intrusion, and that intrusion is the cause of ouster; or, his entry into office being lawful, something has been done or suffered whereby his farther continuance in office became illegal and intrusive, and such act or omission is the cause of ouster.

"The documentary evidence fixes all dates in respect to the appointment and installation of Dr. Beecher into his present office as Professor of Theology, etc., and shows also the period when he became *de facto* the Professor, etc.

"He was appointed January 23d, 1832. His appointment was ratified by the board in October, 1832, and upon the 26th of December, in the same year, he actually entered upon the performance of the duties, and into the enjoyment of the rights, profits, and privileges of his professorship. He has been professor *de facto* ever since.

[1] Salmon P. Chase (1808–1873), who attended Beecher's Cincinnati church, was anti-slavery senator from Ohio (1849–1855) as a result of a coalition between Free Soilers and anti-slavery Democrats. A leader of the new Republican Party, he became Lincoln's Secretary of the Treasury (1861–1864), and Chief Justice of the Supreme Court (1864–1873).

[2] Charles Telford (1816–1856?) was a member of Beecher's church and a professor in the law school of Cincinnati College.

"Now, upon the hypothesis that his appointment was irregular, and that he was ineligible and unqualified at the date of it, and at the date of his actual entry into office, the statute must have commenced running, at the latest, on the 26th of December, 1832, for on that day he consummated his usurpation and investment of office. From that day there was cause of ouster; and from that until the commencement of proceedings in this case, more than twelve years elapsed.

"But the only serious claim on the part of the relation in this case is, that a cause of ouster intervened subsequent to the appointment. In one word, that Dr. Beecher, at some period subsequent to his installation, ceased to be 'a member of the Presbyterian Church in good standing, under the care of the General Assembly of that Church in the United States,' and thereby became disqualified to hold his professorship, and that the cause of ouster arose when that disqualification supervened.

"The only matter of forfeiture or disqualification suggested is not personal to the defendant. It embraces and unchurches one half of those who esteem themselves, even yet, members of the Presbyterian Church, under the care of the General Assembly of that Church in the United States. The matter of disqualification out of which the forfeiture of defendant's right of office accrued is that convulsion which, in the language of *Gibson, Ch. J.*, 1 *Sergeant & Watts*, 9, 'dismembered the Presbyterian body.'

"In that great division of the Presbyterian body into two masses of nearly equal magnitude, it was the fortune or the choice of the defendant to tabernacle with the heretics, himself an arch heresiarch.

"It is not a lack of learning, or a want of diligence and fervor in the service of his Master, that works the forfeiture. These are disqualifications which might have crept upon him so gradually that no mortal eye could discern the point of decline, or coldness or imbecility which unfitted him for his duties, and at which the forfeiture of his rights became consummate.

"We have no such vague, dubious, and conjectural elements to deal with here. The point of time at which the connection of Dr. Beecher with the Old School General Assembly was sundered is fixed and distinct, and that is the time when the cause of ouster arose. Dr. Beecher was a commissioner to the General Assembly which met at Philadelphia on the 17th day of May, 1838. He took part in those scenes in the church at Ranstead Court which form the crisis of the controversy and dissolution of the Presbyterian

Church. See *M'Elroy's Report*, pages 242 and 246, *apud* the testimony of Charles F. Worrall and of Dr. Hill.

"According to the recollection of Mr. Worrall, Dr. Beecher was a most prominent actor and most emphatic voter on that occasion. Speaking of the motion made by Mr. Cleaveland, nominating Dr. Beman to the chair, Mr. Worrall states: 'Some were standing on the seats, some on the tops of the pews. Immediately I heard a general yell of "*ay*," and there was one "*ay*" louder than the rest. It was Dr. Beecher, of Cincinnati, who made the loud yell.' It is true that the testimony of the venerable Dr. Hill, who sat in the pew immediately behind Dr. Beecher, contradicts this witness in the matters of indecorum which are imputed to the defendant, but establishes the fact of his presence, of his calm, deliberate vote upon the motion referred to, and that he took the side, on that day, of those who have since been designated as the New School Presbyterians.

"On that day, when Dr. Beecher and his associates adjourned in a body, with their moderator at their head, from the church in Ranstead Court to the church in Washington Square, he ceased to be a member of that body which the relator esteems and claims to be the General Assembly of the Presbyterian Church of the United States. That was the day on which he forfeited his rights to the professorship in the seminary, and on that day the Statute of Limitations began to run against the relators of his heresy and attainder. * * *

"And surely, if ever there was a defendant in whose behalf this statute of peace might well be pleaded, he is now before the court in the person of this venerable servant of God and man.

"He was the pioneer professor of the seminary from which this court is invoked to remove him. It was the *prestige* of his name which secured the foundation and endowment of its professorships; and his personal and zealous devotion of fifteen years of labor, in every useful capacity of instruction, of government, of farther endowment, of nursing, economizing, and consolidating the scanty and miscellaneous resources of the institution, would be most ungratefully requited by a judgment of this court expelling him from his seat as an intruder and a heretic. We make no appeal, however, to these considerations, except to justify before the court our desire to avoid the discussion of the old and envenomed topics of controversy which are involved in some of the issues submitted."

We do not propose a very minute examination of the case, which properly pertains to the history of the institution. The following is the only allusion to the subject we ever recollect to have heard from Dr. Beecher's lips. It occurred in the course of a conversation on his success in building up the Second Church and the seminary together:

"That was an interesting era in my life. I did more good by coming there and having a pastoral charge, for my success in that was equal to ordinary, and the congregation was built up, besides establishing a first-rate theological seminary. I preached to my congregation as well as if I had been altogether with them, and lectured in the seminary much better than if I had had no congregation.

"But one of the chief things, I consider, in building up Lane Seminary was the power of mind and the wealth that was in the Second Church. There was Judge Burnet, and Mr. Groesbeck, and Wright, and Starr, and others, who came forward and subscribed largely, or we should not have got half through, especially during the time of those trials. The trustees wanted me to draw out a regular history of that business.

"It was a vexatious suit, and vexatious enough they found it. A very large sum of money was spent in trying to turn the faculty out of office; but the fact is, we outwinded them. We served them just as they ought to be served."

LV

FRATERNAL REMINISCENCES

THE following letter was written by Rev. Thomas Brainerd, D.D., of Philadelphia, and published in the New York Evangelist. We offer no apology for its preservation here.

"When Dr. Beecher reached Cincinnati in 1832, he found me there a young man of twenty-eight years of age, engaged in pastoral labor in the Fourth Presbyterian Church. In about one year I left the Church to become editor of the Cincinnati Journal, then the leading religious newspaper of the Great Valley. As Dr. Beecher resided two miles from the city, and held a professorship in Lane Seminary, he and his session desired me, as I had no pastoral care, to aid him in his pastoral supervision of the Second Presbyterian Church.

"To this I consented, and this brought me into intimate and almost daily intercourse with him for two years. I generally worshiped in his Church on the Sabbath, and attended with him upon his lectures, prayer-meetings, funerals, and many of his pastoral visitations. This continued about two years, so that I had ample opportunities to know Dr. Beecher and to estimate his character. Besides this, he has been at my house half a score of times, and spent weeks with us. I have now lived over fifty years, with all of my professional life in the crowd of cities, and must say that no man except Dr. Beecher ever waked in my mind the reverence, admiration, confidence, and affection which for the time absorbed heart and will, and led me captive, a willing devotee. Toward him alone have I had the enthusiasm by which I could cheerfully suffer *for* him and *with* him, both of which I have repeatedly done. I believe Dr. Beecher had kindled the same sentiments in many others East and West.

"How he did this it may be difficult to explain, but I can give my own experience. He brought with him to the West a great reputation. We all regarded him as the first minister of New England; and while this reputation invested him with power, the perfect absence of magisterial dignity and pretense allowed us easy approach, and a familiarity that flattered us all. He was a mount that burned with fire 'that might be touched.' We soon saw and felt that he came among us for no selfish ends. He held his whole being subject to the promotion of Christ's kingdom, and he rejoiced in all the genius, learning, eloquence, and influence of all or any of his brethren, regarding their gifts as his capital with which the good cause might be advanced. If any other one rejoiced in his own abilities or good work, 'he more.'

"He had no small ambitions. He left to his brethren, unchallenged, all the influence they could gain by person, dress, and address, social assiduities, minute learning, and niceties of style; he left to his brethren, if they desired it, all ecclesiastical offices and preaching prominence, if the people would consent, at ordinations and installations; he left to his brethren so much that he hardly seemed to be in the way of any, while all felt his deference to their persons and claims, and, therefore, they all rose to aid and bless him in the great field of thought and enterprise which he occupied; and he was so willing to invite the sympathy and aid of others in all his great efforts, that they seemed to share with him in all the good effected. If good was done, he cared little by whom, or who had the credit for it. He made all around him feel that they were necessary to him. If he had a grand thought or splendid scheme, he shared it with them, and took their suggestions, so that, when the matter was accomplished, all said 'we did it.'

"His hopefulness gave cheerfulness, and his wit frequent merriment to every circle he met; and while all felt the majesty of his great genius, there was in him enough of plainness, naïveté, and peculiarity to disarm envy or jealousy. So far from his general bearing indicating hauteur and self-satisfaction, there seemed to be exactly the opposite — a self-forgetfulness and humility that allowed and invited the sympathy and sustaining efforts of his friends. He had naturally great confidence in others, and was not so satisfied with himself, his opinions, or his plans as to be indifferent to the judgment of his friends. Like a great ship turned by a very small helm, he let his friends have the satisfaction of feeling that he was not insensible to their influence.

"But all these would have failed in creating his surprising influence with his friends, had they been separated from an admiration of his great genius, and a love for his great purity and goodness of heart. He united a wonderful originality of thought, a fertile imagination, with a power of language by which he could originate a maxim of wisdom, condense it in the smallest compass, incase it in a striking and beautiful illustration, and then throw it out with a force of manner almost to keep it moving forever. Thus in regard to the Shepherd Church of Cambridge. Some one said it would die in the shade of Harvard College. 'No,' said Dr. Beecher, ' 'twill live; the blood of atonement beats in its veins.' In a lecture on education, he said, 'Uneducated mind is educated vice.' On the effect of a state religion he says, 'They brought the world into the temple and turned the Church out.' He thus put in the minds of hearers maxims of wisdom which they used and circulated as proverbs, and they are circulating them yet.

"His sayings have been more frequently quoted in public and private life than those of any other American, Benjamin Franklin alone excepted. He thus had an influence denied to those who seemed his equals or superiors in genius. Men quoted his sayings not alone as oddities, or witticisms, or coruscations, not for their shining originality, but for their profound wisdom. He was regarded as a deep, broad, comprehensive, and safe man, whom it was wise to trust. His congregations left his preaching presence not in giddy admiration of his genius, originality, and dramatic power, but penetrated by the great truths he had lodged in their memories. Others have shared richly in his genius, but, as they have failed to inspire confidence in their wisdom, they will never reach his world-wide influence. Their sayings are quoted for amusement, for admiration of their wit and originality, but seldom as maxims of truth or rules for thought and life. Hence they sustain to Dr. Lyman Beecher the relation of comets to a fixed star. One is of the month, the other of ages upon ages.

"And here I may allude to a fact which I have not seen noticed. There was about Dr. Beecher great 'hidings of power.' He threw around him an atmosphere which his brethren felt to be peculiar. You are at an anniversary in Boston. One hundred clergymen of the first class are on the platform. You know them, respect them, and perhaps admire them. But when Lyman Beecher enters you have a new sensation. There is mystery and majesty about that plain, ruddy, nervous old man, which begets awe and reverence. Have we not all felt this in his best days, and had a shading of it on us even to the close of his life? We have felt that, like a great sea or a great mountain, Lyman Beecher had heights and depths of greatness which we had never exhausted. He was most ready and frank in communication, but the depth, and force, and fertility of the stream only led us to a higher estimate of the resources of the hidden, exhaustless fountain. I mean no disrespect to any body when I express the opinion that in massive talent Lyman Beecher stood among his brethren like Daniel Webster in the Senate — alone.

"I have no space here to trace any proper delineation of Dr. Beecher. I owe to the memory of his love, confidence, and steady friendship a debt which I shall not attempt to discharge. In what remains of this communication I desire to recall him to his friends and to his ministerial brethren in some of his marked peculiarities. Dr. Beecher's wit was perennial, and it derived an attraction from his blunt, quaint mode of expression. I close with a few specimens, which I heard from his own lips. I could furnish a great store of similar ones.

"I was dining with him in Cincinnati in 1833. His daughter, coming in from a ride, told how a little dog had started from a door-step as she passed, rushed through the door-yard, around through the fence, came to her horse, opened his mouth, and was — silent. 'Don't you know the cause of that?' said the doctor. 'No,' said Catharine. 'Why, it was a case of *vox hœsit faucibus*,' said the doctor.

"A brother minister was making a lame argument in Presbytery. 'Brainerd,' said the doctor, 'I had rather be before that gun than behind it.'

"Another minister of the Presbytery, who, by-the-by, was a New England man, but greatly alarmed for the orthodoxy of the Church, had a habit of looking up and swinging his head to and fro while he belabored the New School. In the midst of one of his prosy speeches the doctor grew impatient. 'Brainerd,' said he, 'did you ever know a man who looked to heaven so much for light and got so little?'

"A newspaper at Oberlin had said that other seminaries only sent out great theological babies. 'Better send out great babies than little ones,' he remarked.

"Rev. Dr. Wilson wished us to try Dr. Beecher on common fame of heresy in the West. Dr. Beecher replied that this common fame was made by Wilson himself. 'One wolf,' said he, 'will howl on the mountains in so many tones you'd think there were a dozen.'

"In traveling with him in the deep mud of Kentucky, in 1834, our stage stuck. The doctor started across the ditch for a rail. 'Stop,' said I, 'doctor, let me go. I have boots on, and you shoes.' 'No,' says he, 'I haven't shoes on; they are both there sticking in the ditch.' On the same journey we were twice upset. Some were timid, but the doctor was entirely unmoved. 'My passage,' said he, 'is paid.' He seemed incapable of fear.

"I once asked him if he found any difficulty in sustaining himself amid the pulpit competitions of great cities. 'No,' said he; 'I have had the hardest race with myself.'

"The question was up in the Presbytery of Cincinnati whether we should divide a village church? 'Make two,' says Dr. Beecher; 'Adam and grace will do twice as much as grace alone.'

"He was urging meekness on his Church in Cincinnati. He told them 'that in the entire constellation of their Christian virtues it would require a telescope of unusual power to discern the grace of meekness.' While he said this he suited the action to the word, as if peering into the heavens.

"In discussing before his class whether the planets were peopled, he said: 'If any body was there and saw our earth, and inferred it was inhabited, they would be right, for we are here. Now,' says he, 'we'll put the bullet into the other end of the gun and fire it back again.'

"I have written enough for the present. I shall be satisfied if this crude sketch shall avail to recall the blessed memory of the dear old doctor to his friends."

LVI

CORRESPONDENCE, 1847–1851

As early as 1843 Dr. Beecher had resigned his pastoral relation to the Second Church. In his letter to the Session he had said,

"This can not be done, I find, without an emotion such as I have never experienced before in resigning a pastoral charge. Each of my three resignations hitherto has been with reference to the anticipated formation of another in the bosom of an affectionate people, while *this* closes probably my pastoral relations and labors, and consigns me wholly to another sphere of employment, that I may be permitted to consecrate my energies wholly to the rearing up a ministry for the West. In this, though my heart must make sacrifices, my judgment and conscience are satisfied."

He still continued, however, to preach on the Sabbath as occasion offered, either at the seminary chapel or in some of the newly-organized churches of the city.

In 1847 (March 22) he writes, "I have been preaching for two months in the Seventh Street Church. Numbers at first small; all Church-members nearly; almost no congregation. I began, six weeks ago, to preach strong revival sermons to the Church and also to sinners, with as strong revival fullness as I ever had, and as great power in preaching. By God's mercy, it has raised up the Church to prayer and effort, in as favorable a state as I ever knew a Church. The congregation is increasing, and sinners begin to be awakened. I attended an inquiry meeting yesterday, and expect to once or twice a week.

"As I have not been able to get my whole salary at the seminary for a number of years past, and as they are now getting out of debt by the rise of land and property, so that they will soon be endowed and able to pay me, I have become quite unexpectedly rich in my old age; so that, if I should be incapable of self-support for a season before being called home, I may perhaps piece out life without calling on children or others for aid."

April 30 of the same year he writes to Esther, then visiting at Fort Wayne: "A letter from you is the greatest of novelties, and of all most welcome. This winter, for the first time since I had children, I have been without one at home or near me, and really good as my wife is, it will seem lonely, and makes time often hang heavy on my spirits. At length I made up my mind firmly to write and tell you it did not signify, you must come on and help to fill the aching void, when lo! your letter came, the more welcome because spontaneous, and evidently the result of vacancies and longings somewhat like my own, and especially as you seemed to have such a kind of longing for me as was prompting me to write to you.

"Our arrangements for the summer are to stay at home and keep house, so come quick and see if we can not alleviate the leaden weight of time by communing of the present and of the unforgotten past, which at length begins to loom up, and seem bigger and brighter in the distance. So pleasant is retrospection, I wonder we did not enjoy it more when we had it in possession.

"As for Scotland, about which you ask, they are all Scotch Yankees; and as for London, they — the middle classes — are well-bred Americans, and London itself is as pretty a city as any in America except New Haven, which is the prettiest in the world, seen or unseen."

Then, after mentioning the conversion of Thomas and the encouraging condition of James, he continues: "Oh what mercies of our God and Savior, in giving us heart and wisdom to guide and guard so large a family, of so much mind and impetus, through such a world as this to himself and to heaven! And how precious to you must be the thought that your presence, and that of your mother in and around my family, with your care, counsel, example, and prayers, will no doubt be found in the last day to have had a deep and decisive influence in their conversion and usefulness, and preparation for heaven. So I, and so all of us think, and in thinking so, I can not open my mouth to thank you, because words are inadequate to express my constant and unsleeping gratitude for your love and care of me and mine in those vicissitudes of sorrow when none but you could have filled a mother's place.

"But pen and ink are cold. Come and let us pray together, and give thanks together for what the Lord has done for us, and, if the Lord will, come to be no more separated from me till he shall call us home to be reunited to those happy spirits, Roxana, Mary Hubbard, Harriet Porter, George Beecher, and the multitude with whom we have taken sweet counsel in joy and sorrow, and Sabbath worship, and missions, and revivals, which have filled up so many of our days.

"Love to all at Fort Wayne. Ask Charles why he don't write to me in my lonely, childless state — that old gentleman that rode seventy miles in twenty hours to see him safely launched in the ministry."

May 6, 1847, he writes to his son William: "I have received a letter from the moderator of Erie Presbytery, saying they have declined to send commissioners to the approaching Assembly at Cincinnati, from disbelief in some, and doubt in others, of the constitutionality of the Assembly, and we hear of some others doing the same; while all accounts agree that the slaveholding portion will send every man, so as to rule Graham's case against us,* which, if they should do it, would split off half our Western Church and more too, and, between vexation and discouragement, send many to Congregationalism, and some to Old School and some to Independent Presbyterianism, and, on the whole, leave us but a remnant to be saved.

"It is not safe to risk it. Analogy shows that the South and West slaveholders in civil matters are mad, and will do what they can, Constitution or no Constitution, and the clergy are bound hand and foot to their chariot-wheels, drive they never so furiously. I hope, therefore, you will be able to make arrangements to come."

July 3, 1847, to his son at Fort Wayne he writes, "Your account of your two children, in their developments, seems as if you had got some of my old letters to Grandmother Foote, from 1808 to 1817, when a succession of young people began to give premonition of an order of mind such as Roxana and I had not seen. Their elements of language are doubtless innate knowledge, or else the dim reminiscences of their pre-existent state, fast vanishing away by the diversions and exigencies of this world. God speed them to good scholarship, and a copious assortment of good thoughts and powerful and burning words, till they shall pass from the dialect of earth to that of heaven — the old forgotten language, I suppose. Don't you think, if we could any how get a peep at the libraries above, we could make some splendid discoveries, which exist, spite of our telescopic minds, very much not '*in*,' but '*ultra nubibus?*' "

November 2, 1847. The following is from a letter to Henry Ward: "Here I am in my study all alone, not a child at home, and having now until bedtime nothing in particular to do, I have concluded to write a letter to every one of my children as fast as I can write them, so as to get an answer at least once a month or six weeks — a swamp of letters around me, the best compensation for

* Mr. Graham had written a book in defense of slaveholding, which the Cincinnati Presbytery had condemned.

their presence; and having now your bright, loving, witty countenance beaming down upon me, I begin to write to you, because, also, you have so recently passed away to other interesting scenes in Brooklyn, about which I wish you to tell me, as historically and chronologically as you can — a letter full, and *quick*, or I shall soon have another letter after you. I know you have many cares, but I have never given a quit-claim to all your time, and I believe your conscience and heart will both say you ought to give me the run of your doings, and contribute your portion to keep me somewhat filled with the conversation of my children.

"For the first time in my public life I have now no pastoral responsibilities and stated preaching on the Sabbath, when my month shall be out at the seminary chapel. What shall I do — a soul without a body? But the Lord will provide, for preach I must, so long as flesh and heart fail not."

January 2, 1848. To the same he writes, "You are a good boy for writing me that long, comforting letter. It cheered us all. I thank you for your Thanksgiving sermon; and though I could not write as you do, it is a pleasure to think that perhaps you have breathed an atmosphere with me without which you might not have been able to do it. You can not conceive how much joy your successful revival labors afford me, and that efficient influence you are beginning to exert on the public mind, somewhat in the way God has helped me to do; and that so near the close of my day I see the wisdom of God and the power of God in younger hands, to send on the glorious, growing work down through another generation. God preserve and bless you!"

In the summer of 1850 Dr. Beecher resigned the Theological Professorship in Lane Seminary. His views and feelings in so doing are expressed in the following extract of a letter written some months previously:

"I approach this change, not with the regrets of mortified ambition, but with the concurrence of my sober judgment in respect to its expediency at my time of life, and from a long-cherished purpose and earnest desire to withdraw from any considerable responsibility as soon as the finances of the seminary would permit, that I may give undivided attention to some of my own writings, which without my revision must be useless, and which, if it pleases God to spare me with health a little longer, I think may be useful to the Church of God, in which I am sustained by the opinions and wishes of many."

Appropriate resolutions were adopted by the trustees, in which, after expressing their high esteem and affection, they declare "that without his generous co-operation they do not believe this school of the Prophets could have been established on its present broad and liberal basis, and appoint him 'Emeritus Professor of Theology,' requesting him, at the same time, to retain the presidency of the institution."

In December, 1850, he writes to Dr. Taylor, expressing his views and feelings in relation to a recent attack on Yale College, with which he had been represented as sympathizing. " * * * As for Yale, she is my mother, the author of my literary and theological being, and of all my labors for the Church of God, and if I do not defend her when assailed, let my tongue cleave to the roof of my mouth.

"And as to you, my brother, with whom for forty years I have been associated in affection, and confidence, and counsels, and prayers, and revivals, and missions, and reformations, and joys, and sorrows, till the shades of evening begin to fall upon us, and the light of other suns through faith begin to brighten upon our upward vision, what shall I say? Had others seen and known what I have seen and known of the integrity of your heart and the grief of your soul from the commencement of these trials, you would need no other exposition or advocate; and all that now I have to say or need to say is, very precious hast thou been unto me, my brother, and precious art thou still, and precious forever wilt thou be, I doubt not, in the presence and glory of our common Lord."

LVII

RETURN TO BOSTON

In May, 1851, Dr. Beecher left the West and returned to New England. His son-in-law, Professor Stowe, had preceded him, and was now residing in Brunswick, Maine. Thither the doctor at first turned his steps, and spent the summer in preparing his writings for the press, with the assistance of his daughter-in-law, Mrs. Louisa Dickinson. In the fall he returned to Boston, where his son, Dr. Edward Beecher, was residing as pastor of Salem Church, having, since 1844, resigned the presidency of Illinois College.

Here, "in his own hired house," at No. 18 Hayward Place, Dr. Beecher pursued his literary labors, issuing the first volume of his works in 1852, and the third in 1853, comprising his Lectures on Political Atheism, his Sermons on Intemperance, his Occasional Sermons, and his Views of Theology.

These volumes were brought out by John P. Jewitt & Co., just after the publication, by the same firm, of Uncle Tom's Cabin, and just before the appearance of The Conflict of Ages, formidable competitors, both, for the public attention. The series of volumes, however, was not destined to be completed. The Autobiography was still to be written. Considerable progress was made, however, in the preparation of materials for the same. Assisted by his daughter-in-law, he collated, endorsed, and arranged a vast mass of papers, and it is truly surprising, considering his apparently careless habits, how careful in some things he was found actually to have been. Of the numerous long and important letters written at different times in his life, he had rarely failed to preserve copies. His papers and MSS. might be, as has been described in a previous chapter, in admirable confusion, but, in spite of the chaos, he held on upon all documents of real value with a tenacity and vigilance nothing could elude. Moreover, although he might generally neglect to cross his t's and dot his i's, it is worthy of special notice that he never failed *to date his letters*, giving both the year, the month, and the day of the month, which is more than can be said of some of his posterity. Hence, when he came to collect and file the correspondence of his life, there was found, together with what came from collateral sources, enough for two biographies. The whole period of his Western life might almost be written anew, with equal fullness, without using any of the material already employed.

During this period of his second residence in Boston, although his memory of names and places, and the copiousness of language necessary for public speaking were failing, his inward trains of thought seemed as strong and as vivid as ever. It was in the course of 1853 and onward that, during successive visits at Mrs. Stowe's, in Andover, he related the reminiscences which have been incorporated with these pages. That his memory was at this time entirely reliable, except in relation to proper names and the chronological order of events, is certain, his statements being in every instance fully corroborated, at a subsequent period, by his correspondence and other infallible data. In some cases we have found incidents better told in contemporary documents, but never contradicted or falsified in any material particular, while in repeated instances the oral narrative was most comprehensive, vivacious, and exact.

Nor was he at this time at all indifferent to the theological controversies of the hour. On the contrary, he felt in them a peculiar interest, as being the logical sequel of those in which he had borne so prominent a part. The same great battle was still raging between Absolutism and Moral Government, although the leading champions and the field of conflict were singularly changed. Around Andover now was concentrating the fire that a while before had blazed against New Haven, and upon the successor of Dr. Woods [1] was beating the storm of accusation which had formerly burst upon Dr. Taylor.

The Panoplist, a thin and airy shadow of the ancient magazine of that name, had recently arisen to proclaim a new crisis like that which had aroused the zeal of a Morse and of an Evarts, and to assert the existence of a widespread and fatal apostasy begun in the nominally orthodox churches of New England. In defense of the great body of New England churches and ministers, an important part was performed by the Congregationalist, a weekly newspaper established in 1850 for that purpose. In a masterly series of articles, through a period of several years, the real char-

[1] Edwards Amasa Park (1808–1900), professor at Andover after 1836, took over Woods' professorship in 1847. Editor of the *Bibliotheca Sacra* after 1844, he was criticized for distinguishing between the "theology of the intellect" and that of "the feelings."

acter and history of New England theology was set forth with comprehensiveness of survey, fullness of reading, and accuracy of discrimination.

Among other articles was one on the philosophy of self-contradiction. Several of the most distinguished New England divines, ancient and modern, were shown to have written on two, and some on three sides of the same question. The causes of the phenomenon were pointed out. One after another of the former assailants of New Haven, now leagued against Andover, was stretched upon the rack by the imperturbable Congregationalist, with the utmost sang froid. Not a syllable of all this was lost on Dr. Beecher, who, while in his third volume successfully retorting a similar charge upon his Princeton accusers, saw more than poetical justice meted out to their New England allies. The closing portion of his third volume, to which we have just referred, entitled "Remarks on the Princeton Review," was the last effort at composition in which the mind of Dr. Beecher was efficiently engaged. Traces of the same hand that indited the leaders of the Congregationalist are throughout that article apparent. It was a joint production, in which is fulfilled the saying of the Psalmist, "As arrows in the hand of a mighty man, so are children of the youth; happy is he that hath his quiver full of them; they shall not be ashamed, but they shall speak with the enemies in the gate."

For several years after his return to Boston, Dr. Beecher continued to preach occasionally wherever his services were required; attending divine worship, when not thus engaged, at Park Street, under the highly-appreciated ministrations of Rev. A. L. Stone, D.D.[2] Nor were his labors at this time barren nor unfruitful in the Lord. Several churches in the vicinity were materially strengthened by his instrumentality. To have a revival was still his beau ideal of earthly felicity, and not a few gems, it is believed, were added to his crown in these autumn gleanings.

The following incident is mentioned by Mrs. Beecher: "Before your father went to the West, at the time when he was laying the foundations of churches all around Boston, he and Dr. Chaplin, of Cambridgeport, had their eye on Watertown, about three miles and a half from the college. There was but one Congregational Church in the place, and that was Unitarian, and as all the influential men belonged to that Church, it was difficult to gain a foothold there. They, however, rode out there one day to see if a

[2] Andrew Stone (1817–1892), Yale graduate, pastor at the Park St. Church (1849–1866).

location could be found on which to build a church, and see what could be done. They found a desirable lot, but somehow it become known that they had been there, and what their object was, and the ground was at once bought by one of the existing society. Dr. Chaplin died soon after, and your father finally left for the West without seeing his intentions realized.

"On our return from the West, after an interval of twenty-five years, a gentleman called on your father to ask him if he would go to Watertown and preach in the Town Hall to a few persons who felt they must have the Gospel established there, and they had confidence, if he would come and preach for them, their number would soon be increased. 'Yes,' he exclaimed, 'that I will; I know of no place where I will so gladly bestow my labors;' and then related to the young men what I have written above.

"After a few weeks a Church was formed at a private house. They immediately, by your father's advice, settled a minister, and commenced and completed one of the most beautiful church buildings in the vicinity of Boston. It was, however, destroyed by fire about five years after it was built, but they have erected another on the site, commodious and ornamental, and are in prosperous condition."

Another scene of successful effort was at Andover, during a revival in Phillips Academy, a year or two after his return from the West. His preaching and private conversations were very much blessed, several of the young men dating their first religious impressions at that time.

As time wore on, and his command of language continued to decrease, he was obliged at length to give up preaching entirely. At the same time, the effort to compose his autobiography was reluctantly abandoned, and all his sermons, letters, and other MSS. confided to the charge of his son.

After the papers had all been given up, he spent several days in going over them, and giving his last directions and any incidents suggested. Every sermon seemed to have a history. There were discourses dating back to East Hampton; others composed in Litchfield; others still in Boston or Cincinnati; and not a few consisting of a composite of all the different eras, showing how the sermon had been revised and rewritten. Here was a page in the old East Hampton handwriting, here another of the Litchfield stamp, and here others of still later appearance.

As he handled them over for the last time his heart was filled with regret. It was the warrior bidding farewell to trusty sword and spear. He gazed upon them with tears. "Oh," he exclaimed, "if I might have but just ten years more, I could preach *so much* better!" But the necessity was inexorable; the sacrifice must be completed; and after all of reminiscence had been caught and preserved that could be, he went his way, sermonless and sorrowful.

After this, the Old South morning prayer-meeting became, while he continued to reside in Boston, his main dependence — a kind of citadel on which he fell back to fight against decay to the last, and many were the brilliant flashes and bold sallies which reminded his brethren of what he had been.

Yet, while his mind was gradually retreating and hiding itself as in some deep mysterious cave, he was still, as to his bodily powers, muscular, healthful, and vigorous. "The day he was eighty-one," remarks Professor Stowe, "he was with me in Andover, and wished to attend my lecture in the seminary. He was not quite ready when the bell rang, and I walked on in the usual path without him. Presently he came skipping along across lots, laid his hand on top of the five-barred fence, which he cleared at a bound, and was in the lecture-room before me."

After leaving the West, all correspondence for the most part ceased. One of the last attempts at letter writing was in October, 1855, on the occasion of a birthday visit from one of his granddaughters named Roxana, to whose mother he wrote,

"You have well done to send the 'well-beloved name,' never forgotten, and more and more appreciated as time brings our long-delayed communion near, with one not separated by a thin partition, but standing at the door."

The last letter, so far as is known, he ever wrote, was addressed to Professor Allen, of Lane Seminary, in September, 1857. "It has," says Dr. Allen, "at once the movement of his magnificent style of thought and expression, and of an intellect struggling to break through the cloud that was steadily gathering over it. It was the result of the sixth distinct effort to a letter inclosing a draft of about $1000, in part payment of his claims against the seminary for unpaid salary. It was as follows:

" 'Dear Friend, — There are moments of hope and fear, and apprehension and relief, that may fill the soul. We knew that you would be pressed to advance the successive portions of our needed income, and of course our hopes left us in not a little doubt.

" 'But when increasing earthquakes swept over you in ceaseless continuousness, our hearts died within us, or waked only to hear that all was lost. When, therefore, on yesterday morning, on our first arrival home, your opened letter told me that all was well, with all the testimonials, it required time and an effort for our astonishment to get up, and to wake up our realizations, and to clothe our thoughts with wonder, gratitude, and praise. As soon as tears and emotion would permit, we bowed to God together, and, as the pious Montauk woman said to her benefactor, "I think, Colonel Gardiner, God inclined you to give me this meat. I thank you, also, Colonel Gardiner"—and in our condition, we think God inclined *you* to do these things, and we thank you too, brother, for all your care of us.' "

It may be stated here that, on his resignation of his professorship at Lane Seminary, the trustees of the institution gave Dr. Beecher their note of $3800 for arrears of salary, on which interest was regularly paid during his residence in Boston. In 1852 a number of gentlemen in Boston, of Dr. Beecher's old friends, presented him with a life annuity of $500, to which several of his children pledged an additional sum of $400 per annum, so that ample provision might not be wanting for the comfort and respectability of his declining years. On his removal to Brooklyn, the note of the trustees of Lane Seminary was paid, and the money appropriated as part of the price of a commodious residence on Willow Street, not far from the spot where he stopped two nights in 1802, with Uncle Justin Foote, when, as already stated, "there was no town there but only his house," and when he sent home his horse by the stage-driver, and returned to East Hampton on board a sloop.

LVIII

THE LAST OF EARTH

IN 1856–7 Dr. Beecher removed to Brooklyn, L.I., where, after a few months' residence with his son Henry Ward, he removed to his own house on Willow Street, an engraving of which appears in the vignette.[1] From the first he became a constant attendant on divine worship at Plymouth Church, both on the Lord's Day, and at all prayer and conference meetings during the week. No longer able to control his own organs, his soul seemed, as it were, to transfuse itself into the person of his son, and enjoy at second-hand that exhilaration of eloquent effort which had been to him as the very breath of his nostrils. Often during these days might he have been seen sitting, during the Sabbath services, with a kind of halo of half-glorified brightness upon his countenance, as one on the very borders of heaven.

Among the last times he ever spoke in the lecture-room of Plymouth Church, he said feebly, "If God should tell me that I *might* choose" (and then hesitating, as if it might seem like unsubmissiveness to the divine will) — "that is, if God said that it was *his* will that I *should* choose whether to die and go to heaven, or to begin my life over again and work once more" (straightening himself up, and his eye kindling, with his finger lifted up), "*I would enlist again in a minute!*"

Of all these years, after public effort ceased, and the veil was being drawn continually closer over his faculties, we have comparatively few memorials. He was always patient and uncomplaining, though evidently restless and suffering for want of mental stimulus and occupation. It devolved upon his daughter-in-law, Mrs. White, in connection with Mrs. Beecher, by reading and conversation to furnish the needed amusement.

Among the most successful expedients resorted to for this end was mentioning the names of former friends — Cornelius, Evarts, Taylor, in connection with their portraits. On one occasion (1859), while looking at Dr. Taylor's likeness, he exclaimed, "O Lord God, bring my soul to see the man with whom I walked in sweet counsel in this world!"

[1] The engraving appears facing page 230 in this volume.

Sometimes, however, even this resource was vain. Thus, one day in 1862, being quite low-spirited, his daughter alluded to several topics, but nothing seemed to cheer him. At length the following dialogue ensued:

"Father, you remember Dr. Taylor?"

"Don't tell me of him now. I can not always bear it to know that my powers are so far below."

"But you will soon be with him, and his equal."

"There is that to go through first that I can not contemplate."

In 1862 he said, while looking at his sister Esther's portrait, "She came very close to me. She was surpassingly lovely in spirit."

In 1859, in speaking of his first wife, he narrated the following incident, already alluded to in a former part of this work:

"I never in any instance had but one trouble with her, and then it was but a word, quickly repented of and as quickly forgiven. I went out one morning in East Hampton to feed the hogs, and somehow they vexed me. I caught up the handiest thing, and was thrashing them, when she came to the door and said, 'Lyman, don't! don't!' I said something sharply, and she turned to go in. But oh, I had not time enough to get to the door, and to say 'I am ashamed, I am sorry,' when one of the sweetest smiles shone out on her face, and that smile has never died and never will. I was forgiven, you may guess. There was another smile I have never lost. It was when she was leaving me. We supposed she was gone, and I had left the bedside, when a friend said, 'Lyman, she is reviving.' She opened her eyes and smiled, and passed away."

"One day in July, 1862," says Mrs. White, "he was quite delighted to see my Henry, and was quite talkative with him, and asked him to accompany him up stairs. When there he knelt and commenced to pray with great earnestness. One expression was this: 'I am sick because I can not reveal the feelings of my heart. Yet we will look up to Thee. We give up all, all, all to Thee. We give up the power. We have seen Thee, heard Thee, felt Thee. God, thou art God!' "

One day his daughter remarked, "Father, I always had a feeling that your prayers prevailed." "Did you?" he replied; "I am glad of it; but if they did, they met heavy clouds between sometimes. I have been in the pulpit sometimes when all power even to pray has been taken away. Oh, I remember such times! and I remember, too, when the light broke in again."

In March, 1860, little Etta White, who was quite a pet with the doctor, was at the point of death when he left to attend church.

On his return he said, "I wept after I got there, but the thought came over me, Why, she's gone across lots, and here I am going all around this long distance; and I wiped my eyes and was *glad for her*."

For the last year of his life all the organs of communication and expression with the outer world seemed to fail. His utterance was, much of the time, unintelligible sounds, with only short snatches and phrases from which could be gathered that the internal current still flowed. Still his eye remained luminous, and the expression of his face, when calm, was marked both by strength and sweetness. Occasionally a flash of his old quick humor would light up his face, and a quick reply would break out in the most unexpected manner. One day, as he lay on the sofa, his daughter, Mrs. Stowe, stood by him brushing his long white hair; his eyes were fixed on the window, and the whole expression of his face was peculiarly serene and humorous. "Do you know," she said, stroking his hair, "that you are a very handsome old gentleman?" Instantly his eyes twinkled with a roguish light, and he answered quickly, "Tell me something new."

In another mood, as he sat gazing apparently into vacancy, a friend drew near and began reading to him a little article cut from the papers, called "The Working and the Waiting Servant." He drew nearer and nearer, listened with fixed attention, and finally covered his eyes with his fingers, and the tears silently coursed down his cheeks. "How *could* you know that was what I needed?" he said. "Keep that and read to me often."

"His ruling purpose," writes one, "never left him. Since his mental faculties have been clouded, a minister, to try his condition, said to him in the presence of several friends, 'Dr. Beecher, you know a great deal — tell us what is the greatest of all things.' For an instant the cloud was rent, and a gleam of light shot forth in the reply, 'It is not theology, it is not controversy, but it is to save souls;' and then the deep shadow came over him again."

Only three or four weeks before his death, one who had the privilege of seeing him tried to make him remember a distinguished pastor in Connecticut who had died twelve years previously, but with whom he had not been particularly intimate. The name, once familiar, recalled no image to his mind. He could not remember the man. Then the question was put, "Do you remember Dr. Taylor?" He answered suddenly, placing his hand on his heart, "Part of *me* — part of *me*." Three or four years before this, though his memory of names and words was almost gone, he requested that he might be buried by the side of that old friend. He wanted to be buried, as he said, "where it would do the most good," and he thought that there was the place; "for," said he, "the young men [the students] will come and see where Brother Taylor and I are buried, and it will do them good."

"It may be interesting to Christians to know," observes one of his sons, "that with all his hopefulness for others during his active ministry, he was not himself exempt from doubts and fears. He was so *hungry* to do the work of Him that sent him, that he really seemed sometimes to have little appetite for heaven. Thus, after he was seventy years old, one of his children congratulated him that his labors were nearly over, and that he would soon be at rest. To his son's surprise, the old man replied quickly, 'I don't thank my children for sending me to heaven till God does!'

"That he believed himself truly converted; that he had consecrated every power to God; that he loved the Redeemer's kingdom more than every other interest on earth; that he was willing to spend and be spent for it, he never doubted for a moment. That he had a prevailing confidence that it would be well with him at death, is also true. Yet such was his sense of his imperfectness before the divine law, and such his profound humility before God, and such his sense of the solemnity of that great change that settles all forever, that he seldom or never spoke of his own condition with assurance, but only of prevailing hope on the whole. After he had been laid aside from preaching, and began to feel that he was breaking, he one day said, with great solemnity and simplicity, 'I have all my life had my doubts and fears; but I have lately been making an examination of my evidences, and I have come to the conclusion that, in view of every thing, I have a good and reasonable ground of hope.' This tenderness of conscience and timidity in his own case was in marked contrast with his great hopefulness for others, and his power of inspiring hope."

"Twice, however, before his departure," writes Mrs. Stowe, "his spirit seemed for a moment to throw off the torpor that was upon it with premonitions of approaching triumph. The first was when he quoted those words of Paul, ' "I have fought a good fight, I have finished my course, I have kept the faith; henceforth there is laid up for me a crown, which God, the righteous Judge, will give me in that day;" ' and added, '*that* is my testimony; write it down; that is my testimony.'

"The other was still more impressive, when the veil was rent for a few hours, and a vision of transfiguration was vouchsafed. He called to his daughter, thinking it was his wife, 'Mother, mother, come sit beside me; I have had a glorious vision of heaven.' His countenance was luminous, his utterance full and strong, as in his best days. He continued, 'I think I have begun to go. Oh, such scenes as I have been permitted to behold! I have seen the King of Glory himself. Blessed God for revealing thyself! I did not think I could behold such glory while in the flesh.' He prayed in an inspired manner for some time, and then soliloquized, 'Until this evening my hope was a conditional one; now it is full, free, entire. Oh, glory to God!'

" 'Had you any fear?' she asked.

" 'No, none at all; and, what is wonderful, I have no pain either,' passing his hand over his head.

"She then repeated the words, 'I shall be satisfied when I awake in thy likeness.'

" 'How wonderful,' he answered, 'that a creature can approach the Creator so as to awake in his likeness! Oh glorious, glorious God!'

" 'I rejoice with you, father.'

" 'I know you rejoice as a pious woman, but you can not enter into my experience now.'

" 'Father, did you see Jesus?'

" 'All was swallowed up in God himself.'

"For an hour he was in this state, talking and praying. The next day he remarked that he had an indistinct remembrance of some great joy. The last indication of life, on the day of his death,* was a mute response to his wife, repeating,

" 'Jesus, lover of my soul,
Let me to thy bosom fly.'

"The last hours of his earthly sleep his face was illuminated with a solemn and divine radiance, and softly and tenderly, without even a sigh, he passed to the everlasting rest."

The following is an extract from a letter of one of the children when assembled to pay the last tokens of filial reverence to his remains:

"We are having a blessed time. All are here except Edward and James. Last evening, and this morning at breakfast, the reminiscences and tone of feeling were inexpressibly rich; lively and not light, brilliant and diversified, and yet full of feeling. This

* January 10, 1863, in his eighty-eighth year.

morning at table, and afterward at family prayer, which was family *praise*, singing being our chief occupation, there was an unpremeditated outburst of memories of the most beautiful and touching character. We feel that our dear father is not taken from us, but given back to us again. The feeling in all our hearts is more of desire for consecration to Christ's work than I ever knew it to be — more as of old when Father was himself among us in the fullness of the Spirit.

"May the Holy Spirit enable us to carry away the new fire in our souls, and kindle others."

The funeral services in Plymouth Church, attended by the clergy of the vicinity in a body, and by a dense throng, were impressive and appropriate.

"It is not in sorrow," said the speaker,* in the peculiarly felicitous introduction to his eloquent discourse, "that we are assembled for these obsequies. Why should we mourn that he who had more than measured the appointed span of human life, and had entered on the eighth year beyond his fourscore years — who had outlived his activity, and even his cognizance of passing events in the great world, and then had outlived almost entirely his own dear remembrance of those that were dearest to him, both the dead and the living — who had waited for death through a long twilight deepening into darkness — has been at length released from the burden, from the prison, from the body of this death? Shall we mourn that, when 'by reason of strength' he had so far survived himself, that lingering strength is at last cut off, and he has flown away? Shall we mourn that the assiduity which, with unwearying tenderness, waited on his helplessness, and which he recognized with responsive affection till consciousness itself had failed, is now at last relieved? No; let us rather give thanks that the mortal has put on immortality, and that it remains for us only to bury in the bosom of its kindred earth this lifeless clay, from which the freed soul has gone to be with Christ. In such a death there is no extinction of hope, no interruption of activity, no anguish of bereaved affection, and (more than all the rest) no awful questioning whether the departed was ready. What tears we shed to-day are tears of love, of gratitude, of homage to a blessed memory, but not of grief. 'Thanks be to God, which giveth us the victory through our Lord Jesus Christ!' "

* Dr. Bacon, of New Haven, Connecticut. [Leonard Bacon (1802–1881), Congregational minister in New Haven, author, editor of the *Independent*.—B.M.C.]

LIX

MISCELLANEA

A volume might be filled with authentic, and another with apocryphal anecdotes of Dr. Beecher. Of these, some of the latter are the best.

At a public meeting of one of our great benevolent societies, a speaker told with effect the story of a minister who exchanged pulpits with a brother minister on a very stormy Sabbath, and preached a rousing sermon to an audience of *one*. Afterward he met that hearer in the ministry, and found he had been converted under that sermon. The speaker elaborated the incident with vivid minuteness, and at the close exclaimed, with a flourish, turning to Dr. Beecher, who was present, "And here is the man himself. Dr. Beecher, am I right?"

"The only fault with that story," said the doctor, "and it's a pity to spoil it, is, that it never happened." The discomfiture of the speaker can easily be imagined.

Of the same description is the anecdote recently circulated in the newspapers, to the effect that, on arriving in his lecture-room at the seminary one morning, long after the bell had done ringing, he turned to the class and said, "Young gentlemen, this seminary bell is no better than a fur cap with a sheep's tail in it." We have heard that saying ascribed to Dr. Bellamy. Dr. Beecher possibly told the story with an immediate application.

But, not to dwell on things that did not happen, let us mention a few that did; though here we observe, in passing, that it has been nearly impossible to arrest and fix in tangible form those fugitive utterances and incidents so vivid at the moment, so evanescent in the retrospect. Individuals have said to us, "Oh, I could tell you a hundred keen things of his," and yet in no one instance has the possibility become fact. So much depended on look, and manner, and magnetic *rapport*, and delicate hues of sentiment, that when they attempted to put their hand on the "keen thing," it was gone.

We have been told that a lady in Litchfield, of literary acquirements, was for some years in the habit of noting down pithy and pungent expressions in Dr. Beecher's sermons and conversation, and that in this way quite a manuscript volume of "life thoughts" was accumulated. But a brother minister, having borrowed the said manuscript, hid its leaven in the three measures of his own dullness, which nevertheless remained unleavened, while the manuscript itself was irrecoverably lost.

The following incident of his East Hampton life is related by Professor Stowe:

"He had some pleasant rencounters on account of his Episcopal connections. Though the old clergyman of Guilford, where they attended church, was rather of the dullest, this in no wise abated their ecclesiastical pretensions. Just after his marriage, passing a field where the quizzical old uncle who had brought him up was mowing, he heard him calling out,

" 'Halloo, youngster! they say you have no right to preach; you have never been ordained.'

" 'Got a good scythe there, Uncle Lot?'

" 'First rate.'

" 'Who made it?'

" 'Dun'no; bought it over to the store.

" 'And if you had another that was made by a blacksmith who you supposed could trace his authority for making scythes all the way up to St. Peter, and yet the scythe wouldn't cut any more than a sheet of lead, which would you take to mow with?'

" 'Go 'long, you rogue; ho, ho, ho!' "

Another incident of his East Hampton life is the following:

Riding on horseback from Southampton homeward one evening, with a heavy folio, which he had just borrowed, under his arm, he saw what he supposed to be a rabbit run across the path and stop by the roadside. It was moonlight, and he could not see very distinctly, but thought to himself, "I'll have a shot at you, any how." So, when he came alongside the supposed rabbit, he poised the ponderous folio and hurled it at the mark, receiving in return a point-blank shot of an unmistakable character, which required him to bury his clothes, folio, and every thing about him in the earth in order to become presentable. In after life, being asked why he did not reply to a certain Mr. ——, who was abusing him through the press, he replied, "I threw a book at a skunk once and he had the best of it. I made up my mind never to try it again."

Professor Stowe gives the following anecdotes of his Boston life:

"The morning after his church on Hanover Street had been burned, and the firemen and the mob had been amusing themselves all night with their noisy jokes about 'old Beecher' and his 'hell-fire,' several of us were assembled in Pierce's book-store in rather a lugubrious state of mind. Presently the doctor, who had been to view the ruins, and saw his proud, substantial stone tower split from top to bottom with the intense heat, came skipping in gay as a lark. 'Well,' said he, 'my jug's broke; just been to see it.' As there was no affectation in this — as it was all simple and hearty as the utterance of a school-boy just let loose from the school-room, what could we do but join in the laugh and partake of the hopefulness? Those who are acquainted with the facts will remember that there were circumstances which made the conflagration rather mortifying, and the doctor's joke peculiarly appropriate.

"The same simplicity, buoyancy, and imperturbable good humor disarmed opposition when he came in personal contact with an opponent. An old wood-sawyer, whom we will call W——, a rough, strong, shrewd man, who belonged to a rival sect, was violently prejudiced against the doctor, especially on account of his total abstinence principles. He had never seen him, and would not hear him preach. This man had a large lot of wood to saw opposite to the doctor's house.

"The doctor depended upon constant manual labor for keeping up his own health; and in Boston, where he could not enjoy the luxury of a garden to dig in, he was often puzzled to find means to keep himself in good working order. The consequence was that he sawed all the wood for his own large family, and, often finding that too little, would beg the privilege of sawing at the wood-pile of a neighbor.

"He was as fastidious in the care of his wood-saw as a musician in the care of his Cremona. In fact, there was an analogy between the two instruments. In moods of abstraction deeper than ordinary, it was sometimes doubtful which the doctor imagined himself to be doing — filing his saw or sawing his fiddle. That the old saw was musical under his hand, none could deny; and that he enjoyed its brilliant notes was clear from the manner in which he kept the instrument always at hand in his study, half concealed among results of councils, reviews, reports, and sermons, ready to be filed and set at any time while he pondered, or even while settling nice points of theology with his boys, or taking counsel with brother ministers.

"Looking out of his study window one day, when his own

wood-pile was reduced to a discouraging state of order, every stick sawed and split, he saw with envy the pile of old W—— in the street. Forthwith he seized his saw, and soon the old sawyer of the street beheld a man, without cravat and in shirt sleeves, issuing from Dr. Beecher's house, who came briskly up, and asked if he wanted a hand at his pile; and forthwith fell to work with a right good will, and soon proved to his brother sawyer that he was no mean hand at the craft.

"Nodding his head significantly at the opposite house, W—— said,

" 'You live there?'

"B. 'Yes.'

"W. 'Work for the old man?'

"B. 'Yes.'

"W. 'What sort of an old fellow is he?'

"B. 'Oh, pretty much like the rest of us. Good man enough to work for.'

"W. 'Tough old chap, ain't he?'

"B. 'Guess so, to them that try to *chaw him up*.'

"So the conversation went on, till the wood went so fast with the new-comer that W—— exclaimed,

" 'First-rate saw that of yourn!'

"This touched the doctor in a tender point. He had set that saw as carefully as the articles of his creed; every tooth was critically adjusted, and so he gave a smile of triumph.

" 'I say,' said W——, 'where can I get a saw like that?'

"B. 'I don't know, unless you buy mine.'

"W. 'Will you trade? What do you ask?'

"B. 'I don't know; I'll think about it. Call at the house to-morrow and I'll tell you.'

"The next day the old man knocked, and met the doctor at the door, fresh from the hands of his wife, with his coat brushed and cravat tied, going out to pastoral duty.

"W—— gave a start of surprise.

" 'Oh,' said the doctor, 'you're the man that wanted to buy my saw. Well, you shall have it for nothing; only let me have some of your wood to saw when you work on my street.'

" 'Be hanged,' said old W——, when he used afterward to tell the story, 'if I didn't want to crawl into an augerhole when I found it was old Beecher himself I had been talking with so crank the day before.'

"It scarcely need be said that from that time W—— was one

of the doctor's stoutest and most enthusiastic advocates; not a word would he hear said against him. He affirmed that 'old Beecher is a right glorious old fellow, and the only man in these parts that can saw wood faster than I can.'

"The doctor's unconscious, rustic simplicity led to many amusing scenes. I was walking one morning with the senior R. H. Dana in one of the narrow streets which lead to the Quincy Market. We soon saw the doctor rushing up on the other side of the street with a bundle of what seemed to be oysters tied up in a silk handkerchief in one hand, and in the other a lobster, which he was holding by the back, with all the claws sprawling outward. Something had happened the night before which had pleased him very much, and, seeing us, he stopped and began to harangue us across the street with great animation, vehemently gesturing with his bundle of oysters and with his lobster alternately. Perceiving that he was becoming rather more conspicuous than was desirable (for there was soon a crowd in the street looking very much amused), he desisted and walked on. 'Well,' said Dana, with a laugh, 'I never before heard the doctor speak with such *éclat* (*a claw*).'"

A ludicrous incident occurred one night during the doctor's residence in Boston. The upper back windows of his house in Sheafe Street commanded an extensive view of the city. The scuttle in the attic, particularly, was always resorted to by the young folks in case of an alarm of fire.

One night the bells gave the alarm all over the wide panorama, and the startled sleepers rushed to their outlook. The jangling din continued for a few minutes and died away. One by one the gazers stole back to bed. The house grew silent. Bell after bell ceased clanging, until at length one lonely tower alone gave tongue. Just then one of the older boys awoke from sound repose, heard the faint strokes of the solitary bell, and sprung to the scuttle.

"There's a fire," he exclaimed, "and nobody is awake! Why don't they cry fire?" and, stretching his neck out of the scuttle, he began to shout in stentorian tones, "Fire! fire! fire!"

The doctor heard the outcry and came to the banisters below, when the following interchange of salutations took place:

"Fire!" (*from above*).

"Booby!" (*from below*).

"Fire!" (*from above*).

"Booby!" (*from below*).

At length the truth began to dawn on the obstreperous somnambulist, and he crept meekly to bed. The last bell stopped — the lights ceased glancing — all was still.

Dr. Beecher was no ascetic. He was fond of good cheer, though obliged to limit himself to plain and substantial fare. Within due limits, however, he enjoyed the pleasures of the table as thoroughly as any *bon vivant*. No man relished a hearty laugh more than he, or appreciated more readily a good story well told, a merry witticism, or crisp repartee.

The law of his family was that, if any one had a good thing, he must not keep it to himself; if he could say a funny thing, he was bound to say it; if a severe thing, no matter — the severer the better, if well *put;* every one must be ready to take as well as give. The doctor never asked any favors of his children, nor stood upon his dignity in encounters of wit or logic. When they grappled him, he taught them to grapple in earnest, and they well knew what they had to expect in return.

It reminds us of a scene in "The Betrothed," where young Damian de Lacy attempts to hurl to the earth his uncle, the Constable of Chester, disguised as a palmer.

" 'And now for the trial,' said Damian, and at the same moment he sprang on the palmer, caught him by the waist, and made three distinct and desperate attempts to lift him up and dash him headlong to the earth — 'this, for maligning a nobleman; this, for doubting the honor of a knight; and this (with a yet more violent exertion), for belying a lady!' Each effort of Damian seemed equal to have rooted up a tree, yet, though they staggered the old man, they overthrew him not; and while Damian panted with his last exertion, he replied, 'And take thou this for so roughly entreating thy father's brother!' and as he spoke, Damian de Lacy received no soft fall on the floor of his dungeon."

And if, in the process of flooring his boys, they "left the impression of their knuckles on his ribs," he said, like the Constable, "There is nothing to excuse. Have we not wrestled a turn before now?"

The doctor would have disowned his children had they refrained, in fair argument, from putting forth every atom of logical strength they possessed. Moreover, in his house, argument was always argument, and fair argument. Opinions were canvassed without ceremony; but there must be no sophistry, no unfairness. He expected originality; he encouraged independence; he inspired boldness; he trained to mental toughness, tenacity, and endurance.

The only law of thought in his household was to keep to the point. Nothing really roused his wrath like an illogical or sophistical course of reasoning.

Against a refusal to argue, or a resort to evasion or trick, his anger burned like fire. Nothing of the kind was possible in his household. All propositions must be discussed. All argument must be free, open, and above board. Every mind must be expected, in supporting its opinions, to exert itself to the utmost. Nobody must find fault if their arguments were roughly handled. No child of his must grumble and get angry at being bruised and floored in fair debate. To look in upon some hotly-contested theological discussion, a stranger might have said the doctor and his children were angry with each other. Never; they were only in earnest.

So, as far as in him lay, the doctor trained his seminary classes. He could not, indeed, bring around him the omnipresent influence of a household training, incessant, perpetual, by day and by night, year in and year out; but, so far as practicable, the atmosphere of the class-room was the atmosphere of the family. He was father; the students were all sons. He was at home with them, and they with him. Never was a student put down for asking hard questions on ticklish points of theology. The trouble was, he could not get them quite unceremonious enough. He wanted them to come in and grapple with him as his own flesh and blood were wont to do. It cost him no small pains to divest them of their too scrupulous reverence. It was this habit of free and fair argument that, next to their practical revival aim, formed the most valuable characteristic of his theological lectures.

"Besides the Bible," says Dr. Allen, "I apprehend there was no book with which he was so familiar as Butler's Analogy,[1] and no portion of his lectures is more worthy of being given to the world than his lectures on Butler. They were generally given at the beginning of his course, and impressioned the student at the outset with the idea that he was in safe and strong hands."

Perhaps no happier illustration of the lifelong unconscious *drift* of Dr. Beecher's mind can be found than in the following extract from this favorite author:

[1] Joseph Butler's *Analogy of Religion* (1736), standard Am. college and seminary text in the first half of the nineteenth century, argued that the natural world presented difficulties to the reason that were analogous to the "difficulties" the Deists had found in the Bible. Though revelation differed from nature by the presence of prophecies and miracles, reason was the proper judge of "the meaning . . . morality and evidence of revelation." Man's present life was a time of trial and probation, but virtue on the whole tended to bring happiness.

"As it is owned the whole scheme of Scripture is not understood, so, if it ever comes to be understood before the restitution of all things, and without miraculous interpositions, it must be in the same way as natural knowledge is come at, by the continuance and progress of learning and liberty, and by particular persons attending to, comparing, and pursuing intimations scattered up and down it, which are overlooked and discarded by the generality of the world; for this is the way in which all improvements are made — by thoughtful men's tracing on obscure hints, as it were, dropped us by Nature accidentally, or which seem to come into our minds by chance. Nor is it at all incredible that a book which has been so long in the possession of mankind should contain many truths as yet undiscovered." *

To hear Dr. Beecher read the Bible at family prayer in such an eager, earnest tone of admiring delight, with such an indescribable air of intentness and expectancy, as if the book had just been handed him out of heaven, or as if a seal therein was just about to be loosed, was enough to impress one with the feeling that he was thus ever on the search into the deep things of God's Word, "attending to, comparing, and pursuing intimations scattered up and down therein."

A new thought suddenly flashed out, a new illustration of his grand theme, Moral Government, appropriately expressed, would at any time moisten his eyes with tears. The joy of his soul in a new idea, a new ray of heaven's glory, a new and more striking embodiment of some old truth, was most intense. It was a ruling passion of his intellectual being. He hungered and thirsted after the knowledge of God and of his glorious government, and of the sublime plan of redemption, with insatiable appetite.

A few characteristic utterances have been preserved by his associate and successor, Dr. Allen, some of which are here given:

"I was present at one of his lectures, in which, as nearly as I now recollect, he was examining the objections against the doctrine of free agency. He had compared the tremendous perils and fearful responsibilities of such an endowment on the one hand, with the glorious privileges and possibilities which it involved on the other, when, suddenly snatching off his spectacles, he drew a picture of an assembly of all God's intelligent universe summoned into a *quasi* state of existence, in which they should be capable of understanding the reasons for and against being created, clothed with the responsibility of free agency, and permitted to decide the

* Butler's Analogy, p. ii., c. iii.

question for themselves. Then, leaping from his chair, and walking back and forth upon the platform, he poured out, in a few short, pithy sentences, the peril of falling and the damnation of hell on the one side, and the blessedness of standing, and the possibility of restoration by divine love, and the heights of immortal glory to be gained on the other, and then, as if standing in the place of the Creator himself, and putting the question to vote, Shall I create or not create? he made the shout go up as the voice of ten thousand times ten thousand, *Create! Create!*"

"On a visit to the Northwest about the year 1845, he was called to attend a missionary meeting, in which a missionary from among the North American Indians gave an account of his labors. It was a very prosy, dull narrative. The speaker seemed to have forgotten, if he had ever known, how to use the English language. Dr. Beecher followed, and, beginning with Henry Obookiah,[2] he traced the history of Foreign Missions, and unfolded its destined results, in a way that held the audience spell-bound for an hour or more. 'Thank God,' said a professor in one of the Western colleges, 'our mother tongue is not yet a dead language.' "

"I recollect a discussion in Presbytery on the profound question whether slaveholding is a *sin per se*, the whole tone of which showed plainly enough that none on either side had been accustomed to bring the question to the test of any *principle*, metaphysical or practical.

"Dr. Beecher rose, and, taking for his starting-point the principle that whatever tends necessarily to undermine God's institutions is in itself wrong, in a speech of about half an hour laid bare the tendencies of slavery, as antagonistic to all the principles of the divine government, with a clearness and force that left nothing more to be said on the subject."

Dr. Allen also mentions, as one source of his power over young men, "the pithy, sententious remarks which flashed out from his living experience, and, fastening themselves in the memory, became like familiar proverbs — practical principles of life. The weekly

[2] Henry Obookiah (1792–1826), Hawaiian native, was brought to New Haven in 1809, and in 1817 went to the Cornwall Mission School, where he translated *Genesis* into his native tongue in preparation for a missionary career. Beecher saw in the "Providential mystery" of his early death divine encouragement to other missionaries.

conferences of the faculty with the students furnished the best opportunities for these, but they were not unfrequent in the lecture-room.

" 'You will have troubles, young gentlemen,' he would say, 'go where you will; but when they come, *don't dam them up, but let them go down stream*, and you will soon be rid of them.'

"A young man said to him, 'What can I do if I am not elected?' 'When you begin to care about being saved, come to me and I will tell you; but while you don't care a snap about it, very likely God doesn't.'

" 'Take care that you don't let down the doctrine of future punishment. Nothing holds the mind so.'

" 'Eloquence is logic set a-fire.'

" 'Walking is not the best exercise for students: you don't *think* with your *legs*.'

" 'I was in his study,' says a pupil, 'the morning he received a letter from H. W. Beecher, at Indianapolis, announcing the reconversion of Charles. With choking utterance he exclaimed, "His mother has been long in heaven, but she bound cords about her child's heart before she left which have drawn him back. He has never been able to break them." '

"Speaking of the happiness which flows from moral freedom, he said, 'God never meant to fill this world with machines, and then create another order of beings to wait upon them.'

" 'Suppose a skillful workman makes a chronometer so perfect that it never varies, no matter how long the voyage; but some intermeddling scoundrel thrusts his hand in and deranges the machinery. As a consequence, the ship is wrecked. Is the maker of the chronometer to be blamed? God made man in his own image, so that his soul contained all the elements of happiness. He was not made to be miserable. But the tempter placed his hand on the beautiful instrument, and death ensued. Was God to be blamed?'

" 'What a preponderance of motives in favor of doing right! how small the inducement to do wrong! The first is to the second as a million to one.'

"In commenting on the sentiment or opinion which seeks to account for the fact that every one sins, not by alleging natural depravity, but by saying that 'the appetites and passions are developed faster than reason; that is, in the nature of things which *God* has constituted, the appetites and passions *necessarily* obtain the ascendency over reason,' Dr. Beecher said, 'It is by this theory as if God had placed a man in a boat with a crowbar for an oar, and then sent a storm on him! Is the man to be blamed if in such a case he is drowned?'

" 'Indolent habits derange the nervous system, and stir up a tyrant capable of making hell on earth. Thus with dyspepsia; and it is most remarkable that Nature, before she surrenders, stoutly resists, and hangs out flags of distress.'

" 'Dr. Ware, Dr. Channing, and others of their school, who are sound reasoners on other subjects, can not construct a logical argument on Christ's divinity.'

" 'Reverie is a delightful intoxication into which the mind is thrown. It is extempore novel-making. I knew a person who was wont to retire into this garden of reverie whenever he wished to break the force of unwelcome truth. I told him he must break up the habit or be damned.

" 'Multitudes never learn to study a subject and unlock it so as to be able to enter it.

" 'Great readers are in danger of filling their minds with undigested facts, which they have not force enough to reduce to general principles.'

" 'All the sciences which, amplified, occupy so much space, might be reduced to their elements so as to be contained in a few pocket volumes.'

" 'Take care, in your contest with intellectual sharpers, how you attempt to prove that *mind is not matter*. The *onus probandi*, in such a case, is on the skeptic. The inability to prove a negative does not falsify an affirmation. Suppose I assert that the spots on the sun are immense rat-holes made by rats a thousand times larger than our rats.'

" 'The soul in the body is inclosed "within mud walls," through the chinks of which the brilliant light of the soul shines.'

" 'Conscience for the obedient has sounds more pleasant than music, but for the transgressor peals more terrific than thunder.'

" 'Death tears off the mask. Then slumbering convictions awake and rage. The soul is then a volcano in its throes.'

" 'Conscience is the executioner of the sentence — the sheriff who unlocks the dungeon, leads forth the criminal, draws the cap, and swings off the culprit.'

" 'Sincerity will never cause tares to produce wheat, nor sowing to the flesh life everlasting.'

" 'Some cry out, "Mysterious! mysterious!" because God has not so created us that we can not make mistakes. There is no mystery about it. As well ask why God has not created tallow candles to light up the universe. He intended man to be happy in the exercise of mental activity in view of motives. How much happiness could be placed in a snail's shell? God did not make man after such a pattern, but according to a law which is common to all intelligences, from man to the highest angels who burn before the throne of God.' "

LX

CONCLUSION

We dare not attempt to paint the portrait of Dr. Beecher. Our plan has been to show him in his acts, and in the authentic utterances of his mind and heart, so that the reader should receive in some degree the impression of having lived with him — the impression made by the whole man as he was, and by his course as it unfolded, and not by any analysis of the elements of his being, however skillful. In what remains to be said, we shall rely more on others than on our own too partial judgment.

The reason why Dr. Beecher's influence was so wide and so beneficial was, in the language of Professor Stowe, "because he was a man always most thoroughly in earnest, of strong powers of observation, a marvelous fertility and felicity of illustration, and living every moment under the impression that he had a great work to do for God and man, which must be done at once — not a minute to be lost." We may add, because he lived under the constant impression that the millennium was close at hand. It has been said that "he had no patience with the millenarian notion of the personal reign of Christ on earth;" yet never did he treat with disrespect that belief as entertained by Professor Stowe, or by members of his family or others. He firmly believed in the national restoration of the Jews; but the connected doctrine of Messiah's premillennial advent he had not found in the Scriptures. To his mind it seemed to involve some disparagement to Gospel instrumentalities and the dispensation of the Spirit, in regard to which he was fond of quoting the question of Father Mills: "Do you suppose God will stretch his teams, as he has done, all the way from Dan to Beersheba, and then back out?"

But, while rejecting the idea in the shape in which it was presented to his mind, he was equally far from entertaining the conception of a slow and gradual introduction of the millennial era. He believed there would be great tribulations, great judgments, great interpositions of Providence, and great outpourings of the Holy Spirit. The crisis, as he anticipated it, was as impressive and sublime as that presented to the imagination of a moderate millenarian, probably he would have said far more so. The influence on Dr. Beecher's life of such an anticipation of a near impending manifestation of God can hardly be over-estimated.

Of his intellectual character and traits of style Dr. Bacon speaks as follows:

"His intellectual character was altogether peculiar. I am at a loss how to speak of it. His thinking faculty — his power of discerning truth — was keen, ready, logical, discriminating. He delighted in an argument. Thought was a pleasure, sometimes a rapture, to his mind. With a ready command of nervous, idiomatic English, his expression of his thought was clear and powerful. He had not a poetic imagination; yet he had just that kind, and degree, and style of imagination which makes a man eloquent. In the play of his faculties, grappling with truth and striving to hold it up for men to see it, imagination was always active, and there would be frequent flashes of wit and humor; and yet, in the relative proportion and the combination of his powers, and in his style of thought and utterance, he was exceedingly unlike even those who have the best right to resemble him.

"If I were to sum up the character of his eloquence in one word, that word would be *electricity*. Even now, if you read attentively one of those great sermons in which his soul still speaks, you see this quality. The whole sequence of thought, from paragraph to paragraph, is charged alike with meaning and with feeling, and each link of the chain sparkles with electric fire. As you think what the effect of such words would be when uttered in his simple but intensely earnest manner, you will realize that, in a congregation, or in a free consultation among ministers and friends on great interests of religion or the commonwealth, he was like a powerful magnetic battery. I remember the remark that was whispered into my ear by one of the most gifted men in New England, as we sat listening to him in such a consultation many years ago: 'That man has done a great deal of magnetizing in his day.' "

In respect to Dr. Beecher's position as a theologian, in addition to what has been already stated of his comprehensiveness, may be noticed his propensity and his power to bring the great doctrines of religion down to the level of the popular apprehension.

If God's government is a moral government, by motive and not by force, then, he reasoned, it must be a reasonable government in all its developments and requirements. If it is reasonable, it can be shown to be reasonable to the joy of all loyal minds and the confusion of all rebels. If people possessed of ordinary common sense are to submit to that government from conviction, then must the policy of that government be examined on common-sense principles, and shown to be fair, and wise, and kind, so that sin shall be seen to be more unreasonable than any thing except impenitence.

Dr. Beecher not only believed this, but felt it in every fibre of his being, and, as an ambassador of the government of God, he went to men in the full and sublime consciousness of power, by the Spirit's aid, to show them that they were wrong and God right, and that all their complaints, cavils, objections, and accusations could be completely answered. His view of theology was that it was best studied in revivals, where the claims of God's government are pressing on revolted minds, and every plea of the rebellion is urged with all the ingenuity of self-defense, aided by the suggestions of the Deceiver, to stave off conviction. He felt that no man could preach the Gospel, in such scenes, under the full baptism of the Holy Ghost, grappling with the souls of men in every stage of conviction, without encountering first or last every great problem in theology, not as it lies in books, but as it exists as a fact in the great working system of the universe.

Into theology thus considered, he went as a war-horse rushes into the battle. He was a man of the people. The people were his peers. Any man who had a soul to save or lose for eternity was his equal. He went to the encounter of the popular mind without a misgiving or a doubt of the absolute goodness of his cause, or of his own ability, under God, to carry the day. For such encounter he was uncommonly well adapted. By his deep, rich, warm emotiveness — by his utter informality and freedom from pretense — by his insight, his intuitive judgment of what not to say, as well as what to say — by his power to shoot arrowy sentences, short but sharp — by his quaint and homely illustrations, and, finally, by the free wit and humor that enlightened and enlivened all he did and said, he was adapted by Him that made him, when filled with the Holy Ghost, to speak to the dead words of resurrection power, and to bring to bear on the desolate captives of the destroyer the redeeming "powers of the world to come."

It has sometimes been alleged against Dr. Beecher's system that he could not command for it the assent of his own children. Particularly has Dr. Edward Beecher been pointedly referred to as having rejected the theology of his father as indefensible. He himself did not so regard it. "I shall attempt," he said, "to redeem the first-named (or Calvinistic) system from a just liability to such attacks as it has sustained, by showing that all of its fundamental elements may be so stated and held as not to be inconsistent with the highest principles of honor and right." *

Nor did Dr. Beecher himself regard his son as abandoning the system in which he had been brought up, but rather as its defender, as the following communication clearly evinces:

FROM REV. EDWARD BEECHER, D.D.

"Galesburg, October 24, 1864.

"DEAR BROTHER, — You ask for information respecting father's statements to me in regard to my views. Those statements were unsolicited, and I made no note of them, since I have carefully avoided all appeal to the authority of names; but, since he is appealed to against me, it is right to state what he did say after calm reflection.

"Two statements of his are indelibly fixed on my mind, and the very nature of them is proof that his mind was acting soundly and clearly. The earliest statement was to this effect:

" 'Edward, I was sorry that you would publish your book, but I am not now. Your solution, if true, does really remove the difficulty, and all things are as they would be if it was true.' Then, after a pause, he added, 'What is proof that it is true, if not that all things are as they would be if it was true?'

"The next voluntary and unsought statement of his to me expressed his relief in defending God on that ground. He said, in substance, 'I have always defended God, in his dealings with men, on the ground of what I believed to be his word, though I saw difficulties that I could not remove. But your defense is real, and relieves the mind. If it is true, other defenses are nothing, and *nothing* is a poor foundation on which to base the defense of such a government as God's.'

"The last remark was so original, so striking, so like him, that it was daguerreotyped on my mind forever, beyond the effacing powers of forgetfulness.

"Both of these statements were made in unexcited, unargumentative states of mind, when love was in the ascendant, and in vital exercise. Both were to me like intuitions of truth in a heavenly light. In both cases they led to no argument, and I did not seek to extend the conversation on that theme.

"According to the best of my memory, the first remark was

* Conflict of Ages, p. 3.

made in Boston, before his removal to Brooklyn, and while he was carrying on revival labors in the academy in Andover. The second was made, as near as I can recollect, soon after his removal to Brooklyn; but, as I made no record, I give these times as according to my best recollections, and not as certainly correct. But as to the clearness and logical power of his mind in both cases, and for years after, my remembrance is definite."

From the same source we derive the following concluding reflections and reminiscences:

"The practical end of my father's theology was that of Christianity, to destroy the works of the devil, to save men from their sins, to sanctify and reunite them to God, and to extend the influence of this change to all departments of human society. He coincided with Edwards, Hopkins, and others in the belief of a spiritual millennium. He regarded this nation as an instrument in God's hand in producing this result, and his mind grasped human society in all its parts. His general views on this theme are sublimely set forth in his sermon on the Memory of our Fathers.

"In the kingdom of Christ he was, in the noblest sense, a general and a statesman. No interest of that kingdom, as affected by education, government, business, social life, or science, escaped his notice. He was ever on the watch, and ever ready to sound the trumpet of alarm at whatever quarter the enemy assailed the interests of the Great King. His writings on the Faith once delivered to the Saints, on the Bible a Code of Laws, on Dueling, on the Sources of National Prosperity, in defense of the Sabbath, on Colleges and Education, on the Building of Waste Places, on the Rights and Duties of Local Churches, on the Resources of the Enemy and the Means of their Destruction, on Intemperance, on the Reformation of Morals, and on the Institutions of Our Fathers in general, all develop the wide range and the practical character of his system as an elementary part of the great war of ages. This characteristic of his mind pervades and gives tone to his whole theology. It is eminently a theology designed not only to produce revivals, but to organize society, to rally God's hosts for action, for universal conflict, and for victory in the holy war.

"His mind was attracted toward what is generally known as the Augustinian or Calvinistic system, because in it he found the most powerful means of accomplishing his great end. In order that man should be restored to God in Christ, and thoroughly regenerated and sanctified, it is necessary that he should be radically convinced of sin, of his lost estate, and of his moral impotence to save himself, and of the power and readiness of Christ to save. In that system he found the elements of this conviction more fully developed than in any other, and in connection with a system of grace through a divine Trinity, revealed in the great works of atonement through Christ and regeneration by the Holy Spirit. Therefore, with all his heart, and without any wavering of faith, he embraced this system as containing substantially the truth of God.

"True views of human depravity, in its depth and power, result, of necessity, in the doctrine of divine sovereignty and eternal election to holiness and good works in the case of all the redeemed, and this doctrine he fully believed, taught, and defended. Of the final perseverance of all the regenerated he had no doubt, nor of the final ruin and eternal punishment of all who reject God's mercy and die in sin.

"The elements of this system he regarded as set forth in substantial correctness by the Westminster Assembly of divines, and among the last acts of his public life was an emphatic declaration to this effect, in rebutting the charges of heresy and hypocrisy by Dr. Wilson — heresy for contravening the doctrines of those standards, and hypocrisy for still professing to believe and revere them. His full, well-considered, and discriminating statements at that time put his relations to the system of those standards beyond all doubt or denial.

"But he did not receive the Westminster standards as given by inspiration of God, and as therefore infallible in all things, nor did he receive them as interpreted under the influence of what he regarded as an erroneous system of mental philosophy. He regarded the human mind as the work of God, and its true laws and revelations as divine disclosures of truth, which God would not contradict in his Word. What those true laws and revelations were he allowed no speculative philosopher — no Des Cartes, Gassendi, or Malebranche — no Berkeley, or Locke, or Reid, or Stewart, to teach him as an inspired oracle.

"He made no effort to develop any philosophical system of a master, as Wolfe, Kant, Schilling, Hegel, or Coleridge, in theological forms. The ages are full of such systems. Germany teems with them. He had no ambition of this kind; yet he had a system of intellectual philosophy. It was essentially that of common sense, as developed by Reid and the Scotch school,[1] and yet not

[1] Thomas Reid (1710–1796) and other Scottish realists were taught in most

derived from them, but from the study of himself, of men, and of the Scriptures.

"The text-book from which Dr. Dwight taught and lectured to his classes when he was in Yale College was Locke. The works of Reid came out after he had entered the field, and were never the subjects of his special study. But when one of his sons (Charles), after a thorough study of his system, stated to him its fundamental principles and great outlines, he was surprised and delighted at the many and striking coincidences in results between himself and the great father of the Scotch school of common sense.

"He did not frame his system abstractly from books and in his study, but in action and among men, when the real and varied workings of the mind were most fully before him; and it was ever his purpose to extricate the doctrines which he taught from theological technics, remote from popular apprehension, and from the corruptions of false philosophy, and to present them as the harmonious parts of a great working system, truly representing the human mind, and instinct with divine life and power.

"We are thus brought to consider his relations to the Scriptures; and here the fundamental fact is, that the manner of his conversion, and the glow and intensity of his religious experience, produced a peculiar, life-long, and increasing divine sympathy between him and them. Read his account of the conversion of a sinner near the close of his sermon on the Government of God desirable, and take it, as it truly is, as an account of his own conversion, and it reveals the manner of his inauguration, by the Divine Spirit, into that study and declaration of the Word of God which were the main employment of his life. He needed no higher proof of the divine origin and inspiration of the Scriptures than he found in their constant, full, experimental revelation of himself, of man, and of God, as disclosed in the great work of redemption. In this light he saw all history, all human society, all life.

To him the Bible was central as a sun and supreme as an authority. By its statement of facts, by its assumption of principles, he regulated his philosophy as well as his theology, for he was wont to say that God could make no mistake as to an assumption or a fact, and that no philosophy could be true which contravened him in any statement of any kind.

American colleges in the first half of the nineteenth century. They held that by "common sense" men knew the existence of external objects and, by the "moral sense," knew certain universal moral principles.

"Though the Bible does not teach philosophy formally, he held that it fixes bounds and establishes principles which no true philosophy can transcend or violate. No one ever felt more deeply than he the fullness and sufficiency of the Bible, and that by it the man of God was thoroughly furnished to every good work. There was a peculiar affinity of his mind to the Bible. No man was more alive than he to the sublime. It was his peculiar characteristic. For this reason he elevated Milton above all human poets. He had an enthusiastic appreciation of this quality every where. I shall never forget the impression made on my mind, when a boy, by the glowing manner in which he translated to me, from the second book of the Æneid, the sublime account of the capture and sack of Troy. This love of the sublime in him no book gratified like the Bible. He felt it through his whole being, as did Milton of old. Hence he transfused it, not only in its doctrines, but in its glowing and fiery sublimity, into his preaching and into his theology. He loved its rapidity of motion, its boldness and fiery condensation of thought, and exulted in defending the government of God in such a style of bold defiance of all the hosts of falsehood and of rebellion. He would willingly have lived another life in so glorious a work.

"The great difficulty with me in speaking of father is that I recollect too much. A thousand things rise up — particular acts, conversations, and expressions, at home or abroad, walking, riding, hunting, or fishing, at East Hampton, Guilford, Litchfield, Boston, and Cincinnati, and yet I can not take out such things from the web and woof of life, and set them forth as striking enough to deserve permanent record, though they all reveal the man and the father. So, too, I can recall his preaching, and his theology, and his revival labors, and yet not so as to furnish any thing more than general statements.

"For many years I lived and thought in him. I never knew the hour when I did not enter into his thinking, planning, and purposing, from the time I was sufficiently developed to apprehend him, and even before that he made the moral atmosphere in which I lived, nor can I form any idea of what I should have been without him.

"The thing of all others in him, however, that affected me most was, not his intellect, or his imagination, or his glowing emotion, but the absoluteness and simplicity of his faith. The intensity and constancy of his faith made eternal things real to me, and impressed me from childhood with the visionary nature of worldly things, so that I never felt any desire to lay plans for this world."

Here our labors close. If, in any degree, this work, despite its manifold imperfections, shall be employed by the Holy Spirit to quicken in the hearts of Christ's ministers and people a spirit of entire consecration, and of deathless affection for dying men, we shall rejoice that our labor of love has not been in vain.

THE END.

INDEX

INDEX TO VOLUMES I AND II

THE JOHN HARVARD LIBRARY

The intent of Waldron Phoenix Belknap, Jr., as expressed in an early will, was for Harvard College to use the income from a permanent trust fund he set up, for "editing and publishing rare, inaccessible, or hitherto unpublished source material of interest in connection with the history, literature, art (including minor and useful art), commerce, customs, and manners or way of life of the Colonial and Federal Periods of the United States . . . In all cases the emphasis shall be on the presentation of the basic material." A later testament broadened this statement, but Mr. Belknap's interests remained constant until his death.

In linking the name of the first benefactor of Harvard College with the purpose of this later, generous-minded believer in American culture the John Harvard Library seeks to emphasize the importance of Mr. Belknap's purpose. The John Harvard Library of the Belknap Press of Harvard University Press exists to make books and documents about the American past more readily available to scholars and the general reader.